Communications
in Computer and Information Science   1979

Rationale

The CCIS series is devoted to the publication of proceedings of computer science conferences. Its aim is to efficiently disseminate original research results in informatics in printed and electronic form. While the focus is on publication of peer-reviewed full papers presenting mature work, inclusion of reviewed short papers reporting on work in progress is welcome, too. Besides globally relevant meetings with internationally representative program committees guaranteeing a strict peer-reviewing and paper selection process, conferences run by societies or of high regional or national relevance are also considered for publication.

Topics

The topical scope of CCIS spans the entire spectrum of informatics ranging from foundational topics in the theory of computing to information and communications science and technology and a broad variety of interdisciplinary application fields.

Information for Volume Editors and Authors

Publication in CCIS is free of charge. No royalties are paid, however, we offer registered conference participants temporary free access to the online version of the conference proceedings on SpringerLink (http://link.springer.com) by means of an http referrer from the conference website and/or a number of complimentary printed copies, as specified in the official acceptance email of the event.

CCIS proceedings can be published in time for distribution at conferences or as post-proceedings, and delivered in the form of printed books and/or electronically as USBs and/or e-content licenses for accessing proceedings at SpringerLink. Furthermore, CCIS proceedings are included in the CCIS electronic book series hosted in the SpringerLink digital library at http://link.springer.com/bookseries/7899. Conferences publishing in CCIS are allowed to use Online Conference Service (OCS) for managing the whole proceedings lifecycle (from submission and reviewing to preparing for publication) free of charge.

Publication process

The language of publication is exclusively English. Authors publishing in CCIS have to sign the Springer CCIS copyright transfer form, however, they are free to use their material published in CCIS for substantially changed, more elaborate subsequent publications elsewhere. For the preparation of the camera-ready papers/files, authors have to strictly adhere to the Springer CCIS Authors' Instructions and are strongly encouraged to use the CCIS LaTeX style files or templates.

Abstracting/Indexing

CCIS is abstracted/indexed in DBLP, Google Scholar, EI-Compendex, Mathematical Reviews, SCImago, Scopus. CCIS volumes are also submitted for the inclusion in ISI Proceedings.

How to start

To start the evaluation of your proposal for inclusion in the CCIS series, please send an e-mail to ccis@springer.com.

Audrius Lopata · Daina Gudonienė ·
Rita Butkienė
Editors

Information and Software Technologies

29th International Conference, ICIST 2023
Kaunas, Lithuania, October 12–14, 2023
Proceedings

 Springer

Editors
Audrius Lopata (ID)
Kaunas University of Technology
Kaunas, Lithuania

Daina Gudonienė (ID)
Kaunas University of Technology
Kaunas, Lithuania

Rita Butkienė (ID)
Kaunas University of Technology
Kaunas, Lithuania

ISSN 1865-0929   ISSN 1865-0937 (electronic)
Communications in Computer and Information Science
ISBN 978-3-031-48980-8   ISBN 978-3-031-48981-5 (eBook)
https://doi.org/10.1007/978-3-031-48981-5

This Springer imprint is published by the registered company Springer Nature Switzerland AG
The registered company address is: Gewerbestrasse 11, 6330 Cham, Switzerland

Paper in this product is recyclable.

Preface

We are happy to present to you the proceedings of the 29th International Conference on Information and Software Technologies (ICIST 2023). This yearly conference was held during October 12–14, 2023, in Kaunas, Lithuania. These proceedings contain a diverse array of research and insights in the field of Information Technology and related areas. The present volume includes four chapters, which correspond to the major areas that were covered during the conference, namely:

I. Intelligent Methods for Data Analysis and Computer-Aided Software Engineering,
II. Intelligent Systems and Software Engineering Advances,
III. Language Technologies and Smart e-Learning Applications,
IV. AI-Based IT Solutions.

Conference participants not only had the opportunity to present their rigorous research in more specialized settings, but also had the possibility to attend high-quality plenary sessions. This year, we had the pleasure of hearing keynote presentations by Marcin Woźniak (Silesian University of Technology) on "Recent Advances in AI Models for IoT Applications," and Chief Scientist at the Institute for Future Intelligence in the USA Charles Xie on "Using Generative AI to Create Adaptive Feedback in Engineering Design". We would like to express our deepest gratitude to the special session chairs Audrius Lopata (Kaunas University of Technology, Lithuania), Zbigniew Marszałek (Silesian University of Technology, Poland), Martyna Kobielnik (Silesian University of Technology, Poland), and Jurgita Kapočiūtė-Dzikienė (Vytautas Magnus University, Lithuania). We acknowledge and appreciate the immense contribution of the session chairs not only in attracting the highest-quality papers but also in moderating the sessions and enriching discussions between the conference participants. The entire team working on organizing the conference is proud that despite the uncertainties of the pandemic period, the conference maintained and attracted the interest of numerous scholars across the globe. Every year ICIST attracts researchers from all over the world, and this year was not an exception – we received 75 submissions from Europe and beyond. This indicates that over the years the conference has truly gained international recognition as it brings together a large number of brilliant experts who showcase the state of the art of the aforementioned fields and come to discuss their newest projects as well as directions for future research. As we are determined not to stop improving the quality of the conference, only 27 scientific papers were accepted to be published in this volume (thus giving a 36% acceptance rate). Each submission was reviewed by at least three reviewers, while borderline papers had an additional evaluation. Reviewing and selection was performed by our highly esteemed Program Committee, who we thank for devoting their precious time to produce thorough reviews and feedback to the authors. It should be duly noted that this year, the Program Committee consisted of 40 reviewers, representing 24 academic institutions. In addition to the session chairs and Program Committee members, we would also like to express our appreciation to the general chair, Audrius Lopata (Kaunas University of Technology, Lithuania), who has taken the responsibility of steering the wheel of ICIST since the 25th anniversary of the conference in 2019. Moreover, we would like to thank the Local Organizing Committee and the Faculty of Informatics at Kaunas University of Technology, for the conference would not have been a great success without their tremendous support. The proceedings of ICIST 2023 are published as an issue of the Communications in Computer and Information Science series. This would not be possible without the kind assistance that was provided by the Springer team, for which we are extremely grateful. We are very proud of this collaboration and believe that this fruitful partnership will be sustained for many more years to come.

October 2023

Audrius Lopata
Daina Gudonienė
Rita Butkienė

Organization

Conference Chair

Rita Butkienė   Kaunas University of Technology, Lithuania

Programme Committee Chair

Audrius Lopata   Kaunas University of Technology, Lithuania

Local Organizing Committee

Daina Gudonienė (Chair)	Kaunas University of Technology, Lithuania
Rita Butkienė	Kaunas University of Technology, Lithuania
Edgaras Dambrauskas	Kaunas University of Technology, Lithuania
Romas Šleževičius	Kaunas University of Technology, Lithuania
Lina Repšienė	Kaunas University of Technology, Lithuania
Julita Pacevičienė	Kaunas University of Technology, Lithuania
Daumantė Varatinskaitė	Kaunas University of Technology, Lithuania

Special Session Chairs

Audrius Lopata	Kaunas University of Technology, Lithuania
Zbigniew Marszałek	Silesian University of Technology, Poland
Martyna Kobielnik Jurgita	Silesian University of Technology, Poland
Kapočiūtė-Dzikienė	Vytautas Magnus University, Lithuania

Programme Committee

Audrius Lopata (Chair)	Kaunas University of Technology, Lithuania
Aleksandras Targamadzė	Kaunas University of Technology, Lithuania
Andre Schekelmann	Hochschule Niederrhein – University of Applied Science, Germany
Andrzej Jardzioch	West Pomeranian University of Technology, Poland

Co-Editors

Audrius Lopata	Kaunas University of Technology, Lithuania
Rita Butkienė	Kaunas University of Technology, Lithuania
Daina Gudonienė	Kaunas University of Technology, Lithuania

Contents

AI-Based IT Solutions

Intelligent Systems and Software Engineering Advances

A Deep Learning Algorithm
for the Development of Meaningful Learning
in the Harmonization of a Musical Melody

Michele Della Ventura[✉]

Music Academy "Studio Musica", Department of Music Technology, Treviso, Italy
micheledellaventura.mdv@gmail.com

Abstract. The interest of musicians and computer scientists in AI-based automatic melody harmonization has increased significantly in the last few years. This
research area has attracted the attention of both teachers and students of Theory,
Analysis and Composition, looking for support tools for the learning process. The
main problem is that the systems designed and developed up to now harmonize
a melody written by a user without considering the didactic and therefore cognitive aspects at the basis of a "significant learning": given a melody, the system
returns a harmonization finished without any user input. This paper describes a
self-learning algorithm capable of harmonizing a musical melody, with the aim of
supporting the student during the study of Theory, Analysis and Composition. The
algorithm, on the basis of the ascending and descending movement of the sounds
of the melody (soprano), proposes the sounds for the bass line: the Viterbi algorithm was applied to evaluate the probability of the best match between the melody
sounds and the provided Markov chains, to reach the "optimal" state sequences.
Subsequently, the algorithm allows the user to complete the chords for each sound
of the bass line (tenor and alto), or to create the complete chords. Examples of
musical fragments harmonized in this way demonstrate that the algorithm is able to
respect the concatenation rules of the tonal functions which characterize classical
tonal music.

Keywords: artificial intelligence · Hidden Markov Model · melodic
harmonization · significant learning · symbolic music generation

1 Introduction

Even if the use of artificial intelligence in the music composition process is nothing
new, in recent years it has become a solid reality, destined to have more and more
space. One of the main fields of research interest concerns the possibility of creating the
accompaniment (or harmonization) of a melody. There have been several efforts made
towards this task in the past, using different approaches: from hidden Markov models
(HMMs) [1–3] to deep learning models [4, 5]. These systems had in common the goal
of educating the computer (so that it could learn autonomously from various situations)
rather than programming it, as happened in Rule-Based Algorithms [6–8]: algorithms
based on specific rules of musical grammar mathematically formalized.

© The Author(s), under exclusive license to Springer Nature Switzerland AG 2024
A. Lopata et al. (Eds.): ICIST 2023, CCIS 1979, pp. 3–12, 2024.
https://doi.org/10.1007/978-3-031-48981-5_1

Nowadays, there are dozens of platforms that use AI for the harmonization of a melody or for automatic musical composition. The most important platforms carried out to date include the following: Flow Machines, IBM Watson Beat, Google Magenta's NSynth Super, Jukedeck, Melodrive, Spotify's Creator Technology Research Lab e Amper Music. Most of these systems work using deep learning networks, a type of artificial intelligence that depends on analyzing large amounts of data.

In many cases, assisted music composition systems are used as a support tool for the teaching and learning activities of the Theory, Analysis and Composition discipline. The aim would be to stimulate the creativity of the student, i.e. his ability to produce ideas and objects that are new, original, appropriate, and to which a value is attributed, which can be of a social, spiritual, aesthetic, scientific and technological nature [9]. However, a passive use of these tools could affect the student's active learning [10]: what is called "meaningful learning" [11, 12] would thus be lacking.

Starting from the assumption that the learning process must allow the student to develop the skills useful for the specific discipline, this paper presents a new algorithm (that taking inspiration from the previous algorithms) able to support the student in harmonizing a musical melody: given the sounds of the melodic line, it is able to define the sounds of the bass line, leaving the student with the possibility of completing the harmony independently. For each melody sound, the Viterbi algorithm was applied to evaluate the probability (defined through the Markov chains) of the best matching of the bass line sound.

The structure of this paper has been organized as follows. In the Introduction, the context of this study is presented, followed by a review of related studies on automatic melody harmonization and an analysis of the characteristics that these systems present in order to define the research goals. Section 2 explores the concept of "significant learning", which is the basis of the proposed algorithm. This is followed (Sect. 3) by a description of the (mathematical) method used to achieve the goal. Section 4 shows some experimental tests that illustrate the effectiveness of the proposed method. Finally, in Sect. 5 the paper ends with concluding remarks on the current issues and future research possibilities with respect to the efficient enhancement of educational practices and technologies.

2 Harmonization and Significant Learning

The first step in the study of musical composition is to know the musical grammar rules through the 4-voice harmonization (bass, tenor, alto and soprano) of a bass line (see Fig. 1b). Above each sound of the bass line, the sounds that make up the respective musical chord must be arranged so as to obtain a melody (soprano), that is, a succession of sounds that have different heights and which together with the sounds of the other voices (bass, tenor and alto) form a harmonic texture, a music that is pleasant and pleasing to the ear [13].

The musical chord (built on a specific degree of the musical scale) is a set of three notes [14]: the root note, and intervals of a third and a fifth above the root note (see Fig. 1a). As can be seen in Fig. 1b, in 4-voice harmonization there is always a sound that is doubled (doubled sound).

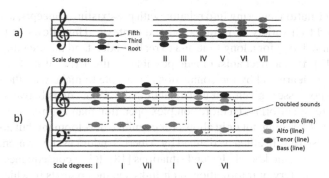

Fig. 1. Example of harmonization of a bass line.

The next step consists in harmonizing (always for 4 voices) a melodic line (soprano). This is a more complex operation than the previous one. The note of the bass line directly represents a degree of the scale with respect to the tonality of the piece of music and therefore it is sufficient to arrange the sounds of the other voices according to the previous chord (concatenation of chords). Instead, for each note of the melody it is possible to find different chords with which to harmonize it, according to the needs and the sound one intends to obtain [15]. This means arranging a melody in a harmonic context, submitting a sound texture to the music [13], choosing and evaluating the alternatives among the possible chords [16]. For example, the note "Do" can belong to the following chords (see Fig. 2):

- all chords where C is the root;
- all chords that contain C as a third;
- all chords that contain C as a fifth;
- all chords that contain C as the seventh.

Fig. 2. Examples of possible chords for the "C" note of the melody.

It is evident that the harmonization of the melody presents greater difficulties and requires more time to carry out than the harmonization of the bass line. Furthermore, the student must possess specific skills and competences which allow him to observe a note from several points of view. All this could become a pretext for the student to justify the use of platforms capable of automatically harmonizing a melody, without being aware of the result obtained.

The type of study that should prevail in the theory, analysis and composition learning process is what is called "significant learning", that is to say the process through which new information, entering into relation with pre-existing concepts, acquire a deep meaning, linked to a variety of information and contexts. This allows us to remember the acquired knowledge for a long time and to really understand the meaning of what we are learning [17]. It is a mechanism made possible by the active attitude towards what the student has to learn and by the connections he is able to make with the information he/she already possesses (given that understanding the connections between the various elements requires an effort and a more complex operation than learning a simple definition). This type of learning not only allows for cognitive development, but also increases the student's sense of self-efficacy, defined by Albert Bandura as the awareness of being able to dominate specific knowledge and situations [18]. It is a consequence that derives from the greater mastery of information, their links and the contexts in which they apply [19].

In order to achieve meaningful learning, therefore, the motivation to learn actively is fundamental, and therefore the tools that the student can use in the learning process are also important.

The algorithm presented in this article is inspired by these considerations and is proposed as a support tool for the teaching activity of the Theory, Analysis and Composition discipline, because, given a melody, it is able to suggest to the student possible solutions for the bass line, leaving the student to complete the tenor and contralto lines, taking care not to make any mistakes in the musical grammar. In this way the student has the possibility to observe (and memorize) how the movements of the melody and the bass line vary without the interference of other sounds. Each bass line proposed by the algorithm tries to respect the harmonic functions of the chords, functions taken from Schenkerian analysis [16] which give a piece of music different intentions depending on their resolution/concatenation with the preceding chords and they follow.

3 Methodology for Melody Harmonization

This paragraph illustrates the method used by the algorithm to analyze the melody and propose the sounds of the bass line consistent with the theories described in the previous paragraphs.

The algorithm takes its cue from an important assumption of the harmonization rules: a bass sound can be harmonized in different ways in order to obtain a better melodic line or to avoid errors in musical grammar [14]. This paper does not illustrate the rules of musical grammar and not even the errors that it asks to avoid in musical harmonization: in the first place because a manual should be illustrated and there would be the risk of creating confusion for the reader who is inexperienced in the field of music; secondly, because the algorithm was designed without presetting any rules of musical grammar, as its goal is to analyze the melody trend and define the sounds of the bass line (and subsequently those of the other voices). Therefore, harmonizing a sound means not only deciding which sounds must compose the chord, but also which sound must be doubled (see example in Fig. 1). The disposition of the sounds in the 4 voices (harmonization) and the trend of the melody are two things connected to each other since the first determines the second and vice versa: in Fig. 3a with the same bass line there is a melody different while in Fig. 3b with the same melody there is a different bass line, according to the sounds of the chord, their disposition and their doublings.

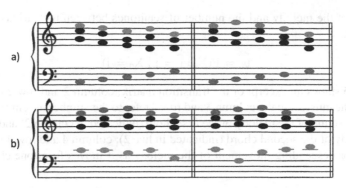

Fig. 3. Example of the relationship between harmonization and melody progression.

Analysis of the Melody

In the previous paragraph it was highlighted that each sound of the melody can belong to different chords and this can determine a different harmonization: a different degree of the musical scale and therefore different sounds and doublings.

The model developed for the automatic harmonization of a melody includes a self-learning phase in which the algorithm, through the reading and analysis of musical scores written in the form of a 4-voice choral, defines:

(1) the degrees of the scale for each chord underlying a sound of the melody (see Fig. 4);
(2) the ascending (a) or descending (d) trend between two consecutive sounds of the melody (see Fig. 4);
(3) the distance (in semitones) between two consecutive sounds of the melody (called musical interval) (see Fig. 4).

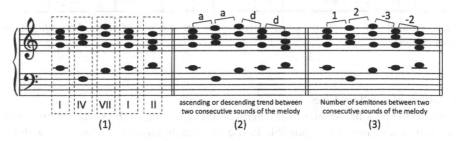

Fig. 4. Analysis of the musical melody.

This type of analysis can be done using the Markov process [20]. From reading musical scores it is possible to construct a transition matrix

$$P = (p_{ij}) \tag{1}$$

in which are represented: the probabilities that one degree of the musical scale X_d resolves on another degree of the musical scale based on the ascending or descending movement of the melody and the number of semitones between the various sounds of the melody:

$$p_{ij} = P(X_{d+1} = j \mid X_d = i) \tag{2}$$

Figure 5 shows an excerpt of the transition matrix: column 2 and row 2 refer to the degrees of the musical scale; column 3 and row 3 refer to the number of semitones which separate the sound of the melody of the first chord (indicated in column 2) and the sound of the melody of the second chord (indicated in line 2); column 4 and row 4 refer to the ascending or descending movement of the melody as it moves from one chord to the next.

Current State	I-1a	I-1d	I-2a	I-2d	I-3a	I-3d	I-4a	I-4d	I-5a	I-5d	...	II-1a	II-1d	II-2a	II-2d	II-3a	II-3d	II-4a	II-4d	II-5a	II-5d	...
I-1-a	0,014				0,014																	
I-1-d														0,014								
I-2-a														0,014				0,040				
I-2-d															0,014							
I-3-a																						
I-3-d															0,014				0,014			
I-4-a																						
I-4-d															0,027				0,027			
I-5-a																						
I-5-d																						
II-1-a																						
II-1-d	0,003																					
II-2-a	0,092		0,153	0,015																		
II-2-d																						
II-3-a																						
II-3-d																						
II-4-a																						
II-4-d																						
II-5-a																						
II-5-d																						

Fig. 5. Example of transition matrix derived from the reading of more than 500 chords concatenation.

Definition of the Bass Line

To define the bass line (which will determine the definition of the sounds of the chord and their arrangement) it is possible to use the Viterbi algorithm associated with the transition matrix represented in Fig. 5 [21]. The probability of the most probable path ending in state k with observation "i" is

$$p_{ij}(i, x) = e_l(i) \max_k (p_k(j, x - 1) \bullet p_{kl}) \tag{3}$$

where "i" represents the probability to observe element "i" in state "l", "j" represents the probability of the most probable path ending at position x-1 in state "k" with element "j", and p_{kl} represents the probability of the transition from state "l" to state "k".

The Viterbi algorithm is used to compute the most probable path (as well as its probability) [22]. It requires knowledge of the parameters of the transition matrix and a particular output sequence and it finds the state sequence that is most likely to have generated that output sequence [23]. It works by finding a maximum over all possible state sequences [24].

Figure 6 shows an example of trellis diagram. The number of possible states depends on the musical scores used for the training phase and therefore the possibility of obtaining a bass line as coherent as possible with the tradition of musical grammar rules is directly proportional to the number of chord concatenations analyzed.

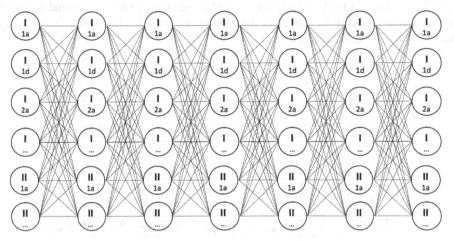

Fig. 6. Excerpt of the trellis diagram.

4 Results and Evaluation

The model presented in this paper is part of a pilot project which aims to investigate the effectiveness of the use of technologies in the teaching/learning process. In the specific case considered in this paper, the research made it possible to develop an algorithm capable of supporting the student in the study of theory, analysis and composition (or autonomously harmonizing a melodic line in the form of a 4-voice choral).

The algorithm does not provide any limitation with respect to the dimensions of the transition matrix, which is automatically dimensioned based on the characteristics of the music scores used during the algorithm training phase: non-modulating musical scores have been used (written in the form of chorale for 4 voices) in order to speed up the procedures for reading and collecting the necessary data (as described in the previous paragraph).

The algorithm was tested in 3 different steps during the training phase:

1) after reading about 500 concatenations of different chords,
2) after reading about 1000 concatenations of different chords,
3) after reading about 3000 concatenations of different chords.

The result supplied important information so as to be able to continue with the test. In particular, in each of the 3 verification steps, some musical melodies were proposed to the algorithm and it was observed that the bass line musically improved as the cases analyzed increased (see Fig. 7). In the first step the algorithm failed (for some proposed melodies) to conclude the bass line: this was determined by the fact that the algorithm found possibilities of movement of the melody, all with the same probability (derived from the transition matrix). In the second step (after reading about 1000 concatenations of different chords), the algorithm was able to finish the bass line even if in some cases in the last sounds (of the bass line) it proposed chords that did not give a final meaning to the musical piece. In the last step, the algorithm concluded the bass line satisfying also the musical cadence aspect.

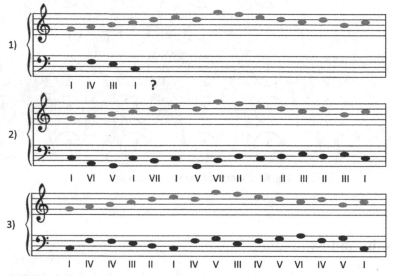

Fig. 7. Example of the results for the 3 steps.

A second type of test was performed to evaluate the algorithm. In this case, 10 students (including 2 dyslexic students) from the third year of a Music High School were involved, and they were asked to use the software while carrying out 2 exercises related to the melody harmonization. To simplify the testing procedures, some fixed test melodies have been chosen. These melodies were not randomly chosen but needed to be relatively simple and in major key rather than minor as our training data had substantially more major key musical pieces.

It was possible to notice that all the students consulted the algorithm to see the bassline it proposed. Three students then partially modified this bass line while the other students limited themselves to completing the other voices: they still had to figure out which type of chord could be inserted, which sounds were missing and which ones could be doubled. Also in this case, 2 students harmonized some sounds in two different ways, respecting (without errors) the melody and the bass.

It is therefore clear that machine learning systems are not born "ready", with a predefined and "embedded" knowledge, but this is acquired over time, as new situations, new documents, data and information are encountered. In this case, if the algorithm encounters new cases in reading new musical scores the solutions can be greater and different.

In order to implement the machine learning mechanisms, and therefore the algorithm begins to "come to life" and to learn automatically according to the preset settings, both the training phase and the subsequent phase are fundamental (bound to the continuous availability of new data on which to retrain the model).

5 Discussion and Conclusions

Research in the field of artificial intelligence has begun to investigate the concept of metacognition [25]: the ability to "learn to learn", knowing how to abstract from a specific domain of knowledge strategies for solving certain problems, even in a new and different context.

In this paper, a method for melody harmonization (mainly for bass line creation) has been presented: it is a part of a pilot project which aims to investigate the effectiveness of the use of technologies in the teaching/learning process. It is a method (algorithm) still under development but the first results have highlighted its potential.

The proposed method allows to obtain a bass line (as a guide for the resolution of a given exercise) to encourage the student to develop new ideas, apply previous knowledge and develop new skills: increasing his involvement and enriching the learning experience. The different harmonization proposed by the algorithm or created by individual students can be analyzed by other students and teachers, thus providing further information to increase the training dataset and refining the transition matrix, useful to guide the Viterbi algorithm to provide more successful harmonization.

New tests must be carried out both as regards the autonomy of the algorithm in harmonizing a melody (through a careful analysis of the proposed results), and as regards the number of students called to use the software as a support during the harmonization of a melody. In the latter case it is possible to evaluate the effectiveness of the algorithm as a teaching tool.

Future work can be directed in two directions. First of all, it is important to extend the training dataset, increasing the number of chord concatenations read and analyzed by the algorithm: including more complicated chords such as those of the seventh and ninth (which offer different possibilities for harmonizing the chords and therefore for their resolutions and doublings). Secondly, in addition to the task of harmonizing the melody (or generating the bass line), it would also be interesting to study the generation of a bass line conditioned by some chords inserted by the user within the melody.

The challenge will be to evolve in two parallel directions: to help students become stylistically unique and competent, and to understand how to use these new tools to enhance their creativity and explore new frontiers.

References

1. Paiement, J.F., Eck, D., Bengio, S.: Probabilistic melodic harmonization. In Conference of the Canadian Society for Computational Studies of Intelligence, pp. 218–229 (2006)
2. Tsushima, H., Nakamura, E., Itoyama, K., Yoshii, K.: Function- and rhythm-aware melody harmonization based on tree-structured parsing and split-merge sampling of chord sequences. In: Proceedings of the International Society for Music Information Retrieval Conference (2017)
3. Ventura, M.D.: A self-adaptive learning music composition algorithm as virtual tutor. In: Maglogiannis, I., Iliadis, L., Macintyre, J., Cortez, P. (eds.) Artificial Intelligence Applications and Innovations. AIAI 2022. IFIP AICT, vol. 646, pp. 16–26. Springer, Cham (2022). https://doi.org/10.1007/978-3-031-08333-4_2
4. Briot, J.P., Hadjeres, G., Pachet, F.D.: Deep learning techniques for music generation: a survey (2017). http://arxiv.org/abs/1709.01620
5. Lim, H., Rhyu, S., Lee, K.: Chord generation from symbolic melody using BLSTM networks. In: Proceedings of the ISMIR 2017 (2017)
6. Boenn, G., Brain, M., De Vos, M., Ffitch, J.: ANTON: a rule based composition system. In: Proceedings of the International Computer Music Conference 2011, University of Huddersfield (2011)
7. Everardo, F., Aguilera, A.: Armin: automatic trance music composition using answer set programming. Fundam. Inform. **113**(1), 79–96 (2011)
8. Kippen, J., Bel. B.: Computers, composition, and the challenge of "new music" in modern India. Leonardo Music Journal, Massachusetts Institute of Technology Press (MIT Press), 1994, vol. 4, pp.79–84 (1994)
9. Bartoli, G.: Psicologia della creatività. Le condotte artistiche e scientifiche. Roma, Monolite, 2005, p. 19 (2005)
10. Ahmed, A.A., Ganapathy, A.: Creation of automated content with embedded artificial intelligence: a study on learning management system for educational entrepreneurship. Acad. Entrep. J. **27**(3), 1–10 (2021)
11. Ausbel D.P.: Educazione e processi cognitivi. Ed. Franco Angeli, Milano 2004 (2004)
12. Novak, J.: L'apprendimento significativo. Ed. Erickson, Trento 2001 (2001)
13. Adorno, T.W.: Kierkegaard. La costruzione dell'estetico, Longanesi, Milano 1983 (1983)
14. Coltro, B.: Lezioni di armonia complementare. Ed. Zanibon (1997)
15. Schoenberg, A.: Theory and Harmony. Univ of California Pr; Reprint edition (1992)
16. de la Motte, D.: Manuale di armonia, Bärenreiter (1976)
17. Novak, J.: L'apprendimento significativo. Erickson, Portland (2001)
18. Bandura, A.: Social Foundations of Thought and Action. Prentice-Hall, Englewood Cliffs, NJ (1986)
19. Bandura, A.: Self-Efficacy: The Exercise of Control. W.H. Freeman, New York (1997)
20. Ames, C.: The Markov process as a compositional model: a survey and tutorial. Leonardo **1989**(22), 175–187 (1989)
21. Viterbi, A.: Error bounds for convolutional codes and an asymptotically optimum decoding algorithm. IEEE Trans. Inf. Theory **1967**(13), 260–269 (1967)
22. Forney, G.: The viterbi algorithm. Proc. IEEE **1973**(61), 268–278 (1973)
23. Bockmayr and Reinert (2011). Markov chains and Hidden Markov Models. Discrete Math for Bioinformatics WS 10/11
24. Della Ventura, M.: Human-centred artificial intelligence in sound perception and music composition. In: Abraham, A., Pllana, S., Casalino, G., Ma, K., Bajaj, A. (eds.) Intelligent Systems Design and Applications. ISDA 2022. LNNS, vol. 646, pp. 217–229. Springer, Cham (2023). https://doi.org/10.1007/978-3-031-27440-4_21
25. Flavell, J.H.: First discussant's comments. What is memory development the development of? Hum. Dev. **14**, 272–278 (1971)

Investigation of the Statistical Properties of the CTR Mode of the Block Cipher Based on MPF

Matas Levinskas, Aleksejus Mihalkovich[✉], Lina Dindiene, and Eligijus Sakalauskas

Faculty of Mathematics and Natural Sciences, Kaunas University of Technology, 51368 Kaunas, Lithuania
aleksejus.michalkovic@ktu.lt

Abstract. In this paper, we investigate the statistical properties of the CTR mode of a previously presented block cipher based on the matrix power function. Relying on the obtained results we propose an improvement of our original idea to achieve a better mixing of bits. We demonstrate that the modified version of our cipher satisfies both the avalanche effect and the bit independence criterion. To evaluate the quality of the obtained results we compare them to the statistical properties of widely used AES-128 and TDES CTR modes of encryption. Additionally, we present the preliminary analysis of collisions for the CTR mode of our cipher.

Keywords: CTR mode · symmetric encryption · matrix power function · avalanche effect · bit independence criterion

1 Introduction

The increasing amount of information encourages attention to the cryptographic systems used to avoid data leakage, disclosure of private information, or damage by malicious adversaries. The ever-growing progress of quantum computers draws the scientific community closer to the day when the currently widely used cryptographic algorithms will be broken in a reasonable time. The latest achievement of IBM is the 433-qubit Osprey quantum computer [1]. In the same paper it is mentioned that IBM plans to develop a 4000-qubit quantum computer by 2025. Therefore, the development of new cryptographic ciphers resistant to quantum cryptanalysis is becoming increasingly actual every day.

Our research group studies encryption algorithms and is currently investigating symmetric block ciphers based on the so-called matrix power function (MPF), previously defined in [2]. In our recent papers [3–5] we have proved that these ciphers possess the perfect secrecy property. The most intuitive definition of a perfectly secure cipher states that the ciphertext c is statistically independent of the initial message m i.e., the following identity holds [6]:

$$\Pr[c = c_0 \mid m = m_0] = \Pr[c = c_0] \qquad (1)$$

where Pr[●] denotes the probability of a random event and c_0, m_0 are fixed. To put it simply, any efficient adversary cannot obtain any useful information about the initial message based on the obtained ciphertext.

For practical implementation, however, the block ciphers are usually used in one of the operation modes [6]. In this paper, we consider the counter (CTR) mode of our cipher since it is currently one of the most widely used modes of encryption. This mode is used to encrypt large messages by splitting them into blocks of fixed size and is probabilistic i.e., the same message is encrypted differently every time, provided that the value of the nonce is chosen randomly.

In this paper, we consider the block cipher previously presented in [7] and investigate its statistical properties namely the avalanche effect and the bit independence criterion [8, 9]. The values of these criteria are commonly calculated by considering the avalanche vector A^{ei}, which describes ciphertext bits change after flipping one bit in the plaintext:

$$A^{ei} = Enc(k, \mu) \oplus Enc(k, \mu \oplus e_i) = \left[a_1^{ei} a_2^{ei} \ldots a_n^{ei}\right], \tag{2}$$

where the vector e_i has all entries equal to 0 except for the i-th one which is equal to 1 whereas the entries $a_j^{ei} \in \{0, 1\}$ for all $j = 1, 2, \ldots, n$ and $Enc(k, \mu)$ is the encryption function mapping the shared key k and the plaintext μ to the ciphertext generally denoted by c.

The avalanche criterion is used to evaluate the probability that a randomly chosen bit of the ciphertext changes its value if the i-th bit of the plaintext is flipped [8]. Using the vector A^{ei} defined by (2) the avalanche criterion is calculated as follows:

$$k_{AVAL}(i) = \frac{1}{n2^n} \sum_{j=1}^{n} W\left(a_j^{ei}\right), \tag{3}$$

where $W\left(a_j^{ei}\right)$ is the Hamming weight of a_j^{ei}. Ideally the avalanche criterion should be equal to 0.5 indicating that the bits in the ciphertext are flipping randomly each time the single bit in the plaintext flips.

The bit independence criterion is used to evaluate the correlation coefficient between the two components of the so-called avalanche vector A^{ei} defined by (2). According to [9] the bit independence criterion is calculated as follows:

$$BIC(a_j, a_l) = \max_{j \leq i \leq n} \left|\text{corr}\left(a_j^{ei}, a_l^{ei}\right)\right|. \tag{4}$$

Moreover, the bit independence criterion of the encryption function can be calculated as follows:

$$BIC(Enc) = \max_{l, l \neq j} BIC\left(a_j, a_l\right). \tag{5}$$

Ideally the bit independence criterion of a statistically secure cipher should tend to 0 indicating that any two bits of the ciphertext act as independent random variables.

However, in practice the near to chaotic flipping of bits can rarely be observed and hence it makes sense to consider the average of correlation coefficients, which is less strict and less sensitive to robust values of $\text{corr}\left(a_j^{e_i}, a_l^{e_i}\right)$ i.e.,

$$BIC(Enc) = \frac{1}{n2^n} \sum_{l \neq j} BIC\left(a_j, a_l\right). \tag{6}$$

These are characteristics that allow us to make assumptions about the resistance of a cipher to cryptographic attacks. In addition to the above-mentioned characteristics, the preliminary analysis of possible collisions was also performed. Although research has shown that sometimes collisions can be found, choosing a sufficient matrix order can yield a large enough set of possible values to ensure that the total scan cannot be done in reasonable time.

This paper is organized as follows: in Sect. 2 we briefly revise the mathematical background of our research; in Sect. 3 we briefly revise the original block cipher and its application in CTR mode; in Sect. 4 we consider the statistical properties of our cipher, discuss the obtained results, and compare them with other widely used block ciphers. Conclusions are presented at the end of the paper.

2 Preliminaries

Our previous research presented in papers [4, 10, 11] was mainly based on the study of the certain two-sided matrix mapping called MPF. This mapping in the general case acts on a base matrix Q defined over some multiplicative semigroup S by raising it from the left and from the right to the matrix powers X and Y defined over the number ring R i.e.

$$MPF_Q(X, Y) : R \times S \times R \mapsto S \tag{7}$$

For simplicity we use the following notation for MPF:

$$\left({}^X Q\right)^Y = E, \tag{8}$$

where E is the matrix exponent value.

It can be easily derived that the cardinality of the so-called power ring R depends on the multiplicative order of the elements of the platform semigroup S. Moreover, the properties of MPF also depend on the properties of the semigroup S. Assuming that S is commutative, MPF is associative and hence the order of actions in expression (8) can be ignored. For this reason, the entries of the exponent matrix E can be calculated as presented below:

$$e_{ij} = \prod_{k=1}^{m} \prod_{l=1}^{m} q_{kl}^{x_{ik}y_{lj}}. \tag{9}$$

However, if S is non-commutative the expression (9) does not hold in general [12]. Hence, we have to define the one-sided MPF in the following way:

$$^X Q = A, \quad a_{ij} = \prod_{k=1}^{m} q_{kj}^{x_{ik}}; \tag{10}$$

$$Q^Y = B, \quad b_{ij} = \prod_{k=1}^{m} q_{ik}^{y_{kj}}. \tag{11}$$

We call mappings defined by expressions (10) and (11) the left-sided and the right-sided MPFs respectively. In our research we use the two-sided MPF to construct a block cipher if S is a commuting platform group [4, 11]. Otherwise, we have to use one-sided MPFs due to the lack of property (9) [5, 7].

In this paper, we use a non-commuting platform group generally denoted by M_{2^t} which is defined in the following way [7]:

$$M_{2^t} = \left\langle a, b \Big| a^{2^{t-1}} = e, b^2 = e, ab = ba^{2^{t-2}+1} \right\rangle, \tag{12}$$

where a and b are two non-commuting generators of this group and e is the identity element. We refer to t as a group-defining parameter, since it determines the cardinality of the set M_{2^t}. In this paper, we consider values of $t \geq 4$.

This family of groups was previously considered in papers [13–15] and drew our attention since it is indecomposable and hence cannot be split into smaller groups of any kind. We have covered the basic properties of a special case of this group, namely M_{16} in our paper [12]. However, we can easily generalize these properties to get the following expressions for the basic operations in M_{2^t}:

$$\left(b^{\beta_1} a^{\alpha_1} \right) \cdot \left(b^{\beta_2} a^{\alpha_2} \right) = \begin{cases} b^{\beta_1+\beta_2} a^{\alpha_1+\alpha_2+2^{t-2}}, & \text{if } \alpha_1 \text{ is odd and } \beta_1 = 1; \\ b^{\beta_1+\beta_2} a^{\alpha_1+\alpha_2}, & \text{otherwise;} \end{cases}$$

$$\left(b^{\beta} a^{\alpha} \right)^n = \begin{cases} b^{\beta n} a^{\alpha n + 2^{t-2} \lfloor \frac{n}{2} \rfloor}, & \text{if } \alpha_1 \text{ is odd and } \beta_1 = 1; \\ b^{\beta n} a^{\alpha n}, & \text{otherwise,} \end{cases}$$

where $\alpha_{1,2} \in \{0, 1, \ldots, 2^{t-2} - 1\}$ and $\beta_{1,2} \in \{0, 1\}$.

Recently we have written several papers [5, 7] introducing the block cipher based on the one-sided MPF mappings. In those papers we have considered cipher block chaining and counter modes of symmetric encryption. Moreover, in [16] we have considered the statistical properties of a block cipher based on the MPF defined over the multiplicative Sylow group [3]. The obtained results have shown that the considered cipher meets the requirements for statistical security for reasonably large values of the main parameters. Furthermore, we also considered the performance of that cipher in [17]. The results have shown that for certain values of the main parameters the proposed cipher can surpass the CBC mode of AES-128.

However, the cardinality of a non-commuting group M_{2^t} is a power of two and hence it makes sense to revisit these properties since we have to consider the effect of our changes on the statistical security of our cipher.

3 Symmetric Block Cipher

In this section we briefly revise the block cipher defined in [7] and its implementation in the CTR mode. Firstly, we define the private key of our block cipher as a triplet of matrices (Δ, X, Y). Matrix Δ is binary i.e., its entries take on values from the set $\{0,1\}$, whereas the entries of matrices X and Y are picked from the set $\mathbf{Z}_{2^t-1}$. In our previous research, we saw that to restore the original plaintext from a ciphertext we need to restrict the matrix Y to be a permutation matrix modulo 2 [5]. In some way this restriction is natural given that the platform group M_{2^t} is non-commuting and hence it ensures that the decryption function correctly recovers the original plaintext.

Let us first assume that we want to encrypt a single block represented in its matrix form M, where each entry is t bits long. We split this matrix into two parts: a binary matrix M_b which contains the leading bits of each entry of the original matrix M and the matrix M_a which contains the rest of bits from M. These matrices represent powers of generators a and b respectively. We now define the following block cipher:

$$C_1 = b^{M_b + \Delta} \odot a^{M_a + X},$$

$$C_2 = {}^Y(C_1)^Y,$$

$$C = Shift_\kappa(\Phi(C_2) \| \Psi(C_2)) + (\Delta \| X),$$

where by $b^{M_b+\Delta}$ and a^{M_a+X} we denote the entry-wise exponentiation of the generators a and b to respective power matrices, $\odot$ denotes the Hadamard product of two matrices, $\|$ denotes the entry-wise concatenation, and the mappings Φ and Ψ output the powers of generators b and a respectively, i.e.

$$\Phi(b^\beta a^\alpha) = \beta,$$

$$\Psi(b^\beta a^\alpha) = \alpha.$$

At the last step of the algorithm the entries of the matrix $\Phi(C_2) \| \Psi(C_2)$ Are shifted by κ bits, where κ is fixed. Hence, denoting the private key $(\Delta, X, Y) = \vec{K}$, we obtain the following encryption function:

$$Enc\left(\vec{K}, M\right) = Shift_\kappa\left(\Phi\left({}^Y(C_1)^Y\right) \middle\| \Psi\left({}^Y(C_1)^Y\right)\right) + (\Delta \| X).$$

To shorten the expression, we omitted substituting C_1 with its value.

The decryption of the original plaintext is performed by reversing each step of the encryption algorithm. However, since the CTR mode makes use of encryption function only (see Fig. 1 for details) we omit the decryption function in this paper. It can be found in [5]. Moreover, due to this feature of the CTR mode, below we consider the possibility of discarding the constraint on matrix Y. Notably this cannot be done for the CBC mode, since it uses both encryption and decryption functions. We think that due to this reason the overall security of the CTR mode of our block cipher may increase.

One of the notable features of the CTR mode is the notion of nonce – a randomly generated string of bits. This string can be viewed as a one-time key and cannot be reused. Also nonce is concatenated with the counter which is used to keep track of the blocks.

Notably, the last step of the CTR mode resembles the one-time pad technique where the original message is XORed (denoted by $\oplus$ in Fig. 1) with a private string of bits represented in CTR mode by the encrypted concatenation of the nonce and the counter.

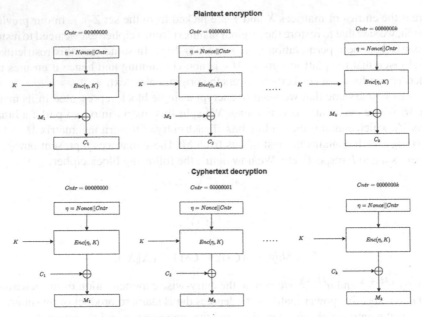

Fig. 1. The general structure of the counter mode of our block cipher.

Furthermore, due to the presented structure of the CTR mode the encryption process is probabilistic. This fact is beneficial when the security of the encryption is considered since it plays a major role in protecting the data against active and passive adversaries [6].

4   Investigation of the Avalanche Effect of Our Cipher

It is important to note that since the encryption function is not applied to the original message, the statistical properties of our block cipher are considered for the concatenation of the nonce and the counter.

Notably, the notion of the avalanche effect appears naturally when CTR mode is considered since the nonce is fixed throughout the encryption process whereas the counter changes. Hence for, say, the first and the third blocks of the original message the considered concatenations differ by exactly one bit. Another case of an occurring avalanche effect is a random flipping of the bit in the nonce when the counter is fixed. This investigation is important since an active adversary has control of the nonce and hence can use the obtained ciphertext as a basis of his statistical analysis.

However, for a secure block cipher we can focus on encrypting a single block, since both the described scenarios are simply special cases of bit flipping. Hence, we vary the main parameters of our block cipher: the matrix order m and the group-defining parameter t. These parameters take on integer values from 4 to 7. For each pair we perform 100 simulations and take the average of the observed avalanche effect. The obtained results are presented in Table 1:

Table 1. Avalanche effect of the original block cipher

	m = 4	m = 5	m = 6	m = 7
t = 4	0.1123	0.0941	0.0841	0.0733
t = 5	0.1316	0.1141	0.1056	0.0982
t = 6	0.1472	0.1302	0.1238	0.1153
t = 7	0.1523	0.1463	0.1397	0.1343

We can see that the results are far from perfect and hence our cipher requires modifications from the statistical point of view. Hence relying on these results, we can see that the MPF mapping by itself cannot ensure bit mixing. Comparing results obtained here to the ones presented in [16] we see that the avalanche effect was higher for the previously chosen algebraic structures. However, the block cipher presented here is better from the point of view of practical implementation since the cardinalities of the algebraic structures are powers of 2. Furthermore, the block cipher considered here is based on non-commuting platform group.

Let us first consider the option of eliminating the constraint on the matrix Y. Then applying the same methodology, we obtained the results presented in Table 2.

Table 2. Avalanche effect of our block cipher after eliminating the constraint on matrix Y.

	m = 4	m = 5	m = 6	m = 7
t = 4	0.2311	0.2272	0.2148	0.2160
t = 5	0.2168	0.2207	0.2153	0.2170
t = 6	0.2272	0.2183	0.2199	0.2224
t = 7	0.2202	0.2219	0.2246	0.2218

Even though the results have improved, and hence the applied change was beneficial, our block cipher still requires modifications to achieve statistical security.

5 Modification of Our Block Cipher

Since the considered cipher was shown to be perfectly secure, to ensure proper mixing of bits we propose to modify the representation of the plaintext in its matrix form. Such an approach was chosen since the proof of the perfect secrecy property does not rely on the way the plaintext is converted into a matrix and hence automatically holds for the modification, presented here.

Note that in this paper we propose just one of the possible ways to improve the mixing of bits. Whether it is the optimal way to achieve our goal is not clear. Additional investigations can be carried out in this area.

We choose p permutation vectors of size m^2, which define the positions of the chunks of bits in the matrix representation of the plaintext. For more clarity, let us assume that we want to encrypt a plaintext $\mu = \mu_1 \| \mu_2 \| \ldots \| \mu_9$ Using a 3×3 matrix and assume that $\vec{v} = (2\,1\,3\,8\,4\,5\,6\,9\,7)$. Then we get the following matrix representation of the considered plaintext:

$$\begin{pmatrix} \mu_2 & \mu_1 & \mu_3 \\ \mu_8 & \mu_4 & \mu_5 \\ \mu_6 & \mu_9 & \mu_7 \end{pmatrix}.$$

Through experiments we have seen that for our purposes it is enough to choose a sufficiently small value of p. Optimal values of the avalanche effect were achieved by choosing $p = 5$.

The representation for each individual block is chosen depending on the sum of the input η (see Fig. 1) bits modulo p. Denoting the i-th bit of η by η_i we have:

$$j \equiv \left(\sum_{i=1}^{m^2 t} \eta_i \right) \bmod p, \tag{13}$$

where j denotes the index of the selected permutation $\vec{v}_j$.

Using this modification and the setup discussed in the previous section we have obtained the results presented in Table 3.

Table 3. Avalanche effect of the modified block cipher

	m = 4	m = 5	m = 6	m = 7
t = 4	0.4742	0.4903	0.4987	0.4973
t = 5	0.4865	0.4926	0.4950	0.5001
t = 6	0.4834	0.4950	0.4961	0.4985
t = 7	0.4913	0.4936	0.4983	0.4984

Relying on the obtained results we claim that the avalanche criterion is satisfied. Furthermore, we have compared these results to AES-128 and TDES. Experimentally we have calculated the avalanche effect for the AES-128 to be 0.5002, and for the TDES it equals 0.5004.

Let us now demonstrate an example of an avalanche effect in the CTR mode of our cipher. We consider a so-called zero message $\mu = \text{'}000\ldots0\text{'}$ of sufficiently large size and compare the ciphertexts of the first and third blocks. For simplicity we chose 4×4 matrices and a platform group M_{16} i.e., $t = 4$. We consider the following matrix forms of η_1 and η_2:

$$H_1 = \begin{pmatrix} 2 & 8 & 14 & 6 \\ 1 & 11 & 10 & 13 \\ 8 & 2 & 14 & 4 \\ 13 & 2 & 8 & 0 \end{pmatrix}, \; H_2 = \begin{pmatrix} 2 & 8 & 14 & 6 \\ 1 & 11 & 10 & 13 \\ 8 & 2 & 14 & 4 \\ 13 & 2 & 8 & 2 \end{pmatrix},$$

where the red entries are counters and everything else is the nonce. Five random permutations $\vec{v}_j$ were chosen.

Note that H_1 contains 27 'ones' and H_2 contains 28 'ones'. Since $27 \equiv 2 \bmod 5$ and $28 \equiv 3 \bmod 5$, the matrix H_1 undergoes through transformation $\vec{v}_2$ whereas H_2 undergoes through transformation $\vec{v}_3$. Then we split off the leading bits of each entry to obtain powers of a and b. For transformed matrices H_1 and H_2 we get respectively:

$$\vec{v}_2(H_1)_b = \begin{pmatrix} 1 & 0 & 0 & 1 \\ 1 & 1 & 1 & 0 \\ 0 & 1 & 0 & 0 \\ 1 & 1 & 0 & 1 \end{pmatrix}, \; \vec{v}_2(H_1)_a = \begin{pmatrix} 0 & 2 & 2 & 0 \\ 0 & 6 & 3 & 0 \\ 6 & 5 & 2 & 1 \\ 2 & 5 & 4 & 6 \end{pmatrix};$$

$$\vec{v}_3(H_2)_b = \begin{pmatrix} 1 & 0 & 1 & 0 \\ 1 & 0 & 1 & 1 \\ 0 & 1 & 1 & 1 \\ 1 & 0 & 0 & 0 \end{pmatrix}, \; \vec{v}_3(H_2)_a = \begin{pmatrix} 6 & 2 & 0 & 4 \\ 6 & 2 & 5 & 0 \\ 2 & 3 & 2 & 0 \\ 5 & 2 & 6 & 1 \end{pmatrix}.$$

By executing our 3-step encryption process we get the following bit strings after concatenating the entries of the obtained matrices $Enc((\Delta, X, Y), \vec{v}_2(H_1))$ and $Enc((\Delta, X, Y), \vec{v}_3(H_2))$ respectively:

'10101111000101011001110001001011001011000100011110101011101101000',

'00010000001111010001110000100100110111110010111010111011101001110'.

The avalanche effect for this example is 0.5313.

We also evaluated the bit independence criterion of the modified cipher by applying two approaches: maximal absolute value of the correlation as presented in (4) and the average absolute value of correlation for the reasons mentioned in the introduction.

Experimentally we got that the maximal value approach is uninformative since we have obtained the value of BIC close to 1 for our block cipher and AES-128. For TDES the maximal value was 0.4367, which considering the requirements of BIC is a reasonably large value.

The average value approach proved to be better for evaluating BIC. Using the same methodology as previously we have obtained the values of BIC for the modified block cipher presented in Table 4.

To evaluate the quality of the obtained results we have compared them to AES-128 and TDES by applying the same approach to calculate BIC. The calculations for these ciphers have shown that the values of BIC are 0.1782 and 0.0993 respectively.

Since the avalanche effect and BIC for the modified version of our block cipher are relatively close to the ones obtained for other widely used ciphers, we think that

Table 4. Bit independence criterion of the modified block cipher

	m = 4	m = 5	m = 6	m = 7
t = 4	0.1931	0.1748	0.1672	0.1599
t = 5	0.1817	0.1669	0.1606	0.1570
t = 6	0.1801	0.1644	0.1598	0.1531
t = 7	0.1773	0.1648	0.1574	0.1485

the statistical security of our block cipher is at the very least comparable to other high-quality techniques of encryption. Moreover, even though the TDES cipher has the best BIC, it has lost the trust of NIST due to possible collisions issue [18].

6 Analysis of the Collisions for Our Cipher

Let us briefly explore the issue of collisions for our block cipher. In other words, we are interested in determining distinct messages M_1 and M_2 which satisfy the following equality:

$$Enc((\Delta, X, Y), M_1) = Enc((\Delta, X, Y), M_2). \tag{14}$$

It can be shown that if the matrix Y is chosen at random, then the following result holds:

$$M - Dec\left(\vec{K}, Enc(\vec{K}, M)\right) \equiv 2^{t-2} U \tag{15}$$

where $\vec{K} = (\Delta, X, Y)$ is a private key, U is a binary matrix and $Dec\left(\vec{K}, C\right)$ is the algorithm which reverses all the steps of the encryption given the ciphertext $C = Enc(\vec{K}, M)$. Note that if Y is a permutation matrix modulo 2, then $Dec\left(\vec{K}, C\right)$ acts as a decryption function. Otherwise, there is no guarantee that $Dec\left(\vec{K}, C\right)$ correctly restores the original message.

Hence it makes sense to search for collisions in the set of matrices:

$$\left\{ M + 2^{t-2} U \,\middle|\, u_{ij} \in \{0, 1\} \right\} \tag{16}$$

Since the cardinality of this set is 2^{m^2} we settle for exploring the case of 4×4 matrices. Moreover, since the restriction on the matrix Y can be removed, we considered two cases:

- the private key matrix Y is invertible;
- the private key matrix Y is singular.

Obviously, there are no collisions if Y is a permutation matrix. However, through experiments we saw that none of the matrices of the considered set (16) are collisions if matrix Y is invertible.

In the case of a singular matrix Y collisions in the considered set were found. The number of collisions depends on the generated key matrices. As of now extra research is needed to estimate this dependence. However, since $2^{m^2} - 1$ matrices must be checked, the total scan becomes infeasible if $m \geq 11$. Also note that in the CTR mode the encryption function acts on the concatenation of the nonce and the counter. Obviously, the counter changes each time the new block is encrypted. For this reason, the matrix M in (16) changes as well. This means that the collision analysis has to be performed separately for each value of η (see Fig. 1).

7 Conclusion

In this paper, we have analyzed the statistical properties of the block cipher based on the one-sided MPF in the CTR mode. Our results have shown that the avalanche criterion for our original cipher was not satisfied. We offered one of the possible solutions to this issue and demonstrated that the statistical properties of the modified scheme have improved. In the future it makes sense to consider other possibilities and settle on the optimal solution to the mentioned issue.

Moreover, we compared our results to other widely used algorithms AES-128 and TDES. The comparison has shown that the statistical properties of our cipher are relatively close to the other two ciphers standardized by NIST.

Recently TDES has lost the trust of NIST due to the collision problem. The preliminary analysis of collisions for our case has shown that this issue can be dealt with either by using invertible matrices, or by increasing the matrix order.

Acknowledgement. This research was funded by the Research Council of Lithuania, activity "Students research during the summer", reg. nr. P-SV-22-86, "The security analysis of the block cipher operating in CTR mode".

References

1. Lardinois, F.: IBM Unveils Its 433 Qubit Osprey Quantum Computer. TechCrunch (2022)
2. Sakalauskas, E., Luksys, K.: Matrix Power S-Box Construction. Cryptol. EPrint Arch. (2007)
3. Sakalauskas, E., Dindienė, L., Kilčiauskas, A., Lukšys, K.: Perfectly secure Shannon cipher construction based on the matrix power function. Symmetry **12**, 860 (2020)
4. Dindiene, L., Mihalkovich, A., Luksys, K., Sakalauskas, E.: Matrix power function based block cipher operating in CBC mode. Mathematics **10**, 2123 (2022). https://doi.org/10.3390/math10122123
5. Mihalkovich, A., Levinskas, M., Dindiene, L., Sakalauskas, E.: CBC mode of MPF based Shannon cipher defined over a non-commuting platform group. Informatica **33**, 833–856 (2022). https://doi.org/10.15388/22-INFOR499
6. Boneh, D., Shoup, V.: A Graduate Course in Applied Cryptography. 900
7. Mihalkovich, A., Levinskas, M., Sakalauskas, E.: Counter mode of the Shannon block cipher based on MPF defined over a non-commuting group. Mathematics **10**, 3363 (2022). https://doi.org/10.3390/math10183363

8. Webster, A.F., Tavares, S.E.: On the design of s-boxes. In: Williams, H.C. (eds.) Advances in Cryptology — CRYPTO '85 Proceedings. CRYPTO 1985. LNCS, vol. 218, pp. 523–534. Springer, Berlin, Heidelberg (1986). https://doi.org/10.1007/3-540-39799-X_41

9. Madarro-Capó, E.J., Legón-Pérez, C.M., Rojas, O., Sosa-Gómez, G., Socorro-Llanes, R.: Bit independence criterion extended to stream ciphers. Appl. Sci. 10, 7668 (2020). https://doi.org/10.3390/app10217668

10. Sakalauskas, E., Luksys, K.: The matrix power function and its application to block cipher S-Box construction. Int. J. Innov. Comput. Inf. Control 8 (2012)

11. Sakalauskas, E., Mihalkovich, A.: Improved asymmetric cipher based on matrix power function resistant to linear algebra attack. Informatica 28, 517–524 (2017)

12. Mihalkovich, A.: On the associativity property of MPF over M16. Liet. Mat. Rink. Liet. Mat. Draugijos Darb. Ser. A 59, 7–12 (2018). https://doi.org/10.15388/LMR.A.2018.02

13. Grundman, H., Smith, T.: Automatic realizability of Galois groups of order 16. Proc. Am. Math. Soc. 124, 2631–2640 (1996). https://doi.org/10.1090/S0002-9939-96-03345-X

14. Grundman, H.G., Smith, T.L.: Realizability and automatic realizability of Galois groups of order 32. Cent. Eur. J. Math. 8, 244–260 (2010). https://doi.org/10.2478/s11533-009-0072-x

15. Grundman, H.G., Smith, T.L.: Galois realizability of groups of order 64. Cent. Eur. J. Math. 8, 846–854 (2010). https://doi.org/10.2478/s11533-010-0052-1

16. Levinskas, M., Michalkovič, A.: Avalanche effect and bit independence criterion of perfectly secure Shannon cipher based on matrix power. Math. Models Eng. 7, 50–53 (2021)

17. Mihalkovich, A., Levinskas, M., Makauskas, P.: MPF based symmetric cipher performance comparison to AES and TDES. Math. Models Eng. 8, 15–25 (2022)

18. Computer Security Division, I.T.L. Update to Current Use and Deprecation of TDEA | CSRC. https://csrc.nist.gov/News/2017/Update-to-Current-Use-and-Deprecation-of-TDEA. Accessed 27 Feb 2023

Online PID Tuning of a 3-DoF Robotic Arm Using a Metaheuristic Optimisation Algorithm: A Comparative Analysis

Muhammad Hamza Zafar[1](ID), Hassaan Bin Younus[2],
Syed Kumayl Raza Moosavi[2](ID), Majad Mansoor[3],
and Filippo Sanfilippo[1,4(✉)](ID)

[1] Department of Engineering Sciences, University of Agder, Grimstad, Norway
`filippo.sanfilippo@uia.no`
[2] National University of Sciences and Technology, Islamabad, Pakistan
[3] Department of Automation, University of Science and Technology of China, Hefei, China
[4] Department of Software Engineering, Kaunas University of Technology, Kaunas, Lithuania

Abstract. This paper presents a metaheuristic algorithm-based proportional-integral-derivative (PID) controller tuning method for a 3 degrees of freedom (DoF) robotic manipulator. In particular, the War Strategy Optimisation Algorithm (WSO) is applied as a metaheuristic algorithm for PID tuning of the manipulator, and the performance of the controller is compared with Particle Swarm Optimisation (PSO) and Grey Wolf Optimisation (GWO) algorithms. According to the simulation outcomes, the WSO algorithm exhibits superior performance compared to the other two algorithms with respect to settling time, overshoot, and steady-state error. The proposed technique provides an effective approach for enhancing the performance of robotic manipulators and can be extended to other applications that require optimal PID controller tuning.

Keywords: Metaheuristic Algorithms · PID Controller · Robotic Manipulator

1 Introduction

1.1 Literature Review

Proportional-integral-derivative (PID) control structures offer straightforward, reliable, and efficient solutions for the majority of control engineering applications. According to Ayala et al. [1], PID controllers account for a whopping 95%

This work is supported by the Biomechatronics and Collaborative Robotics Group at the Top Research Centre Mechatronics (TRCM), University of Agder, Grimstad, Norway.

of all controller usage in industrial operations. Accurate tuning of the controller gains is necessary to maintain the beneficial properties of PID controllers. However, it was demonstrated by Desborough et al. [6] that approximately 80% of the existing PID controllers are not operating at peak efficiency, with improper controller tuning being one of the key contributing factors. Robotic manipulators, which are multi-input multi-output (MIMO) dynamic systems, are highly nonlinear and exhibit strong coupling. Although PID controllers are commonly used to control robotic manipulators, conventional tuning techniques that rely on manual or experimental approaches do not always yield satisfactory results for such complex systems, as noted in [8].

In situations where a robot's tasks change frequently or its configuration and shape are variable (such as in modular robots), traditional manual tuning and experimental approaches become more challenging. Therefore, an auto-tuning technique is essential in such scenarios. Auto-tuning techniques that utilise optimisation approaches have been increasingly applied to nonlinear systems in recent years to enhance their performance based on predetermined fitness functions that are relevant to the particular task being performed. This has been made possible by the significant advancement in computer power. Trajectory tracking tasks frequently use the integral of the absolute error (IAE) or the integral of the square error (ISE) as fitness functions.

Optimisation techniques like Particle Swarm Optimisation (PSO) [10] and Genetic Algorithms (GA) [11] have been utilised in the domain of robotic manipulators to automatically adjust PID controllers. Various studies have also been conducted to compare the efficacy of different algorithms. For example, in a study by Kapoor et al. [7], a GA algorithm was compared with a PSO approach and shown to produce superior tracking accuracy. On the other hand, in a comparative study by Ouyang et al. [15] involving GA, PSO, and Differential Evolution (DE), it was found that DE outperformed the other two algorithms across several performance-measuring functions. However, it should be noted that these findings were based on simplified simulations of serial robots. In addition to optimisation techniques, other methods such as fuzzy logic and neural networks have also been utilised in the design of PID tuning systems for robotic manipulators. This is because typical manual or experimental tuning methods may not yield satisfactory results for highly nonlinear and strongly coupled MIMO dynamic systems like robotic manipulators [8]. Several studies, including [3,13], and [22], have developed such systems that transform traditional controllers into adaptive ones by allowing the PID gains to adjust their values dynamically based on real-time measurements of the robot joint positions.

Another method for optimising the PID's parameters is fuzzy logic. PIDs are commonly used to control rehabilitation robots, while fuzzy logic is used to optimise their parameters. Triangular membership functions and various sets of fuzzy rules are utilised to characterise each parameter of the PID controllers. When compared to conventional PID controllers, experimental results demonstrated that fuzzy PIDs deliver better and more effective trajectory-tracking capability. In [14], another strategy has been suggested: a hybrid PID regulator tuning method was created using both the GA methodology and fuzzy logic. This approach transformed the classic controller into an adaptive controller, which provided the PID gains with changing values based on real-time measurements of the robot joint positions. In [14], another strategy has been suggested. Here, a hybrid PID regulator tuning method was created using both the GA methodology and fuzzy logic. While these techniques have demonstrated improved performance over traditional methods, there is a clear research gap in terms of optimising PID controllers for increasingly complex robotic manipulators.

1.2 Contributions and Paper Organisation

The contribution of the paper are as follows:

1. A 3 degree of freedom (DoF) robotic manipulator is designed in MAT-LAB/Simulink;
2. a novel War Strategy Optimisation Algorithm (WSO) is used for optimal PID tuning of the considered robotic manipulator;
3. A comparison is made with PSO and GWO based PID tuners for the presented robotic manipulator;
4. WSO effectively tunes the PID controller by achieving less cost function value during tuning.

The remainder of the paper is structured as follows: Sect. 2 presents the proposed methodology, wherein first the robotic arm kinematic model is described, then the War strategy optimisation algorithm is presented with the PID controller for a 3 DoF robotic manipulator and WSO based PID tuning method is elaborated. Section 3 of the paper presents the results and discussion, while Sect. 4 summarises the conclusion of the study.

2 Proposed Methodology

2.1 Robotic Arm

A critical component of the robotic arm control system is the kinematic model describing the motion and position of the end effector (EE) of a robotic arm in three-dimensional space. The model typically consists of a set of equations that describe the relationship between the joint angles and positions of the end-effector. There are two main types of kinematic models: forward kinematics and inverse kinematics. To determine a generalized solution for the kinematic model for the Denavit-Hartenburg parameters are used as a numerical approach to the problem. The methodology of DH tables stipulate that any serial manipulator can be described as a kinematic model by specifying four parameters for each link: a_i length of the link, α_i twist of the link, d_i offset of the link, and θ_i angle of the joint. With the development of soft-computing methods, researchers have focused on alternative solutions of machine learning to devise approaches that bypass the traditional numerical approaches.

According to the study in [5], the neural network approach demonstrated superior performance in solving the forward kinematics problem of the HEXA parallel manipulator. Sanfillipo et al. [17] proposed a flexible control system architecture and a genetic algorithms that can automatically learn the inverse kinematic properties of different models. In [9], the authors proposed the use of neural networks and particle swarm optimization to develop a kinematic model for hybrid robots with parallel-serial structure, Fig. 1 (a) shows a three revolute joint robotic manipulator on three linkages that will be used for the purposes of this study.

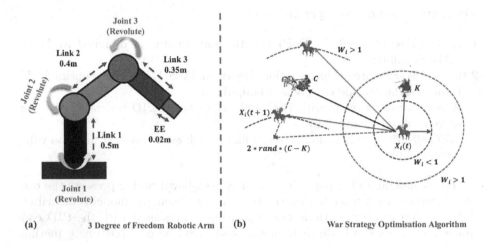

(a)   3 Degree of Freedom Robotic Arm   (b)   War Strategy Optimisation Algorithm

Fig. 1. (a) Robotic Manipulator Description (b) Operating Principle of WSO algorithm

2.2   War Strategy Optimisation Algorithm (WSO)

In this section, we develop the mathematical model of the WSO algorithm, as described in [2]. This is a swarm intelligence algorithm inspired by the strategy employed by military forces in battles. The Commander and the King both act as leader on the battlefield. The remainder of the army will follow the King and Commander's commands as they march around the battlefield. Based on their Combating Strength, all troops have an equal chance of becoming King or Commander at each iteration (Fitness Value). The enemy's soldier, who is strong enough to capture the Leaders, may put up a difficult fight against the King or the Commander. To avoid this, soldiers will follow the Commander and King's position in combat as well as their synchronised movement patterns. The working principle of WOS is shown in Fig. 1 (b).

Attacking Policy: We have developed two plans for a potential war scenario. In the first plan, each soldier will adjust their position according to the locations of the King and Commander. The method of updating positions aims to position the monarch in the best possible location to launch a successful offensive against the enemy. The monarch is expected to have the highest level of fitness or assault force in this plan. When the conflict begins, all soldiers are assigned the same rank and weight. However, their respective ranks and weights will adjust as the plan is executed and its effectiveness is evaluated. Effective tactics will lead to a rise in rank and weight for soldiers, while ineffective strategies will cause their ranks and weights to decrease.

$$X_j(t+1) = X_j(t) + 2 \times \rho \times (C - K) + (W_j \times K - X_j(t)) \times rand, \qquad (1)$$

where $X_j(t+1)$ denotes the next position, X_j the original position, ρ the commander position, K the king position, and W_j the weight. When $W_j > 1$, the new location of the agent that is the soldier will be away from the position of the agent that is the commander because $W_j \times K - X_j(t)$ lies outside the King's position. On the other hand, when $W_j \leq 1$, the updated location of the soldier will be between their current position and the King's position, and it will be determined by $W_j \times K - X_j(t)$.

When compared to the prior scenario, the soldier's revised position is closer. If W_j approaches zero, the soldier's new and better updated position moves nearer to the position of the commander. This indicates the final part of the war strategy.

Ranking Update Methodology: The positions of all agents are updated by taking into account the interplay of ranks of the three pieces in the war i.e., King, Commander, and regular soldier. Each soldier's rank is determined by his record of success in battle, as determined by Eq. 4, which in turn influences the weighting factor W. Each soldier's rank represents how near the soldier is to the goal. It should be noticed that the weighting factors in other competing algorithms vary linearly, but the weight (W_i) in the present suggested WSO method exponentially using e as the growth factor. Provided that the new position of the assault force (F_n) is lesser than the strike force in its prior position, the soldier then assumes the former stance.

If the new position of the assault force (fitness) (F_n) is smaller from the strike force (fitness) in the prior position (F_p), the soldier assumes the former stance.

$$X_j(t+1) = X_j(t) \times F_n \geq F_p + R_j \times F_n \geq F_p \qquad (2)$$

Provided the soldier agent successfully adjusts the location, the soldier's rank/weight R_j will be improved accordingly from the Equation provided as under:

$$R_j = (R_j + 1) \times F_n \geq F_p + R_j \times F_n \geq F_p \qquad (3)$$

The current rank/weight determines the next rank/weight based on the following equation:

$$W_j = W_j \times (1 - R_j/Max_j)^\alpha \qquad (4)$$

Defensive Strategy: Unlike the first plan, the second strategic position update considers the location of the key players in the war namely the King, Commander, and a random soldier chosen from the army, while maintaining a constant ranking and weighting of the soldiers.

$$X_j(t+1) = X_j(t) + 2 \times \rho \times (K - X_j(t)rand) + rand \times W_j(C - X_j(t)) \quad (5)$$

Since it includes the position of a random soldier, this combat strategy examines a larger search space than the preceding method. Soldiers take significant steps and update their position when W_j is high. W_j troops take modest moves while updating the position for small values of W_j.

Replacement of Weak Soldier: To identify weak soldiers in each iteration, various replacement strategies were attempted. One simple approach involved using a random soldier from the army population to replace the weakest soldier, as shown in Eq. 6.

$$X_j(t+1) = Bound_{Lower} + rand \times (Bound_{Upper} - Bound_{Lower}) \quad (6)$$

The second technique involves moving the weak soldier to a location close to the middle of the army population in the conflict zone, using Eq. 7 described below. This technique improves the convergence factor of the algorithm.

$$X_j(t+1) = -(1 - rand) \times (X_j(t) - median(X_j)) + K \quad (7)$$

2.3 PID Controller for Robotic Manipulator

A PID (Proportional-Integral-Derivative) controller is a common control algorithm used in many applications. A feedback controller uses the error between the desired setpoint and the actual process variable to adjust the control signal [12]. The PID controller comprises three components: the proportional term, the integral term, and the derivative term. The mathematical equation of a PID controller is given by:

$$u(t) = K_p e(t) + K_i \int_0^t e(\tau)d\tau + K_d \frac{de(t)}{dt}, \quad (8)$$

where the control signal $u(t)$ in a feedback control system is calculated based on the error signal $e(t)$, which is the difference between the desired setpoint and the actual process variable. The values of the proportional gain K_p, integral gain K_i, and derivative gain K_d are used to determine the behaviour of the system.

The proportional term provides an immediate response to the error, while the integral term sums up the past errors to eliminate the steady-state error. The derivative term anticipates the future error by calculating the rate of change of the error. The PID controller combines these three terms to achieve a stable and accurate control of the system. The tuning of the PID gains is critical to achieve the desired performance, and various methods can be used to determine the optimal gains.

PID controllers are widely used in robotic manipulators to achieve precise and stable control of the joint angles and velocities [21]. A PID controller can be designed to track the desired trajectory of the end-effector or to maintain a specific configuration of the manipulator [18,19]. The proportional term of a PID controller provides the immediate response to the error in the joint position or velocity, while the integral term eliminates the steady-state error caused by external disturbances or system uncertainties. The derivative term in a PID controller can enhance the system's response speed and mitigate overshoot and oscillations. The tuning of the PID gains for robotic manipulators can be challenging due to the complex dynamics and nonlinearities of the system, and various optimization techniques can be used to determine the optimal gains.

2.4 WSO Based PID Tuning

Metaheuristic optimisation algorithms are popular techniques for tuning the PID gains in robotic manipulators due to their ability to search the large parameter space and find the optimal solution efficiently [23]. These algorithms utilise a heuristic approach to search for the optimal solution by iteratively enhancing the candidate solutions based on the fitness function which is a measure towards the performance of the system, and in the case of PID tuning, it is typically defined as a combination of the tracking error and the control effort. One such cost function is the Integrated Time Error Absolute (ITEA) index, which is given by [16]:

$$ITEA = \int_0^T |e(t)|dt + \alpha \int_0^T |u(t)|dt, \qquad (9)$$

where $e(t)$ is the tracking error, $u(t)$ is the control signal, T is the simulation time, and α is a weighting factor that balances the tracking error and the control effort. The ITEA index measures the cumulative error and control effort over the entire simulation time, and the optimisation algorithm seeks to minimise this index by adjusting the PID gains. The effectiveness of tuning the PID gains using metaheuristic optimisation algorithms has been demonstrated in various studies, and these techniques have been shown to provide improved performance compared to traditional methods of PID tuning. In this study, the WSO is used for tuning of PID gains for robotic manipulator. Figure 2 shows the detailed overview of proposed technique. Table 1 shows the parameters for tuning of PID using metaheuristic techniques.

3   Results and Discussion

3.1   Simulation Model

The simulation setup consists of a 3 DoF robotic manipulator designed in MAT-LAB/Simulink, controlled by a PID controller tuned using a metaheuristic optimisation algorithm implemented in MATLAB. The cost function for the optimisation algorithm is the ITEA (Integrated Time Error Absolute) index, which

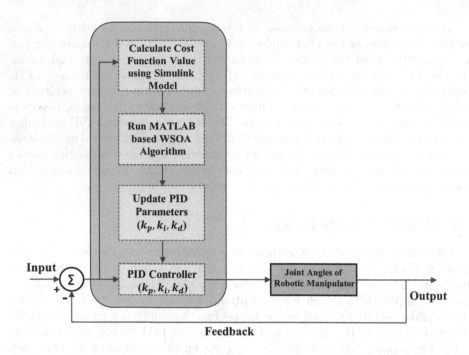

Fig. 2. WSO based PID tuning of Robotic manipulator in MATLAB/Simulink

Table 1. Simulation Parameters for Metaheuristic Algorithms based PID Tuning

Technique	Parameter	Values
PSO	Max Iterations	50
	Population Size	10
	$C1$	0.25
	$C2$ Text follows	0.1
	W	0.6
GWO	Max Iterations	50
	Population Size	10
	a	2–0
WSO	Max Iterations	50
	Population Size	10
	ϕ_r	0.5

Table 2. Comparative analysis of cost reduced during training by the proposed algorithms

Technique	Joint 1	Joint 2	Joint 3
PSO	0.0013	0.0027	0.3081
GWO	0.0012	0.0025	0.2667
WSO	0.00006	0.0007	0.1106

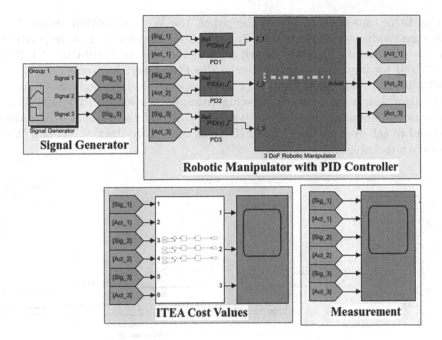

Fig. 3. 3-DoF Simulation model with PID control in MATLAB/Simulink

measures the performance of the system in terms of the tracking error and the control effort. The simulation setup is shown in Fig. 3. This simulation setup aims at achieving precise and efficient control of the robotic manipulator by optimising the PID controller gains through the metaheuristic algorithm. The results obtained from this simulation can be used to validate the proposed control strategy's effectiveness and provide insights for the design and optimisation of robotic manipulators in various applications.

3.2   PID Tuning Error Comparison

In this section of the paper, the authors have compared three different optimisation algorithms, namely PSO [20], GWO [4] and WSO for the purpose of tuning the PID control of a robotic manipulator. The aim of this study was to determine which of the three algorithms would result in the best performance in terms of the cost function and the number of iterations required to achieve a satisfactory result. The cost function used in this study was the Integral Time Absolute Error (ITAE) between the reference trajectory and the actual trajectory of the robotic manipulator. According to the findings of the research, the WSO algorithm demonstrated superior performance compared to the two algorithms namely; PSO and GWO in terms of achieving the best cost and the number of iterations necessary to attain that cost. The best cost versus iteration graphs presented in the paper clearly show that the WSO algorithm consistently outperforms the other two algorithms, with the PSO algorithm performing the worst. The minimisation of cost function by PSO, GWO and WSO is shown in Fig. 4. As shown in Table 2 of the paper, the WSO algorithm attained the lowest cost values of 0.00006, 0.0007, and 0.1106 for joint 1, 2, 3, respectively. On the other hand, the GWO algorithm achieved cost values of 0.0012, 0.0025, and 0.2667 for joint 1, 2, 3, respectively. The PSO algorithm achieved a cost of 0.0013, 0.0027, and 0.3081 for joint 1, 2, 3 respectively. This indicates that the WSO algorithm is the most effective algorithm for tuning the PID controller of a robotic manipulator, in terms of both the cost and the number of iterations required to achieve that cost. The PID gains tunned by PSO, GWO and WSO are shown in Table 3.

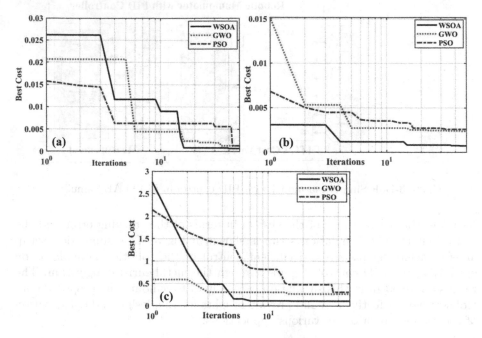

Fig. 4. Best Cost vs Iterations in Tuning of (a) Joint 1 (b) Joint 2 (c) Joint 3

Table 3. Optimised Values of PID Parameters by Algorithms

Technique	Joint	Kp	Ki	Kd
PSO	1	1.504	0.7577	0.0017
	2	2.411	0.3922	−0.0023
	3	1.868	0.6555	0.0039
GWO	1	1.725	0.1712	−0.0025
	2	2.473	0.7060	0.0070
	3	1.129	0.0318	0.0017
WSO	1	1.654	0.2769	−0.00063
	2	2.674	0.0462	0.0026
	3	0.485	0.0971	0.0016

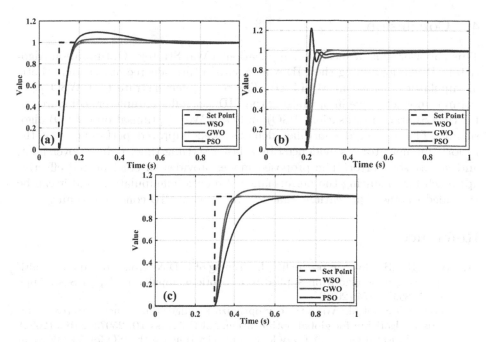

Fig. 5. Step Response Comparison of (a) Joint 1 (b) Joint 2 (c) Joint 3

3.3   Step Response Comparison

In this section of the paper, the authors have compared the step response of all three joints of a robotic manipulator controlled by PID controllers tuned using three different optimisation algorithms, PSO, GWO, and WSO. The step response refers to the duration it takes for a system to react to an abrupt change in input. In this study, the step response of all three joints of the robotic manipulator was measured and compared for each of the three algorithms. The comparison of the step response is shown in Fig. 5.

The results of the study indicate that the WSO algorithm produces the best step response for all three joints of the robotic manipulator. The step response plots presented in the paper clearly show that the WSO-tuned PID controller produces a faster response with less overshoot compared to the PSO and GWO-tuned controllers. The PSO-tuned controller shows some oscillations and overshoots, especially in the second and third joints of the robotic manipulator. The GWO-tuned controller shows less overshoot compared to the PSO-tuned controller, but the response is slower. In contrast, the WSO-tuned PID controller produces a faster and smoother step response with minimal overshoot for all three joints of the robotic manipulator.

4   Conclusion

This paper presents a successful application of War Strategy Optimisation Algorithm (WSO) for tuning the PID controller of a three-degree-of-freedom robotic manipulator designed in MATLAB. The results demonstrate that WSO algorithm is more effective in optimising the PID controller parameters compared to Particle Swarm Optimisation (PSO) and Grey Wolf Optimisation (GWO) algorithms. The optimised controller demonstrated improved performance of the robotic manipulator, as evidenced by a faster settling time, reduced overshoot, and steady-state error. The proposed model provides an efficient and effective approach for enhancing the performance of robotic manipulators, and it can be extended to other applications that require optimal PID controller tuning.

References

1. Ayala, H.V.H., dos Santos Coelho, L.: Tuning of PID controller based on a multi-objective genetic algorithm applied to a robotic manipulator. Expert Syst. Appl. **39**(10), 8968–8974 (2012)
2. Ayyarao, T.S., et al.: War strategy optimization algorithm: a new effective meta-heuristic algorithm for global optimization. IEEE Access **10**, 25073–25105 (2022)
3. Bingül, Z., Karahan, O.: A fuzzy logic controller tuned with PSO for 2 DOF robot trajectory control. Expert Syst. Appl. **38**(1), 1017–1031 (2011)
4. Das, K.R., Das, D., Das, J.: Optimal tuning of PID controller using GWO algorithm for speed control in dc motor. In: 2015 International Conference on Soft Computing Techniques and Implementations (ICSCTI), pp. 108–112. IEEE (2015)
5. Dehghani, M., Ahmadi, M., Khayatian, A., Eghtesad, M., Farid, M.: Neural network solution for forward kinematics problem of HEXA parallel robot. In: 2008 American Control Conference, pp. 4214–4219. IEEE (2008)
6. Desborough, L., Miller, R.: Increasing customer value of industrial control performance monitoring-Honeywell's experience. In: AIChE Symposium Series, pp. 169–189. New York; American Institute of Chemical Engineers; 1998 (2002)
7. Gani, M.M., Islam, M.S., Ullah, M.A.: Optimal PID tuning for controlling the temperature of electric furnace by genetic algorithm. SN Appl. Sci. **1**, 1–8 (2019)
8. Johnson, M.A., Moradi, M.H.: PID Control. Springer, London (2005). https://doi.org/10.1007/1-84628-148-2_1
9. Kang, R., Chanal, H., Bonnemains, T., Pateloup, S., Branson, D.T., Ray, P.: Learning the forward kinematics behavior of a hybrid robot employing artificial neural networks. Robotica **30**(5), 847–855 (2012)
10. Kapoor, N., Ohri, J.: Improved PSO tuned classical controllers (PID and SMC) for robotic manipulator. Int. J. Mod. Educ. Comput. Sci. **7**(1), 47 (2015)
11. Kim, E.J., Seki, K., Iwasaki, M., Lee, S.H.: Ga-based practical auto-tuning technique for industrial robot controller with system identification. IEEJ J. Ind. Appl. **1**(1), 62–69 (2012)
12. Knospe, C.: PID control. IEEE Control Syst. Mag. **26**(1), 30–31 (2006)
13. Lochan, K., Roy, B.K.: Control of two-link 2-DOF robot manipulator using fuzzy logic techniques: a review. In: Das, K.N., Deep, K., Pant, M., Bansal, J.C., Nagar, A. (eds.) Proceedings of Fourth International Conference on Soft Computing for Problem Solving. AISC, vol. 335, pp. 499–511. Springer, New Delhi (2015). https://doi.org/10.1007/978-81-322-2217-0_41

14. Nahapetian, N., Motlagh, M.J., Analoui, M.: PID gain tuning using genetic algorithms and fuzzy logic for robot manipulator control. In: 2009 International Conference on Advanced Computer Control, pp. 346–350. IEEE (2009)
15. Ouyang, P., Pano, V.: Comparative study of DE, PSO and GA for position domain PID controller tuning. Algorithms 8(3), 697–711 (2015)
16. Rawat, D., Gupta, M.K., Sharma, A.: Intelligent control of robotic manipulators: a comprehensive review. Spat. Inf. Res. 1–13 (2022)
17. Sanfilippo, F., Hatledal, L.I., Schaathun, H.G., Pettersen, K.Y., Zhang, H.: A universal control architecture for maritime cranes and robots using genetic algorithms as a possible mapping approach. In: 2013 IEEE International Conference on Robotics and Biomimetics (ROBIO), pp. 322–327. IEEE (2013)
18. Sanfilippo, F., Hatledal, L.I., Zhang, H., Fago, M., Pettersen, K.Y.: Controlling Kuka industrial robots: flexible communication interface JOpenShowVar. IEEE Robot. Autom. Mag. 22(4), 96–109 (2015)
19. Sanfilippo, F., Hatledal, L.I., Zhang, H., Fago, M., Pettersen, K.Y.: JOpenShowVar: an open-source cross-platform communication interface to Kuka robots. In: Proceedings of the IEEE International Conference on Information and Automation (ICIA), pp. 1154–1159 (2014)
20. Solihin, M.I., Tack, L.F., Kean, M.L.: Tuning of PID controller using particle swarm optimization (PSO). In: Proceeding of the International Conference on Advanced Science, Engineering and Information Technology, vol. 1, pp. 458–461 (2011)
21. Su, Y., Müller, P.C., Zheng, C.: Global asymptotic saturated PID control for robot manipulators. IEEE Trans. Control Syst. Technol. 18(6), 1280–1288 (2009)
22. Tuan, H.M., Sanfilippo, F., Hao, N.V.: A novel adaptive sliding mode controller for a 2-DOF elastic robotic arm. Robotics 11(2), 47 (2022)
23. Valluru, S.K., Singh, M.: Optimization strategy of bio-inspired metaheuristic algorithms tuned PID controller for PMBDC actuated robotic manipulator. Procedia Comput. Sci. 171, 2040–2049 (2020)

Multivariate Bitcoin Price Prediction Based on Tuned Bidirectional Long Short-Term Memory Network and Enhanced Reptile Search Algorithm

Ivana Strumberger[1] , Miodrag Zivkovic[1] , Venkat Ram Raj Thumiki[2] ,
Aleksandar Djordjevic[1] , Jelena Gajic[1] , and Nebojsa Bacanin[1(✉)]

[1] Singidunum University, Danijelova 32, 11000 Belgrade, Serbia
{istrumberger,mzivkovic,adjordjevic,jgajic,nbacanin}@singidunum.ac.rs
[2] Modern College of Business and Science, Muscat, Oman
venkat@mcbs.edu.om

Abstract. Cryptocurrency price prediction and investment is a popular and relevant area of business nowadays. It involves analyzing historical data to forecast future trends and movements in asset prices. Bitcoin has gained significant prominence in the worldwide financial market as an investment asset. However, the high volatility of its price has attracted considerable attention from researchers and investors alike, leading to a growing interest in understanding the factors that drive its movement. This paper builds upon a research and conducts an empirical approach into the time-series data of a diverse range of exogenous and endogenous variables. Specifically, in this paper, the closing prices of Bitcoin, Ethereum and the daily volume of Bitcoin-related tweets are examined. For forecasting closing Bitcoin price based on the above mentioned predictors, bidirectional long-short term memory (BiLSTM) network tuned by hybrid adaptive reptile search algorithm is proposed. The analysis covers a three-year period from January 2020 to August 2022 and employs a three-fold split of the data to train, validation, and testing datasets. The best generated model by algorithm introduced in this manuscript is compared to other BiLSTM networks tuned by other cutting-edge metaheuristics and achieved results revealed that the method introduced in this research outperformed all other competitors regarding standard regression metrics.

Keywords: Cryptocurrency price forecasting · Bitcoin, neural networks · bidirectional long short-term memory · metaheuristic optimization · reptile search algorithm

1 Introduction

Financial time series prediction is a process that utilizes statistical or machine learning methods to evaluate historical financial data and forecast future financial trends, including stock prices, exchange rates, or commodity prices [30]. The

A. Lopata et al. (Eds.): ICIST 2023, CCIS 1979, pp. 38–52, 2024.
https://doi.org/10.1007/978-3-031-48981-5_4

primary goal is development of the model that could learn from patterns and trends in the past performance of a financial asset and leverage this knowledge to make predictions about its future performance. Such predictions can be used to support investment decisions, risk management strategies, or financial policy decisions [4]. To achieve accurate predictions, financial time series models usually consider several variables such as historical price and volume data, economic indicators, news articles, and other external factors that may influence the price of the asset being analyzed.

In comparison, cryptocurrency price prediction and investment is more popular and relevant area of business nowadays. It involves analyzing historical data to forecast future trends and movements in asset prices. The primary difference between traditional financial assets and cryptocurrencies is the fact that the crypto is a relatively new and volatile asset class, with prices that can be influenced by a wide range of factors, including technological innovations, regulatory changes, and social media sentiment including Twitter feeds [16,21].

Although the research presented within this manuscript uses only the number of tweets as the predictor, due to its importance, the sentiment analysis of tweets to establish its influence on the crypto prices should be mentioned. Sentiment analysis can be conducted using natural language processing (NLP) techniques, which entail analyzing the language used in tweets to establish their sentiment [5]. Machine learning algorithms can then be trained on this sentiment data to make predictions about cryptocurrency prices.

Mohapatra et al. [23] used KryptoOracle trading platform to predict cryptocurrency price based on Twitter sentiment analysis. Park and Lee [24] employed social network analysis to the Twitter profiles related to cryptocurrencies and found that networking strategies of cryptocurrencies affected their credit scores. Aslam et al. [5] performed sentiment analysis using tweets related to cryptocurrencies to predict their market prices and found that machine learning models can be helpful in this process.

Additionally, while comparing financial and cryptocurrency prices, the availability and quality of data may differ. For example, cryptocurrency data is often limited to a few years, whereas data on more established financial assets may span several decades. Consequently, different techniques and models may be more effective for predicting cryptocurrency prices compared to traditional financial assets. Sentiment analysis of social media may be more useful for predicting cryptocurrency prices, which can lead to more suitable accumulated parameters for proposed models, whereas economic indicators and historical price data may be more effective for predicting the prices of traditional financial assets [25]. Overall, while there are similarities between financial time series prediction and cryptocurrency price prediction, the unique characteristics of cryptocurrencies may require different approaches and models.

In recent years, Bitcoin has gained significant prominence in the worldwide financial market as an investment asset [21]. However, the high volatility of its price has attracted considerable attention from researchers and investors alike, leading to a growing interest in understanding the factors that drive its movement. This paper builds upon a research and conducts an empirical approach into the time-series data of a diverse range of exogenous and endogenous variables. Specifically, in this paper, the closing prices of Bitcoin, Ethereum and the daily volume of Bitcoin-related tweets are examined. The analysis covers a three-year period from January 2020 to August 2022 and employs a three-fold split of the data into train, validation, and testing datasets.

This manuscript suggest Bidirectional Long Short-Term Memory (BiLSTM) structure to execute multivariate Bitcoin price prediction. As it is the case with other neural networks, the important requirement is to determine the appropriate values of the model's hyperparameters for each individual prediction problem. Metaheuristics algorithms have proven to be powerful stochastic optimizers, and this approach was used in this research as well. Moreover, a novel improved variant of the powerful recent reptile search algorithm (RSA) [1] that deals with the limitations of the basic variant was proposed, and later employed to determine the hyperparameters of the BiLSTM network for the Bitcoin price forecasting task. The BiLSTM control parameters that were subjected to the optimization were learning rate, training epochs, dropout rate, count of hidden layers, and cells' count in the hidden layers.

The structure of the manuscript has been separated to following sections: Sect. 2 provides the background of BiLSTM and metaheuristic optimization, along with the literature survey. Afterwards, in Sect. 3, the original reptile search algorithm and the hybrid adaptive version are explained. Following these Sections, Sect. 4 presents the overall experimental concept, the optimization challenge and the outcomes compared with other methods for Bitcoin price prediction.

2   Background

The following section of the paper begins with descriptions of BiLSTM and metaheuristic optimization (focusing on nature-inspired algorithms), considering that these models and their utilization are crucial in this research for cryptocurrency price prediction optimization problem. Afterwards, literature survey of research involving this topic is shown.

2.1   Bidirectional Long Short-Term Memory Network

BiLSTM represents a sort of recurrent neural network (RNN) devised to better capture dependencies between the past and future inputs in sequential data. Comparing with traditional RNNs, BiLSTMs process input sequences in both directions, from the beginning to the end (known as forward pass) and from the end to the beginning (known as backward pass), allowing the network to capture both dependencies and give the optimal result.

A single BiLSTM cell is formed as a combination of a forward LSTM cell and a backward LSTM cell, with their outputs concatenated at each time and in each step. LSTM cells can be defined as a type of RNN cell that are designated to address the vanishing gradient problem, happening during train process of deep neural networks. The LSTM cell contains an internal state that allows it to selectively "forget" or "remember" information over time, which is important when processing long sequences of data while predicting the output. By processing input sequences in both directions, a BiLSTM is able to capture more complex patterns and dependencies in the data compared to a traditional RNN or a unidirectional LSTM.

The network consists of multiple LSTM units, each of which has a cell state, an input gate, a forget gate, and an output gate. Equation (1) represents the forward LSTM unit:

$$\overrightarrow{h}_t = \sigma(\overrightarrow{W}_i x_t + \overrightarrow{V}_i \overrightarrow{h}_{t-1} + \overrightarrow{b}) \qquad (1)$$

where $\overrightarrow{h}_t$ depicts the hidden state at time step t for the forward LSTM, x_t denotes the input vector at time step t, $\overrightarrow{W}_i$ and $\overrightarrow{V}_i$ are the weight matrices for the input and the hidden state of the forward LSTM, respectively, and $\overrightarrow{b}$ is learnable parameter that allows the model to shift the output of the activation function up or down. The parameter $\overrightarrow{b}$ is added to the input of the activation function of the forward and backward LSTMs, respectively. The σ function represents the sigma activation function.

Equation (2) represents the backward LSTM unit:

$$\overleftarrow{h}_t = \sigma(\overleftarrow{W}_i x_t + \overleftarrow{V}_i h_{t+1} + \overleftarrow{b}) \qquad (2)$$

where $\overleftarrow{h}_t$ depicts the hidden state at time step t for the backward LSTM, $\overleftarrow{W}_i$ and $\overleftarrow{V}_i$ are the weight matrices for the input and the hidden state of the backward LSTM, respectively, and $\overleftarrow{b}$ is added to the input of the activation function of the forward and backward LSTMs, respectively.

Equation (3) represents the output layer of the BiLSTM model:

$$y_t = \sigma(U[\overrightarrow{h}_t; \overleftarrow{h}_t] + c) \qquad (3)$$

where y_t denotes the predicted output at time step t, U is the weight matrix for the output layer, $[\overrightarrow{h}_t; \overleftarrow{h}_t]$ denotes the merging of the forward and backward hidden states at time step t, and c for the output layer. Parameter c allows the output of the network to be shifted up or down along the y-axis, which can be useful for adjusting the output of the network to better match the target values. The value of c is learned during the training process along with the other parameters of the network. The output layer employs the sigma activation function to produce the predicted output value.

BiLSTM neural network can be used for time series prediction, including cryptocurrency price prediction, taking into consideration historical price data and other relevant variables, such as trading volume, social media sentiment, and economic indicators, which can be used as input to the network [27]. The network can then be trained on this data using a supervised learning approach or adding a modification method, where the goal is to predict future price movements based on past data.

During training, the network can learn to identify patterns and trends in the input sequence that are relevant for predicting future prices. Once the network is trained, it can be used to make predictions about future price movements based on new input data.

It's worth mentioning that the effectiveness of a BiLSTM network for cryptocurrency price prediction depends of the quality and relevance of the information fed to the inputs, as well as the specific architecture and parameters of the network, and can be modified and enhanced with other methods [13]. Additionally, like any prediction model, the accuracy of the forecasts depends of the unpredictability of the cryptocurrency market.

2.2 Metaheuristic Optimization

In the fields of computer science and mathematical optimization, metaheuristics present high-level procedures or heuristics that are designed to identify, generate, adjust, or to choose partial search algorithms that could potentially offer satisfactory solutions to optimization problems. These methods are particularly useful for tackling problems that have incomplete or imperfect information or when computational resources are limited. Metaheuristics are applicable to various problems since they offer a way to explore a limited set of solutions that would otherwise be too vast to examine fully, without relying on many assumptions about the problem being solved.

Swarm intelligence algorithms (SI), belong in the category of nature-inspired metaheuristics. They model the swarm bearings depicted by decentralized, self-organizing systems, either natural or artificial. SI draws inspiration from the cooperative behavior and intelligence found in biological systems like ant colonies, bird flocks, animal herds etc. In their structure, the significant aspect involves a concept of a population of simple units that perform local interaction with each other as well as surrounding area, resulting in emergent global behavior that appears "intelligent".

Swarm intelligence algorithms have gained popularity in recent years for solving complex optimization problems, including NP-hard problems. Examples of swarm intelligence methods devised from nature include the artificial bee colony [20], firefly algorithm [31], while others can be incorporated with mathematical concepts, such as the sine cosine algorithm [22] and the arithmetic optimization algorithm [2]. The hybridization and enhancement of other methods also aims to find the best performance in finding optimal or suboptimal solution for the specific problem. However, experimentation is crucial because no singular method works best in all situations.

Swarm intelligence approaches have been successful in different practical areas such as medical and healthcare applications [26], optimizing energy problems and localization of the sensor nodes in wireless sensor networks [6,9], solving problems in cloud computing [10,12] as well as resolving issues and problems regarding the COVID-19 pandemic [32,33].

Other swarm intellgence algorithms that surfaced recently include the Harris hawks optimizer (HHO) [14], as well as the particle swarm optimizer (PSO) [29], reptile search algorithm (RSA) [1]. These algorithms have been successful in tackling problems in security [17], finance [11, 18] as well as medicine [19, 26].

In the context of cryptocurrency price prediction, swarm intelligence can be used to aggregate the opinions of multiple traders or investors to make more accurate predictions. One approach is to create a prediction market, where traders can buy and sell contracts that represent the future price of a cryptocurrency [28]. The collective behavior of traders in the market can then be used for predicting the future prices trend of the cryptocurrency.

Another approach for using swarm intelligence is to create a model that aggregates the opinions of multiple experts or analysts. This model can be trained using historical data and the opinions of the experts, and can then be used to make predictions about future price movements which is also an inspiration for our research.

In terms of using swarm intelligence in conjunction with the BiLSTM structure for cryptocurrency price forecasting, the BiLSTM network can be used to process and analyze historical data, while the swarm intelligence model can aggregate the opinions of multiple experts or traders, or even Twitter input [15]. The output of the BiLSTM network and the swarm intelligence model can be utilized using an ensemble approach, where the predictions of both models are combined to generate a final prediction. This can help in reduction of the effect of individual prediction errors and improve the overall prediction accuracy, while comapring to other models with the same data ranging sets.

Empirical studies have demonstrated that this combined approach can improve the prediction accuracy of bitcoin prices in comparison to using either method alone, which can be seen in the experimental part of this paper. However, there are not many papers in literature that combine these methods, but the combination of metaheuristics with BiLSTM, LSTM structures were implemented in various time-series tasks such as forecasting gold price predictions [3], energy load forecasting [8], pollution prediction [7], oil price prediction [18] etc.

3   Methods

The baseline RSA metaheuristic algorithm is presented in this chapter, followed by the hybrid adaprive RSA version, developed to enhance and overcome the limitations, while combining with BiLSTM neural network for Bitcoin price prediction problem.

3.1   Original Reptile Search Algorithm

Reptile Search Algorithm (RSA), created by Abualigah et al. [1], is a swarm intelligence method inspired by predatory hunting behavior of Crocodiles.

Survival instinct of Crocodiles can be characterized in two steps: the process of encircling and the process of hunting. Encircling is a form of distinctive twofold walking and being aware of surroundings, while hunting is a precise coordinated action while tackling the prey. These actions are utilized in exploitation and exploration phases of RSA algorithm.

By populating a matrix X with stochastic solutions $x_{i,j}$ in the optimization initialization phase, Eq. (4), defines i as index of a solution, j denotes its momentary location, N is the count of candidate individuals, while n signifies the dimension size of a specific challenge:

$$X = \begin{bmatrix} x_{1,1} & \cdots & x_{1,j} & x_{1,n-1} & x_{1,n} \\ x_{2,1} & \cdots & x_{2,j} & \cdots & x_{2,n} \\ \cdots & \cdots & x_{i,j} & \cdots & \cdots \\ \vdots & \vdots & \vdots & \vdots & \vdots \\ x_{N-1,1} & \cdots & x_{N-1,j} & \cdots & x_{N-1,n} \\ x_{N,1} & \cdots & x_{N,j} & x_{N,n-1} & x_{N,n} \end{bmatrix} \tag{4}$$

The following Eq. (5) randomly generates these solutions. In this Equation, $rand$ is a random number in the range [0,1], LB denotes the lower boundary, and UB presents the upper boundary of the problem.

$$x_{ij} = \text{rand} \times (UB - LB) + LB, j = 1, 2, \ldots, n \tag{5}$$

With encircling and hunting, the search process can be incorporated into four behavioral strategies to emphasize the importance of exploration and exploitation. Two walking techniques are used during exploration: elevated walking and stomach walking. The primary goal of this phase is to broaden the search field in order to support the second phase of the hunt. The elevated walking strategy executed when $t \leq \frac{T}{4}$, while the stomach walking behavior is determined by $t > \frac{T}{4}$ and $t \leq 2\frac{T}{4}$.

Equation (6) presents the position updating for the exploration phase:

$$x_{(i,j)}(t+1) = \begin{cases} \text{Best}_j(t) \times -\eta_{(i,j)}(t) \times \beta - R_{(i,j)}(t) \times \text{rand}, t \leq \frac{T}{4} \\ \text{Best}_j(t) \times x_{(r_1,j)} \times ES(t) \times \text{rand}, t > \frac{T}{4} \text{ and } t \leq 2\frac{T}{4} \end{cases} \tag{6}$$

$$\eta_{(i,j)} = \text{Best}_j(t) \times P_{(i,j)} \tag{7}$$

where $Best_j$ is the current best solution at location j, t denotes the current iteration, and T is the maximum number of iterations. The hunting operator $\eta_{(i,j)}$ as presented in Eq. (7,) is defined by $Best_j$ the current best solution at location j and $P_{(i,j)}$, where $P_{(i,j)}$ presents the percentage difference between the j_{th} position of te current solution and the j_{th} position of the best calculated solution, with the sensitive sensitive parameter β positioned at value 0.1 significantly important for precision process in the exploration.

Following the Eq. (7) the search area is narrowed down by employing a reduction function, presented in Eq. (8):

$$R_{(i,j)} = \frac{\text{Best}_j(t) - x_{(r_1,j)}}{\text{Best}_j(t) + \epsilon} \tag{8}$$

where r_1 is a random number in the range $[1, N]$, $x_{r_1,j}$ presents the i_{th}'s solution random location, while ϵ denotes small value.

The calculation of the probability ratio $ES(t)$ is represented in Eq. (9) with randomly decreasing values between –2 to 2 as iterations progress:

$$ES(t) = 2 \times r_2 \times \left(1 - \frac{1}{T}\right) \tag{9}$$

where r_2 signifies a random number in the range $[-1, 1]$.

$$P_{(i,j)} = \alpha + \frac{x_{(i,j)} - M(x_i)}{\text{Best}_j(t) \times \left(UB_{(j)} - LB_{(j)}\right) + \epsilon} \tag{10}$$

Equation (10) calculates the percentage difference of the corresponding locations of the current and best-obtained solution:
where α as the sensitive parameter is determined to 0.1, which controls the fluctuation between potential solutions for the hunting cooperation. The corresponding upper and lower bound of the j_{th} location are given as $UB_{(j)}$ and $LB_{(j)}$. The $M(x_i)$ is the average ith solution calculated as in Eq. (11):

$$M(x_i) = \frac{1}{n} \sum_{j=1}^{n} x_{(i,j)} \tag{11}$$

The exploitation phase of the RSA is defined by hunting coordination (when $t \leq 3\frac{T}{4}$ and $t > \frac{T}{2}$) and hunting cooperation (when $t \leq T$ and $t > 3\frac{T}{4}$) given in Eq. (12):

$$x_{(i,j)}(t+1) = \begin{cases} \text{Best}_j(t) \times P_{(i,j)}(t) \times \text{ rand}, \, t \leq 3\frac{T}{4} \text{ and } t > \frac{T}{2} \\ \text{Best}_j(t) - \eta_{(i,j)}(t) \times \epsilon - R_{(i,j)}(t) \times \text{ rand}, \, t \leq T \text{ and } t > 3\frac{T}{4} \end{cases} \tag{12}$$

where $\text{Best}_j(t)$ presents the j_{th} position in the best solution that is obtained thus far, ϵ a small value, while $\eta_{(i,j)}$, $R_{(i,j)}$ and $P_{(i,j)}$ can be referenced in Eq. (7), Eq. (8) and Eq. (10).

3.2 Hybrid Adaptive RSA (HARSA)

Although the original RSA is recognized as a suitable optimization technique, it has certain limitations like other metaheuristics depending on a type of problem during the implementation. Research on benchmark functions has demonstrated that while RSA is adept at exploring the search space, it is deficient in exploiting the search space during subsequent iterations, when it should be focusing on narrowing down the search. In contrast, the firefly algorithm ([31]) is well-known for its robust exploitation capabilities, and it can be effective when tackling time-series problem like cryptocurrency price prediction

Within this manuscript, a hybrid adaptive RSA approach is presented to overcome a limitation of the original RSA algorithm by combining its exploration capabilities with the exploitation strengths of the firefly algorithm. Initially, solutions are updated through the RSA search equation (Eq. (6)). As the algorithm progresses and favorable areas of the search domain are discovered, the firefly search equation (Eq. (13)) is employed to enhance exploitation:

$$X_i^{t+1} = X_i^t + \beta_0 \cdot e^{-\gamma r_{i,j}^2}(X_j^t - X_i^t) + \alpha^t(\kappa - 0.5) \tag{13}$$

where the randomization factor in the equation is denoted by α, κ is a value chosen from a Gaussian distribution. The distance among individuals i and j has been defined as $r_{i,j}$.

Along with the FA enhanced exploitation, in this hybrid adaptive method, two new control parameters are being introduced. The first is the varying search vs parameter, which enables the combined search mode when the number of iterations surpasses vs.

Another control variable is the search mode sm, which decides whether RSA or FA search is executed for each individual solution based on an arbitrary number rnd generated for each individual. The sm parameter is gradually reduced over the iterations, shifting the focus towards more fine-tuned FA search as the algorithm converges. The initial value of sm was set to 0.8 and reduced using Eq. (14) based on empirical analysis.

$$sm_t = sm_{t-1} - (sm_{t-1}/10) \tag{14}$$

The pseudo-code of HARSA is provided in Algorithm 1.

4   Experiments and Comparative Analysis

4.1   Simulation Setup

This research employed an empirical approach to compare various swarm intelligence algorithms in order to identify satisfying BiLSTM parameters for Bitcoin price prediction. The dataset used for this analysis included Bitcoin Close, number of Bitcoin Tweets, and Ethereum Close features, spanning from January 1, 2020 to August 31, 2022. The dataset is divided into training, validation and testing by using 70%/10%/20% split rule, as it is shown in Fig. 1.

The algorithms that are compared in this study are the original RSA, HARSA, particle swarm optimization (PSO), firefly algorithm (FA) and chimp optimization algorithm (ChOA) that were all employed for BiLSTM tuning with the same experimental setup. The MAE, MSE, $RMSE$, and R^2 metrics have been utilized to evaluate the outcomes.

Algorithm 1. Pseudo-code of the HARSA metaheuristics

Produce a random starting population of N solutions
Initialize RSA control variables α, β, etc.
Initialize $sm = 0.8$ and $vs = 3$
while $(t < T)$ **do**
   for Every solution X in the population **do**
      if $t < vs$ **then**
         Execute RSA search, according to the procedure given in Alghorithm (1).
      else
         Generate random value rnd.
         if $rnd > sm$ **then**
            Execute FA search, according to the Eq. (13).
         else
            Execute RSA search, according to the procedure given in Algorithm (1).
         end if
      end if
   end for
   Update parameters' of algorithm.
   Update candidate solutions' positions.
   Update sm according to (14)
   $t = t + 1$
end while
return Best discovered solution

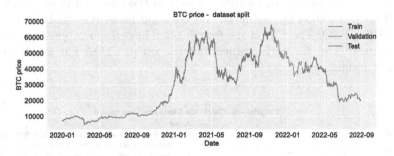

Fig. 1. BTC price dataset with data split visualization

Each assessed generated BiLSTM architecture by metaheuristics has the assigned role of three-step ahead predicting. The BiLSTM control parameters that were optimized accompanied by their respective limits are as follows: $[0.0001, 0.01]$ for the learning rate, $[300, 600]$ for the count of training epochs, $[0.05, 0.2]$ regarding dropout rate, $[1, 2]$ regarding the hidden layer boundaries, and $[100, 200]$ with respect to the count of cells within the hidden layers.

For improving the efficiency of BiLSTM networks, metaheuristic algorithms were run in 8 iterations using a population of 5 search agents. To account for the inherent volatility of these algorithms, 30 separate runs were conducted due to their significant processing requirements.

4.2 Results and Discussion

The scores of the overall fitness function (MSE) for each metaheuristic, averaged across 30 separate executions, are presented in Table 1.

Table 2 yields a detailed statistics of the metrics of the top-performing BiL-STM architecture established for a 3-step ahead prediction, following diagram in Fig. 2 where BiLSTM-HARSA 3-steps ahead best forecast is presented. Additionally, Table 3 shows the parameter choices generated by each metaheuristic.

Table 1. Overall fitness function scores of each individual algorithm.

Method	Best	Worst	Mean	Median	Std	Var
BiLSTM-HARSA	**0.001001**	0.001040	**0.001024**	0.001027	1.48E-05	2.19E-10
BiLSTM-RSA	0.001007	0.001085	0.001044	0.001039	2.82E-05	7.97E-10
BiLSTM-PSO	0.001031	0.001042	0.001038	0.001041	4.86E-06	2.36E-11
BiLSTM-FA	0.001024	**0.001026**	0.001025	**0.001025**	**8.49E-07**	**7.21E-13**
BiLSTM-ChOA	0.001023	0.001040	0.001034	0.001035	6.50E-06	4.23E-11

Table 1 shows the overall metrics for each of the observed models. The proposed HARSA method has achieved the best and mean results, in front of the original RSA, PSO. The FA on the fourth place has shown promising results in the median,std and var performance metrics, where ChOA has stable but not significant results.

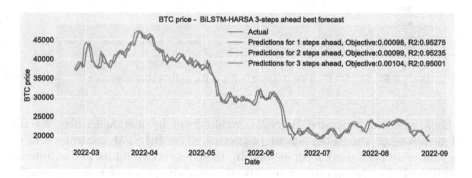

Fig. 2. BTC price BiLSTM-HARSA 3-steps ahead best forecast

Table 2 presents the metrics of the top-performance BiLSTM structure for 3 steps ahead where best metrics are shown in bold font. As in previous analysis the proposed HARSA has the best results in R^2 indicator and MSE in one step ahead where original RSA methods has shown great results in three step ahead for R^2, MAE, MSE and $RMSE$,but the overall results are significantly better in overall results for hybrid adaptive RSA while comparing with RSA, PSO, FA and ChOA metaheuristics.

Table 2. Metrics of the top-performing BiLSTM architectures for 3 steps ahead.

	Error indicator	BiLSTM-HARSA	BiLSTM-RSA	BiLSTM-PSO	BiLSTM-FA	BiLSTM-ChOA
One-step ahead	R^2	**0.952755**	0.952164	0.950038	0.951471	0.951329
	MAE	0.023165	**0.022976**	0.023760	0.023166	0.022977
	MSE	**0.000979**	0.000991	0.001035	0.001006	0.001008
	RMSE	**0.031288**	0.031483	0.032175	0.031710	0.031757
Two-step ahead	R^2	**0.952347**	0.951537	0.951295	0.950706	0.950623
	MAE	0.023483	0.023290	0.023557	**0.023250**	0.023334
	MSE	**0.000987**	0.001004	0.001009	0.001021	0.001023
	RMSE	**0.031423**	0.031688	0.031768	0.031959	0.031986
Three-step ahead	R^2	0.950010	**0.950529**	0.949447	0.949529	0.949895
	MAE	0.024192	**0.023636**	0.024088	0.023781	0.023684
	MSE	0.001036	**0.001025**	0.001047	0.001046	0.001038
	RMSE	0.032184	**0.032016**	0.032365	0.032338	0.032221
Overall Results	R^2	**0.951704**	0.951410	0.950260	0.950569	0.950616
	MAE	0.023613	**0.023301**	0.023802	0.023399	0.023332
	MSE	**0.001001**	0.001007	0.001031	0.001024	0.001023
	RMSE	**0.031634**	0.031730	0.032103	0.032003	0.031988

Hyperparameters' values for the best obtained BiLSTM model by each metaheuristics are shown in Table 3. One interesting remark to note is that all methods generated BiLSTM structure with 2 layers.

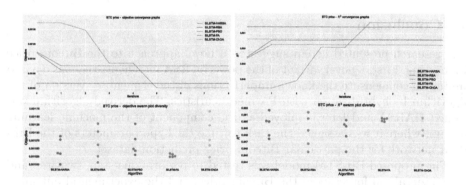

Fig. 3. Swarm diagrams, fitness function and indicator convergence

Table 3. Selection of control parameters for metaheuristic algorithms.

Method	L1 NN	LR	Epochs	DR	No.lay	L2 NN
BiLSTM-HARSA	200	0.010000	375	0.128817	2	133
BiLSTM-RSA	140	0.008358	500	0.161122	2	192
BiLSTM-PSO	200	0.010000	600	0.099543	2	180
BiLSTM-FA	200	0.010000	545	0.200000	2	200
BiLSTM-ChOA	116	0.006496	591	0.160379	2	117

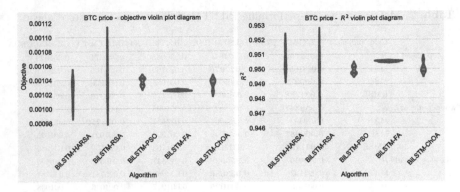

Fig. 4. BTC price R^2 box plot and violin plot diagrams

The best predicted values attained by the introduced HARSA method are depicted in Fig. 2. Swarm and violin diagrams of the fitness function and indicator (R^2) rates for time-series bitcoin price prediction, accompanied by the convergence diagrams of all methods implemented for this optimization problem, are depicted within Fig. 3 and Fig. 4 to highlight the improvements contributed to the introduced approach's convergence rates. The proposed hybrid adaptive metaheuristic outscores the baseline method regarding the convergence rates.

5   Conclusion

The research presented herein suggested a novel approach to the Bitcoin price forecasting. First, a novel variant of the powerful RSA metaheuristics was devised aiming to compensate the known imperfections of the elementary version of the algorithm by hybridization with FA metaheuristics. The derived algorithm was named HARSA and later employed as the component of the machine learning system, where it was assigned the task to tune the hyperparameters of the BiL-STM network for the particular Bitcoin price prediction dataset.

The proposed BiLSTM model was tested to perform one-step, two-step and three-step ahead forecasts of the Bitcoin price, and the experimental outcomes were collated to the scores attained by four powerful contending metaheuristics methods. The overall results have shown the supremacy of the proposed BiLSTM-HARSA method, allowing the conclusion that the suggested method is suitable to perform time-series predictions.

The future work in this area will be focusing on evaluating the suggested model to supplementary real-world datasets, and also on testing other metaheuristics' performance in tuning different neural network models.

References

1. Abualigah, L., Abd Elaziz, M., Sumari, P., Geem, Z.W., Gandomi, A.H.: Reptile search algorithm (RSA): a nature-inspired meta-heuristic optimizer. Expert Syst. Appl. **191**, 116158 (2022)

2. Abualigah, L., Diabat, A., Mirjalili, S., Abd Elaziz, M., Gandomi, A.H.: The arithmetic optimization algorithm. Comput. Methods Appl. Mech. Eng. **376**, 113609 (2021)
3. Alameer, Z., Elaziz, M.A., Ewees, A.A., Ye, H., Jianhua, Z.: Forecasting gold price fluctuations using improved multilayer perceptron neural network and whale optimization algorithm. Resour. Policy **61**, 250–260 (2019)
4. Alhnaity, B., Abbod, M.: A new hybrid financial time series prediction model. Eng. Appl. Artif. Intell. **95**, 103873 (2020)
5. Aslam, N., Rustam, F., Lee, E., Washington, P.B., Ashraf, I.: Sentiment analysis and emotion detection on cryptocurrency related tweets using ensemble LSTM-GRU model. IEEE Access **10**, 39313–39324 (2022)
6. Bacanin, N., Sarac, M., Budimirovic, N., Zivkovic, M., AlZubi, A.A., Bashir, A.K.: Smart wireless health care system using graph LSTM pollution prediction and dragonfly node localization. Sustain. Comput. Inform. Syst. **35**, 100711 (2022)
7. Bacanin, N., Sarac, M., Budimirovic, N., Zivkovic, M., AlZubi, A.A., Bashir, A.K.: Smart wireless health care system using graph LSTM pollution prediction and dragonfly node localization. Sustain. Comput. Inform. Syst. **35**, 100711 (2022)
8. Bacanin, N., Stoean, C., Zivkovic, M., Rakic, M., Strulak-Wójcikiewicz, R., Stoean, R.: On the benefits of using metaheuristics in the hyperparameter tuning of deep learning models for energy load forecasting. Energies **16**(3), 1434 (2023)
9. Bacanin, N., Tuba, E., Zivkovic, M., Strumberger, I., Tuba, M.: Whale optimization algorithm with exploratory move for wireless sensor networks localization. In: Abraham, A., Shandilya, S.K., Garcia-Hernandez, L., Varela, M.L. (eds.) HIS 2019. AISC, vol. 1179, pp. 328–338. Springer, Cham (2021). https://doi.org/10.1007/978-3-030-49336-3_33
10. Bacanin, N., Zivkovic, M., Bezdan, T., Venkatachalam, K., Abouhawwash, M.: Modified firefly algorithm for workflow scheduling in cloud-edge environment. Neural Comput. Appl. **34**(11), 9043–9068 (2022)
11. Bacanin, N., Zivkovic, M., Jovanovic, L., Ivanovic, M., Rashid, T.A.: Training a multilayer perception for modeling stock price index predictions using modified whale optimization algorithm. In: Smys, S., Tavares, J.M.R.S., Balas, V.E. (eds.) Computational Vision and Bio-Inspired Computing. AISC, vol. 1420, pp. 415–430. Springer, Singapore (2022). https://doi.org/10.1007/978-981-16-9573-5_31
12. Bezdan, T., Zivkovic, M., Bacanin, N., Strumberger, I., Tuba, E., Tuba, M.: Multiobjective task scheduling in cloud computing environment by hybridized bat algorithm. J. Intell. Fuzzy Syst. **42**(1), 411–423 (2022)
13. Chen, Q., Zhang, W., Lou, Y.: Forecasting stock prices using a hybrid deep learning model integrating attention mechanism, multi-layer perceptron, and bidirectional long-short term memory neural network. IEEE Access **8**, 117365–117376 (2020)
14. Heidari, A.A., Mirjalili, S., Faris, H., Aljarah, I., Mafarja, M., Chen, H.: Harris hawks optimization: algorithm and applications. Futur. Gener. Comput. Syst. **97**, 849–872 (2019)
15. Hitam, N.A., Ismail, A.R., Saeed, F.: An optimized support vector machine (SVM) based on particle swarm optimization (PSO) for cryptocurrency forecasting. Procedia Comput. Sci. **163**, 427–433 (2019)
16. Huang, X., et al.: LSTM based sentiment analysis for cryptocurrency prediction. In: Jensen, C.S., et al. (eds.) DASFAA 2021. LNCS, vol. 12683, pp. 617–621. Springer, Cham (2021). https://doi.org/10.1007/978-3-030-73200-4_47
17. Jovanovic, D., Antonijevic, M., Stankovic, M., Zivkovic, M., Tanaskovic, M., Bacanin, N.: Tuning machine learning models using a group search firefly algo-

rithm for credit card fraud detection. Mathematics **10**(13) (2022). https://www.mdpi.com/2227-7390/10/13/2272

18. Jovanovic, L., et al.: Multi-step crude oil price prediction based on LSTM approach tuned by salp swarm algorithm with disputation operator. Sustainability **14**(21), 14616 (2022)

19. Jovanovic, L., Zivkovic, M., Antonijevic, M., Jovanovic, D., Ivanovic, M., Jassim, H.S.: An emperor penguin optimizer application for medical diagnostics. In: 2022 IEEE Zooming Innovation in Consumer Technologies Conference (ZINC), pp. 191–196. IEEE (2022)

20. Karaboga, D., Basturk, B.: On the performance of artificial bee colony (ABC) algorithm. Appl. Soft Comput. **8**(1), 687–697 (2008)

21. Khedr, A.M., Arif, I., El-Bannany, M., Alhashmi, S.M., Sreedharan, M.: Cryptocurrency price prediction using traditional statistical and machine-learning techniques: a survey. Intell. Syst. Account. Financ. Manag. **28**(1), 3–34 (2021)

22. Mirjalili, S.: SCA: a sine cosine algorithm for solving optimization problems. Knowl.-Based Syst. **96**, 120–133 (2016)

23. Mohapatra, S., Ahmed, N., Alencar, P.: Kryptooracle: a real-time cryptocurrency price prediction platform using twitter sentiments, pp. 5544–5551 (2019)

24. Park, H.W., Lee, Y.: How are twitter activities related to top cryptocurrencies' performance? Evidence from social media network and sentiment analysis. Drustvena istrazivanja **28**, 435–460 (2019)

25. Patel, M.M., Tanwar, S., Gupta, R., Kumar, N.: A deep learning-based cryptocurrency price prediction scheme for financial institutions. J. Inf. Secur. Appl. **55**, 102583 (2020)

26. Prakash, S., Kumar, M.V., Ram, S.R., Zivkovic, M., Bacanin, N., Antonijevic, M.: Hybrid GLFIL enhancement and encoder animal migration classification for breast cancer detection. Comput. Syst. Sci. Eng. **41**(2), 735–749 (2022)

27. Q. Chen, W.Z., Lou, Y.: Forecasting stock prices using a hybrid deep learning model integrating attention mechanism, multi-layer perceptron, and bidirectional long-short term memory neural network. IEEE Access **8**, 117365–117376 (2020)

28. Thakkar, A., Chaudhari, K.: A comprehensive survey on portfolio optimization, stock price and trend prediction using particle swarm optimization. Arch. Comput. Methods **28**, 2133–2164 (2021)

29. Wang, D., Tan, D., Liu, L.: Particle swarm optimization algorithm: an overview. Soft Comput. **22**, 387–408 (2018)

30. Yan, H., Ouyang, H.: Financial time series prediction based on deep learning. Wirel. Pers. Commun. **102**, 683–700 (2018)

31. Yang, X.S., Slowik, A.: Firefly algorithm. In: Swarm Intelligence Algorithms, pp. 163–174. CRC Press (2020)

32. Zivkovic, M., et al.: COVID-19 cases prediction by using hybrid machine learning and beetle antennae search approach. Sustain. Urban Areas **66**, 102669 (2021)

33. Zivkovic, M., Petrovic, A., Venkatachalam, K., Strumberger, I., Jassim, H.S., Bacanin, N.: Novel chaotic best firefly algorithm: COVID-19 fake news detection application. In: Biswas, A., Kalayci, C.B., Mirjalili, S. (eds.) Advances in Swarm Intelligence. Studies in Computational Intelligence, vol. 1054, pp. 285–305. Springer, Cham (2023). https://doi.org/10.1007/978-3-031-09835-2_16

Android Malware Detection Using Artificial Intelligence

Rebecca Kipanga Masele and Fadoua Khennou[✉]

Perception, Robotics and Intelligent Machines (PRIME), Moncton University, Moncton, Canada
fadoua.khennou@umoncton.ca

Abstract. Malware poses a significant global cybersecurity challenge, targeting individuals, businesses, institutions, and nations by compromising sensitive information and causing disruptions, incurring substantial costs. Android devices, with relatively lower security measures allowing installations from unknown sources, face notable malware prevalence, creating opportunities for cybercriminals to engage in illicit activities. To address this issue, numerous research studies have focused on harnessing the power of artificial intelligence (AI) to develop effective solutions. Notably, research utilizing the CICMalDroid2020 dataset has achieved promising results by employing Deep Learning and Machine Learning approaches for Android malware detection. However, to the best of our knowledge, no prior studies utilizing this dataset have explored the potential of the Extra-Tree Machine Learning classifier.

In our research, we endeavored to fill this gap by implementing the Extra Tree classifier in conjunction with cross-validation techniques. Additionally, we employed the SelectFrom-Model feature selection method to enhance the accuracy of malware detection. Through our investigation, we found that the ExtraTree classifier exhibited good performances, achieving an accuracy rate of 96.7%.

Keywords: Machine Learning · Malware · ExtraTree · Cross validation · Artificial intelligence

1 Introduction

In February 2023, a U.S. government agency experienced a cyberattack by the ransomware known as "Hook," compromising sensitive files and disrupting its operations [1]. Another concerning incident involved the emergence of a dangerous Android malware called "Hook," capable of remote device control and stealing banking login information from around 467 applications [2]. Additionally, the first quarter of 2023 witnessed a surge in crypto jacking attacks, targeting cell phones to mine cryptocurrencies [3].

Supported by the New Brunswick Innovation Foundation.

Malware employs various techniques to disguise itself and evade detection, including anti-debugging, obfuscation, packing, polymorphism, and metamorphism [9]. Specifically, crypto ransomware utilizes polymorphism and metamorphism to change its behavior and structure, making it highly challenging to detect [9]. This evasion approach allows the malware to remain undetected by security measures. Static analysis extracts characteristics that include permissions, API calls, Java code and network permissions, activities, etc [10,11]. This process does not include the execution of the malware samples [12]. Dynamic analysis focuses on understanding and revealing malware behavior and extracting attribute information related to it. Malware samples are carefully studied and decomposed to understand their activities. This is done in a special environment where their behavior is uncovered [14,15]. The result of this analysis provides attributes such as System calls, CPU usage, file system operations, registry key changes, etc., which are descriptive of the activity of the studied malware [11,12]. It is possible to combine the two previous methods, resulting in a hybrid method that combines the advantages of both [11,12].

To deal with this phenomenon, several research have already been conducted to find a solution using AI. Research using the CICMalDroid2020 dataset with Deep Learning and Machine Learning approaches for malware detection on Android has proven successful. To the best of our knowledge, no research using the same databases has used the Extra-Tree Machine Learning classifier. Therefore, in our research, we used Extra Tree with cross-validation, as well as Select-FromModel feature selection method for malware detection. Extra Tree is a DT-based ensemble learning method. It is also known for its ability to handle overfitting and the use of averaging improves the model performance [].

Our research contribution encompasses several key aspects. Firstly, we have devised an efficient and straightforward method that yields high accuracy in the context of malware detection. Specifically, we employed the Extra Tree classifier in conjunction with cross-validation techniques, leveraging the CIC2020 dataset. Additionally, we explored the efficacy of the Extra Tree classifier when combined with the SelectFromModel feature selection method. Furthermore, we conducted extensive experimentation with the Bagging algorithm, employing various classifiers.

To address the issue of imbalanced datasets, we applied the Synthetic Minority Over-sampling Technique (SMOTE), which effectively increases the representation of malware samples and subsequently enhances accuracy. Our investigation encompassed the training and evaluation of a diverse range of Machine Learning techniques, enabling a comprehensive comparison of their respective results. Furthermore, we conducted a comparative analysis, benchmarking our findings against previous studies. The remaining sections of this paper are organized into five main parts, namely the introduction, related work, ML algorithms, proposed method, and conclusion. Through these sections, we aim to provide a comprehensive overview of our research methodology, results, and concluding remarks.

2   Related Works

In this section, we delve into the extensive body of research and articles that revolve around the implementation of machine learning and deep learning for malware detection. Our focus lies specifically on the renowned CICMal-droid2020 dataset, which has served as a cornerstone for numerous studies in this domain. Furthermore, the authors have employed a combination of dynamic and static analysis techniques to enhance the effectiveness of malware detection. These approaches provide a comprehensive understanding of malware behavior and enable robust identification and mitigation strategies.

The authors [15] performed a classification problem by merging two datasets, including CICMaldroid2020 (8750 Android samples) and CIC-InvesAndMal2019 (250 ransomware samples). The dataset used was large and contained a total of 9000 malware. Their goal was to perform two classification tasks. One is for malware and the other for ransomware. To do this, they used the APK tool, manifest analyzer, and ML algorithm to analyze, extract, and select features. A total of 140 permission features are obtained for the classification task. The best result was obtained with the Meta-Multiclass (KNN and RF) classifier with 95/% accuracy for malware classification. For ransomware classification, they achieved 80/% accuracy with an ensemble approach (RF, SMOTE, and Genetic Algorithms to fit the model). To classify the malware (1422 adware, 2506 banking and 4821 SMS malware), the authors used the Meta-Multiclass classifier (KNN and RF). The classification was performed using the DT algorithm. The result was underfitting with an accuracy of 60%. Therefore, they solved this situation using three different approaches. SMOTE was used to balance and augment the data set. To adjust the parameters to find the best parameter with the genetic algorithm . Finally, the RF performed the classification. This resulted in an accuracy of 80/%.

They [16] created a new CICMalDroid2020 dataset of size 17,341. They used the copperdroid tool to analyze and extract the dynamic and static features. After analysis, the size of the dataset used is 11,598. The dynamic features also include system calls and composite behavior. All the characteristics were resized to 470 and normalized (12). They then trained a pseudo-label deep neural network (7-layer PLDNN) on a 70–30% ratio dataset for training and testing. The results showed an accuracy of 96.7, F1 score of 97.84, and an FPR of 2.76. They used many hidden layers to learn deep features and increase the accuracy. They also got good results (91% F1-score) with 1% of labeled data in the training set. They achieved 97.84 of F1-score with 10% of labelled data in the training set. They obtained a good, robust, and stable model which performs well with less labeled data.

The aim of this paper [17] is to classify malware using a combination of text and images features. This article uses two datasets: the CICMalDroid 2020(size 17,341) and CIC-InvesAndMal2019(426 malware and 5065 benign). The authors also employed 2 types of features: images and texts. They first used the BERT model to process the network byte stream and extract the textual features. They then extracted, labeled, and then described the textual features. To do this, they used tools such as the Features from Accelerated Segment Test (FAST) extractor and the Binary Robust Independent Elementary Features (BERT) descriptor. They employed the voting classifier which involves 5 ml algorithms (GNB, SVM, DT, LR, RFL) to train the two datasets. The classification accuracy is 99.16% for the CIC-InvesAndMal2019 dataset and 98.8 for the CICMalDroid 2020 dataset.

Table 1. Related Works.

Authors	Data Source	Analysis	Method	Features	Accuracy
[15]	CICMaldroid2020, CICInvesAndMal2019	Static	MetaMulticlass(KNN and RF)	Text:140 permissions	95
[16]	CICMaldroid2020	Dynamic	PLDNN(7layer-neurones)	System calls, binders, compositebehaviors	96.7
[17]	CICMaldroid2020, CICInvesAndMal2019	Static	VC(GNB, SVM, DT,LR,RF)	Image and Text	99.16
[18]	CIC-AndMaldroid2017, CICAndMalDroid2020	Static	GA-StakingMB(SVM, KNN, LGBM, CatBoost, and RF)	Text and Image: Permission, API, Dalvik, Intent, Hardware	98.45
[19]	CICMalDroid2020	Dynamic Static	PLSAE	40 Features	98.3
[20]	CIC-AndMaldroid2017, CICMalDroid2020	static	VGG16	NA	97.81
[13]	Debrin, CICMalDroid2020	Static	CNN	Permission	92 and 94.6
[4]	CICMalDroid2020	Static	DesNet121	Not mentionned	96.4
[6]	Debrin, CICMalDroid2020, AndroidMalgenome	Dynamic Static	GTB	261 Features	96.3

This work [18] presents a detection method based on feature selection and a Machine Learning stacking model. They considered two datasets named CIC-AndMal2017 and CICMalDroid2020. Using static analysis, the malware code is decompiled to extract features that were then digitized. Chi-square and Info-Gain are used to select important features. Then, they use the staking model to train the first and second layers of ML algorithms. Then, they applied Genetic Algorithm (GA) on the staking model for hyperparameter optimization. They achieved an accuracy of 98.45 on the CIC-AndMal2017 dataset and 98.66 on CICMalDroid2020.

The authors [20] implemented a framework using CNN and VGG16 to detect malware. They used APK files of benign and malicious software and converted them into RGB images. The dataset used consists of 957 malware samples and 647 benign software samples. The performance of the CNN was 93.43 accuracy and 93.42 F1. They also used VGG16, a transfer learning method, to train the RGB images. The best result is obtained with VGG16, with 97.81 accuracy and 97.78 F1 score.

This work [13] aims at classifying android files using Static analysis, CNN and the network-based fuzzy inference system (ANFIS). They used two datasets: Drebrin (5,560 malware: 179 different malware families) and CICMalDroid2020 (17,34 samples: 5 different categories). After analysis, they used both datasets containing: Debrin (250 malware and 250 benign) and CICMalDroid 2020 (250 malware and 250 benign). They reverse engineered the APK files.

This paper [4] aims at identifying malware using CNN-transfer learning using grayscale images. APK files are converted into images. The CICMaldroid2020 used contained 10,878 balanced malicious and benign samples. The ratio of the data set split includes validation (5%), train (90%) and test (5%). Then feature selection was performed with CNN helped to obtain a subset of features. The CNNs used includes the RMSprop as optimizer, max-pooling and 37,975,105. parameters, fully connected layers, etc. They trained and tested a bunch of transfer learning approaches. DeseNet121 obtained the best accuracy with 96.4%.

In this section, we compare different approaches using the CICMALdroid2020 dataset for malware detection. VC [18] achieved the highest accuracy (98.8%) by employing text and images as features. Their approach utilized the FAST extractor and BERT descriptor, extracting 400 essential features. To address class imbalance, SMOTE was used for dataset augmentation. Training with VC's majority voting technique contributed to their outstanding performance. Table 1 provides an overview of the techniques and results obtained. Using the ExtraTree (ET) classifier and cross-validation, we addressed the malware problem, seeking better generalization on new data. Through a for loop with 10 to 19 folds, we compared training-test splitting and cross-validation, achieving 96.7% accuracy with 16 folds, a satisfactory result for our straightforward approach.

3 Machine Learning Algorithms

3.1 K-Nest Neighbour(KNN)

K-Nest Neighbour is a simple classification algorithm. This Machine learning approach takes into account the distance of each class from the training data to give a result. It considers the class with the most data points or the class with K data points closest to the training data as the majority and predicts it. Thus, K represents the number of nearest input vectors belonging to a class label, which are closest, taken as the predicted class. It is easier to define the parameter K, but the cross-validation procedure is reliable to find the optimal value of K. However, knn requires more memory usage and its computation time is higher. K-Nest Neighbour (K-NN) is not a good choice for large data sets, moreover it gives a bad result if a data set is not evenly distributed. [10, 21–23, 33, 34]

Using distances such as Euclidean distance, hamming distance, Minkowsky distance, cosine similarity, etc., we can determine which category the nearest k belongs to. As a result, the Euclidean distance between two points of data can be represented by the following equation:

$$d(p,q) = \sqrt{(p_1 - q_1)^2 + \cdots + (p_n - q_n)^2} \qquad (1)$$

In addition, the Hamming distances (HD) are a measure of how many letters, symbols separate similar strings.It is describe by the following formula where q and p represent the 2 symbols words that separates two words:

$$HD(\mathbf{Q}, \mathbf{P}) = \sum_{i=1}^{m} \mathbf{Q}_i \oplus \mathbf{P}_i \tag{2}$$

3.2 Decision Tree (DT)

Decision Tree supervised ML algorithm. It uses a data set to grow trees based on certain criteria. During the splitting process, the features are analyzed and evaluated. The evaluation is done based on the same criteria such as "information gain ratio". In DT, the splitting process is recursive. When the "information gain ratio" is high, a node is split, and stops when the "information gain ratio" is lower. DT involves a pruning procedure that removes nodes that are not needed. This solves over fitting by reducing the complexity of the algorithm. Each decision path affects the outcome of a prediction. It is possible to select variables in decision trees through Entropy, Information Gain and Gini index [18, 23, 24]. Here is the formula to calculate the entropy of the target variable T:

$$E(T) = \Sigma - P_i \log P_i \tag{3}$$

Info-Gain Is used as feature selection to process datasets to reduce entropy [18]. The calculation of the "information gain" is as follows:

$$\text{Gain}(T, X) = E(T) - E(T, X) \tag{4}$$

where E(T) represent the entropy of the dataset T
    E (T, X) represents the entropy of a feature X.

3.3 Random Forest (RF)

Random Forest (RF), a popular ML algorithm using the bagging procedure with multiple decision trees, performs well in situations like noisy, small, and imbalanced data. While RF is a simple, flexible approach using divide and conquer, it lacks full control over its behavior. The algorithm constructs a decision tree forest randomly based on specific criteria, without involving pruning. At each iteration, a tree is built, and the final result is obtained through majority voting [23, 25–27].

Let define t(X) as a Decision Tree model. Several DT represent a Random Forest. Let P be the Model parameter. So, t(X) = t(X—P) represents a Decision Tree model.

The Random Forest model will be represented as an ensemble of Decision Trees defines as:

$$R = t(X1), t(X2), t(X3), t(X4) \tag{5}$$

3.4 Extra Tree (ET)

Extra tree is a meta estimator which used Decision Trees as base learner. Consequently, it is used for classification and regression. In ExtaTree, the Decision Trees are random, which allows to obtain a good accuracy. Each decision path affects the outcome of a prediction. There is a threshold assigned to each feature that is selected at random. In comparison to Random Forest, it's faster and enhances randomness. The result is an average of all the randomized decision trees. Averaging improves the performance of the model. In addition to managing overfitting, it also minimizes the variance. All the datasets contribute to the growth of the trees. It is possible to select variables in decision trees through Entropy, Information Gain and Gini index. In order to reduce impurities, the Gini index is calculated. Gini index is nn alternative way to split a decision tree. The Gini index analyzes a data set to identify impurities. The Gini index of an attribute must be smaller [22, 25, 28, 29].

$$\text{gini}(D) = 1 - \sum_{i=1}^{m} {p_i}^2 \tag{6}$$

The number of classes in the target variable is indicated by m. Pi represents the likelihood/ probability that a sample belongs to a particular output.

3.5 Ensemble Learning

In ensemble learning, different Machine Learning models are assembled to improve the final result of the classifiers. This approach performs well in multiclass problems. Among several ensemble learning approaches, we used the Voting Classifier, Gradient Tree Boosting, Adaboost and Bagging algorithms in this paper [30].

3.6 Voting Classifier

(VC) trains all classifiers with the same data set. The results produced by each classifier are merged into one final output. In our case, we used the KNN, RF, ExtraTree and DT models to build the voting classifier.

3.7 Bagging

Using a bagging method, each classifier is trained separately on a portion of the data set selected at random. In RF, the decision tree forest is constructed randomly choosing a portion of dataset based on certain criteria. The RF classifier is therefore a bagging classifier [31].

3.8   Boosting

The boosting algorithm is a machine learning algorithm that aims to build a robust and efficient final classifier. The final classifier is the result of training several weak candidates one by one in a consecutive manner. Weak candidates are trained one by one in a sequential method to produce the final classifier. We used two boosting algorithms: Gradient Tree Boosting and Adaboost [10].

3.9   Gradient Tree Boosting

Gradient tree boosting is an ensemble model, a ML aglo which generally provide good prediction for classification and regression problem. It's a meta-estimator using DT as base learners as well can accept additive ML model. Each model in the GB series aims to minimize mistakes made in the predecessor. In this technique, weak learners are added to minimize the loss function. This is achieved by gradient descent [32]. The following equation the negative gradient gt(x):

$$g_{t(x)} = E_y \left(\partial\varphi \frac{\delta f(x)}{y \cdot f(x)} \mid x \right)_{f(x)=f^{t-1}(x)} \tag{7}$$

Here the least-squares minimization is one of the function to study the Gradient tree boosting:

$$\rho_t, \theta_t = \arg\min_{\rho,\theta} \sum_{i=1}^{N} \left(-g_t(x) + \rho h \left(x_i, \theta \right) \right)^2 \tag{8}$$

In the following equation, L represents the loss function and gamma is the predicted value. F0(x) is the calculation of the optimal value for each region of the tree.

$$F_0(x) = \arg\min_{\gamma} \sum_{i=1}^{n} L \left(y_i, \gamma \right) \tag{9}$$

In the following equation, L represent the log-likelihood loss function to be minimized.

$$L = \frac{1}{n} \sum_{i=0}^{n} \left(y_i - \gamma_i \right)^2 \tag{10}$$

4   Methodology

4.1   Metrics

Metrics are used in measuring the performance of a Machine Learning algorithm. Therefore, using the F1, precision (P), recall (R), and accuracy (ACC); we could verify the performance of the different models used in this paper. Precision True positives are divided by predicted positives to calculate precision. In other word, precision represent the predictions which were correct out of all the positive predictions. The term True Positive (TP) refers to a malicious file that has been detected as malicious. The False Positive (FP) refers to a benign sample that is detected as malware.

$$P = TP/(TP + FP) \tag{11}$$

Recall

A measure of the number of true positive samples that were identified. In other words, recall is A successful identification of positive samples. The term True Negative (TN) refers to a benign sample that is detected as benign. False Negative (FN) refers to a malicious file that is detected as benign. Recall is also referred to as the true positive rate.

$$R = TP/(TP + FN) \tag{12}$$

Accuracy

The accuracy of a data set can only be computed when the data set is balanced. The accuracy of a model is calculated on the basis of the frequency of correct predictions. We calculate the accuracy of the different ML models after balancing the dataset with SMOTE.

$$A = (TP + TN)/TotalPredictions \tag{13}$$

F1-score

An average of precision and recall. F1-score is usually employed when the data set is imbalanced.

$$F1 = 2 * (precision * recall)/(precision + recall) \tag{14}$$

4.2 Dataset

We obtained the CICMalDroid2020 dataset from the Canadian Cybersecurity Institute, comprising 139 features extracted from 11,598 APKs. The dataset contains system call frequencies and was checked for missing values, duplicates, and outliers. It consists of 5 unbalanced classes: Adware (1,253), Banking (2,100), SMS malware (3,904), Riskware (2,546), and Benign (1,795). To address the imbalance, we applied SMOTE, generating synthetic samples by considering distances between minority and neighboring category samples, resulting in improved representation.

4.3 Machine Learning Algorithms

Several Machine Learning algorithms (RF, DT, KNN, VC and ET) were tested on the dataset. First, we used the Machine Learning techniques alone, without SMOTE and without feature selection. Second, we applied the SMOTE technique to the dataset and trained and tested the models. Finally, we combined the Machine Learning algorithms with SelectFromModel feature selection approaches on a balanced data set. Figure 1. Machine Learning Methods

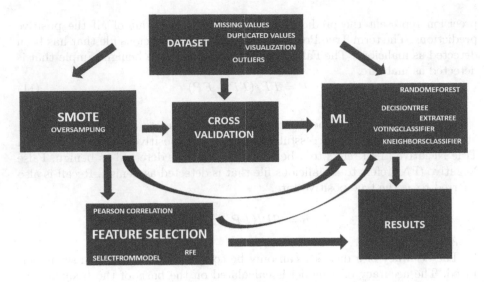

Fig. 1. Proposed Methodology.

Ensemble methods such as bagging was also tested as meta-classifier. The purpose of cross-validation (CV), which is a resampling approach, is to obtain results about the behavior of models across different folds. Cross-validation (CV), which is a resampling approach, provides results on the behavior of models on different folds tested. Cross-validation divides the data set into n folds. With a ratio of n-1 training samples and 1 validation sample. The classifiers run in a loop of n-1 times selecting a new subset of the dataset at each iteration. In this work, we run a for loop between 10 and 15, defined as the number cv. We selected the number cv that gives the best result. Feature selection selects the important and significant features that somehow increase the performance of the classifiers. We applied SelectFromModel feature selection approach. We use SMOTE to augment and obtain a balanced data set. RF, DT, KNN, VC, and ExtraTree are the main machine learning methods used in this study.

4.4 Experiments and Results

First, we train different ML algorithms, namely RF, KNN, ExtraTree, DT, and GT. The dataset used contains 11,598 APKs samples. The split ratio of the dataset was 80% for training and 20% for the test set. We used Anaconda3 with Jupiter notebook version 6.4.3 as the development environment. The result of this first experiment is described in the Table 2. The evaluation was performed using the accuracy, recall, F1, and precision. The results in Table 2 show that the ExtraTree classifier performs best.

Table 2. Machine Learning Classifiers.

Classifier	Recall	Accuracy	Precision	F1
RF	90.7	92	89.9	90.2
ET	**91.5**	**93**	**91.3**	**91.3**
KNN	82.1	85.3	82	81.9
DT	87.5	89.9	87.5	87.5
VC	86.6	88	89	87.5

To improve results, in a second step we use the SMOTE algorithm which improves the classification performance. The data set was increased from 11,598 to 19520 samples. We kept the same training-test ratio of 80 and 20%. Our results with the same algorithms are shown in Table 3. These results are good compared to the previous results. All classifiers improved their performance, with ExtraTree once again coming out on top. Followed by RF and DT.

Table 3. Machine Learning Classifiers with SMOTE.

Classifier	Recall	Accuracy	Precision	F1
RF	95.5	95.5	95.5	95.5
ET	**96**	**96**	**96**	**96**
KNN	91.5	91.5	91.5	91.5
DT	92.4	92.4	92.4	92.4
VC	93.9	93.9	94	93.9

At this point, we applied the CV approach, which is well known for providing insight into how new data sets affect the behavior of a model. We run a for loop to calculate the best number of CVs for each algorithm. Our for loop goes from 2 to 15 folds. The results obtained are shown in Table 4. All classifiers generalized quite well, with ExtraTree once again coming out on top in all the metrics.

Then we applied SelectFomModel features selections algorithm. When determining if a feature is significant, SelectFomModel compares the threshold value to the weight. This algorithm choosed important feature for each trained model. The result obtained (Table 5) show that there is not much change compared with the result in Table 3.

Table 4. Machine Learning Classifiers with CV and SMOTE.

Classifier	Recall	Accuracy	Precision	F1	Folds
RF	95.2	95.2	95.2	95.1	10
ET	**96.7**	**96.7**	**96.7**	**96.7**	**29**
KNN	93.4	93.4	93.5	93.4	14
DT	92.4	92.4	92.3	92.2	12
VC	94	94.1	94.4	94.2	11

Table 5. Machine Learning Classifiers with SelectFromModel and SMOTE.

Classifier	Recall	Accuracy	Precision	F1
RF	95.6	95.6	95.7	95.6
ET	**95.9**	**95.9**	**95.9**	**95.8**
DT	92.1	92.1	92	92

Bagging algorithm allow to train many estimators, or base models. Bagging can increase the performance of a model. It reduces the variance of a model. So, we further used bagging algorithm on the augmented dataset. The result of bagging is given in Table 6. The result has been slightly reduces compared to the result on Table 3 and 4.

Table 6. Machine Learning Classifiers with Bagging and SMOTE.

Classifier	Recall	Accuracy	Precision	F1
RF	95.2	95.2	95.2	95.2
ET	**95.7**	**95.7**	**95.8**	**95.7**
KNN	82.1	85.5	82.6	82.3
DT	91.5	92.9	91.3	91.4

We find that the use of the SMOTE approach has impacted the performance of the classifier shown in Table 2. The increase in the data set from 11,598 to 19520 is quite significant. This raises the overall performance of the models. The cross-validation gives an accurate result of the classifiers. This shows that the models can generalize in Table 3. Bagging and selectFromModel did not affect the results at all. Although bagging is an accurate technique that reduces the variance, it can introduce a bias in the model. Extratree performs well over all the different methods. It is also a robust and stable algorithm that is not influenced by certain features. Random Forest has the advantage to perform well on noisy and imbalanced dataset. However, the behavior of the RF cannot be fully controlled. Our best result is obtained with ExtraTree used with Cross validation which got 96.7 on all the metrics.

In comparison with other papers, our methods can also be considered among those that have performed well. We used a simple and straightforward method that relies on tabular data and ET classifier which uses the Averaging of randomized DT to improve the performance of the model . Some papers required text data set, other images, while some mixed the advantages of text and images data which had an impact on the developed frameworks. Our method uses only text data and still performs well. According to the needs of different research authors, optimization techniques, feature selection, oversampling (SMOTE) method and, or hyperparameter adjustment have built powerful frameworks that boost the performance of ML techniques. Deep Learning methods, including transfer learning and Cconvolutional Neural Network, which are capable of learning from many deep features and extracting them for a proper generalization. To capture the features that distinguish malware from benign files, static analysis, dynamic analysis or hybrid analysis have been employed. With dynamic or hybrid analysis, new sophisticated malware is likely to be captured to overcome attacks such as zero-day. Our approach does not use dynamic or hybrid analysis and therefore cannot capture advanced malware. It can therefore be enhanced with dynamic or hybrid methods to deal with different aspects of a malware.

5 Conclusion

Our approach leverages machine learning techniques to accurately differentiate between malware and benign files. In the field of Android malware detection, extensive research has explored multiple methods, including Meta-Multiclass, CNN, GA-StackingMD, GTB, transfer learning, and semi-supervised algorithms. Among these classifiers, the ExtraTree classifier achieved an impressive 96.7% accuracy when combined with 29-fold cross-validation. Despite its simplicity, our method effectively identifies malware amidst benign samples. Further improvements can be implemented to tackle the intricate nature of sophisticated malware and capture its diverse behaviors.

Acknowledgments. This research was enabled in part by support provided by the New Brunswick Innovation Foundation.

References

1. US Marshals Service hit by ransomware and data breach. https://www.malwarebytes.com/blog/news/2023/02/us-marshals-service-hit-by-ransomware-and-data-breach. Accessed 11 Apr 2023
2. New ËHook' Android malware lets hackers remotely control your phone. https://www.bleepingcomputer.com/news/security/new-hook-android-malware-lets-hackers-remotely-control-your-phone/. Accessed 11 Apr 2023
3. 10 Most Dangerous Virus & Malware Threats in 2023, SafetyDetectives, 22 March 2021. https://www.safetydetectives.com/blog/most-dangerous-new-malware-and-security-threats/. Accessed 23 Apr 2023

4. Al-Fawa'reh, M., Saif, A., Jafar, M.T., Elhassan, A.: Malware detection by eating a whole APK. In: 15th International Conference for Internet Technology and Secured Transactions (ICITST), vol. 2020, pp. 1–7. IEEE (2020)
5. Baltazar, P.: List of Android Viruses and How to Protect in 2023, MalwareFox, 16 March 2023. https://www.malwarefox.com/android-virus-list/. Accessed 12 Apr 2023
6. Hadiprakoso, R.B., Kabetta, H., Buana, I.K.S.: Hybrid-based malware analysis for effective and efficiency android malware detection. In: 2020 International Conference on Informatics, Multimedia, Cyber and Information System (ICIMCIS), Jakarta, Indonesia: IEEE, November 2020, pp. 8–12 (2020)
7. Wang, Z., Liu, Q., Chi, Y.: Review of android malware detection based on deep learning. IEEE Access 8, 181102–181126 (2020)
8. Liu, K., Xu, S., Xu, G., Zhang, M., Sun, D., Liu, H.: A review of android malware detection approaches based on machine learning. IEEE Access 8, 124579–124607 (2020)
9. Olaimat, M.N., Aizaini Maarof, M., Al-Rimy, B.A.S.: Ransomware anti-analysis and evasion techniques: a survey and research directions. In: 2021 3rd International Cyber Resilience Conference (CRC), pp. 1–6, January 2021
10. Singh, J., Singh, J.: A survey on machine learning-based malware detection in executable files. J. Syst. Archit. 112, 101861 (2020)
11. Kouliaridis, V., Kambourakis, G.: A comprehensive survey on machine learning techniques for android malware detection. Information 12(5), 185 (2021)
12. Yadav, P., Menon, N., Ravi, V., Vishvanathan, S., Pham, T.D., et al.: EfficientNet convolutional neural networks-based Android malware detection. Comput. Secur. 115, 102622 (2022)
13. Jang, J.S.: ANFIS: adaptive-network-based fuzzy inference system. IEEE Trans. Syst. Man Cybern. 23(3), 665–685 (1993)
14. Alzaylaee, M.K., Yerima, S.Y., Sezer, S.: DL-Droid: deep learning based android malware detection using real devices. Comput. Secur. 89, 101663 (2020)
15. Odat, E., Alazzam, B., Yaseen, Q.M., Detecting malware families and subfamilies using machine learning algorithms: an empirical study. Int. J. Adv. Comput. Sci. Appl. 13(2) (2022)
16. Mahdavifar, S., Kadir, A.F.A., Fatemi, R., Alhadidi, D., Ghorbani, A.A.: Dynamic android malware category classification using semi-supervised deep learning. In: IEEE International Conference on Dependable, Autonomic and Secure Computing, Intl Conf on Pervasive Intelligence and Computing, Intl Conf on Cloud and Big Data Computing, Intl Conf on Cyber Science and Technology Congress, pp. 515–522. IEEE (2020)
17. Ullah, F., Alsirhani, A., Alshahrani, M.M., et al.: Explainable malware detection system using transformers-based transfer learning and multi-model visual representation. Sensors 22(18), 6766 (2022)
18. Xie, N., Qin, Z., Di, X.: GA-StackingMD: android malware detection method based on genetic algorithm optimized stacking. Appl. Sci. 13(4), 2629 (2023)
19. Mahdavifar, S., Alhadidi, D., Ghorbani, A.A.: Effective and efficient hybrid android malware classification using pseudo-label stacked auto-encoder. J. Netw. Syst. Manag. 30, 1–34 (2022)
20. Ksibi, A., Zakariah, M., Almuqren, L.A., et al.: Deep Convolution Neural Networks and Image Processing for Malware Detection (2023)
21. Nagano, Y., Uda, R.: Static analysis with paragraph vector for malware detection. In: Proceedings of the 11th International Conference on Ubiquitous Information Management and Communication, pp. 1–7 (2017)

22. Abhishek, L.: Optical character recognition using ensemble of SVM, MLP and extra trees classifier. In: International Conference for Emerging Technology (INCET), pp. 1–4. IEEE (2020)
23. Ganta, V.G., Harish, G.V., Kumar, V.P., Rao, G.R.K., et al.: Ransomware detection in executable files using machine learning. In: 2020 International Conference on Recent Trends on Electronics, Information, Communication Technology (RTE-ICT), pp. 282–286. IEEE (2020)
24. Ye, J., Yang, J., Yu, J., et al.: A Chi-MIC based adaptive multi-branch decision tree. IEEE Access **9**, 78962–78972 (2021)
25. Kasongo, S.M.: An advanced intrusion detection system for IIoT based on GA and tree based algorithms. IEEE Access **9**, 113199–113212 (2021)
26. Tie, J., Lei, X., Pan, Y.: Metabolite-disease association prediction algorithm combining DeepWalk and random forest. Tsinghua Sci. Technol. **27**(1), 58–67 (2021)
27. Dong, L., Du, H., Mao, F., et al.: Very high resolution remote sensing imagery classification using a fusion of random forest and deep learning technique-Subtropical area for example. IEEE J. Sel. Top. Appl. Earth Obs. Remote Sens. **13**, 113–128 (2019)
28. Li, Y., Bao, T., Gong, J., et al.: The prediction of dam displacement time series using STL, extra-trees, and stacked LSTM neural network. IEEE Access **8**, 94440–94452 (2020)
29. Du, Y., Liu, Y., Yan, Y., et al.: Risk management of weather-related failures in distribution systems based on interpretable extra-trees. J. Mod. Power Syst. Clean Energy (2023)
30. Aziz, R.H.H., Dimililer, N.: Twitter sentiment analysis using an ensemble weighted majority vote classifier. In: 2020 International Conference on Advanced Science and Engineering (ICOASE), pp. 103–109. IEEE (2020)
31. Jia, J., Cao, X., Gong, N.Z.: Intrinsic certified robustness of bagging against data poisoning attacks. In: Proceedings of the AAAI Conference on Artificial Intelligence, pp. 7961–7969 (2021)
32. Usharani, S., Sandhya, S.G., et al.: Detection of ransomware in static analysis by using gradient tree boosting algorithm. In: 2020 International Conference on System, Computation, Automation and Networking (ICSCAN), pp. 1–5. IEEE (2020)
33. Rabie, A.H., Mohamed, A.M., Abo-Elsoud, M.A., et al.: A new COVID-19 diagnosis strategy using a modified KNN classifier. Neural Comput. Appl. 1–25 (2023)
34. Yang, L., Huang, X., Li, Y., et al.: Self-selective memristor-enabled in-memory search for highly efficient data mining. InfoMat e12416 (2023)

Intelligent Methods for Data Analysis and Computer Aided Soft-ware Engineering

Autoencoder as Feature Extraction Technique for Financial Distress Classification

Dovilė Kuizinienė(✉), Paulius Savickas, and Tomas Krilavičius

Vytautas Magnus University, Universiteto str. 10–202, 53361 Akademija, Kaunas District, Lithuania
if@vdu.lt
https://if.vdu.lt, https://if.vdu.lt/en/contacts/

Abstract. Financial statements are typical financial distress identification data for the enterprise. However, nowadays, the valuable data source characterizing enterprise could be expanded, including data from legal events, macro, industry, government register center, etc. This data creates valuable information, which could lead to more accurate financial distress classification model creation. On the other hand, the new data source involvement expands the dimensional space of features and increases the data sparsity. In order to reduce dimensions and have maximum information retention from the initial data space is used feature extraction techniques. This study uses an autoencoder as a nonlinear feature extraction method. Moreover, we compared several structure composition strategies for autoencoders: 1) all data compress; 2) union of the several autoencoders (i.e. data compress of each data type separately and the union of these separate autoencoders). After implementing different autoencoder strategies, eight machine-learning models for financial distress classification were used. The results demonstrated that features retrieved from the union data source strategy outperform the features extracted all at once. These findings create a novelty of autoencoder usage as a feature extraction technique for financial distress key feature's identification and better financial distress issue classification.

Keywords: Autoencoder · Feature extraction · Bankruptcy · Financial distress

1 Introduction

Financial distress significantly negatively impacts creditors, employees, management, shareholders, and other interested parties. As a result, many stakeholders, including rating agencies, investors, financial institutions, management, and shareholders, have long been particularly interested in the topic of detecting enterprise failure. To ensure the stability of the financial markets, financial institutions can identify early warning signals with the aid of an accurate and effective

A. Lopata et al. (Eds.): ICIST 2023, CCIS 1979, pp. 71–86, 2024.
https://doi.org/10.1007/978-3-031-48981-5_6

Financial Distress Prediction (FDP) model, which also enables enterprise managers to make operational decisions [22]. The financial distress or bankruptcy prediction topic is widely explored in the financial and informatics fields, creating one of the fintech branches. For machine learning experts, this topic is interesting due to case scenarios implementation when algorithms have to deal with complex problems: dimensionality, outbalance, and different types of data.

According to the "curse of dimensionality", the cost of a machine-learning system increases exponentially with the number of dimensions [12]. A new feature (dimension) increases the sparsity of the data, which leads to difficulties in achieving better model results [11]. In scientific literature is a tendency to combine various other indicators with the financial data to improve the model results: macroeconomic [3,5], sector [3], boards [7], legal [1], etc. However, it is essential to apply the dimensionality reduction techniques, divided into feature selection and extraction, to construct realistic financial distress models. The main advantage of feature extraction is to maximize the kept information, while feature selection uses a narrow subset from the original data set.

This study for financial distress classification uses an autoencoder as a nonlinear feature extraction technique. Lithuanian business data has been gathered, and new features are produced. A data collection with 972 distinct features in total has been developed. This article's main novelty is using different autoencoder's structure composition strategies, with merged or separated data sources, to determine the optimal set of features for financial distress classification.

The rest of this paper is structured as follows: Sect. 2 reviews financial distress and autoencoder's related topic's literature, Sect. 3 presents the data and its preparation steps, the methodology part is presented in Sect. 4, the research results and main findings are presented in Sects. 5 and 6.

2   Review of Research for Features Extraction for Financial Distress Classification

The majority of articles on financial distress and bankruptcy prediction either use data from stock market markets or internet data sources that use information from financial statements. However, the interest in dimensionality reduction techniques implementation in this contest is growing. According to the systemic review [11]. The researchers often use feature selection techniques instead of extraction due to an achievable understanding of the significance of the feature. However, from a feature extraction perspective most often used linear technique - principal component analysis (PCA), from a nonlinear perspective: multidimensional scaling (MDS) [10,14,19], t-distributed stochastic neighbor embedding (tSNE), [23] and autoencoder [17]. MDS and tSNE techniques are used for clusterization, not classification tasks.

For bankruptcy prediction, the Stacked Autoencoders (SAE) method was used for two different data sets [16,17]. The first data set had an accuracy of 87.9%, which was 1.11% points higher than the best-performing FS-Boosting method accuracy. The second data set had an AUC of 96.1%, which was 0.8%

points higher than the XGBoost method. Compared to other authors' studies, which were performed on the same data sets but did not use an autoencoder, but only machine learning methods, the results were also better.

2.1 Autoencoder

An autoencoder is a method of unsupervised learning for neural networks that train the network to ignore signal "noise" to learn efficient information representations (encoding).

A neural network architecture that forces a knowledge representation of the original input that is compressed because of a bottleneck we impose on the network. It would be incredibly challenging to compress the input features and then reconstruct them if they were all independent of one another. A structure in the data, such as correlations between input features, can be learned and subsequently used to force the input through the network's bottleneck if it exists.

The autoencoder network has three layers [4]:

1. **Encoder:** A feedforward, the fully connected neural network called an encoder compresses input data into a latent space representation and encodes the input data as a compressed representation in a smaller dimension. The input data is deformed in the compressed version.
2. **Hidden layer:** The input that the decoder receives is decreased in representation in this network area.
3. **Decoder:** Similar in construction to the encoder, the decoder is also a feedforward network. This network is in charge of translating the input from the hidden layer back to its original dimensions.

By setting the target output values to equal the inputs, the unsupervised algorithm continuously trains itself using backpropagation [9,18]. The middle ('bottleneck') hidden encoding layer is compelled to use dimensional reduction to remove noise and reconstruct the inputs.

The scheme of the autoencoder is shown in Fig. 1.

3 Data

Lithuanian Enterprise's data from different LT registers are aggregated and provided by LTD "Baltfakta". Analyze period is from 2015.01.01 to 2022.05.30. It contains 81202 unique Lithuanian enterprises. In analyses, period included only active enterprises: a) age is ≥ 1.5 years; b) has the legal status of private limited liability, public limited liability; an individual enterprise or small community; c) in last six months has ≥ 1 social insured employee; d) it has passed ≥ 1.5 years after additional registration of good company conditions (e. g. the company has a history of the bankruptcy case in court, but after a change in circumstances, the company's activities continue); e) non-financial sector enterprise. Financial distress is defined as a "bad" situation of the company, which was detected at least in one Lithuanian government register. Financial distress events consist of 2.88% of the entire sample.

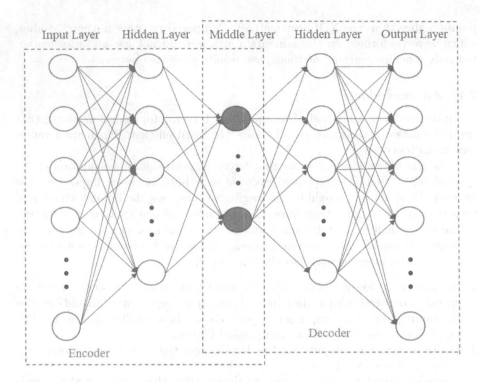

Fig. 1. Autoencoder scheme

3.1   Features

The data contains different LT registers information, such as the Register center, The State of Social Insurance, The State Tax Inspectorate, The State data agency, etc. The data is aggregated by its type in 12 different categories:

1. Board, Directors, Shareholders contains information about the age, the last change, and quantity.
2. Financial statements ratios include the last two years of annual financial ratios information: ROA, ROE, Net profit, Change in Assets, etc.
3. Financial statements records include the last two years of basic annual reports information: assets, equity, liabilities, sales, net profit, etc.
4. Firm type is a binary indicator for the legal status of the enterprise (e. g. individual enterprise).
5. Legal events contain information about history in low-suits, asset seizures from the debtor, and creditor perspectives.
6. Microeconomics indicators include the last three years' quarterly and monthly indicators of inflation, unemployment, GDP, etc.
7. Sector class is a binary indicator for each NACE category.
8. Sector's ratios include the last three years' yearly financial statements ratios and other statistics, which are grouped by each sector.

9. Sodra (The State Social Insurance Fund Board under the Ministry of Social Security and Labour) taxes delay or debt contains the last three years' monthly information about companies' delay to pay tax for Sodra or its provision.
10. Sodra employees include the last three years' monthly information about employee quantity, range, and average salary.
11. Taxes include the last three years' monthly information about paid taxes to the government.
12. Other includes the features not assigned before, such as a history of bad events, age, enterprises name change, etc.

In the Table 1, the number of analyzed features is assigned to these categories. It is important to mention, that in some categories, the number of features is reduced due to missing values, and in others, it is increased by deriving change and other statistical indicators.

Table 1. Distribution of features in different sources

Data type	Quantity	Autoencoder						
		I-a	I-b	I-c	II-b	III-b	S1	S2
Board, Directors, Shareholders	21	32	64	100	64	64	2	2
Financial statements ratios	89						8	8
Financial statements records	71						8	4
Firm type	4						1	1
Legal events	13						2	2
Macroeconomic indicators	247						16	2
Sector's class	17						2	2
Sector's ratios	104						8	8
Sodra taxes delay or debt	241						16	8
Sodra employ's	150						8	2
Taxes	5						1	1
Other	10						2	2
Total number of features	**972**	**32**	**64**	**100**	**64**	**64**	**74**	**42**
Percentage, %	100.00%	3.29%	6.58%	10.29%	6.58%	6.58%	7.61%	4.32%

Sodra - The State Social Insurance Fund Board under the Ministry of Social Security and Labour. Autoencoder I, II, III - identifies a number of hidden dense layers between the input layer and the middle ('bottleneck') layer. Letters a, b, c - the number of units in the middle ('bottleneck') layer (a-32, b-64, c-100). Autoencoder S - identifies separate autoencoders for each data type.

3.2   Data Preparation

The data is split to train and test sets. The train data contains 202010 unique records, and the test data 72095 (it is last year's information). The data is normalized [21], and the range of values of each indicator is maintained between [0, 1]. Here, x_{min} and x_{max} are the minimum and maximum values of an indicator, respectively:

$$x' = \frac{x - x_{min}}{max(x) - min(x)} \tag{1}$$

Before normalization, several financial indicators are assigned to the outliers category due to unrealistic values of the indicator. These values are replaced with NA (not available data). After normalization, all NA values are changed to a minimal value (=0).

The training set is balanced using the SMOTE-NC [20] method due to its suitability for nominal and continuous variables. After balancing, the training data consists of 392734 unique records.

4 Methodology

The purpose of the study is to classify the enterprises as financial distress or not with an optimal set of features. For this reason, the data is presented as follows: the class is determined from the following year, and the features until its beginning, e.g. if the enterprise class is determined in 2018, the feature set is from 2015.01.01 till 2017.12.31. The training set is made from 2018, 2019, 2020, 2021 class information, and the test set - 2022. If the enterprise was not financially distressed in 2019, it might fall into the 2020 sample.

This research used autoencoder as a nonlinear relationship extraction technique and analyzed several different autoencoder structure composition strategies. The first compresses all the data, and the second compresses by data type, creating 12 different autoencoders with each extract data set. The first strategy is developed five different autoencoders: I-a, I-b, I-c, II-b, and III-b (see Table 1). The number of hidden dense layers is identified by Roman numerals, and between two or more hidden layers is implemented drop-out layer, e.g. II autoencoder structure would be input layer - hidden layer - drop out layer - hidden layer - middle layer - hidden layer - drop out layer - hidden layer - output layer. The number of units in the middle layer represents the letters a, b, and c. The better results have 64 units set; for this reason, a more deep autoencoder has been created. The second strategy creates two different sets of autoencoders. In S1, the extracted values from the autoencoder are observed to be highly correlated ≥0.7. Thus, the number is narrowed down until the feature passes the <0.7 correlation condition and completes the S2 set.

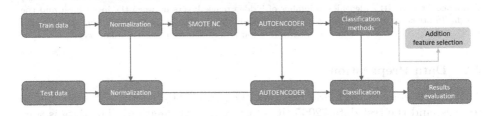

Fig. 2. The research process

The research process is presented in Fig. 2. After the training and testing data split, training and testing data are normalized. Still, testing data is normalized based on normalization parameters from training data to adapt to unknown data criteria. The test sample is then balanced, and since a few features are nominal, the synthetic minority over-sampling technique for the nominal and continuous (SMOTE-NC) metric is used [20]. The autoencoder for the test sample is implemented as the normalization parameter based on the trained autoencoder of the training sample. This is followed by the classification method training, the test sample classification, and evaluation results.

We also have implemented the results benchmark score, which is achieved from the usage of financial statements data (records and ratios). For benchmark score, we have implemented five different autoencoders:

1. FS-records (Financial statements records) autoencoder – uses only data from financial statements records, e.g. Fix assets, Current assets, Equity, etc.;
2. FS-ratios (Financial statements ratios) autoencoder – uses ratios from financial statements, e.g. Current ratio, ROA, ROE, Net profit, etc.;
3. FS (Financial statements) autoencoder – uses ratios and records from financial statements;
4. FS-S1 (Financial statements) autoencoder – combines separate autoencoders values from FS-records and FS-ratios autoencoders;
5. FS-S2 (Financial statements) autoencoder – modification of S1 autoencoder, the features are narrowed down until the <0.7 correlation criteria is fulfilled.

4.1   Methods for Classification

Based on the analysis [11], the most commonly used and neural network methods for the financial distress issue are selected:

1. Commonly used:
   (a) Logistic regression (LG) - a logistic function that delivers a straightforward indication of the likelihood that an event will occur [2], usually used as the benchmark model.
   (b) Decision tree (DT, CART) - a decision support method based on the tree-like model, which consists of a root, inter/decision node, and leaf node [11].
   (c) Random forest (RF) - an ensemble data mining technique that creates a small number of tightly connected Decision Trees by randomly choosing a set of prediction parameters [8].
   (d) XGBoost - well-performing boosted decision tree approach [15], that improves the efficiency and speed of tree-based machine learning methods (including sequential decision trees) [8].
2. Neural network methods:
   (a) Artificial neural network (ANN), Multilayer perceptron (MP - MLP), or Deep neural network (DNN) - the imitation of biological neuron system process which neuron connectivity. A number of hidden layers separate ANN from DNN [11].

(b) Convolutional neural network (CNN) - is separated into two main parts: feature detection and classification. Convolution, pooling, and fully linked layers make up the architecture, which is utilized for automatic and adaptive learning of features for classification problems [11].

(c) Extreme learning machine (ELM) - is a single-hidden layer feedforward network, which performs faster than ANN due to different weights assignment [11].

(d) Self-organizing map (SOM) - unsupervised neural network model, which concurrently quantizes the input data and projects the output space's regular two-dimensional grid from the data space while maintaining topology [13]. Its modification applies to supervised learning.

Addition feature selection is adopted for LG, RF, and XGBoost models. If the analyzed data set has more than 35 features, it is retrained which 30 features set. After the first training, a feature selection method for each method is used, and the model is retrained with a set of 30 features. For LG, three feature selection methods are used: coefficients, Anova, and import.

4.2   Evaluation Matrix

The six evaluation matrix is used for unseen data (test data) performance evaluation. The definitions of each accuracy metric are presented in Eqs. (2)–(7) [2,6]:

$$AUC = \int_0^1 (TPR)d(FPR) \tag{2}$$

$$Precision = \frac{TP}{TP + FP} \tag{3}$$

$$Recall = \frac{TP}{TP + FN} \tag{4}$$

$$Specificity = \frac{TN}{TN + FP} \tag{5}$$

$$F1score = 2 * \frac{precision * recall}{precision + recall} \tag{6}$$

$$ACC(accuracy) = \frac{TP + TN}{TP + TN + FP + FN} \tag{7}$$

where TP = true positives, FP = false positives, TN = true negatives, FN = false negatives, TPR = sensitivity = recall, and FPR = 1 - Specificity.

5   Results

The autoencoder, as a feature extraction technique and classification method, is used for Lithuanian enterprises' financial distress classification. First of all, for all the experiments outcomes has been implemented the effectiveness criteria, which requires to classify financial distress cases ≥ 1000, and not financial distress cases ≥ 35000 due to an unbalanced test set. If this criterion is not fully filled the experiment outcome is not further analyzed. The Table 2 presents only the remaining significant model results that will be evaluated further. "Max no" represents the number of experiments with the concrete method for each autoencoder type, e.g. four ANN models are built, each with a different number of hidden layers, three CNN, etc. LG, RF, and XGBoost are retrained with 30 feature sets. In addition, XGBoost is trained with Binary and Softmax functions. In total, each compiled autoencoder is tested 23 times (see Table 2). However, certain outcomes are not evaluated, i.e. if the model groups the results into one class. To prevent this, it has been decided to effectiveness criteria implementation that the model should correctly categorize around half of the negative and positive occurrences. In Table 2 the percentage represents the models left after effeteness condition implementation.

Table 2. Table of effective methods

Method	Autoencoder type							
	Max no.	I-a	I-b	I-c	II-b	III-b	S1	S2
LG	4	–	–	–	2	–	4	4
DT	1	–	–	–	1	1	1	1
RF	2	–	–	–	1	1	2	2
XGBoost	4	–	–	–	4	–	4	4
ANN	4	–	4	–	4	3	4	4
CNN	3	–	2	–	3	2	3	3
ELM	4	–	–	–	4	4	4	4
SOM	1	–	–	1	1	1	1	0
Total	**23**	**0**	**6**	**1**	**20**	**12**	**23**	**22**
Percentage, %	100.00%	0.00%	26.09%	4.35%	86.96%	52.17%	100.00%	95.65%

Secondly, we have created the benchmark score, which in the analysis includes only financial statements data (records, ratios). In Fig. 3 and Table 3 are presented the outcomes after the effectiveness criteria implementation and ranked by AUC score performance. For the benchmark score has been implemented five different autoencoders (FS-records, FS-ratios, FS, FS-S1, FS-S2); however Fig. 3. is not presented FS-records outcomes due to not fully filled effectiveness criteria, i.e. all the methods results have been grouped to the not-bankrupt class category. The best AUC score is 71.61%, which becomes the benchmark for further autoencoder's structure analyzes. This autoencoder has 16 features in the middle layer using all FS data, and for classification is used an artificial neuron network. Moreover, using the F1 metric, the benchmark score becomes 90.99%, the autoencoder with 8 features in the middle layer using only FS ratio data set and logistic regression method for bankruptcy prediction.

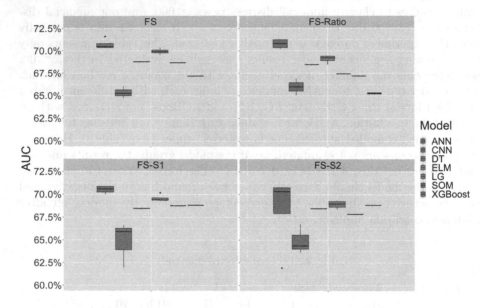

Fig. 3. AUC score boxplots for the benchmark analysis (using only FS data)

Finally, comparing the autoencoders structure strategies, it is found that the method of developing many autoencoders according to the type of data is more effective; this is confirmed by Tables 2, 5 and 6, Figs. 4 and 5. Comparing the AUC metric, it is noticeable that the data sets created by S1 and S2 autoencoders have higher results regardless of the chosen classification model (Fig. 4). This suggests that good feature extraction increases the effectiveness of all classifiers. Moreover, the benchmark score illustrates the new data implementation effectiveness, if it is used second strategy (S1 or S2). Comparing the methods' outputs for each autoencoder's feature extrapolation set, it becomes clear that ANN, CNN, and LG produce better results than other classificational approaches. The results of the F1 score are presented in Fig. 5, which reveals that the best F1 score results are achieved by RF and XGBoost methods (Table 6).

Table 3. Performance results ranged by AUC score metrics for the benchmark data (using only FS data)

#	Type	No.	Method	Accuracy	AUC	F1	Precision	Recall	Specificity
1	FS	16	ANN-1	67.96%	**71.61%**	80.43%	**98.96%**	67.74%	**75.48%**
2	FS-Ratio	8	ANN-1	68.83%	**71.27%**	81.07%	**98.91%**	68.68%	**73.86%**
3	FS-Ratio	8	ANN-2	67.99%	**71.22%**	80.46%	**98.93%**	67.80%	**74.64%**
4	FS-S1	16	ANN-1	68.19%	**70.87%**	80.61%	**98.89%**	68.03%	**73.71%**
5	FS-S1	16	ANN-2	74.12%	**70.86%**	84.81%	**98.74%**	74.32%	67.41%
6	FS-S2	12	ANN-1	67.47%	**70.81%**	80.08%	**98.91%**	67.27%	**74.35%**
7	FS-S2	12	ANN-3	71.08%	**70.73%**	82.70%	**98.81%**	71.10%	**70.36%**
8	FS	16	ANN-4	**78.61%**	**70.56%**	**87.79%**	98.63%	**79.09%**	62.04%
9	FS-Ratio	8	ANN-4	69.80%	**70.40%**	81.78%	**98.81%**	69.76%	**71.05%**
10	FS	16	ELM_100	76.19%	**70.39%**	86.20%	98.66%	76.53%	64.25%

Table 4. Performance results ranged by F1 score metrics for the benchmark data (using only FS data)

	Type	No.	Method	Accuracy	AUC	F1	Precision	Recall	Specificity
1	FS-Ratio	8	LG	**83.70%**	67.45%	**90.99%**	98.32%	**84.68%**	50.22%
2	FS-S2	12	LG	**83.67%**	67.86%	**90.97%**	98.35%	**84.61%**	51.11%
3	FS	16	LG	**82.16%**	68.69%	**90.04%**	98.43%	**82.96%**	54.41%
4	FS-S1	16	LG	**82.13%**	68.77%	**90.02%**	98.44%	**82.93%**	54.60%
5	FS-Ratio	8	CNN-3	**78.89%**	65.07%	**88.01%**	98.23%	**79.71%**	**50.42%**
6	FS	16	ANN-4	**78.61%**	70.56%	**87.79%**	98.63%	**79.09%**	62.04%
7	FS-S2	12	CNN-2_a	**78.53%**	66.74%	**87.76%**	98.35%	**79.23%**	54.26%
8	FS-Ratio	8	XGBoost (Softmax)	**78.34%**	65.14%	**87.65%**	98.24%	**79.13%**	**51.16%**
9	FS-Ratio	8	XGBoost (Binary)	**78.33%**	65.42%	**87.65%**	98.26%	**79.10%**	51.75%
10	FS-S1	16	CNN-3	**77.77%**	65.93%	**87.28%**	98.31%	**78.48%**	**53.37%**

The top ten performance results range by AUC, and F1 scores are presented in Tables 5 and 6. Table "Type" identifies autoencoders creation strategy name, "No" - the number of features used in the classification method, "Method"- classification method, and all evaluation metrics scores presented in %. If a score is highlighted, it is one of the top 10 results for that statistic. In the Table 6, all scores in accuracy, F1, and recall are highlighted even if it is ranged by F1 score; it is due to the top 10 rank being the same for all parameters. It is evident that in both rankings, the top models come from either type S1 or S2. In the Table 5, the number of ANNs identifies the hidden layers. It is observed that a simple network with I-II hidden layers can produce high results. LG regression achieves better results which fewer feature sets, 30 or 42. In the Table 6, the best results achieved by RF and XGBoost methods and their modifications with S1 or S2 autoencoders type. The results are so near that identifying the best model modification is difficult. This leads to the conclusion that the modification of the model is not very important; the basic principle of the model is essential.

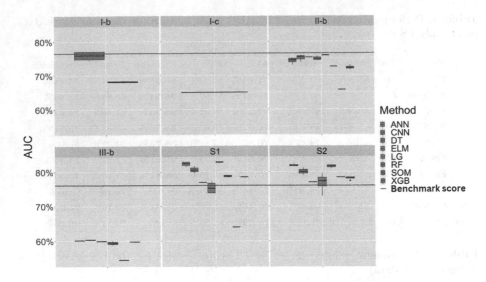

Fig. 4. AUC score boxplots distributed by different autoencoders structure and classification methods

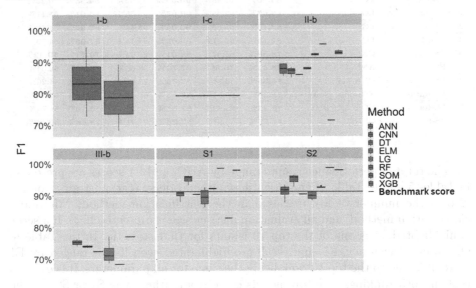

Fig. 5. F1 score boxplots distributed by different autoencoders' structure and classification methods

The Table 7 is compiled, leaving one best model from the group based on the AUC metric, i.e. if the S1-ANN group consists of 4 different models (from I to IV hidden layers), only the best one according to the AUC score is left. This table shows a more diverse spectrum of models: LG, RF, XGBoost, ANN, CNN, and ELM. However, the diversity of autoencoder types has not changed. Now

Table 5. Performance results ranged by AUC score metrics for all data

#	Type	No	Method	Accuracy	AUC	F1	Precision	Recall	Specificity
1.	S2	42	ANN-2	84.13%	**83.16%**	91.16%	**99.39%**	84.19%	**82.13%**
2.	S1	30	LG Coefficients	85.67%	**83.12%**	92.09%	**99.34%**	85.83%	**80.40%**
3.	S1	74	ANN-1	83.26%	**82.95%**	90.63%	**99.40%**	83.28%	**82.62%**
4.	S1	30	LG VarImport	86.30%	**82.94%**	92.47%	**99.31%**	86.51%	79.37%
5.	S1	74	ANN-2	79.28%	**82.93%**	88.12%	**99.52%**	79.06%	**86.80%**
6.	S1	74	LG basic	85.95%	**82.92%**	92.26%	**99.32%**	86.13%	**79.71%**
7.	S1	30	LG VarAnova	85.56%	**82.63%**	92.02%	**99.31%**	85.73%	**79.52%**
8.	S2	42	ANN-3	87.65%	**82.29%**	93.27%	99.24%	87.97%	76.61%
9.	S1	74	ANN-3	84.98%	**82.09%**	91.68%	99.29%	85.16%	79.03%
10.	S2	30	LG Coefficients	86.37%	**81.97%**	92.51%	99.25%	86.64%	77.30%

Table 6. Performance results ranged by F-1 score metrics

#	Type	No	Method	Accuracy	AUC	F1	Precision	Recall	Specificity
1.	S2	42	RF	**97.74%**	78.42%	**98.84%**	98.78%	**98.89%**	57.95%
2.	S2	30	RF	**97.45%**	78.44%	**98.68%**	98.79%	**98.58%**	58.30%
3.	S1	74	RF	**97.41%**	78.37%	**98.67%**	98.79%	**98.55%**	58.20%
4.	S1	30	RF	**97.24%**	79.15%	**98.58%**	98.83%	**98.32%**	59.97%
5.	S2	42	XGBoost (Binary)	**96.37%**	78.38%	**98.12%**	98.80%	**97.44%**	59.33%
6.	S1	74	XGBoost (Binary)	**96.33%**	78.39%	**98.10%**	98.81%	**97.40%**	59.38%
7.	S2	42	XGBoost (Softmax)	**96.28%**	77.36%	**98.07%**	98.75%	**97.41%**	57.31%
8.	S1	30	XGBoost (Softmax)	**96.26%**	78.48%	**98.06%**	98.81%	**97.33%**	59.63%
9.	S2	30	XGBoost (Softmax)	**96.11%**	78.26%	**97.98%**	98.80%	**97.18%**	59.33%
10.	S1	74	XGBoost (Softmax)	**95.99%**	78.60%	**97.92%**	98.82%	**97.02%**	60.17%

Table 7. Performance results ranged by AUC score metrics after leaving one model from the group using all data

#	Type	No	Method	Accuracy	AUC	F1	Precision	Recall	Specificity
1.	S2	42	ANN	84.13%	**83.16%**	91.16%	**99.39%**	84.19%	**82.13%**
2.	S1	30	LG	85.67%	**83.12%**	92.09%	**99.34%**	85.83%	**80.40%**
3.	S1	74	ANN	83.26%	**82.95%**	90.63%	**99.40%**	83.28%	**82.62%**
4.	S2	30	LG	**86.37%**	**81.97%**	92.51%	**99.25%**	**86.64%**	**77.30%**
5.	S1	74	CNN	**87.68%**	**81.76%**	93.28%	**99.20%**	**88.03%**	75.48%
6.	S2	42	CNN	**92.04%**	**81.20%**	95.77%	**99.06%**	**92.69%**	69.72%
7.	S2	42	ELM	80.86%	**79.56%**	89.15%	**99.22%**	80.93%	**78.19%**
8.	S1	30	RF	**97.24%**	**79.15%**	98.58%	98.83%	**98.32%**	59.97%
9.	S1	74	XGBoost	**95.99%**	**78.60%**	97.92%	98.82%	**97.02%**	60.17%
10.	S2	30	RF	**97.45%**	**78.44%**	98.68%	98.79%	**98.58%**	58.30%

the variation of the results is better, but the best model determination depends on the main evaluation metrics. AUC score identifies the S2-ANN model with 83.16%, F1 score - S2-RF with 98.68%.

6   Conclusion

In this paper, we propose a novel approach to using an autoencoder as a feature extraction technique for financial distress classification. We have analyzed two different strategies for the application of autoencoder:

1. The first strategy has compressed all the data simultaneously.
2. The second has created 12 different autoencoders for each extract data set.

Eight main methods (with their modifications) have been implemented during the classification phase. Since the classes are unbalanced, financial distress cases contain 2.88% entire sample; the model's results have been reduced to ensure the analysis of significant ones. In addition, it has been required to correctly classify financial distress cases ≥ 1000, not financial distress cases ≥ 35000. The main conclusions have been grouped into four main categories:

1. **The best strategy of autoencoder structure composition.** Better results have been achieved in the second autoencoder's structure composition strategy by creating 12 different autoencoders for each data type;
2. **Number of features.** From the first autoencoder's strategy, the optimal set contains 64 features, while the second is difficult to determine due to close results. However, fewer features lead to lower computational resources and a simpler model. This means reducing the number of "bottleneck" units until it passes the <0.7 correlation condition helps to create a more effective model;
3. **Performance of the models.** The ANN and LG model's have been determined as the best by AUC sore; RF and XGBoost - by F1 score using the second autoencoder's structure composition strategy.
4. **Modification of models.** The model's modification is not particularly relevant; the most important is the model's fundamental idea.

The research development could contain a variety of feature selection and extraction methods and new machine learning algorithms implementation. Moreover, more separate models could be created depending on the size of the enterprise or sector.

Acknowledgements. We wish to thank Viktoras Vaitkevičius from Baltfakta for providing data and fruitful discussion, Rimantė Kunickaitė, Rūta Juozaitienė, Milita Songailaitė for discussions on the application of different methods and technical support.

References

1. Alshahrani, F., Eulaiwi, B., Duong, L., Taylor, G.: Climate change performance and financial distress. Bus. Strategy Environ. bse.3298 (2022). https://doi.org/10.1002/bse.3298. https://onlinelibrary.wiley.com/doi/10.1002/bse.3298
2. Ben Jabeur, S., Serret, V.: Bankruptcy prediction using fuzzy convolutional neural networks. Res. Int. Bus. Financ. **64**, 101844 (2023). https://doi.org/10.1016/j.ribaf.2022.101844. https://linkinghub.elsevier.com/retrieve/pii/S0275531922002306

3. Bozkurt, B., Kaya, M.V.: Foremost features affecting financial distress and Bankruptcy in the acute stage of COVID-19 crisis. Appl. Econ. Lett. 1–12 (2022). https://doi.org/10.1080/13504851.2022.2036681. https://www.tandfonline.com/doi/full/10.1080/13504851.2022.2036681

4. Dertat, A.: Applied deep learning - part 3: Autoencoders (2017). https://towardsdatascience.com/applied-deep-learning-part-3-autoencoders-1c083af4d798

5. Figlioli, B., Lima, F.G.: A proposed corporate distress and recovery prediction score based on financial and economic components. Expert Syst. Appl. **197**, 116726 (2022). https://doi.org/10.1016/j.eswa.2022.116726. https://linkinghub.elsevier.com/retrieve/pii/S0957417422001993

6. Garcia, J.: Bankruptcy prediction using synthetic sampling. Mach. Learn. Appl. **9**, 100343 (2022). https://doi.org/10.1016/j.mlwa.2022.100343. https://linkinghub.elsevier.com/retrieve/pii/S2666827022000494

7. Gerged, A.M., Yao, S., Albitar, K.: Board composition, ownership structure and financial distress: insights from UK FTSE 350. Corporate Gov.: Int. J. Bus. Soc. (2022). https://doi.org/10.1108/CG-02-2022-0069. https://www.emerald.com/insight/content/doi/10.1108/CG-02-2022-0069/full/html

8. Hossain, T., Ferdous, T., Bahadur, E.H., Masum, A.K.M., YasirArafat, A.: Data mining for predicting and finding factors of bankruptcy. In: 2022 International Conference on Innovations in Science, Engineering and Technology (ICISET), Chittagong, Bangladesh, pp. 504–509. IEEE (2022). https://doi.org/10.1109/ICISET54810.2022.9775887. https://ieeexplore.ieee.org/document/9775887/

9. Jordan, J.: Introduction to autoencoders (2018). https://www.jeremyjordan.me/autoencoders/

10. Khoja, L., Chipulu, M., Jayasekera, R.: Analysis of financial distress cross countries: using macroeconomic, industrial indicators and accounting data. Int. Rev. Financ. Anal. **66**, 101379 (2019). https://doi.org/10.1016/j.irfa.2019.101379. http://www.sciencedirect.com/science/article/pii/S1057521919300869

11. Kuizinienė, D., Krilavičius, T., Damaševičius, R., Maskeliūnas, R.: Systematic review of financial distress identification using artificial intelligence methods. Appl. Artif. Intell. **36**(1), 2138124 (2022). https://doi.org/10.1080/08839514.2022.2138124. https://www.tandfonline.com/doi/full/10.1080/08839514.2022.2138124

12. Kuo, F.Y., Sloan, I.H.: Lifting the curse of dimensionality. Not. AMS **52**(11), 9 (2005)

13. Li, S.T., Kuo, S.C., Tsai, F.C.: An intelligent decision-support model using FSOM and rule extraction for crime prevention. Expert Syst. Appl. **37**(10), 7108–7119 (2010). https://doi.org/10.1016/j.eswa.2010.03.004. https://linkinghub.elsevier.com/retrieve/pii/S0957417410001855

14. Mokrišová, M., Horváthová, J.: Bankruptcy prediction applying multivariate techniques. Sci. J. Faculty Manag. Univ. Presov in Presov **12**, 52–69 (2020). http://www.journalmb.eu/archiv/JMB-2-2020.pdfpage=52

15. Qian, H., Wang, B., Yuan, M., Gao, S., Song, Y.: Financial distress prediction using a corrected feature selection measure and gradient boosted decision tree. Expert Syst. Appl. **190**, 116202 (2022). https://doi.org/10.1016/j.eswa.2021.116202. https://linkinghub.elsevier.com/retrieve/pii/S0957417421015177

16. Smiti, S., Soui, M.: Bankruptcy prediction using deep learning approach based on borderline. SMOTE **22**(5), 1067–1083 (2020). https://doi.org/10.1007/s10796-020-10031-6

17. Soui, M., Smiti, S., Mkaouer, M.W., Ejbali, R.: Bankruptcy prediction using stacked auto-encoders. **34**(1), 80–100. https://doi.org/10.1080/08839514.2019. 1691849. https://www.tandfonline.com/doi/full/10.1080/08839514.2019.1691849
18. GL Team: Introduction to autoencoders? What are autoencoders applications and types? (2022). https://www.mygreatlearning.com/blog/autoencoder/
19. Štefko, R., Horváthová, J., Mokrišová, M.: The application of graphic methods and the DEA in predicting the risk of bankruptcy. J. Risk Financ. Manag. **14**(5), 220 (2021). https://doi.org/10.3390/jrfm14050220. https://www.mdpi.com/1911-8074/14/5/220
20. Wongvorachan, T., He, S., Bulut, O.: A comparison of undersampling, over-sampling, and SMOTE methods for dealing with imbalanced classification in educational data mining. Information **14**(1), 54 (2023). https://doi.org/10.3390/info14010054. https://www.mdpi.com/2078-2489/14/1/54
21. Xu, W., Fu, H., Pan, Y.: A novel soft ensemble model for financial distress prediction with different sample sizes. Math. Probl. Eng. 1–12 (2019). https://doi.org/10.1155/2019/3085247. http://search.ebscohost.com/
22. Zhang, Z., Wu, C., Qu, S., Chen, X.: An explainable artificial intelligence approach for financial distress prediction. Inf. Process. Manag. **59**(4), 102988 (2022). https://doi.org/10.1016/j.ipm.2022.102988. https://linkinghub.elsevier.com/retrieve/pii/S0306457322001030
23. Zoričák, M., Gnip, P., Drotár, P., Gazda, V.: Bankruptcy prediction for small-and medium-sized companies using severely imbalanced datasets. Econ. Model. **84**, 165–176 (2020). https://doi.org/10.1016/j.econmod.2019.04.003. http://www.sciencedirect.com/science/article/pii/S0264999318315438

Scope Assessment Methodology for Agile Projects Using Automated Requirements Gathering from Models

Lina Bisikirskiene[✉] and Egle Grigonyte

Kaunas University of Technology, Studentu str. 50, 51368 Kaunas, Lithuania
lina.bisikirskiene@ktu.edu

Abstract. This article discusses the importance of effective scope assessment in Agile projects. The adoption of Agile principles and methods has replaced the traditional waterfall approach, leading to better involvement of clients and teams in gathering requirements, regular review of results, and flexible adaptation to changes. However, Agile implementation projects lack the opportunity to pay detailed attention to the analysis phase, which makes scope assessment crucial. The article proposes using Story Map and UML models to analyze the scope of Agile projects, as their ability to visualize information and act as a source of truth. The methodology helps to integrate models, compile functional and non-functional requirements, perform cross-checking of the requirements, and create an initial scope assessment. Proper preparation for scope assessment is necessary for successful Agile implementation and can lead to understanding project goals and objectives, prioritizing work, managing stakeholder expectations, estimating timelines, and enhancing team collaboration.

Keywords: Agile Project · Scope Assessment · UML Models · Story Map · Requirements-gathering

1 Introduction

Since development trends of information systems evolve a lot, efficiency becomes the main competitive advantage. The variety of possible solutions has expanded significantly. This is influenced by various technological possibilities, as well as increased attention to customer needs and competitiveness in the markets. The specific technologies chosen will depend on the nature of the system, the organization's requirements, and the available resources. The implementation methods of IT projects started adapting to the changes. Step-by-step waterfall work principles have been replaced by Agile principles and methods based on it, such as Scrum, and Kanban. The journey from waterfall to Agile has its pros and cons [1]. The main success factors that allow Agile principles to be competitive could be distinguished as follows: involvement of the client and the team in gathering requirements, regular (usually bi-weekly) review of results and providing feedback, and flexible adaptation to changes. For this process to go smoothly, it needs

A. Lopata et al. (Eds.): ICIST 2023, CCIS 1979, pp. 87–101, 2024.
https://doi.org/10.1007/978-3-031-48981-5_7

proper preparation. Preparation starts very early when gathering of requirements (scope, duration, etc.) with the client is initiated. If waterfall made it possible to pay a lot of attention to the analysis phase and thus have a more accurate assessment of the scope of work, then agile implementation projects do not have such an opportunity. Assessment is fast, do not pay a lot of attention to the details, expecting to solve all the challenges during the implementation phase. To accomplish the scope assessment task, companies use various methods to collect functional and non-functional requirements, restrictions, risks, integrations, and technological dependencies as accurately as possible. Assessing scope is crucial in agile projects [11] as it enables the team to understand project goals and objectives, prioritize work, manage stakeholder expectations, estimate project timelines accurately, and enhance team collaboration.

The purpose of this article is to present the methodology that allows making a scope assessment of Agile project integrating the automated requirements gathering from the UML models. Even if they are often used in the waterfall, their ability to visualize information and be a source of truth [17] brings valuable experience in analyzing the scope of an Agile project, including the automated scan of models, cross-checking of requirements, and the creation of an initial scope assessment.

2 Literature

A project is a temporary and unique endeavor that is designed to achieve a specific goal or objective. Projects are usually initiated to create or deliver a product, service, or result that is different from the usual routine operations of an organization. Projects have a defined scope, budget, and timeline, and they typically involve a team of people working together to complete the project [9]. Agile project life cycle is a framework for managing and delivering projects in an iterative and incremental approach [2]. The Agile methodology emphasizes flexibility, adaptability, and customer satisfaction. The Agile project life cycle typically consists of the following stages [10]:

- Planning: In this stage, the project team identifies the project requirements, goals, and objectives, and creates a plan for how to achieve them. The team also defines the scope of the project and identifies the stakeholders.
- Analysis and Design: In this stage, the project team analyzes the requirements and designs a solution that meets those requirements. The team also identifies any potential risks and develops a plan to mitigate them.
- Development: In this stage, the project team creates the product or solution in iterations, with each iteration adding new features and functionality to the product.
- Testing: In this stage, the project team tests the product to ensure that it meets the requirements and is functioning as expected. The team also performs user acceptance testing to ensure that the product meets the needs of the users.
- Deployment: In this stage, the product is deployed to the production environment and made available to the users.
- Monitoring and Maintenance: In this stage, the project team monitors the product to ensure that it is functioning properly and performs any necessary updates.

Agile project life cycle is iterative, meaning that each stage is repeated in multiple cycles until the final product is delivered. The Agile methodology allows for flexibility and adaptability throughout the project life cycle, enabling the project team to respond to changes and adapt to the evolving needs of the stakeholders.

Assessing scope in the Planning stage helps to establish clear project boundaries and ensures that the project team and stakeholders understand the goals and objectives of the project. This enables the team to focus on the essential requirements and avoid unnecessary work. Work must be prioritized based on its value and importance to the project. The team should understand the most critical features, functionalities, and deliverables, enabling them to prioritize their work accordingly [4]. Expectations management is another area that ensures that everyone is on the same page. It helps to prevent scope creep, which is when project requirements increase beyond what was initially planned. By understanding the project's scope, the team can identify the number of tasks required to complete the project, the resources required, and the timeframes needed to complete each task. Assessing scope promotes team collaboration by enabling the team to work together towards a shared goal. It helps the team to understand each other's roles and responsibilities, which enhances communication and collaboration throughout the project [3]. Since the Planning stage is a cornerstone of the project, several methodologies help to deal with the project scope assessment.

2.1 Methodologies for Project Scope Estimation

Various methodologies can be used to estimate project scope. They define the principles of how to deal with large projects, scaling, and requirement gathering. Even though initially they were dedicated to waterfall projects, the main principles can be reused in Agile projects.

A **Work Breakdown Structure (WBS)** is a hierarchical breakdown of the project deliverables into smaller, more manageable components or work packages [12]. Each task or activity in the WBS is defined in terms of its scope, duration, and resources needed to complete it. The WBS provides a structured approach to organizing and defining the scope of the project, making it easier to plan and manage. The WBS is typically created at the beginning of the project planning phase and is used throughout the project life cycle.

Mind Mapping involves brainstorming and visualizing the project scope using a diagram [13] that represents ideas, concepts, or tasks and their relationships to one another. The diagram is created by starting with a central idea or concept and then branching out into subtopics or related ideas. Each subtopic can then be further expanded into smaller ideas or tasks. Mind mapping helps to identify project objectives, deliverables, and constraints in a structured way. Since Mind Mapping does not support any specific standard or process, the team has to be very specific about what kind of outcome they are expecting. Mind Mapping is a sub-activity of the Lean Requirement Workshop [7] described in the offered methodology.

Feature Driven Development (FDD) is an iterative and incremental approach that focuses on delivering features [14]. It is an Agile software development methodology that breaks down the project scope into small, feature-sized components that can be delivered incrementally. Each feature is then developed in a series of short iterations that typically last no more than two weeks. The features are developed and tested individually, and then integrated into the system as a whole. The attitude that features can be developed, and released separately is very valuable in Agile projects. Such principles must be included in requirements-gathering practices.

Function Point Analysis (FPA) is often used in Agile software development projects to estimate the size of a software system or application based on the functionality it provides [15]. FPA is based on the concept of breaking down a software system into a set of logical functions, each of which can be measured and quantified. These functions are then categorized into different types, such as input, output, inquiry, and internal logical files. Each type of function is assigned a weight based on its complexity, and the total number of weighted functions is used to calculate the size of the system. Once the size of the system has been determined, FPA can be used to estimate the effort required to develop and maintain the system. This information can then be used to help plan and manage the project, as well as to track progress and identify potential issues.

Use Case Points (UCP) is a software estimation technique used in agile projects to estimate the size of a software application or system [16]. UCP is based on the number of use cases and actors in a system and assigns a point value to each one based on complexity factors such as technical complexity, business criticality, and user interaction. UCP consists of three main components: Use Case Weight (the level of complexity based on the number of transactions, input and output points, and the technical complexity); Actor Weight (complexity of the actors involved, including a number of transactions performed and the technical complexity); Technical Complexity Factor (technical environment in which the software will be developed and deployed, including a number of interfaces, and the level of security required). By combining these three components, UCP provides an estimate of the size of a software system, which can be used to estimate the effort required to develop the system, as well as the time and cost required for the project.

However, despite the advantages of these techniques, experts argue that traditional scope assessment methodologies, such as Work Breakdown Structure (WBS) or Function Point Analysis (FPA), may not be well-suited for Agile projects. This is because these methodologies typically require a more rigid and structured approach to requirements gathering, which may not align with the flexible and iterative nature of Agile development. Although the decomposition principles always help to clarify and identify the goals that should be reached in the project. Analysis of various aspects of the system ensures that key influencers will not be left behind.

2.2 UML in Agile Projects

UML stands for Unified Modeling Language, which is a standardized visual modeling language used to design and model software systems. UML has become the de facto standard for software modeling and is widely used by software engineers, architects, project managers, and other stakeholders involved in the software development process. UML has several benefits when applied in Agile projects [17]:

- Visualization: UML provides a graphical notation that can help project team members communicate more effectively. UML diagrams can be easily understood by both technical and non-technical stakeholders, which can facilitate better collaboration and reduce misunderstandings.

- Flexibility: UML can be used to model different aspects of a system, such as a user interface, data structures, or behavior. This flexibility allows Agile teams to adapt the modeling approach to the specific needs of the project and to evolve the models as the project progresses.
- Traceability: UML models can be used to trace requirements, design decisions, and test cases throughout the project lifecycle. This can help ensure that the final product meets the stakeholders' needs and that changes are properly managed.

Combining principles from project scope assessment methodologies and modeling benefits can lead to successful planning in Agile projects as long as they are used in a lightweight and iterative way that supports the principles of agility, such as collaboration, feedback, and continuous improvement. These principles are combined with the proposed methodology below.

3 Methodology for the Assessment of the Project Scope

To solve the challenges of assessing the scope of the project, a methodology has been proposed that allows the necessary information to be collected and evaluated in one place. The main goal is to avoid multiple sources, Excel files, and information traveling through e-mails and be competitive in time.

Pre-conditions play important role in this methodology. The main purpose is to identify what information we already have gathered before starting. The collected information depends on several factors: the process of gathering requirements in the company; the competencies of the project manager/analyst/architect/client to collect information; the knowledge base of the subject area; and its complexity. If the requirement gathering is struggling, the methodology helps to tighten the collection and focus on the most important parts.

The pre-condition chosen in this article is that the requirements are collected during the Lean Requirements Workshop [7]. During the workshop, the following outcomes are identified: Product Charter (current challenges, vision, success metrics) [8], user roles, user journey map, and story map. After the session with the client must be collected, reviewed, and the proposal with the estimates sent to the client.

Collecting and consolidating the requirements is a complex process. This process is complicated by the fact that people see and record different things while participating in the workshop. The methodology must ensure that their vision and understanding of the requirements are smooth and allows a proper assessment of the scope of the project. Sometimes for Scrum-based projects, only a story map is created. In most cases, it is not enough to have a clear picture of the scope. For such reason, other helpful models are introduced in the methodology.

3.1 Algorithm of the Methodology

The methodology of the project scope assessment consists of an algorithm and the steps describing it (see Fig. 1). The algorithm consists of eight main steps, indicating the output of each of them. The first two steps allow us to identify the problem of the project (Step "1. Identify Problem") and define expected results (Step "2. Define Results").

These steps are directly related to the Product Charter deliverables during the Lean Requirements Workshop.

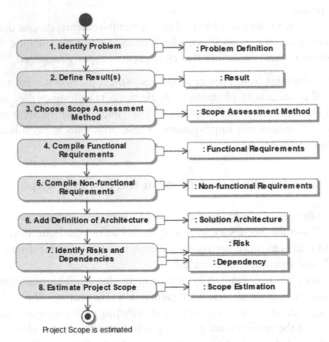

Fig. 1. The algorithm of the method of the project scope estimation

The third step is to choose which assessment method the user wants to use (Step "3. Choose Scope Assessment Method"). He chooses the units of measurement. Although Story Points are recommended for Agile projects, some IT companies still prefer hours. It is the choice of the unit of measurement that depends only on the internal agreement of the project participants performing the evaluation. The following measurement units are available in the methodology:

• Story Points (Fibonacci sequence 0, 0.5, 1, 2, 3, 5, 8, 13, 21, 34, ∞) [6];
• Hours (minimum unit is one hour);
• T-shirt size (XS (extra small), S (small), M (medium), L (large), and XL (extra large), and
• Function Points (complexity weights of function points for external inputs, external outputs, internal logical files, external user interfaces, and external queries [55]).

Steps 4–6 are intended to evaluate the product (project) from different perspectives, including functional requirements (Step 4. Compile Functional Requirements), non-functional requirements (Step 5. Compile Non-functional Requirements), and architectural requirements (Step 6. Add Definition of Architecture). The user may choose what kind of information they want to upload, i.e. selected type model, excel list. The ability to upload different types of models allows for cross-checking of requirements. It is a benefit from the competencies of the persons gathering the requirements perspective. They can be familiar with UML knowledge, Story Map, etc. It can be an internal agreement as well that different team members will write and collect the requirements using different methods. In this way, it is possible to determine whether all users see the scope of the project in the same way, as well as whether there were no omissions in the identification of requirements. The steps are not mandatory, but their completion directly affects the estimation of the scope of the project. A detailed description of the steps is provided below.

The seventh step is the identification of risks and dependencies (Step 7. Identify Risks and Dependencies). The user can enter them by hand or upload a list. The eighth step is to add the estimates to all available requirements or any additional information that is needed to calculate the scope of the project according to the formula.

For representation purposes, the "Animal Shelter app" model fragments and requirements are shown next to each step. The experiments are described in the Sect. 4.

3.2 Requirements Gathering

Steps 4–6 require a detailed description to reveal the principles of the algorithm.

Step "4. Compile Functional Requirements"
The process of creating functional requirements is presented in Fig. 2. When starting the collection of functional requirements, the user can choose whether to import models (Step 4.1. Choose Type of Model) or enter them manually (Step 4.12. Add Additional Requirements). Since the process can be repeated as many times as needed, the user can first import the models and then add additional requirements to them. Five types of models can be imported: Story Map (Step 4.2.), UML Use Case model (Step 4.3.), UML Activity model (Step 4.4.), UML Domain (Class) model (Step 4.5.), SysML Requirement model (Step 4.6.) and Excel spreadsheet with functional requirements (Step 4.7.). The order of the model import does make an impact, the user may choose later which model is the primary one.

In step 4.8, the elements of each model are identified. Each model defines a certain set of elements that are analyzed in the methodology. They are used to form the functional requirements and identify their overlapping:

- Story Map: Use, Goals, Epic, User Story, Priority;
- SysML Requirement model: Requirement;
- UML Use Case model: Actor, Use Case, Association, Include, Extend;
- UML Activity model: Swimlane (Activity Partition), Action, Object Node, Object/Control Flow, Input/Output pin, Decision, Merge, Fork, Join, Send Signal, Accept Event, Time Event;
- UML Domain Model: Class, Association, Generalization, Composition, Aggregation, Property;
- Excel spreadsheet structure: ID (hierarchical structure), name, description, priority, type.

After adding the elements and the relationships between them into the methodology, functional requirements are formed by combining the previously mentioned types of elements and relationships between them according to the established rules (Step 4.8. Form Functional Requirements). Compilation rules and examples are given in the table below.

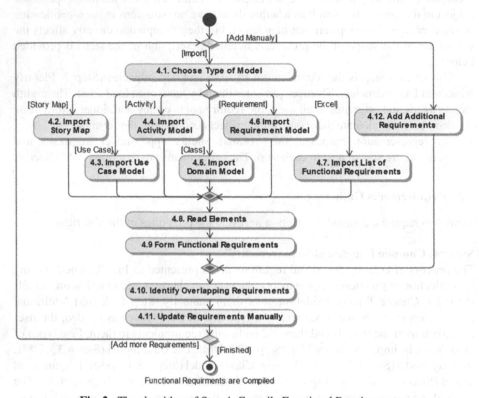

Fig. 2. The algorithm of Step 4. Compile Functional Requirements

The story map has one rule for creating the functional requirements and it is displayed in Table 1. Requirement's text is formed from separate elements. The SysML Requirement model has one rule for creating the functional requirements and it is displayed in Table 2. Requirements may have a hierarchical structure which is shown using the Owner of each requirement. The rule is applied to all the elements. The UML Use Case model has four predefined rules for creating the functional requirements and one of them is displayed in Table 3.

UML Activity model has the largest number of elements that are used to form the functional requirements. The rules cover:

- Activity partition;
- Call Behavior Action (CBA);
- CBA with Input Pin or combination with Object Flow and Object Node;
- CBA with Output Pin or combination with Object Flow and Object Node;
- CBA interaction with Decision/Fork/Join/Merge;

Table 1. Requirement structure for Story Map elements

Story map	Structure	Example
Rule:	Requirement text: "User Role" may "Story" in the "Epic" context	Pet Adopter (*User Role*) may List available pets (*Story*) in the Search (*Epic*) context
Additional information about the requirement:	- Parenting element: "Epic" - Sequence number: Story number on the "Epic" - Priority	- Search - 3 - High

Table 2. Requirement structure for Requirement model elements

Requirement model	Structure	Example
Rule:	Requirement text: Requirement. Name	The list of the available pets must be sortable (*Requirement*)
Additional information about the requirement:	- Parenting element: - "Requirement.Owner" - Sequence number: ID - Priority	- Home page functionality - 7 - High

Table 3. Requirement structure for Use Case model elements

Use Case model	Structure	Example
Rule:	Requirement text: "Actor. Name" may "Use Case. Name [1]" and also has to "Use Case. Name [2]"	Pet Adopter (*Actor*) may Fill out application (*Use Case* [1]) and also has to Sign documents (*Use Case* [2])
Conditions:	Include relationship exists and Use Case [1] is Including Case and Use case [2] is Addition	
Additional information about the requirement:	- Sequence number: ID	- 3 (*Use case* [1]) - 4 (*Use case* [2])

- CBA interaction with Fork;
- Hierarchy of CBAs using Activities.

Once the pattern of the rule is identified it can be combined with other rules, e.g. Input and Output rules and Activity Partition rules for one Call Behavior Action. Also, FOR cycle is used to gather all related elements using the same rule. An example of the predefined rule is displayed in Table 4. UML Class model also has combined rules to form functional requirements. They cover attributes, association/generalization/composition/aggregation relationships, and constraints. An example of the predefined rule is displayed in Table 5.

Table 4. Requirement structure for Activity model elements

Use Case model	Structure	Example
Rule:	Requirement text: "Call Behavior Action. Name" gives "Object Node. Name or Type" as a result (s)	Register animal in the system (*Call Behavior Action*) gives Registered Animal (*Object Node*) as a result
Conditions:	Object Flow exists or Output Pin with Type = "Animal" or Name "Registered Animal" exists	
Additional information about the requirement:	- Sequence number: ID	- 3 (*Call Behavior Action*)

Table 5. Requirement structure for Class model elements

Use Case model	Structure	Example
Rule:	Requirement text: "Class. Name [1]" "Association. Name" 'Association. Property [2]. Multiplicity" "Class. Name [2]"	Pet Adopter (*Class* [1]) adopts (*Association*) many (*Multiplicity*) Animal(s) (*Class* [2])
Conditions:	Association relationship exists	

Once all the functional requirements are scanned and in place, the next step is to evaluate their overlap automatically (Step 4.11. Identify Overlapping Requirements). Even though different models analyze the project from different perspectives, the gathered requirements allow for assessing whether all needs are identified. In this way, it is possible to ensure that the estimation of the scope will be more accurate. The user's involvement at this stage is very important. In parallel with automatic recommendations for overlapping, he can manually adjust the requirements himself (Step 4.12. Update Requirements Manually).

The following rules apply when assessing the overlap of requirements:

- Name matching is performed. This includes both full name matching and identification of certain recurring elements or their combinations, e.g. Actor, Actor + Action.
- User can manually filter and sort requirements to eliminate overlaps. Since requirements are composed of elements from models, filtering and grouping capabilities can include and offer semantic searches.

- The user can choose which model is the leading model and according to it, the comparison of requirements will be performed.
- The user can consider the recommendations of the methodology for the overlapping of requirements. Requirements that have a hierarchical structure (Requirements, Activity, Story Map, Excel) are displayed in parallels and it is allowed to identify which parent elements overlap, thus child elements fall into the group of compared elements. The number of analyzed requirements is reduced.
- The user can decide which requirements to remove and which to leave.

In the scope assessment phase, the main focus is not on the accuracy of the requirements' details, but on their identification. For this reason, requirements can be gathered by any role that is familiar with the product/project. Details in the Agile process are analyzed at the implementation phase of the project.

Non-functional Requirements, Architecture, Risks, and Dependencies
Steps 5–7 are necessary to add additional information about the project. Non-functional requirements (Step 5. Compile Non-functional Requirements) come as an Excel spreadsheet. The main categories are performance, accessibility, security, and compatibility. User can add them manually as well. They can be linked to functional requirements.

Technical requirements about architecture are defined in Step 6. (6. Add Definition of Architecture). It covers: Architecture model (UML Deployment or UML Component models); Technical description (Excel spreadsheet); Manually described architectural requirements.

Risks and dependencies are identified in step 7 (Step 7. Identify Risks and Dependencies). These are not project requirements, but their existence may increase project costs (e.g. time, and amount of resources). For this reason, after identifying them, the user should evaluate and include them in the scope calculation formula.

It is recommended to determine the general risks of the project, and for each requirement, predict whether there are possible risks, which may result in the requirement not being implemented. It is important not only to predict each risk but also to control and regularly monitor it during the entire life of the project to be able to react and take timely action against the losses incurred. The probability of risk is divided by criteria: high, medium, and low. It also indicates the impact that will be made on the solution: high, medium, or low. All the requirements are added to the general list.

3.3 Principles of Project Scope's Estimation

After collecting the requirements and other additional information, the project scope assessment is performed (Step 8. Estimate Project Scope). This step consists of the following steps.

A **level of clarity** is identified for each requirement. There are times in projects when a certain requirement raises a lot of questions, ambiguities, and uncertainties that can only be answered after the implementation of other related functions. Levels are: 1(very clear and its purpose is understandable); 2 (raises questions and is not completely clear); 3 (has several solution options, it is not clear which way will have to be done); 4 (is not clear and raises many questions that will be answered after additional analysis or implementation of other functionalities). User may give the coefficient to each level if needed, e.g. 1 for 1, 1.3 for 2, 1.5 for 3, 2 for 4. In such a way, it increases the amount of work that potentially will be needed. The same increase can be included in Story Points or T-shirts already. It depends on the team which approaches they are planning to choose.

Priorities are identified for each requirement to clarify which requirements are important and must be implemented as soon as possible. Prioritization of requirements is very important when creating a project plan, as it determines the sequence of tasks and their completion on time. Priorities are stacked in an automated way according to how they appear in the sequence and hierarchy. This is a recommended step. The user can do this completely manually. The priority does not affect the scope formula. Possible priorities: 1 (Very high); 2 (High); 3 (Average); 4 (Low); 5 (Very low ("nice to have")).

The **dependencies** of requirements must be clarified. If the requirements were formed from a model, the dependencies are assembled automatically. If they were formed from a list or entered manually, then the dependencies must be clarified. This will ensure that the requirements will be implemented sequentially without misunderstandings or disruptions in achieving the desired result.

Assess the scope of each requirement according to the chosen methodology (Step 3. Choose Scope Assessment Method). If the scope of tasks is very small, they can be grouped to make the list clearer and easier to control. If the scope of the tasks is very large, it should be broken down to make its components clear.

After entering the necessary information, the algorithm evaluates all criteria and provides an estimate of the scope of the project.

The project scope formula (1) consists of these arguments: Scope of all functional and non-functional requirements (*Scope of all Req*); Scope of all architectural requirements (*Scope of all ArchReq*); and Scope of all risks (*Scope of all Risks*).

$$Project\ Scope = Scope\ of\ all\ Req + Scope\ of\ all\ ArchReq$$
$$+\ Scope\ of\ all\ Risks \tag{1}$$

The formula of *Scope of all Req* (2) consists of these arguments: Scope of all Parental Requirements and Scope of all nonparental Requirements. Parental requirements are the ones that have a hierarchical structure.

$$Scope\ of\ all\ Req = Scope\ of\ all\ Parental\ Req$$
$$+\ Scope\ of\ all\ nonparental\ Req \tag{2}$$

The formula of *Scope of all parental Req* calculates the scope of each child (*Scope of Req*) for all parental requirements. If the requirement has a hierarchical structure, its whole scope is calculated. There are two options to calculate scope: 1. Parental requirement is a sum of children's scope; 2. Parental requirements has it is own evaluation.

The formula of *Scope of Req* includes story points and coefficient of clarity (3) for each functional and non-functional requirement.

$$Scope\ of\ Req = Story\ Points\ of\ Req * Coefficient\ of\ Clarity \tag{3}$$

Scope of ArchReq and *Scope of Risk* use the same formula (3) to calculate the weight. All *Scopes of ArchReq* and *Scopes of Risks* are summed and added to the formula (1).

Since all the requirements are constructed from separate parts, the user may analyze which requirements influence the scope the most. If it is necessary, they may evaluate only the mandatory requirements, e.g., with high and very high priorities. The methodology ensures the flexibility to perform cross-functional impact analysis.

4 Experiments

The prototype of the methodology is a web application. It supports all the main steps of the algorithm and allows the user to make a project scope assessment. Models are imported using XML and Excel formats. Based on the described methodology, experiments were conducted with different development projects. The experiments are dedicated to answer these research questions: can the methodology improve the overlap of the gathered requirements; is it possible to improve the project coverage by the requirements. The experiments are described here:

- **Project 1. Development of a mobile application for the management of train driver tasks**. Problem: there is an application where the station attendant manually creates a route for the driver. He enters the actions, such as refueling, maneuvering, etc. Information about the locomotive is entered into the application, but later the responsible persons must manually enter it into the planning system. Definition of the desired result: to have a single application that will manage crew tasks and automatically transfer information between the related systems. The aim is to optimize processes to avoid manual work and human errors.
- **Project 2. Development of an information system for an animal shelter**. Problem identification: there are a lot of pets that do not have home. Animal shelters are overcrowded, and people keep buying animals from breeders and other untrustworthy places where animals are kept in poor conditions and simply bred. Definition of the desired result: we want to create a website where you can see animals in shelters, with their descriptions. People could fill out an application to adopt an animal and give it a loving home.

A summary of the experiments is given in Table 6. Conclusions based on the experiments are given below:

- The biggest overlap of the requirements is in Requirements + Story map + Use case models. Project1 has in total for these models 91 and 49 removed as duplicates. The primary model is the Requirement model. Project 2 has in total 76 and 21 are removed as duplicates. The primary model is the Story map.
- In both projects, Activity and Class (only in Project 1) models brought more detailed requirements (Project 1 added 45 and Project2 added 15 additional requirements) and helped to fulfill the requirements hierarchy.
- Since the number of non-functional requirements, architectural requirements, risks, and dependencies is not a big one compared to functional requirements, and usually, they are clearly defined, they do not have many adjustments. In both projects, they were left unchanged.

- Both projects helped to understand that one model (the primary one) cannot support all the functionalities. Additional models can identify either the new requirements or clarify (decompose) the existing ones
- Supporting manually several models would be an ineffective decision, but automated requirements gathering eliminate manual work and helps to read the requirements even if the user does not know how the model is constructed.
- Project Scope Assessment is a number that is meaningful to the team and the client of the project. Even the same team can have different approaches once they estimate two projects. T-shirt sizing and Story Points enable a comparative approach in the estimation session and allow user to compare and estimate.

Table 6. Summary of experiments

Use Case model	Project 1	Project 2
Scope assessment method:	T-Shirt size	Story Points
No of req from Requirement model	35	15
No of req from Story Map model	24	40
No of req from Use Case model	32	21
No of req from Activity model	47 (3 diagrams)	35 (4 diagrams)
No of req from Class model	15	–
No manually added req	2	–
No non-functional req	12	5
No architectural req	7 (Deployment diagram)	4 (Excel)
No risks and dependencies	5 (Manual list)	2 (Manual list)
No removed req from the list	66	21
Total number of requirements	113	81
Project scope assessment	XS – 17; S – 22 M – 48; L – 11; XL – 15	700

5 Conclusions and Directions for Future Research

In Agile projects, scope assessment can be challenging because of the iterative and incremental nature of Agile development.

The pressure to have a quick estimate of the project scope can have negative consequences on project execution. Traditional scoping methods provide guidelines but do not help to achieve a more accurate scoping of an Agile project with limited estimation time. To make proper use of the collected information in requirements-gathering events (e.g., Requirement Gathering Workshops), the proposed methodology allows include not only the Story Map but also UML models in the process of the project scope estimation. Automatic extraction of requirements from models and identification of their overlap saves time and ensures that even people without knowledge of requirements gathering will be able to understand the expressed needs and approve them. Further research will be aimed at improving the requirements overlap algorithm and the representation of overlaps in models. Also, the scope assessment and priorities should be reflected in resource planning, time planning, roadmap creation, and the identification of risky areas of the project.

References

1. Thesing, T., Feldmann, C., Burchardt, M.: Agile versus waterfall project management: decision model for selecting the appropriate approach to a project. Procedia Comput. Sci. **181**, 746–756 (2021)
2. Beng Leau, Y., Khong Loo, W., Yip Tham, W., Fun, S.: Software development life cycle AGILE vs traditional approaches. IPCSIT **37**, 162–167 (2012)
3. Dvir, D., Raz, T., Shenhar, A.J.: An empirical analysis of the relationship between project planning and project success. Int. J. Project Manag. **21**, 89–95 (2003)
4. Rajabi Asadabadi, M., Zwikael, O.: Integrating risk into estimations of project activities' time and cost: a stratified approach. Eur. J. Oper. Res. **291**(2), 482–490 (2021)
5. Sarmad Ali, S., Shoaib Zafar, M., Tallal Saeed, M.: Effort estimation problems in software maintenance – a survey. In: 3rd International Conference on Computing, Mathematics and Engineering Technologies (iCoMET), pp. 1–9 (2020)
6. Ravi Kiran, M., Manmohan, S.: Study on agile story point estimation techniques and challenges. Int. J. Comput. Appl. **174**, 9–14 (2021)
7. Adomavicius, A.: The Secret Source. ASIN: B0937NCNHC. Publisher: Devbridge; 1st edition (April 21, 2021). Publication date, 21 April 2021
8. Bart, C.K.: Product innovation charters: mission statements for new products. R&D Manag. **32**(1), 23–34 (2002)
9. Cooke-Davies, T.: The, real success factors on projects. Int. J. Project Manag. **20**(3), 185–190 (2002)
10. Serrador, P., Pinto, J.K.: Does agile work? - A quantitative analysis of agile project success. Int. J. Project Manag. **33**(5), 1040–1051 (2015)
11. Primadhika, M., Raharjo, T., Hardian, B., Prasetyo, A.: Agile project management challenge in handling scope and change: a systematic literature review. Procedia Comput. Sci. **197**, 290–300 (2022)
12. Sharon, A., Dori, D.: A model-based approach for planning work breakdown structures of complex systems projects. IFAC Proc. Vol. **45**(6), 1083–1088 (2012)
13. Abd El Hameed, T., Abd EL Latif, M., Kholief, S.: Identify and classify critical success factor of agile software development methodology using mind. Int. J. Adv. Comput. Sci. Appl. **7**(5), 83–92 (2016)
14. Williams, L.: Agile software development methodologies and practices. Adv. Comput. **80**, 1–44 (2010)
15. Di Martino, S., Ferrucci, F., Gravino, C., Sarro, F.: Web effort estimation: function point analysis vs. COSMIC. Inf. Softw. Technol. **72**, 90–109 (2016)
16. Azzeh, M., Bou Nassif, A., Basem Attili, I.: Predicting software effort from use case points: a systematic review. Sci. Comput. Program. **204**(1), 102596 (2021)
17. Liebel, G., Knauss, E.: Aspects of modeling requirements in very-large agile systems engineering. J. Syst. Softw. **199**, 111628 (2023)

User Interaction and Response-Based Knowledge Discovery Framework

Martins Jansevskis[(✉)] and Kaspars Osis

Vidzeme University of Applied Sciences, Terbatas st. 10, Valmiera 4201, Latvia
{martins.jansevskis,kaspars.osis}@va.lv

Abstract. The World Economic Forum in Davos in 2022 raised the issue of knowledge by describing the situation as follows: "It could be that we are drowning in content, but starved of knowledge and therefore often fail to connect the dots to anticipate change before it becomes mainstream. With over four billion pieces of content being created each day, keeping abreast of all that is happening far exceeds our capacity to do so. The business models of social media organizations and news outlets have been increasingly focused on giving people more of what they like, leading to echo chamber effects and making it easy to lose sight of the big picture [10]." In recent decades a shift to the knowledge society has been acknowledged, characterized by its ability to identify, create, process, transform, disseminate and use information to generate and use knowledge for the development of individuals [2]. In such a society, intellectual capital is considered to be the most important indicator of wealth, ahead of assets. The acquisition, application and creation of knowledge is more important to the knowledge society than the creation and consumption of information. In regards to knowledge society requirements this paper presents a conceptual knowledge discovery framework: User Interaction and Response-based Knowledge Discovery Framework – UIS-KDF. The framework introduces a meta-level approach for knowledge discovery system design principles.

Keywords: Knowledge Discovery · Knowledge Discovery Framework · Knowledge Discovery Systems

1 Introduction

The most important features of the knowledge society can be described as follows: mass production, transmission and application of knowledge; the value of services is determined by the knowledge required for the development of products; the majority of the population has access to information and communication technologies and the Internet; a large proportion of the workforce are knowledge workers; substantial funds are invested in education, research and development; organizations need to continuously innovate [9]. For the knowledge society, more important than the creation and consumption of information is the acquisition, application and creation of knowledge. The economic requirements of companies and organizations, the efficiency of knowledge retrieval and the knowledge society's demand for continuous innovation are enabled by information technologies and knowledge discovery systems.

A. Lopata et al. (Eds.): ICIST 2023, CCIS 1979, pp. 102–112, 2024.
https://doi.org/10.1007/978-3-031-48981-5_8

Ackoff [1] defines data as symbolic representations of properties associated with objects, events, and the environment, arising from the process of observation. As data undergoes processing, it transforms into information, taking on a meaningful form. Knowledge, in this context, is depicted as the understanding of how a system operates, representing a form of "know-how." Understanding involves the ability to identify errors and rectify them effectively. According to Ackoff [1], at the pinnacle lies wisdom, which encompasses the highest level of proficiency, empowering individuals with the capacity to augment their effectiveness and bring added value to the decision-making process.

Knowledge discovery systems consist of a wide range of technologies that are able to ensure the operation of the systems. The amount of technologies and the amount of impacting factors make the development of knowledge discovery systems a complex and time-consuming process, which is facilitated by knowledge discovery frameworks that aim to provide development guidelines. Frameworks helps to speed up the development process, encourage reuse and problem isolation, and provide architects with the information to create more flexible and less error-prone systems. Prior literature research reveals that there is a limited amount of knowledge discovery frameworks and a discussion about the characteristics of those frameworks are still necessary [6].

2   Knowledge Discovery Systems

Big data technologies are applied to the development of knowledge discovery systems, data analysis and data sharing and have created considerable economic benefits. The acquired knowledge provides decision-making strategies for social and economic development. Big data service architecture is a new service economic model that uses data as a resource and loads and extracts information from various data sources [17]. The big data are closely related with knowledge discovery systems as the combination provides customized data processing methods, data analysis and visualization services enabling data-driven decision making. The service architecture, according to literature, is composed of three (application, processing and collection & storage [17]) or five main layers (collection, storage, processing, analytics and application [20]). Regardless of the number of layers, there are always enabling technologies.

2.1   Technologies

Data storage in knowledge discovery systems mainly includes batch data and dynamically streamed data. Packet data is stored in static form, while streaming data is a sequence of continuous real-time data records [8]. Accumulation of streamed data in knowledge discovery systems requires solutions capable of providing immediate operation, fault tolerance, stability and reliability – for batch processing there usually is Hadoop and MapReduce and for stream data processing Storm, Spark, Samza [17, 20].

The large amount of data has set new requirements for data storage and systems are more often using distributed file systems: NoSQL, NewSQL and other data management systems. HDFS (Hadoop Distributed File System) is considered the most widely used large data storage file system that supports redundancy and scalability in parallel distributed architecture systems [3].

NoSQL databases are designed for operational requirements - real-time applications. NoSQL provides high-performance, agile information processing at large volumes. Data is stored unstructured in several processing nodes, as well as in several servers, therefore NoSQL distributed database infrastructure is one of the most suitable solutions for knowledge discovery systems with large data warehouses [14].

The advantages of cloud computing technology are its distributed processing capabilities, distributed databases and virtualization technologies. According to literature it is necessary to use cloud computing platforms in the knowledge discovery system development [17, 20]. There are three types of cloud computing architectures – SaaS (Software as a Service), PaaS (Platform as a Service), IaaS (Infrastructure as a Service). By using any of the architecture types organizations do not need to maintain their own servers' rooms or develop specific solutions, cloud services are available for the performance of certain tasks. The most well-known and largest cloud service providers are Amazon Web Services, Microsoft Azure, Google Cloud Platform. Service providers offer infrastructure, according to various data development needs, which is capable of providing a full cycle of knowledge discovery system creation and data processing. For the development of machine learning algorithms, service providers support regression, classification, clustering and other algorithms, and also offer well-known learning systems such as TensorFlow, MXNet, Caffe, PyTorch. Computing power is necessary not only for technological processes, but also for data processing. Creating, maintaining and providing appropriate solutions with only developer or customer resources is potentially possible, however this type of approach would increase the complexity of technical processes.

Batch data is often static and the data volume is large, data processing is performed using a processing method capable of parallel computing. In 2004, Google introduced MapReduce, a programming framework for processing large data sets. MapReduce enables users to perform complex computations on large data sets while ensuring synchronization, fault tolerance, reliability, and availability [17].

The streaming data approach is suitable for processing data that requires almost instantaneous response, therefore streaming data requires systems capable of achieving high speeds. A number of streaming data processing products are available - Storm is an open source real-time streaming data processing framework that is capable of high performance and low execution latency and is suitable for streaming data processing. An alternative to Storm is the Apache Samza streaming data processing system, which can efficiently process large amounts of user response data. The combination of Samza and Kafka enables better use of the advantages of both systems - Kafka can provide fault tolerance, data buffering and state storage [11]. Certain data preprocessing tasks can include both batch data processing and streaming data processing, some data processing systems support both batch and stream data. Apache Spark is a batch data processing framework with streaming data processing capabilities.

Data storage, processing, visualization and application of cloud computing resources are only part of the technological considerations of knowledge discovery systems. Knowledge discovery systems must also comply with legal standards governing data collection and storage, as well as include preventive and corrective measures for cybersecurity.

2.2 Legislations

One of the goals of knowledge discovery systems is to accumulate data in order to process, analyze, create added value and make decisions. On the other hand, the personal data protection regulation stipulates that only the minimally necessary data sets should be used for certain and defined purposes [5]. The principles of the General Data Protection Regulation (GDPR) apply to the processing of personal data, organizations must assess whether the use of specific personal data meets the reasonable expected requirements of the relevant data subject, which in turn contradicts the practice of systems for accumulating large amounts of data [7]. The accumulation, storage, analysis and use of knowledge discovery system data in order to extract useful knowledge from them is in contrary to what is guaranteed to individuals by the Charter of Fundamental Rights of the European Union and the GDPR. Accordingly, personal data must be protected and processed in a fair manner for defined and specific purposes and must not be stored for longer than necessary [5].

One of the options for making knowledge discovery systems GDPR compliant is by anonymizing or pseudonymizing data. Anonymization refers to the practice of making data non-identifiable in such a way that the identity of the data subject cannot be obtained. If the data is anonymized, the GDPR regulation does not apply to it [5].

According to Article 22 (1) of the GDPR, individuals have the right not to be subjected to automated decision-making, including profiling. Profiling is most often performed using machine learning algorithms, thus GDPR also restricts machine learning algorithms of knowledge discovery systems. Organizations may still use automated decision-making where it is necessary to perform or enter into contracts permitted by national law or where the data subject has given explicit consent. Profiling in knowledge discovery systems is often invisible to individuals, a practice against which data protection law seeks to protect individuals by requiring organizations to provide clarity and the option to opt out of automated profiling [5].

An important limiting factor is the possibility for the data subject to receive an understandable explanation. The data subject should be given the opportunity to understand the logic of data processing and its impact. Article 13 (2) (f) of GDPR establishes the right of data subjects to receive meaningful information about the logic involved, as well as the meaning and expected consequences of such processing [5]. So, if personal data is used in the algorithms of the knowledge discovery system, then the data subject has the right to receive an understandable explanation of the execution of these algorithms - the algorithms must be explained to subjects without knowledge of how the algorithms are working.

Computer security, cybersecurity, or information technology security is the protection of computer systems and networks from information disclosure, theft or damage to their hardware, software, or electronic data, and from service interruption or misdirection [15]. The field of cybersecurity is becoming increasingly important due to the ever-increasing dependence on computer systems, the Internet and wireless network standards such as Bluetooth and Wi-Fi, as well as "smart" devices, including smartphones, televisions and various devices that make up the "Internet of Things". Cybersecurity is also one of the most significant challenges in today's world due to its complexity, both in terms of political application and technology [15, 18]. The knowledge discovery system must incorporate cybersecurity requirements into the development lifecycle.

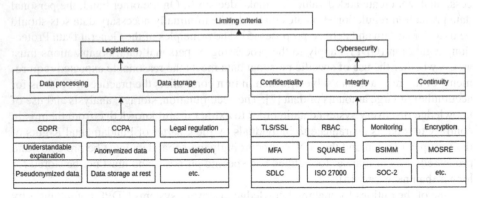

Fig. 1. Knowledge discovery systems limiting criteria.

The development of knowledge discovery systems is impacted by both the legal regulation in a given region of operation and cybersecurity factors (for example GDPR in Europe, CCPA in the USA) (see Fig. 1). When developing a knowledge discovery system, it is necessary to include the security requirements already during system planning, and it is also necessary to use some security requirements methodology, it may also be necessary to obtain appropriate certificates (ISO 27000 in Europe, or SOC-2 in the USA).

3   Conceptual Framework

Knowledge discovery systems consist of a complex set of technologies that are able to ensure the operation of the systems. The set of technologies and the range of impacting factors make the development of knowledge discovery systems a complex and time-consuming process. A framework is an abstraction that describes a general arrangement of components that can be selectively changed according to the requirements thereby providing specific behavior. The amount of frameworks available for the development of knowledge discovery systems is limited and they can be applied in a certain field, which are often not directly transferable between different sectors [6].

Since there is a limited amount of knowledge discovery frameworks and they are not directly transferable between different sectors, the authors are introducing a conceptual knowledge discovery framework: User Interaction and Response-based Knowledge Discovery Framework – UIS-KDF. The conceptual framework is divided into five logical layers - public applications, management applications, machine learning, limiting criteria (described in Sect. 2.2) and technology (see Fig. 2).

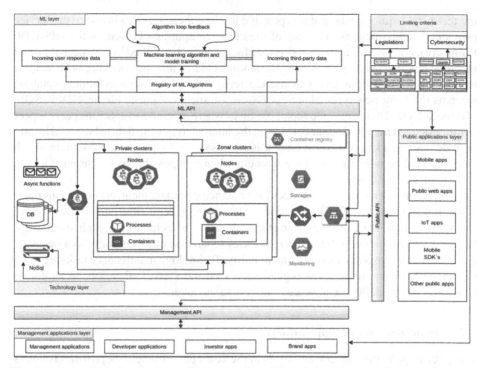

Fig. 2. Proposed User Interaction and Response-based Knowledge Discovery Framework – UIS-KDF.

3.1 Technology Layer

Technologies and infrastructure provide the functionality of knowledge discovery systems, support business processes and helps to make data-driven decisions. Technology layer ensures the separation of technology from business, application and machine learning functionality. Technology layer includes technology stacks, operating systems, containers, processes, communication protocols, databases, gateways, monitoring and management solutions. Essential conditions for the layer are the ability to dynamically increase and decrease computing capabilities, as well as multi-level user authentication, full audit logs and role based access control.

The recommended approach for creating a flexible technology layer is to apply containers such as Docker, LXD, Containerd, container orchestration platforms and cluster technologies such as Kubernetes, Rancher, Google Cloud Run, AWS Fargate. Figure 2 includes the technology layer using Kubernetes, Docker, Cloud Run and Containerd solutions. The technology layer must utilize the advantages of cloud computing technologies such as the potential of distributed computing, distributed databases and virtualization technologies, as well as automated vertical and horizontal scalability. The technology layer therefore requires the application of cloud computing services, such as Amazon Web Services, Microsoft Azure, Google Cloud Platform or similar.

A data storage placed on a cloud computing platform provides functionality such as data continuity, integrity and availability. The choice of cloud storage services depends on the technical requirements, and it is possible to place these services in one of the service providers' infrastructures. The role of the cloud computing platform in the UIS-KDF framework is to provide an application interface that can be applied by private, public and machine learning layer applications. The storage of large amounts of data can be realized using database solutions and database clusters, such as traditional relational database systems (SQL) or new types of storage (NoSQL), such as Apache Flume, HDFS, SQL, MongoDB, etc. There are some separable cases where machine-to-machine peer-to-peer communication may be disconnected from the internet, requiring data to be stored locally on a device. To address this use case, it is necessary to implement a scenario in which data is stored on machines until the moment when it is possible to synchronize it with web databases for further use.

The technology layer also includes load balancing management, asynchronous operation management, monitoring solutions, system image registries, public and management application APIs, and supporting technologies. The technology layer in the conceptual knowledge discovery framework provides separation of technology from business, application, and machine learning functionality. Technology maintenance tasks are often significantly different from the organization's business goals, therefore technologies providing functionality are allocated into a separate layer.

3.2 Public and Private Applications

The public application layer (see Fig. 2) in the conceptual framework provides business functionality requirements for the end users. The public application layer works with the APIs of the technology layer, providing the flexibility to modify, customize, add and replace public applications. The management applications layer (see Fig. 2) contains a set of management applications for the organizations internal processes and procedures, layers goal is to provide management and control functionality in accordance with the company's business requirements.

Both the public and management application layers include web-based, mobile, hybrid, and desktop applications for all platforms and systems, as well as both open source and closed source applications. An essential requirement for these applications is the ability to work with API's, regardless of the type of API technology (REST, GraphQL, RPC, SOAP).

A key differences between public and management applications is the end users and the potential loads that the specific applications are capable of generating. The number of users of management applications will always be limited and controllable, while the number of users of public applications may not be limited. The API development process for public applications needs to consider scalability, load management, and strict authentication methods.

The business goals of companies and organizations are focused on providing services to end consumers, and they are powered by public applications. Management applications, on the other hand, are intended for internal use. Therefore, it is necessary to separate the functionality of management and public applications.

3.3 Machine Learning

The machine learning (ML) layer (see Fig. 2) provides knowledge discovery functionality from user response data and management of knowledge discovery models. The essential requirements for a layer are to provide the capabilities and placement of machine learning models. The purpose of knowledge discovery systems is to provide data-driven decision making and knowledge extraction from data. The mentioned tasks are enabled by machine learning, which provides an opportunity for knowledge discovery systems to predict results with a certain accuracy, as well as to improve the services provided by organizations, for example, by providing the functionality of chatbots.

The machine learning layer includes the algorithm registry, feedback data of algorithm loops, third-party data and user response data (see Fig. 2). The ML layer includes a registry of ML algorithms, providing the ability to apply multiple ML algorithms for different purposes. The ML register provides the possibility to replace a certain algorithm if there is such a need, as well as to place them in a unified system. By separating the ML layer for the knowledge discovery system, the machine learning functionality and training process can be separated from the functionality of public and management applications.

ML algorithm models are often developed taking into account the most important factors of the considered domain and using available historical user response data. By applying machine learning technologies, algorithms can be developed that are able to extract knowledge from large volumes of user response data. Machine learning has gradually taken an important role in various social fields, such as language processing, natural language understanding, neuroscience, Internet of Things, etc. [19].

ML creates challenges in attracting specialists to organizations, there are almost no experts who have all the necessary skills - data processing, statistical analysis, the domain understanding, database technologies, backend technologies, development languages and application development. Attempts are gradually being made to develop information systems that are easier to understand and use for non-specialists [19]. To address these challenges, knowledge discovery systems must separate the ML layer, thus separating the specific functionality and requirements of specialists from the overall operation of the knowledge discovery system.

Data processing operations must ensure added value and sufficiently fast data processing. Data analysis and application of ML algorithms create added value, which provides support in predicting future trends and understanding the situation. Separating the machine learning layer provides the ability to abstract from technology and application specific requirements and functionality.

3.4 UIS-KDF

Knowledge discovery refers to the process of extracting knowledge from data and emphasizes the implementation of specific data mining techniques. The purpose of knowledge discovery is to extract applicable and useful knowledge from data. Knowledge is retrieved using data mining algorithms to extract insights from data according to defined conditions and specifications [16]. Knowledge discovery processes are also described by several process models developed in both academic and industry environments. The knowledge discovery process is described as several basic activities that are included in the general principles of project management [6, 12].

The implementation of knowledge discovery processes in the operation of organizations is associated with several problem situations. Some knowledge discovery algorithms and tools stop at building and delivering models that satisfy technical requirements. Knowledge discovery models are developed and the organization might not always have the capabilities and understanding to apply the models in business decision-making [4]. Knowledge discovery is a closed problem-solving process that includes a series of targeted activities: problem definition, framework/model development to provide operational business rules that can be seamlessly linked or integrated with business processes and systems [4]. On the other hand, there is still a growing tendency in IT systems to use available data to obtain information and hidden correlations. The most important factors that have contributed to this is the desire to provide better services to end users [13].

In order for organizations to provide better services to the end users, there is a need for a way to extract knowledge from user response data, and this can be obtained using knowledge discovery systems. The development of knowledge discovery systems is a complex and time-consuming process that is facilitated by knowledge discovery frameworks that provide development guidelines. Knowledge discovery frameworks from user response data are applied in the early development stage of knowledge discovery system architecture.

The division of the conceptual framework into layers (see Fig. 2) ensures flexibility according to changing business goals. In the UIS-KDF, technologies, management and public applications, limiting criteria and machine learning are separated as loosely connected layers. The technology and infrastructure requirements for development processes are significantly different from those for management and public applications, as well as for machine learning processes. On the other hand, for organizations, the mutual interaction of all the mentioned components is important for the data-based decision-making process.

The pace of technology change, along with the adoption of lean and flexible agile methods that enable rather fast delivery cycles, learnings and data-driven decisions have made conventional technology development an unwieldy process. Deadlines are often missed, technology becomes obsolete, priorities and customer expectations change and competition increases. As a result, organizations are increasingly caught between the choice of implementing changes or following the original plan.

The UIS-KDF framework is intended for the early stage of knowledge discovery system development – to support infrastructure planning processes. The goal of the UIS-KDF framework is to ease the complex and time-consuming process of developing knowledge discovery systems by providing guidelines for architectural planning and organization.

4 Conclusions

Frameworks speed up the development process, encourage reuse, problem isolation and provide developers with the tools to develop more flexible and less error-prone applications and systems. Prior literature research reveals that there is a limited amount of knowledge discovery frameworks and a discussion about the characteristics of those frameworks are still necessary [6]. Whenever a knowledge discovery system is developed, it is necessary to include the security requirements early in the system planning, and it is also necessary to use security requirements methodology as well as it might be necessary to obtain appropriate certificates.

Knowledge discovery systems consist of a complex set of technologies that are interconnected in order to enable data-driven decision making, therefore the development of knowledge discovery systems is a complex and time-consuming process. From prior research it was clear that knowledge discovery systems have to be layered to separate the different functionality of each of the parts, therefore the proposed UIS-KDF framework introduces five-layer design.

Based on the UIS-KDF the authors are working on defining knowledge discovery system development phases and implementation roadmap as well as testing the layered design in field projects.

References

1. Ackoff, R.L.: From data to wisdom: presidential address to ISGSR. J. Appl. Syst. Anal. **16**, 3–9 (1989)
2. Bindé, J., Matsuura, K., (eds.): Towards Knowledge Societies. UNESCO Publications (2005)
3. Bok, K., et al.: An efficient distributed caching for accessing small files in HDFS. Clust. Comput. **20**(4), 3579–3592 (2017). https://doi.org/10.1007/s10586-017-1147
4. Cao, L., Zhao, Y., Zhang, H., Luo, D., Zhang, C., Park, E.K.: Flexible frameworks for actionable knowledge discovery. IEEE Trans. Knowl. Data Eng. **22**(9), 1299–1312 (2010). https://doi.org/10.1109/TKDE.2009.143
5. General Data Protection Regulation (GDPR) (2016). https://gdpr-info.eu/. Accessed 13 Mar 2023
6. Jansevskis, M., Osis, K.: State of knowledge discovery process models and frame-works. In: SOCIETY. TECHNOLOGY. SOLUTIONS. Proceedings of the International Scientific Conference, vol. 2, p. 14. (2022). https://doi.org/10.35363/via.sts.2022.81
7. Jeren, A.: The impact of the GDPR on big data. Tech GDPR (2020). https://techgdpr.com/blog/impact-of-gdpr-on-big-data. Accessed 13 Mar 2023
8. Karunaratne, P., Karunasekera, S., Harwood, A.: Distributed stream clustering using micro-clusters on Apache Storm. J. Parallel Distrib. Comput. **108**, 74–84 (2017). https://doi.org/10.1016/j.jpdc.2016.06.004
9. Knowledge Society. International Encyclopedia of the Social Sciences. https://www.encyclopedia.com/social-sciences/applied-and-social-sciences-magazines/knowledge-society. Accessed 27 Feb 2023
10. Marshall, J., Mergenthaler, S.: These are the 3 ways knowledge can provide strategic advantage (2022). https://www.weforum.org/agenda/2022/01/this-is-how-knowledge-can-bring-you-strategic-advance. Accessed 12 Mar 2023
11. Oussous, A., Benjelloun, F.-Z., Ait Lahcen, A., Belfkih, S.: Big data technologies: a survey. J. King Saud Univ. Comput. Inf. Sci. **30**(4), 431–448 (2018). https://doi.org/10.1016/j.jksuci.2017.06.001
12. Osei-Bryson, K.-M., Barclay, C. (eds.): Knowledge Discovery Process and Methods to Enhance Organizational Performance. CRC Press, Taylor & Francis Group (2015)
13. Osman, A.M.S.: A novel big data analytics framework for smart cities. Future Gener. Comput. Syst. **91**, 620–633 (2019). https://doi.org/10.1016/j.future.2018.06.046

14. Richa, B.: NoSQL vs SQL — which database type is better for big data applications (2017). https://analyticsindiamag.com/nosql-vs-sql-database-type-better-big-data-applications. Accessed 13 Mar 2023
15. Schatz, D., Bashroush, R., Wall, J.: Towards a more representative definition of cyber security. J. Digit. Forensics Secur. Law (2017). https://doi.org/10.15394/jdfsl.2017.1476
16. Technopedia Inc. Knowledge discovery (2017). https://www.techopedia.com/definition/25827/knowledge-discovery-in-databases-kdd. Accessed 15 Mar 2023
17. Wang, J., Yang, Y., Wang, T., Sherrat, R.S., Zhang, J.: Big data service architecture: a survey. J. Internet Technology 21(2), 393–405 (2020)
18. Xin, Y., et al.: Machine learning and deep learning methods for cybersecurity. IEEE Access 6, 35365–35381 (2018). https://doi.org/10.1109/ACCESS.2018.2836950
19. Zhou, L., Pan, S., Wang, J., Vasilakos, A.V.: Machine learning on big data: opportunities and challenges. Neurocomputing 237, 350–361 (2017). https://doi.org/10.1016/j.neucom.2017.01.026
20. Zhu, J.Y., Tang, B., Li, V.O.K.: A five-layer architecture for big data processing and analytics. Int. J. Big Data Intell. 6(1), 38–49 (2019). https://doi.org/10.1504/ijbdi.2019.097399

Privacy Risks in German Patient Forums: A NER-Based Approach to Enrich Digital Twins

Sergej Schultenkämper[✉] and Frederik Simon Bäumer

Bielefeld University of Applied Sciences and Arts, Bielefeld, Germany
{sergej.schultenkaemper,frederik.baeumer}@hsbi.de

Abstract. The online sharing of personal health data by individuals has raised privacy concerns. This paper presents a Named Entity Recognition (NER)-based analysis to detect potential privacy risks in German patient forums. The objective is to extract sensitive information from user-generated texts and augment existing digital profiles of users to demonstrate the potential threats posed by the aggregation of information. To achieve this, we trained a NER model on a large corpus of German patient forum texts and evaluated its performance using standard metrics. The results show that the NER model can effectively extract health-related information from German texts with a micro-average precision of 0.8666, a recall of 0.9633 and an F_1-score of 0.9124. This enables the creation of Digital Twins that accurately reflect the health-related characteristics of individuals. However, when this information is combined with data from different platforms, it poses a potential threat to users' privacy and underlines the need to warn users.

Keywords: Privacy · Health · Digital Twin · Online Social Networks

1 Introduction

In the modern era, where Web 2.0 is a prevalent tool for individuals to exchange and accumulate information, the extensive data collection that results from it also creates new threats. This collection of centralized data comprises text, images, news, health information, and more. Many users have limited trust in the ability of these collections to be adequately secured against unauthorized access [18]. However, much of the disclosed information has been voluntarily made available to the public, such as to connect with other individuals. This information, sometimes shared anonymously, can also entail risks, particularly if the anonymity can be partially or entirely revoked at a later point.

An instance of this is patient forums that encourage the exchange of information about diseases and treatments, and which typically allow participation via pseudonyms. These patient forums can serve as a valuable resource for individuals seeking information and support related to their health conditions. However, using these forums also poses significant privacy risks for users [8]. When individuals post on patient forums, they may disclose sensitive information about their medical conditions, treatments, and personal lives (cf. Fig. 1).

A. Lopata et al. (Eds.): ICIST 2023, CCIS 1979, pp. 113–123, 2024.
https://doi.org/10.1007/978-3-031-48981-5_9

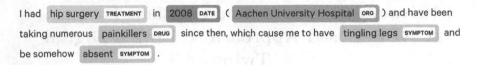

Fig. 1. Detected entities in disease description of a user.

One of the primary risks associated with posting on patient forums is the potential for doxing [14]. Doxing refers to the malicious act of publicly revealing previously private information about an individual, often with the intention of causing harm, humiliation, or harassment. In the context of patient forums, doxing can occur when a person gathers information from a user's posts, including the topics they discuss, the language they use, and the entities they reference. This information can be used to construct a profile of the user, which can then be linked to other online profiles or pieces of information, thus exposing their personal and medical history. The possible consequences of being doxxed through patient forum posts are severe. Users may be subjected to online harassment, shaming, or even potential physical threats. This has the potential to have serious implications for the user's personal life and well-being [4,14].

All of these considerations are taking place as part of the *Authority-Dependent Risk Identification and Analysis in online Networks* (ADRIAN) research project, which investigates the risk and defense of profiling in Web 2.0. ADRIAN focuses on researching and developing AI-based methods for identifying potential threats to individuals and institutions based on heterogeneous, online data sets [6]. Digital Twins (DTs) of users are created to visualize the currently available dataset of individuals and educate about the threats. In this sense, the research project uses the same ways that doxing uses to warn and educate users. To highlight the privacy risks associated with patient forum posts, we propose using NER models on user-generated texts and to show users the possible threats posed by combined information. These models are well-suited for our task because they are pre-trained on large corpora of text and can be fine-tuned on our specific corpus of patient forum posts. We evaluate the performance of our NER models using standard metrics, including precision, recall, and F_1-score, and achieve high accuracy in identifying medical entities. German BERT and XLM-RoBERTa are powerful tools for identifying medical entities in user-generated texts on patient forums, which is a critical step in protecting the privacy of forum users. Furthermore, we include the latest technical developments (e.g., GPT-3) in our considerations. Finally, our approach can be extended to other domains, such as financial forums, where users may also disclose sensitive information.

In the following, we discuss related work in the context of privacy and NER methods in Sect. 2 and describe the data acquisition and processing in Sect. 3. Our NER approach and the evaluation is described in Sect. 4. Finally, we discuss our findings in Sect. 5 and draw our conclusions in Sect. 6.

2   Related Work

This section covers privacy in Web 2.0 and in the online health domain (s. Sect. 2.1), DTs (s. Sect. 2.2), and NER (s. Sect. 2.3). We discuss challenges and approaches to protecting privacy, the potential impact of DTs on privacy, and how NER can be used to instantiate and enrich DTs. Additionally, we examine the use of NER in the German medical domain.

2.1   Threats from User-Generated Content

User-generated content refers to data, information, or media in the form of text, images, and videos that are created by everyday people and shared online [19]. The sharing of sensitive content may place users at risk of privacy breaches. Their personal information may be exposed or misused, which can lead to different threats, e.g., deanonymization and doxing. While deanonymization aims to find out the true identity of users [23], doxing is the intentional collection and publication of personal information about an individual by a third party, often with the intent to harm the identified individual [11]. These threats are called modern threats because they usually use the infrastructure of social networks on the Internet to violate the security and privacy of users [15].

The potential risk associated with the usually constant and extensive sharing of information is increased by the sensitive nature of the data. In the case of privacy in the online health domain, multiple studies examine which data is disclosed by physicians and patients on physician review websites (PRWs) [8,9]. It is not only the obvious data (e.g., diseases, treatments) that are a threat, but also the latent information that has been given out without intention (e.g., gender, place of treatment, family relationships). That said, it is reasonable to presume that the social networks issues and potential privacy breaches are applicable to PRWs as well. For this reason, there is already preparatory work that warns users against too extensive information disclosure in online portals, especially those with a medical focus: By applying natural language processing (NLP) techniques, such as hand-crafted patterns and NER, a web application, called *Text Broom*, can highlight potential data exposures related to users [7]. The work in this paper goes beyond this and develops the methods further in that the information is not only highlighted (prevention) but can also be merged with other information that is already published and acquired and may be on other platforms on the web and displayed as comprehensive modeling.

2.2   Digital Twins in the Privacy Context

The concept of DT encompasses a wide range of applications and interpretations across various fields such as mechanical engineering, medicine, and computer science [2]. Developments in the field of artificial intelligence have given the term a wider usage. More generally, "DTs can be defined as (physical and/or virtual) machines or computer-based models that are simulating, emulating, mirroring, or 'twinning' the life of a physical entity, which may be an object, a process, a human, or a human-related feature" [2].

In the ADRIAN project, we use the term for the digital representation of a real person instantiated by information available on the Web [6]. The DT can never reflect the entire complexity of a real person, but it reproduces features that, alone or in combination with other characteristics, can pose a threat to the real person. In this way, the DT makes it possible to model and measure the vulnerability of a person. The modeling of DTs is based on established and freely available standards of the semantic web, such as Schema.org and FOAF (*Friend of a Friend*). This makes it possible to easily connect and extend DTs.

2.3   Named Entity Recognition for Digital Twin Enrichment

In the context of instantiating and expanding digital twins of internet users, NER plays a crucial role in making sense of unstructured textual data. NER enables the extraction and categorization of named entities such as names, locations, organizations, and dates from free-text sources such as social media posts, web pages, and chat logs [25]. These entities provide valuable contextual information that can enhance the accuracy and granularity of digital twins, enabling them to more accurately reflect the behaviors and preferences of their real-world counterparts. As such, NER is a key technology for developing more comprehensive and effective digital twin models for internet users. Fortunately, developments in NLP in recent years have made it very easy to fine-tune existing language models to specific tasks, so that solid results can already be expected even for data-poor tasks. This is especially important in our context, where only few data are available and furthermore sensitive data are involved.

In the medical domain, NER is already a used method. For example, GERN-ERMED is a NER model for German medical texts [16]. The model was trained on a newly created German dataset by extracting, translating, and aligning masked English texts. The texts were taken from the publicly available training data from the n2c2 NLP 2018 Track 2 dataset (ADE and Medication Extraction Challenge) [17]. The analyzed entities in their study were *Drug*, *Strength*, *Route*, *Form*, *Dosage*, *Frequency*, and *Duration*. The best performing entities were *Strength*, with an F_1-score of 91.66, and Form, with an F_1-score of 90.57, whereas the worst performing entities were *Duration*, with an F_1-score of 59.37, and *Drug*, with an F_1-score of 66.74. Overall, the model achieved an F_1-score of 81.54. This shows that a fundamentally robust extraction of medical entities is possible, but leaves out the additional challenges of user-generated content.

3   Data Acquisition and Data Processing

We have obtained the fundamental information required for the training and evaluation of our models from various German patient forums. In the context of our research project, we encountered a dearth of appropriate datasets in the

NER domain that catered to our research query. Unlike conventional training data, which is gleaned from assorted publications or health-related documents, this data focuses on identifying user-generated content. To overcome this predicament, we painstakingly crafted our very own dataset. Our exposition will commence with an overview of the descriptive statistics for the data procured, followed by a presentation of the selected entities earmarked for annotation, culminating in an illustration of the entity distribution within the annotated dataset. For a comprehensive snapshot of the acquired data, Table 1 provides a detailed account of the descriptive statistics.

Table 1. Descriptive statistics for the acquired data.

Description	#
Topics	309,642
Posts	1,431,696
User Profiles	108,998
Avg. Posts per User	13.15
Avg. Sentences per Post	5.82
Avg. Tokens per Post	82.98
Avg. Unique Tokens per Post	62.89
Avg. Tokens per Sentence	14.36
Avg. Unique Tokens per Sentence	11.83

The data was acquired on January 11, 2023. The data consists of 309,642 topics, 1,431,696 posts, and 108,998 user profiles. On average, each user has contributed 13.15 posts. Posts in the dataset are on average 5.82 sentences and 82.98 tokens (words and punctuation) long per post. The posts also exhibit some diversity in vocabulary, with an average of 62.89 unique tokens per post. At the sentence level, the average length is 14.36 tokens per sentence, and the average number of unique tokens per sentence is 11.83.

From our data, we annotated 2,736 sentences using Prodigy[1]. Also, to allow for the annotation of relationships between entities in future research, the sample was purposely selected to contain only sentences containing at least two entities. In this study, we focused on annotating medical entities relevant to the DT, including *"Anatomy"*, *"Diagnosis"*, *"Diseases"*, *"Substances"*, *"Symptoms"*, and *"Treatment"*. These entities were selected because of their high information value and the availability of this information in German patient forums. This will enable us to provide a detailed representation of the DT.

---

[1] Available at https://prodi.gy, last accessed 2023-03-27.

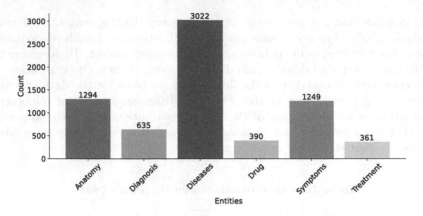

Fig. 2. Distribution of entities in the dataset.

Figure 2 indicates that the distribution of entities is uneven. There is a higher occurrence of *"Diseases"* and *"Anatomy"* entities, followed by *"Symptoms"* and *"Diagnosis"*. The *"Treatment"* and *"Drug"* entities are less frequent in the dataset. In Table 2, examples referring to each entity are shown.

Table 2. Examples of entities for the dataset.

Entity	Examples	Expression Count
Anatomy	Eyes, Vessels, Intestine	191
Diagnosis	ECG, Ultrasound, Gastroscopy	147
Diseases	Flu, Hemorrhoids, Stroke	945
Drug	Omeprazol, Fluoxetine, Ibuprofen	174
Symptoms	Headache, Fever, Tired	347
Treatment	Eyeglasses, Massage, Physiotherapy	135

As the examples of the different entities in these forums show, we can gain insight into patient concerns and the information content in these forums. Furthermore, the unique values for *"Anatomy,"* *"Diagnosis,"* *"Drug,"* and *"Treatment"* are limited. This low variant richness of entities is, in our opinion, what will explain in the following why it is straightforward to achieve very good results.

4   NER Models and Evaluation

Our work is based on achievements in NLP of the past years in particular transformers like Bidirectional Encoder Representations from Transformers (BERT). BERT is a state-of-the-art pre-training technique for text processing [13]. BERT has been trained on the BooksCorpus [26] and the English Wikipedia, allowing it to learn representations that can be fine-tuned for a variety of NLP tasks. BERT and further models based on the Transformer architecture have proven to achieve state-of-the-art results in downstream NLP tasks, such as NER, Question Answering, and Text Classification [20].

In this work, we use GBERT and XLM-RoBERTa in combination with our NER dataset. GBERT is a variant of the BERT model and was trained on German data [10]. For the dataset construction, the authors have used OSCAR [1], OPUS [24], Wikipedia, and OpenLegalData [22] as sources. XLM-RoBERTa is a multilingual language model, that improves cross-lingual language understanding (XLU) and achieves state-of-the-art performance for various languages in different tasks [12]. It has been trained on monolingual data from 100 languages.

As the split between the training and test datasets we use 80% (2,168 Sentences) and 20% (569 Sentences). For the purpose of hyperparameter optimization and experiment tracking, we used the Weights & Biases Library [3]. For the optimization, we used the parameters that are shown in Table 3.

Table 3. Parameters for optimization with Weights & Biases.

Model	Epochs	Learning Rate	Batch Size
GBERT (*gbert-large*)	3, 4, 5	5e−5, 3e−5, 2e−5	8, 16, 32
XLM-RoBERTa (*xlm-roberta-large*)	2, 4, 6, 8, 10	5e−5, 3e−5, 2e−5	8, 16, 32

For GBERT, the best performance was achieved with a learning rate of 5e−5, 5 training epochs, and a train batch size of 16. In comparison, XLM-RoBERTa exhibited optimal results with the same learning rate of 5e−5 but required 10 training epochs and a train batch size of 8. This indicates that the adjustment of parameters during the fine-tuning of models leads to an improvement in their overall performance. The results of the evaluation are shown in Table 4.

Table 4. Comparison of GBERT and XLM-RoBERTa Results.

Entity	GBERT				XLM-RoBERTa			
	P	R	F_1	Support	P	R	F_1	Support
Anatomy	0.8686	0.9643	**0.9140**	336	0.8705	0.9461	0.9067	334
Diagnosis	0.8803	0.9470	**0.9124**	132	0.8243	0.9242	0.8714	132
Diseases	0.8732	0.9718	**0.9198**	496	0.8601	0.9332	0.8951	494
Drug	0.8000	1.0000	0.8889	48	0.8704	0.9792	**0.9216**	48
Symptoms	0.8895	0.9441	**0.9160**	179	0.7731	0.9489	0.8520	176
Treatment	0.7792	0.9524	0.8571	63	0.8382	0.9048	**0.8702**	63
Micro Avg.	0.8666	0.9633	**0.9124**	1254	0.8448	0.9383	0.8891	1247
Macro Avg.	0.8485	0.9633	**0.9014**	1254	0.8394	0.9394	0.8862	1247
Weighted Avg.	0.8675	0.9633	**0.9126**	1254	0.8461	0.9383	0.8894	1247

Evaluation metrics used for this comparison include Precision (P), Recall (R), and F_1-score (F_1). In addition, the support specifies the number of instances associated with each class for the evaluation of the fine-tuned models. Differences in performance can be seen among the various entity classes. GBERT outperforms XLM-RoBERTa in terms of F_1-score for the following entity classes: *Anatomy, Diagnosis, Diseases*, and *Symptoms*. Conversely, XLM-RoBERTa shows a superior F_1-score for the *Drug* and *Treatment* classes. Interestingly, XLM-RoBERTa performs better on entities with a low number of labels, such as *Drug* and *Treatment*. Considering the average metrics, GBERT shows slightly better performance compared to XLM-RoBERTa. The micro, macro, and weighted average F_1-scores are 0.9124, 0.9014, and 0.9126 for GBERT and 0.8891, 0.8862, and 0.8894 for XLM-RoBERTa, respectively. In summary, both models performed well on the task. While each model excels in certain entity classes, the overall performance of GBERT is slightly superior to that of XLM-RoBERTa.

5   Discussion

In the context of German patient forums, the GBERT and XLM-RoBERTa models are both suitable for recognizing medical entities. Our evaluation has shown that both models exhibit high accuracy for all entities. The differences in their performance can be attributed to the distribution and expression of the entities. As depicted in Fig. 2, the distribution of entities in patient forums is highly imbalanced, with the most common entities being diseases. This suggests that people seek advice before receiving a medical diagnosis from a doctor, and only share such information in patient forums once they have received a diagnosis or treatment. Additionally, we observed that the expressions used to denote entities in our annotated data are limited, which can influence the results. To address this, annotating more data to increase the diversity of variants would be beneficial. By considering these factors, we can further enhance the performance of NER models and safeguard the privacy of forum users.

Recent progress in language modeling, particularly with Large Language Models, has cast doubt on the approach presented in this paper. Some argue that fine-tuning smaller models like BERT may not achieve the same level of performance as larger models like OpenAI GPT-3 [5]. However, it has already been shown that finetuned models can often better capture the properties of a specific domain and an explicit task [21]. Moreover, we believe that two additional aspects need to be considered: 1) the costs that arise from mass entity extraction, and 2) the relatively slower processing speed. Additionally, we conducted experiments with GPT-3 on our training data and found that the quality of results, even on user-generated content, is good. Nevertheless, closed-source models, coupled with significant cost factors and potential privacy concerns, present an application barrier for our use case.

6   Conclusion and Future Work

In this paper, we have presented a NER-model that can detect privacy-relevant entities in German patient forums, enabling us to enhance existing user DTs. Our results indicate that our NER model can effectively extract sensitive health-related information from user-generated text with high precision and recall, which has crucial implications for individual privacy. This data, in combination with latent information that was not intended to be disclosed, provides a valuable resource for learning more about the contributors. Nonetheless, it is crucial to establish a threshold for when to warn users - that is, when there is sufficient information with the potential for threats.

Our current approach discussed here only focuses on identifying entities in the text, without taking into account the relationships between them. In future research, we intend to expand our NER model to capture entity relationships, such as medication and dosage, as well as diseases. This will enable us to create more comprehensive DTs. Hence, our upcoming research will concentrate on labeling the relationships between these NER entities to provide a more holistic picture of the context and facilitate information extraction. For instance, exploring the relationship between anatomy and disease entities can help identify which part of the body a certain disease affects, such as internal organs, parts, or external body parts and regions. Furthermore, extracting relationships between drug dosages and durations can furnish valuable information for clinical decision-making. This can contribute to enhancing relationship extraction techniques and investigating the performance of different models based on data from German patient forums.

Overall, our proposed method – as one puzzle piece among many in our project – has the potential to enhance the quality of the DT in the healthcare field. We aspire to inspire further research in this domain and promote privacy solutions via the utilization of machine learning techniques.

Acknowledgments. This research is funded by dtec.bw – Digitalization and Technology Research Center of the Bundeswehr. dtec.bw is funded by the European Union – NextGenerationEU.

References

1. Abadji, J., Suárez, P.J.O., Romary, L., Sagot, B.: Ungoliant: an optimized pipeline for the generation of a very large-scale multilingual web corpus. In: CMLC 2021– 9th Workshop on Challenges in the Management of Large Corpora (2021)
2. Barricelli, B.R., Casiraghi, E., Fogli, D.: A survey on digital twin: definitions, characteristics, applications, and design implications. IEEE Access **7**, 167653–167671 (2019). https://doi.org/10.1109/ACCESS.2019.2953499
3. Biewald, L.: Experiment tracking with weights and biases (2020). https://www.wandb.com/. Accessed 19 July 2023
4. Bilge, L., Strufe, T., Balzarotti, D., Kirda, E.: All your contacts are belong to us: automated identity theft attacks on social networks. In: Proceedings of the

18th International Conference on World Wide Web, WWW 2009, pp. 551–560. Association for Computing Machinery, New York (2009). https://doi.org/10.1145/1526709.1526784

5. Brown, T.B., et al.: Language models are few-shot learners (2020)
6. Bäumer, F.S., Denisov, S., Geierhos, M., Lee, Y.S.: Towards authority-dependent risk identification and analysis in online networks. In: Science, N., Organization, T. (eds.) STO-MP-IST-190. NATO Science and Technology Organization (2021)
7. Bäumer, F.S., Geierhos, M.: Text broom: a ML-based tool to detect and highlight privacy breaches in physician reviews: an insight into our current work. In: European Conference on Data Analysis 2018: Multidisciplinary Facets of Data Science - Book of Abstracts (2018)
8. Bäumer, F.S., Grote, N., Kersting, J., Geierhos, M.: Privacy matters: detecting nocuous patient data exposure in online physician reviews. In: Damaševičius, R., Mikašytė, V. (eds.) ICIST 2017. CCIS, vol. 756, pp. 77–89. Springer, Cham (2017). https://doi.org/10.1007/978-3-319-67642-5_7
9. Bäumer, F.S., Kersting, J., Orlikowski, M., Geierhos, M.: Towards a multi-stage approach to detect privacy breaches in physician reviews. In: Khalili, A., Koutraki, M. (eds.) Proceedings of the Posters and Demos Track of the 14th International Conference on Semantic Systems Co-Located with the 14th International Conference on Semantic Systems (SEMANTiCS 2018). CEUR Workshop Proceedings, vol. 2198. CEUR-WS.org (2018)
10. Chan, B., Schweter, S., Möller, T.: German's next language model. In: Proceedings of the 28th International Conference on Computational Linguistics, pp. 6788–6796. International Committee on Computational Linguistics, Barcelona (2020). https://doi.org/10.18653/v1/2020.coling-main.598
11. Chen, M., Cheung, A.S.Y., Chan, K.L.: Doxing: what adolescents look for and their intentions. Int. J. Environ. Res. Public Health 16(2), 218 (2019). https://doi.org/10.3390/ijerph16020218
12. Conneau, A., et al.: Unsupervised cross-lingual representation learning at scale. In: Proceedings of the 58th Annual Meeting of the ACL, pp. 8440–8451. ACL (2020). https://doi.org/10.18653/v1/2020.acl-main.747
13. Devlin, J., Chang, M.W., Lee, K., Toutanova, K.: BERT: pre-training of deep bidirectional transformers for language understanding. In: Proceedings of the 2019 Conference of the North American Chapter of the Association for Computational Linguistics: Human Language Technologies, Volume 1 (Long and Short Papers). pp. 4171–4186. Association for Computational Linguistics, Minneapolis (2019). https://doi.org/10.18653/v1/N19-1423
14. Eckert, S., Metzger-Riftkin, J.: Doxxing. In: The International Encyclopedia of Gender, Media, and Communication, pp. 1–5 (2020). https://doi.org/10.1002/9781119429128.iegmc009
15. Fire, M., Goldschmidt, R., Elovici, Y.: Online social networks: threats and solutions. IEEE Commun. Surv. Tutor. 16(4), 2019–2036 (2014). https://doi.org/10.1109/COMST.2014.2321628
16. Frei, J., Kramer, F.: GERNERMED: an open German medical NER model. Softw. Impacts 11, 100212 (2022). https://doi.org/10.1016/j.simpa.2021.100212
17. Henry, S., Buchan, K., Filannino, M., Stubbs, A., Uzuner, Ö.: 2018 n2c2 shared task on adverse drug events and medication extraction in electronic health records. J. Am. Med. Inform. Assoc. (JAMIA) 27(1), 3–12 (2020)
18. Karahasanovic, A., Brandtzæg, P.B., Vanattenhoven, J., Lievens, B., Nielsen, K.T., Pierson, J.: Ensuring trust, privacy, and etiquette in web 2.0 applications. Computer 42(6), 42–49 (2009)

19. Krumm, J., Davies, N., Narayanaswami, C.: User-generated content. IEEE Pervasive Comput. **7**(4), 10–11 (2008). https://doi.org/10.1109/MPRV.2008.85

20. Lothritz, C., Allix, K., Veiber, L., Bissyandé, T.F., Klein, J.: Evaluating pretrained transformer-based models on the task of fine-grained named entity recognition. In: Proceedings of the 28th International Conference on Computational Linguistics, pp. 3750–3760. International Committee on Computational Linguistics, Barcelona (2020). https://doi.org/10.18653/v1/2020.coling-main.334

21. Moradi, M., Blagec, K., Haberl, F., Samwald, M.: GPT-3 models are poor few-shot learners in the biomedical domain. arXiv preprint arXiv:2109.02555 (2021)

22. Ostendorff, M., Blume, T., Ostendorff, S.: Towards an open platform for legal information. In: Proceedings of the ACM/IEEE Joint Conference on Digital Libraries in 2020, JCDL 2020, pp. 385–388. Association for Computing Machinery, New York (2020). https://doi.org/10.1145/3383583.3398616

23. Tian, W., Mao, J., Jiang, J., He, Z., Zhou, Z., Liu, J.: Deeply understanding structure-based social network de-anonymization. Procedia Comput. Sci. **129**, 52–58 (2018). https://doi.org/10.1016/j.procs.2018.03.045

24. Tiedemann, J.: Parallel data, tools and interfaces in OPUS. In: Proceedings of the Eighth International Conference on Language Resources and Evaluation (LREC 2012), pp. 2214–2218. European Language Resources Association (ELRA), Istanbul (2012)

25. Tjong Kim Sang, E.F., De Meulder, F.: Introduction to the CoNLL-2003 shared task: language-independent named entity recognition. In: Proceedings of the Seventh Conference on Natural Language Learning at HLT-NAACL 2003, pp. 142–147 (2003)

26. Zhu, Y., et al.: Aligning books and movies: towards story-like visual explanations by watching movies and reading books. In: 2015 IEEE International Conference on Computer Vision (ICCV), pp. 19–27 (2015). https://doi.org/10.1109/ICCV.2015.11

Application of Machine Learning in Energy Storage: A Scientometric Research of a Decade

Samuel-Soma M. Ajibade[1,7,8](✉), Faizah Mohammed Bashir[2], Yakubu Aminu Dodo[3], Johnry P. Dayupay[4], Limic M. De La Calzada II[5], and Anthonia Oluwatosin Adediran[6]

[1] Department of Computer Engineering, Istanbul Ticaret Universitesi, Istanbul, Türkiye
asamuel@ticaret.edu.tr
[2] Department of Interior Design, University of Hail, Hail, Kingdom of Saudi Arabia
fai.bashir@uoh.edu.sa
[3] Architectural Engineering Department, Najran University, Najran, Kingdom of Saudi Arabia
yadodo@nu.edu.sa
[4] College of Education, Cebu Technological University, Moalboal, Cebu, Philippines
johnry.dayupay@ctu.edu.ph
[5] College of Engineering, Cebu Technological University, Moalboal, Cebu, Philippines
limic.delacalzada@ctu.edu.ph
[6] Faculty of Architecture and Urban Design, Federal University of Uberlandia, Uberlândia, Brazil
[7] Department of Computing and Information Systems, Sunway University, Selangor, Malaysia
[8] Department of Data Science, Miva University, Abuja, Nigeria

Abstract. The publication trends and bibliometric analysis of the research landscape on the applications of machine/deep learning in energy storage (MES) research were examined in this study based on published documents in the Elsevier Scopus database between 2012 and 2022. The PRISMA technique employed to identify, screen, and filter related publications on MES research recovered 969 documents comprising articles, conference papers, and reviews published in English. The results showed that the publications count on the topic increased from 3 to 385 (or a 12,733.3% increase) along with citations between 2012 and 2022. The high publications and citations rate was ascribed to the MDLES research impact, co-authorships/collaborations, as well as the source title/journals' reputation, multidisciplinary nature, and research funding. The top/most prolific researcher, institution, country, and funding body on MDLES research are; is *Yan Xu, Tsinghua University*, China, and the National Natural Science Foundation of China, respectively. Keywords occurrence analysis revealed three clusters or hotspots based on *machine learning, digital storage*, and *Energy Storage*. Further analysis of the research landscape showed that MDLES research is currently and largely focused on the application of machine/deep learning for predicting, operating, and optimising energy storage as well as the design of energy storage materials for renewable energy technologies such as wind, and PV solar. However, future research will presumably include a focus on advanced energy materials development, operational systems monitoring and control as well as techno-economic analysis to address challenges associated with energy efficiency analysis, costing of renewable energy electricity pricing, trading, and revenue prediction.

© The Author(s), under exclusive license to Springer Nature Switzerland AG 2024
A. Lopata et al. (Eds.): ICIST 2023, CCIS 1979, pp. 124–135, 2024.
https://doi.org/10.1007/978-3-031-48981-5_10

Keywords: energy storage · machine learning · artificial intelligence · scientometric analysis

1 Introduction

Energy is regarded as one of the most crucial resources needed for socioeconomic development and long-term infrastructure development worldwide [1, 2]. 733 million people worldwide still lack access to electricity, while 2.4 billion rely on dangerous or polluting fuels for their lighting, cooking, and other home energy requirements, according to the United Nations (UN) [3]. This situation has brought about an energy and environmental crisis that could seriously impede global growth and development. As a result, the UN created the Sustainable Development Goals (SDG) in 2015 to address a variety of concerns, including lack of access to electricity. As a result, Goal 7 of the UN-SDG aspires to ensure that everyone has access to reliable, affordable, clean, and modern energy services [3]. By 2030, it also hopes to significantly increase the global percentage of renewable energy sources in the world's energy mix [4]. The Paris Agreement, also proposed in 2015, states that in order to address global warming and climate change, humanity must reduce greenhouse gas (GHG) emissions from the current levels of 50 billion tonnes per year to zero by 2050.

2 Literature Review

The use of computational methods like machine learning (ML) for energy storage study has gained popularity over time. According to Luxton's definition [5], machine learning (ML) is a key component of AI that enables computers to learn how to carry out tasks without being explicitly programmed. The definition includes computer programs or other devices that carry out tasks after being exposed to or using data. Typically, a computer learns to comprehend the data that is already present before using that understanding to forecast upcoming or newly emerging data. Nevertheless, Bhavsar and Safro [6] describe ML as a collection of methods that let computers create data-driven models by logically identifying patterns within the data sets that are statistically significant. Similar to this, Edgar and Manz [7] defined ML as a branch of research that investigates the use of computer algorithms to convert experience data into functional models (ML was derived from classical statistics and artificial intelligence). Considering the benefits of ML, several researchers have attempted to investigate and make use of the use of such computation tools in tackling the problems associated with energy storage. Similar to this, numerous studies have looked into the opportunities and difficulties of using ML in energy storage research across the globe. For instance, ML has been used to design and build innovative ionic/nano liquids, polymer composites, and nanocomposites [8–10] as well as energy materials and storage devices [11–13]. ML has the potential to hasten the development of materials for energy conversion and storage, claim Chen and Zhang [14]. In other noteworthy research, the use of ML was investigated for smart grid optimization [15], RET performance analysis [16], and transportation/vehicular systems [17, 18].

A few scholars have reviewed the many advancements in the area. The research on the use of ML in the modeling of materials and interfaces for energy conversion and storage was most recently reviewed by Artrith [19]. Similar to this, Qian and Sun [20] evaluated the most recent developments in ML investigations on MXenes for energy storage and conversion. The review by Barrett and Haruna [21] identified and underlined the potential of ML as a useful tool for computing the physico-chemical properties and time scales of energy materials. The authors also emphasized the existing capacity of ML for application in data analysis in compared to computational quantum mechanical modeling techniques like density functional theory. Additional literature reviews on the ML applications on energy storage (MES) research reveal that around 1,301 publications, including articles, conference papers, and reviews, have been published on the topic over the years. Considering the abundance of publications on MES research, no study has yet looked at the research environment, publishing trends, and stakeholders' analyses of the subject.

3 Methodology

The main goal of this research is to examine the landscape of publications and research trends on the use of ML in energy storage is the paper's main goal. The PRISMA (Preferred Reporting Items for Systematic Reviews and Meta-analysis) technique, which is used to find and screen published documents from particular scientific databases, was utilized to conduct the analysis. The Elsevier Scopus database was chosen for this study in order to identify published papers on machine/deep learning in energy storage research, abbreviated MES research in the following.

The published documents or publications on the MES research were identified using the "TITLE-ABS-KEY" search criteria: ("machine learning" OR "deep learning" AND "energy storage") AND PUBYEAR > 2011 AND PUBYEAR < 2023 which was executed in Scopus to recover related documents published on the topic between 2012 and 2022. The search was executed on 24th January 2023 and recovered 1,122 results comprising numerous document types (e.g., notes, erratum, letters, and data papers, etc.) and source types (trade journals, book series, and books, etc.) published in various languages (e.g., Chinese, Korean). Consequently, the document screening process was performed to eliminate the non-peer reviewed, duplicates, and unrelated as well as non-English publications from the recovered list of documents. The screening process was performed using the "LIMIT-TO" and "EXCLUDE" refine functions of Scopus, which resulted in 969 published documents after eliminating 153 documents from the list. The resulting document types were articles, conference papers, and reviews, whereas the source types are journals and conference proceedings, all published in the English language.

Using the published data recovered from Scopus and Scientometric analysis, the analysis stage involved looking at the trends in publishing and the research landscape on MES studies. The trends analysis of the publication looked at the output of the publication as well as the productivity of the top authors, affiliations, institutions, and nations. Additionally, the effects of research financing and the leading funding organizations on the subject were examined. Finally, the co-authorship and citation analysis features were used to analyze the research landscape with VOSviewer (version 1.6.17). The BA analysis was used to identify the present hotspots and future directions for MES as well as assess the effects of collaborations on the productivity of the key research actors.

4 Results and Discussion

This Section shows the results of the scientometric analysis which includes the publication trends, the top cited articles, top authors and affiliations and then the top active nations in the research of machine learning and energy storage.

4.1 Publication Trends

Figure 1 illustrates the plot of the total publications and citations on MES research against the year of publication. The analysis of the general publication trends shows that the number of published documents increased from 3 to 385 (or a 12,733.3% increase) between 2012 and 2022.

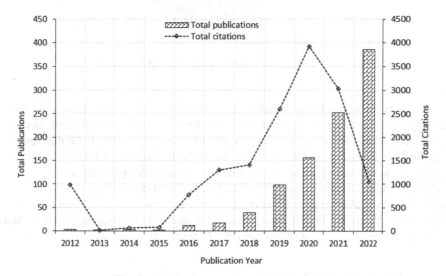

Fig. 1. Publication trends on MES research.

88.09 publications, or 9.09% of all publications (TP), are published on the topic annually, according to the data. Similar to this, it was discovered that the overall citation count (TC) increased with time, rising from 989 in 2012 to 1,061 in 2022, however the greatest total (TC = 3,928) was noted in the year 2020. The metrics show that the topic of MES has a very high research impact, with an h-index of 59 based on TC = 15,256. High citation rates are typically attributed to elements like publication type/quality, scientific journal reputation, or multidisciplinary character of article and journal [22–24].

The distribution of topics for publications on the topic, as inferred from the Scopus database from 2012 to 2022, is shown in Fig. 2. As shown, the Engineering category has 591 publications indexed under it. Engineering is followed by the categories of

Energy (496) and Computer Science (303). Chemistry (110), Materials Science (156), and Mathematics (182) are additional noteworthy categories. The results show that, even though the majority of the publications are in the STEM fields, the subject area analysis shows that MES research is broad-themed, complementary, and interdisciplinary, which may account for the significant amount of publications and citations the topic has accumulated over time.

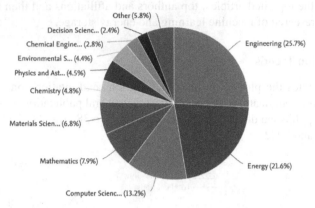

Fig. 2. Distribution of subject areas for MES research.

The many studies on ML applications in energy storage research clearly demonstrate the growing significance of applying math and computer science to problems in energy engineering. Battery development is one of the most famous scientific fields that benefited from the interdisciplinary nature of MES. To study the lifespan of lithium-ion (Li-ion) batteries in electric vehicles, Hu, Jiang [25] used sophisticated sparse Bayesian predictive modeling. The study found that ML might be helpful in monitoring and assessing the condition of Li-ion batteries in EVs. In a related study, Hu and Li [26] looked at Li-ion batteries in EVs using the ML-based State-of-Charge (SOC) estimator and a unique genetic algorithm-based fuzzy C-means (FCM) clustering technique.

4.2 Top Cited Articles (TCA)

The relationship between high citation rates and research impact has been the subject of numerous studies [27, 28]. Therefore, study of the most-cited articles is necessary for determining the research landscape in any topic. The number of publications in the Scopus database that have received 100 or more citations as on this study's definition of the highest publication citation. The top 10 TCA on MES research articles from 2012 to 2022 are displayed in Table 1. The data analysis reveals that the top 30 most TCA works, which have cumulatively acquired between 104 and 892 citations (5,971 total or 199.03 on average) over the time investigated in this study, comprise of 66.67% articles and 33.33% review papers.

Table 1. Top 10 most cited publications on MES

Authors/References	Paper Title	Source Title	Citations	Document Type
Foley, Leahy [32]	Current methods and advances in forecasting of wind power generation	Renewable Energy	892	Review
Hwang, Rao [33]	Perovskites in catalysis and electrocatalysis	Science	792	Review
Hu, Jiang [25]	Battery health prognosis for electric vehicles using sample entropy and sparse Bayesian predictive modelling	IEEE Transactions on Industrial Electronics	340	Article
Chemali, Kollmeyer [27]	State-of-charge estimation of Li-ion batteries using deep neural networks: A machine learning approach	Journal of Power Sources	308	Article
Chen, Hou [34]	Combining theory and experiment in lithium-sulphur batteries: Current progress and future perspectives	Materials Today	235	Review
Hu, Li [26]	Advanced Machine Learning Approach for Lithium-Ion Battery State Estimation in Electric Vehicles	IEEE Transactions on Transportation Electrification	219	Article
Zheng, Yao [35]	A review of composite solid-state electrolytes for lithium batteries: Fundamentals, key materials, and advanced structures	Chemical Society Reviews	208	Review

(*continued*)

Table 1. (*continued*)

Authors/References	Paper Title	Source Title	Citations	Document Type
Wang, Zhang [29]	Recent progress of biomass-derived carbon materials for supercapacitors	Journal of Power Sources	196	Review
Ng, Zhao [36]	Predicting the state of charge and health of batteries using data-driven machine learning	Nature Machine Intelligence	190	Review
Feng, Weng [11]	Online State-of-Health Estimation for Li-Ion Battery Using Partial Charging Segment Based on Support Vector Machine	IEEE Transactions on Vehicular Technology	155	Article

4.3 Top Authors

The top 5 authors on MES research from 2012 to 2022 are shown in Fig. 3. As seen, the authors have written at least six publications on the subject. Yan Xu, who is based in Singapore and has 9 publications, is the top author (h-index = 6). Her works have received a total of 100 citations. The article "Data-Driven Game-Based Pricing for Sharing Rooftop Photovoltaic Generation and Energy Storage in the Residential Building Cluster under Uncertainties" by the author, which appeared in the IEEE Transactions on Industrial Informatics and has been cited 21 times, is his most significant work.

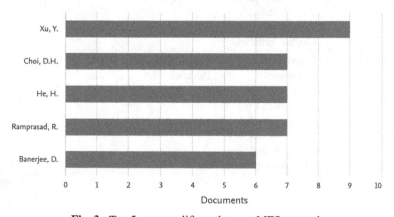

Fig. 3. Top 5 most prolific authors on MES research

The co-authorship network visualization map (NVM) for MES research from 2012 to 2022 is depicted in Fig. 4. The findings indicated that 61 authors—out of a possible 3,166—have five or more articles with more than 50 citations within the study's time period. The top 61 authors on MES, or 57 of them, or 93.44% of them, have co-authored works on the subject. Additionally, the cluster analysis reveals eight clusters with three to thirteen authors each, 244 links, and a TLS of 334. Therefore, it could be wisely concluded that co-authorship had a major effect on the writers' work on the subject.

4.4 Top Affiliations

The top five most active affiliations in MES research are presented in Fig. 5 for the period of 2012 to 2022. As can be seen, over the time period considered in this analysis, the top 5 most productive associations have produced 15 or more articles on the subject. Tsinghua University (32), the Chinese Academy of Sciences (28), the Ministry of Education of China (27), Nanyang Technological University (NTU, 21), and Shanghai Jiao Tong University (18) are the top affiliations, along with the number of publications they have each produced. The other four most prevalent affiliations, with the exception of NTU Singapore, are based in China, suggesting that Chinese-based institutions are the leading actors or stakeholders in the application of ML in energy storage.

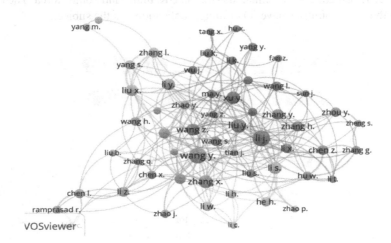

Fig. 4. Network visualization map for co-authorship among authors on MES

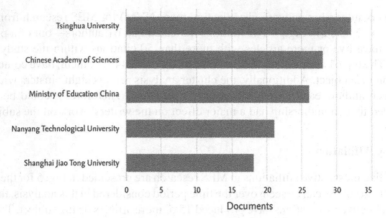

Fig. 5. Top 5 affiliations on MES research

4.5 Top Active Countries

In Fig. 6 the top 5 most active countries conducting MES research globally was displayed. According to the statistics, the countries that conducted the most research on the subject between 2012 and 2022 were China, the US, the UK, India, and South Korea. The results indicate that all 5 countries have 50 or more publications on the subject.

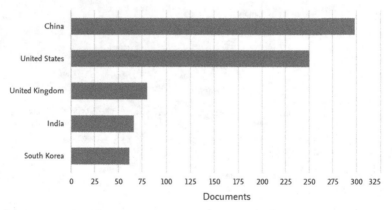

Fig. 6. Top 5 most active on MES research

As shown, China has produced the most articles in MES research with 298; these publications have received 5,249 citations and have an h-index of 38 throughout time. Researchers from Tsinghua University including Xiang Chen (3) and Longqing Chen (2), as well as Hongwen He (7) and Shuangqi Li (5) who are based at the Beijing Institute of Technology, have contributed to China's productivity. Researchers from China and other countries, including Yan Xu of Nanyang Technological University in Singapore, Zhe Chen of Aalborg University in Denmark, and Xinhua Liu (5) of Imperial College London in London (UK), have collaborated to increase production in the country.

5   Conclusion

The study looked at bibliometric data and publishing patterns related to the application of ML in energy storage. The PRISMA method is used to locate, evaluate, and filter published documents. According to the distribution of published documents, numerous English-language articles, conference papers, and reviews have been published in high-impact journals like Energies, Applied Energy, and Journal of Energy Storage. According to a subject-area study, MES research articles are included in a number of categories, including engineering, energy, and computer science, indicating that the field is multi-disciplinary and has a wide range of themes. The multidisciplinary character of MES and research funding have been determined to be the causes of the topic's high publication and citation rates. According to publication trends, Yan Xu (Nanyang Technological University) is the most productive researcher, while Tsinghua University (China) is the most productive institution. According to the financing landscape, Chinese and American institutions are the leading sponsors of MES research, which explains why there are so many publications, citations, and stakeholders interested in the field worldwide. The authors predict that future research on the subject will probably concentrate on ML and computational applications for synthesis of energy materials, analysis of energy efficiency, monitoring and control of operational systems, and techno-economic analysis for electricity pricing, trading, and revenue forecasting. Overall, the report used the Scopus database, and Bibliometric analysis to provide complete insights into the publication's patterns and the research environment on MES.

References

1. Wysokiński, M., et al.: Economic and energy efficiency of agriculture. Agric. Econ.-Zemedelska Ekonomika **66**(8), 355–364 (2020)
2. Antai, A.S., Udo, A.B., Ikpe, I.K.: A VAR analysis of the relationship between energy consumption and economic growth in Nigeria. J. Econ. Sustain. Dev. **6**(12), 1–12 (2015)
3. United Nations. Goals 7: Ensure access to affordable, reliable, sustainable and modern energy for all. Sustainable Development Goals 2015. https://bit.ly/3DHOTp3. Cited 3 Jan 2023
4. Timilsina, G., Shah, K.U.: Energy technologies for sustainable development Goal 7. In: Science, Technology, and Innovation for Sustainable Development Goals: Insights from Agriculture, Health, Environment, and Energy, p. 36 (2020)
5. Luxton, D.D.: An introduction to artificial intelligence in behavioral and mental health care. In: Artificial Intelligence in Behavioral and Mental Health Care, pp. 1–26. Elsevier (2016)
6. Bhavsar, P., et al.: Machine learning in transportation data analytics. In: Data Analytics for Intelligent Transportation Systems, pp. 283–307. Elsevier (2017)
7. Edgar, T., Manz, D.: Research Methods for Cyber Security. Syngress (2017)
8. Zahid, T., Xu, K., Li, W.: Machine learning an alternate technique to estimate the state of charge of energy storage devices. Electron. Lett. **53**(25), 1665–1666 (2017)
9. Henri, G., Lu, N.: A supervised machine learning approach to control energy storage devices. IEEE Trans. Smart Grid **10**(6), 5910–5919 (2019)
10. Ajibade, S.S.M., Ahmad, N.B.B., Zainal, A.: A hybrid chaotic particle swarm optimization with differential evolution for feature selection. In: 2020 IEEE Symposium on Industrial Electronics & Applications (ISIEA), pp. 1–6. IEEE (2020)
11. Feng, Y., et al.: Machine learning and microstructure design of polymer nanocomposites for energy storage application. High Voltage **7**(2), 242–250 (2022)

12. Said, Z., et al.: Experimental analysis of novel ionic liquid-MXene hybrid nanofluid's energy storage properties: model-prediction using modern ensemble machine learning methods. J. Energy Storage **52**, 104858 (2022)
13. Yue, D., et al.: Prediction of energy storage performance in polymer composites using high-throughput stochastic breakdown simulation and machine learning. Adv. Sci. **9**(17), 2105773 (2022)
14. Chen, A., Zhang, X., Zhou, Z.: Machine learning: accelerating materials development for energy storage and conversion. InfoMat **2**(3), 553–576 (2020)
15. Zsembinszki, G., et al.: Deep learning optimal control for a complex hybrid energy storage system. Buildings **11**(5), 194 (2021)
16. Moradi-Sepahvand, M., Amraee, T., Gougheri, S.S.: Deep learning based hurricane resilient coplanning of transmission lines, battery energy storages, and wind farms. IEEE Trans. Ind. Inform. **18**(3), 2120–2131 (2022)
17. Fu, T., Wang, C., Cheng, N.: Deep-learning-based joint optimization of renewable energy storage and routing in vehicular energy network. IEEE Internet Things J. **7**(7), 6229–6241 (2020)
18. Bansal, S., Dey, S., Khanra, M.: Energy storage sizing in plug-in Electric Vehicles: driving cycle uncertainty effect analysis and machine learning based sizing framework. J. Energy Storage **41**, 102864 (2021)
19. Artrith, N.: Machine learning for the modeling of interfaces in energy storage and conversion materials. J. Phys. Energy **1**(3), 032002 (2019)
20. Qian, C., Sun, K., Bao, W.: Recent advance on machine learning of MXenes for energy storage and conversion. Int. J. Energy Res. **46**(15), 21511–21522 (2022)
21. Barrett, D.H., Haruna, A.: Artificial intelligence and machine learning for targeted energy storage solutions. Curr. Opin. Electrochem. **21**, 160–166 (2020)
22. Bordons, M., Aparicio, J., Costas, R.: Heterogeneity of collaboration and its relationship with research impact in a biomedical field. Scientometrics **96**(2), 443–466 (2013). https://doi.org/10.1007/s11192-012-0890-7
23. Bong, Y., Ale Ebrahim, N.: Increasing visibility and enhancing impact of research. Asia Research News (2017)
24. Carroll, C.: Measuring academic research impact: creating a citation profile using the conceptual framework for implementation fidelity as a case study. Scientometrics **109**(2), 1329–1340 (2016). https://doi.org/10.1007/s11192-016-2085-0
25. Hu, X., et al.: Battery health prognosis for electric vehicles using sample entropy and sparse Bayesian predictive modeling. IEEE Trans. Ind. Electron. **63**(4), 2645–2656 (2016)
26. Hu, X., Li, S.E., Yang, Y.: Advanced machine learning approach for lithium-ion battery state estimation in electric vehicles. IEEE Trans. Transp. Electrification **2**(2), 140–149 (2016)
27. Chemali, E., et al.: State-of-charge estimation of Li-ion batteries using deep neural networks: a machine learning approach. J. Power. Sources **400**, 242–255 (2018)
28. Feng, X., et al.: Online state-of-health estimation for Li-ion battery using partial charging segment based on support vector machine. IEEE Trans. Veh. Technol. **68**(9), 8583–8592 (2019)
29. Wang, J., et al.: Recent progress of biomass-derived carbon materials for supercapacitors. J. Power. Sources **451**, 227794 (2020)
30. Foley, A.M., et al.: Current methods and advances in forecasting of wind power generation. Renew. Energy **37**(1), 1–8 (2012)
31. Ajibade, S.S.M., Ahmad, N.B.B., Shamsuddin, S.M.: A novel hybrid approach of Adaboostm2 algorithm and differential evolution for prediction of student performance. Int. J. Sci. Technol. Res. **8**(07), 65–70 (2019)

32. Cherchali, N.O., Tlemçani, A., Boucherit, M.S., Morsli, A.: Elimination of low order harmonics in multilevel inverter using nature-inspired metaheuristic algorithm. Int. J. Energy Power Eng. **13**(9), 638–644 (2019)
33. Hwang, J., et al.: Perovskites in catalysis and electrocatalysis. Science **358**(6364), 751–756 (2017)
34. Chen, X., et al.: Combining theory and experiment in lithium–sulfur batteries: current progress and future perspectives. Mater. Today **22**, 142–158 (2019)
35. Zheng, Y., et al.: A review of composite solid-state electrolytes for lithium batteries: fundamentals, key materials and advanced structures. Chem. Soc. Rev. **49**(23), 8790–8839 (2020)
36. Ng, M.F., et al.: Predicting the state of charge and health of batteries using data-driven machine learning. Nat. Mach. Intell. **2**(3), 161–170 (2020)

Access Control Approach for Controller Management Platforms

Tomas Adomkus[1]([✉]), Klaidas Klimakas[1], Rasa Brūzgienė[1][iD],
and Lina Narbutaitė[2]

[1] Department of Computer Sciences, Kaunas University of Technology,
Studentu str. 50-204a, 51368 Kaunas, Lithuania
{tomas.adomkus,rasa.bruzgiene}@ktu.lt
[2] Department of Software Engineering, Kaunas University of Technology,
Studentu str. 50-415b, 51368 Kaunas, Lithuania
lina.narbutaite@ktu.lt

Abstract. Controller management platforms are part of the rapidly growing IoT infrastructure. Platforms manage physical devices and collect, process and integrate data, making them an attractive target for cybercriminals. Weak access control is one of the key cybersecurity threats in this area. This paper aims to provide a secure platform for remote control of controllers using a tailored access control approach. It also aims to evaluate the effectiveness of the proposed access control method. The implemented platform is configured for smart home solutions. Experiments on the administrative cost, speed and security of the method are carried out in scenarios.

Keywords: Access control · Security threats · Risk score · Decision-making · Riskiness of the context

1 Introduction

The Internet of Things is a fast-growing area of IT, where solutions combine both physical devices and information systems. Sensors monitor and record environmental parameters, actuators perform specified actions in the physical environment, and controllers manage these devices. Controllers also provide data processing and communication with platforms. Platforms at the application layer act as an intermediary: they store and process sensor data, allow users to remotely control devices, analyze data, provide interfaces between different services, and take care of security. Controller control platforms are characterized by weak access control. The traditional solutions used are static and therefore not suitable for dynamic IoT environments. Hence, there is a need to find authorization methods suitable for this environment. This paper addresses the problem of efficiency and security of access control decision-making. By designing an access control method, the following results are sought: granularity, flexibility and simplicity.

2 Security Threats to Controller Management Platforms

IoT applications, like all IT systems, inevitably face security challenges. According to Nokia Corporation's enterprise data, the percentage of IoT devices infected in 2020 has risen from 16.17% in 2019 to 32.72% [1]. This area poses specific cybersecurity challenges that require unique approaches given the unique nature of IoT infrastructure. This requires specialized security tools and practices to protect IoT solutions from potential threats [2].

2.1 Security Threats to IoT Infrastructure and Platforms

Security threats to Internet of Things (IoT) infrastructures and platforms include potential risks and hazards that jeopardise the security of the entire IoT system. These threats can include unauthorised access, data theft, cyber-attacks, inadequate data encryption, insufficient attack detection and many other potential security vulnerabilities. Enhancing the security of IoT infrastructure and platforms requires careful assessment of these threats and appropriate measures to address them. Based on the OWASP (Open Web Application Security Project) 2018 list and a summary of problematic IoT challenges, Table 1 shows the architectural layers with their inherent security issues.

Table 1. Security challenges for IoT solutions at different architectural layers [3–9].

Security challenge	Application layer	Network layer	Perception layer
Weak or encrypted passwords		√	√
Insecure network services		√	√
Insecure interfaces	√		
Insecure device updates	√		√
Use of insecure components	√		√
Inadequate privacy protection	√	√	√
Insecure data transfer and storage	√	√	√
Lack of device management	√		
Insecure settings provided by manufacturers		√	√
Lack of physical security		√	√

Thus, cybersecurity issues arise at all layers of the IoT ecosystem. Some of them are similar, and some of them differ. However, a large part of the threat lie at the application layer, where IoT platforms operate. These threats are important because they can affect the security of IoT platforms and devices, and measures must be taken to address them and ensure the secure operation of IoT. A detailed analysis of the security threats to IoT platforms reveals that a significant part of the problems is related to weak access control. Platforms do not have effective authorization mechanisms tailored for IoT environments. It can be observed that access control problems occur both in generic IoT platforms and in domain-specific platforms. The most common problem is that smaller system components, prevailing contextual information, attributes of objects, entities or environments are not taken into account, and only roles are used. In summary, further analysis of access methods and solutions used on IoT platforms is needed.

3   Proposed Access Control Method

The analysis of the publications shows that IoT applications are dominated by a dynamic and ever-changing environment with low-resource devices. It also concludes that controller management platforms face the problem of authorization security, where traditional static access control methods do not take into account the dynamic nature of the IoT environment and thus fail to ensure the principle of least privilege. When designing an access control method, it was decided that for the granularity and flexibility of the method, standard architectural blocks of the Attribute-Based Access Control (ABAC) type of methods should be used.

Typically, there are 3 main actors involved in the operation of ABAC-type methods: the administrator, the subject and the object. The main task of the administrator is to create access policy rules, while the main task of the subject, or user, is to make access requests to the access method in order to perform certain operations on the object. The controller plays the role of an object, or resource. Since the access control method is developed for control platforms, both the subject and the administrator perform actions using the interface provided by the platform.

The components of the access control method and the overall operation of the method is visualised in Fig. 1.

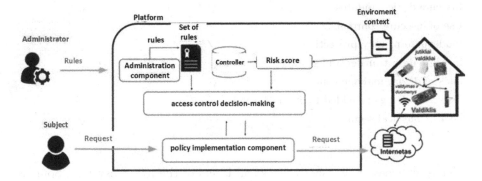

Fig. 1. Vision of an access control approach for controller management platforms

The platform implementation and the network of controllers communicate remotely, i.e. via the Internet. The application environment of the method may include various types of input and output devices. The controller is controlled from the platform, and the data is transmitted to the platform using the controller's available communication modules, which access the network. Consideration of the dynamically changing context of the environment is important in the decision-making process.

Environmental conditions are not directly assessed in the decision-making process but are used for both the risk score and the situational assessment. The risk score is calculated by considering the environmental context and the attributes of the site. This is done using the sensitivity of the controller and the criticality of the desired operation. The risk assessment provides a simple way of evaluating the different attributes and providing an overall risk score. The detailed process of risk calculation is described in the next subsection.

In summary, access control decision-making is carried out in accordance with the access policy rules established for each entity role. The specified maximum permissible risk score for a role is compared with the calculated risk score for an entity request, taking into account environment and resource attributes.

3.1 Calculation of the Risk Score

To calculate the risk score, it is necessary to define which risk factors will be used in the calculation. In the case of the method to be developed, the following attributes are used:

- **Resource sensitivity.** This attribute describes the level of sensitivity of the resource, or controller, that the subject is trying to access. The higher the level of sensitivity, the worse the expected consequences of an unauthorized or improperly authorized operation. Thus, a higher sensitivity of a resource will result in a higher overall risk score.
- **Impact of the action.** Different actions, or operations, may have different consequences, so each operation is assigned a specific impact that describes the negative consequences. The higher the impact, the higher the overall risk score.
- **The riskiness of the context of the query.** Certain conditions in the context of the request environment (e.g. a request from a certain IP address or from a certain device type) may have negative consequences and therefore pose a risk. To assess this risk, environmental context conditions may be assigned a higher risk score based on system configurations.

Once the key factors that make up the final risk assessment have been identified, it is important to choose the method for calculating the risk. There are a variety of such methods [10]: fuzzy logic, machine learning, game theory, the standard risk assessment method or other mathematical equations. Due to its simplicity, the access control method to be developed uses a standard risk calculation (Eq. 1):

$$SR = P \cdot I, \tag{1}$$

where: SR – Standard risk estimate, P – Probability, I – Impact.

In the case of a method under development, the likelihood of negative consequences is determined by the impact of the action to be performed by the subject.
This means that different operations on a resource (controller) may have different probabilities of negative consequences. Meanwhile, the negative impact, or
consequence, of an event is determined by the sensitivity of the resource and
its data. Thus, in the general case of the approach, the baseline risk score is
calculated using the following formula (Eq. 2):

$$BS = E \cdot S, \tag{2}$$

where: BS – Baseline risk estimate, E – Effect of the action, S – Sensitivity of
the resource.

It is also important to consider the riskiness of the context of the query, as the
method should take this into account in the case of different contextual riskiness.
To assess the environmental context conditions, the standard risk estimation
formula introduces an additional variable describing the riskiness of the context,
so the generalized risk estimation formula of the method is as follows (Eq. 3):

$$RS = BS \cdot RC, \tag{3}$$

where: RS – Risk score, BS – Baseline risk estimate, RC – Riskiness of the
context.

Environmental riskiness can be a result of a number of environmental contextual conditions. Thus, the total riskiness of an environmental condition is the
sum of all possible environmental contextual conditions divided by the number
of such conditions (Eq. 4):

$$RC = \frac{\sum_i C}{N} \tag{4}$$

where: RC – Riskiness of the context, C – Context conditions i riskiness, N –
Number of context conditions.

The calculation of the risk score presented here is only carried out under
normal environmental conditions. The environmental assessments can be split
into two thresholds:

– **Critical situation.** This means that in this situation the decision-making
  component ignores the calculated baseline risk estimate. A critical situation
  is defined as a situation where there is an urgent situation where a person's
  health or property becomes more important than the information being protected. In this case, the method is able to take this into account and the
  decision-making mechanism does not assess the risk score but gives immediate access to the subject.
– **Typical situation.** This situation is normal and stable and therefore poses
  no threat to the subject. Information security is essential in this case and no
  exceptions to the risk are made by the access control method.

To assess these situations, it is necessary to set thresholds for the environmental attributes being assessed, beyond which the situation becomes critical.
This is done by the administrator of the Controller Management Platform when

configuring the access method. In summary, the decision-making logic discussed allows the criticality of the environmental conditions to be taken into account, thus ensuring the flexibility of the access control method.

The final risk score is calculated using the numerical values mentioned above and the risk calculation formula below (Eq. 5):

$$RS = (E \cdot R) \cdot RC, \tag{5}$$

where: RS – Risk score, E – Effect of the action, R – Resource sensitivity, RC – Riskiness of the context.

The resulting risk score is used directly in the decision-making process by comparing it with the maximum risk score specified in the risk policy rules. The range of risk values is broken down into 5 risk levels:

- 0 to 3.6, which means that the risk score is very low, i.e. negligible;
- 3.6 to 7.2 - low risk values;
- 7.2 to 10.8 are medium risk values;
- 10.8 to 14.4 are high risk values;
- 14.4 to 18 means very high risk, i.e. critical in terms of information security.

Taking into account the above ranges and their explanations, the administrator of the Controller Management Platform shall create access policy rules specifying the user roles and the maximum risk scores assigned to them.

3.2 Detailed Decision-Making Process for the Access Method

In particular, the method administration component needs to have access policy rules in place that define the maximum risk score allowed for each role in the user environment. These rules shall guide the decision-making process. The assignment of a role to an entity, as well as the prediction of entity, resource, operation and environment states, is necessary in order to be able to assess all of this when making access control decisions. Prior assignment of resource sensitivity, action effects and the addition of environmental context conditions are required. Once all these data are defined, the smooth operation of the method is possible.

The access control method shall start to operate upon receipt of an access request from an entity. The initial processing of this request is carried out by the decision execution component. This part of the method performs a minimal processing of the request, reads the data and passes it on to the decision-making component.

The decision-making component reads the role of the subject. It also reads the impact of the operation to be performed in the request, the sensitivity of the object (resource) to which the subject intends to gain access. The access control approach reads the rules and values of the environmental context conditions in preparation for the situation assessment.

After the initial steps, the decision-making component performs an assessment and determines whether the current environmental situation is normal or critical. Two options are possible:

– if the situation is critical, the method grants access to the subject without taking into account the riskiness, as the security of people and assets is judged to be more important than the security of information;
– if the situation is normal, the method continues to calculate the risk score of the request made. The score assesses the sensitivity of the resource, the impact of the operation and evaluates the riskiness of the context of the request.

4   Prototype Implementation and Research on the Access Control Approach for Controller Management Platforms

4.1   Prototype Hardware

The following hardware is used to implement the prototype access control method: Raspberry Pi 4 model B microcomputer; ESP8266 NodeMCU micro-controller; sensors and output devices.

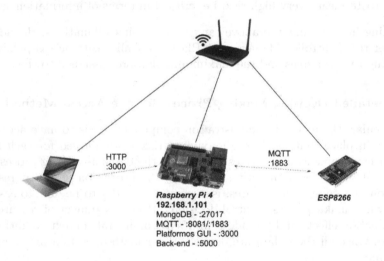

Fig. 2. Hardware subsystem diagram

The hardware chosen is that typical of conventional IoT infrastructures. This choice aims to bring the control platform and approach closer to real IoT infras-tructures. The implementation of the access control approach uses software on both the controller and the microcomputer. Figure 2 shows a diagram summa-rizing the software as well as the hardware of the prototype.

Such software is often used in IoT solutions and in implementations of con-troller management platforms. It provides fast, simple and efficient communica-tion with controllers.

4.2 Controller Management Platform

In order to test the performance of the access control method, a prototype controller management platform has been implemented in a closed network. To ensure the security of the controller management platform and the functioning of the access control method, the system adds the possibility for the administrator to select the sensitivity of the controllers and the impact of actions on those controllers.

Table 2. Controls and related actions with the risk impact on these actions.

Controller ID	Sensitivity	Action	Imitation	Effect
100001	Medium	Raise gate	Sound buzzer	High (3)
100001	Medium	Lower gate	Sound buzzer	Medium (2)
100001	Medium	Get status	Informative info	Low (1)
100002	Large	Switch on fireplace	Red LED	Medium (2)
100002	Large	Switch off fireplace	Off LED	Low (1)
100002	Large	Switch on light	Yellow LED	Low (1)
100002	Large	Switch off light	Off LED	Low (1)
100002	Large	Alarm on	Blue LED	Low (1)
100002	Large	Alarm off	Off LED	High (3)
100003	Small	Start/Stop sprinkler	Flashing LED	Medium (2)
100003	Small	Get status	Informative info	Low (1)
100003	Small	Get network settings	Important info	High (3)

The administrator shall also have the possibility to add context conditions and to specify high-risk or critical thresholds for them. The monitoring of context conditions is performed by the MQTT protocol in the *homeDeviceContext* topic according to the added function paths. The resulting data shall be recorded in a database. Context conditions can also be checked against functions implemented in the system. 3 such functions have been implemented:

- Daytime. This function checks if the query is made during the day. Queries made during the night are considered more risky.
- Network. This function checks whether the IP address of the subject is on an internal network. A request coming from an external network is considered riskier.
- Location. This function checks whether the request created by the subject originates from Lithuania. If the request comes from elsewhere, it is considered to be a risk and therefore the risk score will be higher.

The administrator configures the access control logic by adding access policy rules in the policy administration component. In order to facilitate the survey and to better understand the results, the control management platform has been configured to fit the smart home environment. In particular, the platform adds users with roles specific to this environment: owner, resident, child, nanny, guest, tenant. 3 controllers will be simulated in the home environment. Table 2 provides information about these controllers and the actions associated with them. It also summarizes the ID of each controller, its sensitivity level, the actions performed, the simulation of the actions, and the impact that these actions may have. This provides a clear structure and makes it easy to understand what actions are associated with each controller and what their risks are.

5   Research Scenarios and Results

The research scenarios are carried out separately for each research parameter. Firstly, **the administrative costs** of the access control method shall be investigated. For this purpose, the number of access policies is calculated. Several scenarios shall be carried out:

- Test 1 - in this case the number of users, objects, actions and context conditions is as defined during the preparation of the environment. Let's say that each object has on average 4 actions.
- Test 2 - in this case the number of users increases by 100%.
- Test 3 - in this case the number of objects increases by 100%.

   The number of policies in a method depends on the roles, contextual conditions, objects and actions and is the product of all of them. If the method is fully configured, then only the number of objects can increase, and the number of users will not be affected due to the roles used.
   The number of policies depends on the access control method used:

- MAC: Policies = (Users × Tags) + (Tags × Objects).
- DAC: Policies = Users × Objects × Actions.
- RBAC: Policies = Roles × Objects × Actions.

A summary of the study on the cost of administering the access control approach for the Controller Management Platform is given in Table 3 below.
   A quantitative comparison of the constructed method with other access control methods shows that the number of policies in the RBAC method depends

Table 3. Study on the cost of administering the access control method for the Controller Management Platform.

	Test 1	Test 2	Test 3
Roles	6	6	6
Context conditions	7	7	7
Objects	3	3	6
Actions per object	4	4	4
Number of policies	504	504	1008

on the number of roles, objects and actions, and is the equivalent of the product of all of them. If the method is fully configured, then only the number of objects can increase, the increase in the number of users will have no effect due to the roles used. If the number of objects is increased by 100%, the number of policies is increased by the same amount. To summarize, it can be seen that the initial configuration of the method built during the work is more difficult due to the context conditions used, which is also typical for other methods using ABAC type logic. In this respect, the method is inferior to the RBAC mechanism. However, the method analyzed in this paper is robust to the growth in the number of users. In this respect, it is superior to the DAC and MAC methods. Thus, the resulting method is relatively complex to configure at the beginning, but convenient to expand the system in the later stages as the number of users increases, as the administration costs do not increase.

Rapidity is another parameter that is being investigated. The study is carried out according to the scenarios presented:

1. a critical situation is identified in the decision-making process;
2. a normal situation without environmental context conditions is identified in the decision-making process;
3. a normal situation with environmental context conditions is established in the decision-making process;
4. the environmental context conditions increase by 100%.

In summary, it is observed that in an emergency situation, the decision-making component takes about 68.67 ms to make an access decision. In a normal situation, but without environmental context conditions, the decision-making process takes twice as long, i.e. about 142.39 ms. Further testing with six environmental context conditions slows down the speed-up by about 33% to 212.19 ms. Increasing the environmental context conditions by 100% slows down the speedup by about 6% to 226.81 ms. Thus, critical situations significantly reduce the time for the decision-making process.

Next, a security study of the constructed method was performed. To do this, firstly, the calculated baseline and overall riskiness for each action of the control platform, according to the object and the action performed is compiled. The overall risk score covers the possible range of values. Some of risky actions (e.g. disarming the alarm, switching on the fireplace, lifting the gate, lowering the gate) are not allowed for roles with a lower maximum risk, such as guest or child. The decision may change depending on the criticality of the environmental situation and the current environmental context conditions, under which the calculated riskiness may remain the same or increase by 100%.

The following assesses how the same access decisions may change depending on the state of the environmental context conditions. According to the configurations carried out previously, there are 5 conditions (time of day, request source, subject country, owner location, alarm operation) on the platform that characterise the environment and can affect the overall risk score. The paper presents some of the results obtained.

Parameters of a subject in the role of nanny submits a request to turn on the fireplace at home shown in Fig. 3a. Parameters of a child subject tries to raise the garage door shown in Fig. 3b.

(a) A subject in the role of nanny submits a request to turn on the fireplace at home

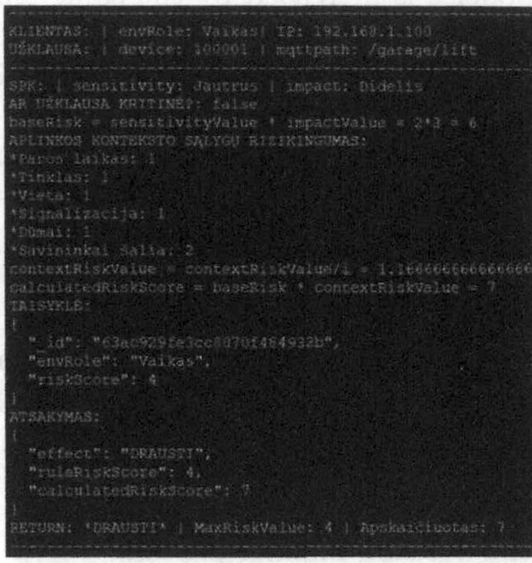

(b) A child subject tries to raise the garage door

Fig. 3. Experimental results

6   Conclusions

It has been observed that in order to add granularity and flexibility to the access approach, it is useful to apply the risk calculation algorithm and the architecture and principles of ABAC methods: to use the component architecture and the assessment of the environmental contextual conditions, to adapt the access solutions to the environmental situations. It was observed that in order to dynamically assess the environment while maintaining the simplicity of the method, it is useful to use the product of a standardized baseline risk score formula and the risk score of the environmental context conditions to calculate the risk score. It is also effective to use roles specific to RBAC method types to maintain simplicity. For flexibility of the method, it is effective to use situational criticality assessment, i.e. in a critical situation, the subject should be granted access to the facility in any case, assuming that the subject is potentially at risk to his/her health or property.

The administrative cost experiments showed that the constructed method is more difficult to configure and audit compared to the DAC, MAC, RBAC methods. The additional administrative costs are due to the desire for granularity, i.e. the configuration of the environmental context conditions as well as the role settings. The method uses roles, and it has been observed that an increase in the number of users on the platform does not lead to an increase in the number of access policies. However, as the number of objects grows, the number of policies grows in parallel, so in this respect the extensibility of the platform suffers as in the other methods mentioned. Speedup studies have shown that the evaluation of environmental context conditions slows down the decision-making component by 33%, and in critical situations decisions are made 3 times faster than in a normal situation with 6 environmental context conditions. This shows that in critical situations the method is flexible and fast in assessing the situation and prioritizing the safety of the subject in the decision to allow access. The security evaluation of the method verifies the flexibility of the method in the presence of the dynamics inherent in the IoT infrastructure. Thus, due to the evaluation of environmental conditions and subject attributes used to calculate the risk score, access rights are not static and unchanging as in traditional methods. It has been observed that risk scoring simplifies the construction of rules compared to other ABAC-type methods.

References

1. Marton, A.: Latest IoT threat statistics. https://iotac.eu/latest-iot-threat-statistics/. Accessed 24 Dec 2021
2. Frustaci, M., Pace, P., Aloi, G., Fortino, G.: Evaluating critical security issues of the IoT world: present and future challenges. IEEE Internet Things J. **5**(4), 2483–2495 (2017)
3. OWASP top 10 (2021). https://owasp.org/Top10/. Accessed 25 Dec 2021
4. Gupta, M., Bhatt, S., Alshehri, A.H., Sandhu, R.: Access Control Models and Architectures for IoT and Cyber Physical Systems [interaktyvus]. Springer, Cham (2022). https://doi.org/10.1007/978-3-030-81089-4
5. Krishna, R.R., et al.: State-of-the-art review on IoT threats and attacks: taxonomy, challenges and solutions. Sustainability **13**(16), 9463 (2021)
6. Babun, L., Kyle, D., Celik, Z.B., Mcdaniel, P., Uluagac, A.S.: A survey on IoT platforms: communication, security, and privacy perspectives. Comput. Netw. **192**, 108040 (2021)
7. Nebbione, G., Calzarossa, M.C.: Security of IoT Application Layer Protocols: Challenges and Findings. Future Internet **12**(3), 55 (2020)
8. Aljeraisy, A., Barati, M., Rana, O., Perera, C.: Privacy laws and privacy by design schemes for the Internet of Things: a developer's perspective. ACM Comput. Surv. (CSUR) **54**(5), 1–38 (2020)
9. Azam, F., Munir, R., Ahmed, M., Ayub, M., Sajid, A., Abbasi, Z., et al.: Internet of Things (IoT), security issues and its solutions. Sci. Heritage J. **3**(2), 18–21 (2019)
10. Atlam, H.F., Wills, G.B.: An efficient security risk estimation technique for Risk-based access control model for IoT. Internet Things **6**, 100052 (2019)

Leveraging Semantic Search and LLMs for Domain-Adaptive Information Retrieval

Falk Maoro[(✉)] [ID], Benjamin Vehmeyer [ID], and Michaela Geierhos [ID]

University of the Bundeswehr Munich, Neubiberg, Germany
{falk.maoro,benjamin.vehmeyer,michaela.geierhos}@unibw.de

Abstract. The rapid growth of digital information and the increasing complexity of user queries have made traditional search methods less effective in the context of business-related websites. This paper presents an innovative approach to improve the search experience across a variety of domains, particularly in the industrial sector, by integrating semantic search and conversational large language models such as GPT-3.5 into a domain-adaptive question-answering framework. Our proposed solution aims at complementing existing keyword-based approaches with the ability to capture entire questions or problems. By using all types of text, such as product manuals, documentation, advertisements, and other documents, all types of questions relevant to a website can be answered. These questions can be simple requests for product or domain knowledge, assistance in using a product, or more complex questions that may be relevant in determining the value of organizations as potential collaborators. We also introduce a mechanism for users to ask follow-up questions and to establish subject-specific communication with the search system. The results of our feasibility study show that the integration of semantic search and GPT-3.5 leads to significant improvements in the search experience, which could then translate into higher user satisfaction when querying the corporate portfolio. This research contributes to the ongoing development of advanced search technologies and has implications for a variety of industries seeking to unlock their hidden value.

Keywords: Vectorization of Enterprise Data · Large Language Models · Semantic Search

1 Introduction

In today's rapidly changing digital landscape, users demand fast, accurate access to information. Existing search solutions on enterprise websites often struggle to capture the semantic context and implicit relationships between data, resulting in poor search results and user dissatisfaction [6]. Traditional keyword-based search techniques often fail to deliver relevant results and understand user intent, leading to suboptimal user experiences and potentially lost business opportunities. This is because they require keyword overlap between the query entered

A. Lopata et al. (Eds.): ICIST 2023, CCIS 1979, pp. 148–159, 2024.
https://doi.org/10.1007/978-3-031-48981-5_12

and the indexed documents. This forces the user to have domain knowledge in phrasing, as synonyms may not be recognized by the search system. In addition, the keyword-based approach does not take into account the context of a text and therefore cannot distinguish between homonyms or find information for complex questions. Information retrieval models, including the Boolean, vector space, and probabilistic models, are essential components of modern search engines. These models attempt to satisfy users' subjective information needs by accurately processing their search queries [13]. Due to their complex and often opaque mechanisms, users often perceive search engines as black boxes, making them difficult to use and reducing customer satisfaction. Another important consideration is the different information needs of different target groups. For example, a typical customer may be looking for in-depth information about a specific product, while a potential business partner may be more interested in understanding the company's technological capabilities and strategic focus.

In this paper, we investigate and present the implementation of a domain-adaptive question-answering framework. For our feasibility study, we use data from an industrial company that develops, produces, and sells high-quality measurement and inspection technology. As these products are often highly specialized, there are many technical documents and user manuals available. The company's current search implementation on the website is based on SOLR[1] (Search on Lucene and Resin), an open-source search engine. It provides a working full-text search server by integrating it into a web server environment. As a result, the site's search function is primarily keyword-based and requires users to enter product numbers or almost exact product names. Technical documentation and other documents are not searchable with the current implementation.

In the future, users should be able to not only search for products but also to ask questions about any information related to those products. This should allow the user to get help with technical details, usage of, or problems with products. For this application, all the currently available content on the site such as user guides, blog posts, or technical documentation, should be searchable. In addition, it should be possible to ask not only questions about specific information but also complex questions that require the aggregation of multiple sources of information. This could then be used for a structured analysis of a company's portfolio. Large language models (LLMs) can help transform unstructured website data into structured, searchable databases, improving accessibility and fostering potential collaborations. This application of large language models not only contributes to corporate transparency but also serves as a powerful tool for optimizing collaborative efforts.

To improve the search experience on enterprise websites, this work proposes an innovative approach that combines semantic search and GPT-3.5, a state-of-the-art LLM [3]. On top of that, when an answer is returned, users can ask follow-up questions and engage in subject-specific communication. The result is a domain-adaptive question-answering framework. The purpose of this study is to accomplish the following tasks:

---

[1] https://solr.apache.org, last accessed 2023-07-24.

– Develop a semantic search system that can provide the appropriate context for a search query.
– Investigate GPT-3.5's ability to understand queries and generate meaningful responses based on the given context.
– Develop a framework combining semantic search and GPT-3.5 to improve corporate website retrieval based on documents like product manuals and other unstructured data.

The proposed solution has the potential to transform the search experience on corporate websites by providing users with more relevant, accurate, and context-sensitive results. By leveraging the power of semantic search and LLMs, this study aims at contributing to the ongoing development of advanced search technologies and improving the overall user experience on corporate websites. Ultimately, this research could have a significant impact on user satisfaction, customer engagement, and business outcomes.

In the following, we first give an overview of the state of the art in the area of LLMs and semantic search in Sect. 2. We then describe our approach for a domain-adaptive question-answering framework in Sect. 3. After that, we describe the implementation of our framework in Sect. 4. There, we discuss the data collection and implementation of the system, describe the evaluation, and present the results. Next in Sect. 5, we discuss our findings and the overall approach. Finally, in Sect. 6, we draw conclusions from our study and outline potential future work.

2   Related Work

In this section, we review the existing literature and related work in Natural Language Processing (NLP), specifically discussing the state of the art in LLMs (c.f. Sect. 2.1) and semantic search (c.f. Sect. 2.2).

2.1   Large Language Models

The emergence of LLMs, particularly those based on transformer architectures [17] such as BERT [5], GPT [9], and their successors, has revolutionized the field of NLP and NLU. Transformer models [17] have become the backbone of many state-of-the-art NLP models due to their ability to capture long-range dependencies and contextual information in text.

One of the most influential transformer-based models is BERT. It uses bidirectional context to pre-train deep neural networks on a large text corpus, which can then be fine-tuned for various NLP tasks [5]. The success of BERT has spurred the development of other LLMs such as GPT (Generative Pre-trained Transformer) [9], RoBERTa [7], and T5 (Text-to-Text Transfer Transformer) [11], among others. GPT and its successor, GPT-2, take a unidirectional approach to language modeling, generating text from left to right, one token at a time. These models have shown impressive performance in several NLP tasks, including text generation and question answering [9,10].

As LLMs have evolved, their accessibility has improved, making them available for practical applications. However, larger models do not inherently align with user intent, sometimes producing untrue, toxic, or unhelpful outputs. Researchers have explored fine-tuning models such as GPT-3 with human feedback to align them with user intent, resulting in models called InstructGPT. In human evaluations of the distribution of prompts, outputs from the 1.3B parameter InstructGPT model are preferred to outputs from the 175B parameter GPT-3 model, even though it has 100 times fewer parameters. Moreover, InstructGPT models show improvements in truthfulness and reductions in toxic output generation, while having minimal performance regressions on public NLP datasets. Although InstructGPT still makes simple mistakes, the results show that fine-tuning with human feedback is a promising direction for aligning language models with human intent [3,8].

Now, models such as GPT-3.5 are easily accessible through APIs provided by organizations such as OpenAI, enabling small and medium-sized enterprises (SMEs) to use these tools without extensive computing resources or expertise in artificial intelligence and NLP. As a result, SMEs can benefit from the cutting-edge capabilities of LLMs to enhance their products, services, and customer experiences and remain competitive in today's rapidly evolving technological landscape [3,8]. Since GPT models are closed source, there is a need for open source alternatives that can be self-hosted, fine-tuned, and extensively evaluated. Models such as OPT [19], MPT [15], LLaMa [16], and Falcon [1] are publicly available and vary in size, performance, training data, hardware requirements, and capabilities.

2.2 Semantic Search

In recent years, advances in semantic search, driven by deep learning techniques, have significantly improved the ability of search engines to understand and process natural language queries [5,10]. Semantic search aims to provide more meaningful and contextual results by analyzing the intent and contextual meaning of search queries, rather than relying solely on keyword matching [2]. As discussed in Sect. 2.1, deep learning models have shown significant effectiveness in many natural language understanding (NLU) tasks. These tasks include but are not limited to question answering, named entity recognition, and sentiment analysis. Models such as the Universal Sentence Encoder [4], SBERT [12], XLNet [18], or DistilBERT [14] can be used to generate sentence embeddings that capture the semantic context within a vector space. These sentence embeddings can be compared semantically by computing distance metrics such as cosine similarity or Euclidean distance. This allows texts to be ranked by their semantic similarity, which is used in semantic search. By storing sentence embeddings in vector databases, it is possible to search for relevant documents for a given query on a large scale. These advances have opened up new possibilities for improving the search experience.

Enterprise search engines can better understand user queries, extract relevant information from unstructured data sources such as documents, product manuals, and customer reviews, and deliver more accurate, relevant, and personalized results by using deep learning-based semantic search techniques. As a result, they can significantly improve user satisfaction, streamline information access, and increase overall business productivity.

3   Domain-Adaptive Question-Answering Framework

Here we describe our approach to integrating semantic search and a conversational LLM as a domain-adaptive question-answering framework. This framework requires two interacting components: The semantic search pipeline (cf. Sect. 3.1) and the conversational question-answering model (cf. Sect. 3.2), which uses the result of the search pipeline as context for answer generation. The framework is adaptable to any domain because any textual data can be stored and retrieved as language-independent embeddings within the search pipeline. Relevant content to the user's query is retrieved by the pipeline so that the question-answering model is able to generate an appropriate response to the user's query. The architecture of the described framework is shown in Fig. 1.

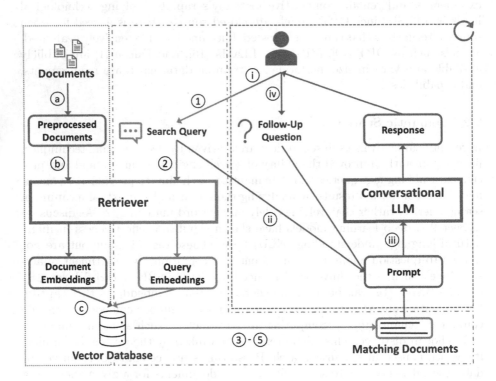

Fig. 1. Framework for domain-adaptive question answering.

3.1   Semantic Search Pipeline

The semantic search pipeline includes a vector database and an embedding model that is referenced as a retriever. The use of this pipeline can be divided into two distinct stages: filling the vector database and querying it.

Filling is performed each time new data is to be uploaded to the database. Three steps are performed: (a) Raw data preprocessing. In this step, the content is extracted from various file formats, such as Portable Document Format (PDF) files, the content of the documents is cleaned to remove irrelevant or noisy information, and then the documents are split using a user-defined chunking algorithm. This splitting algorithm can be applied at different levels of granularity, such as words, sentences, or passages, and can also use a sliding window approach. (b) Compute embedding representations. Each document chunk is passed to the retriever to compute an embedding. (c) Store the document chunks. The chunks are stored in the database together with their metadata and embedding representations.

The database query stage is performed when a user query is entered and matching documents need to be retrieved. (1) Enter the user query. The user query is entered and sent to the pipeline. (2) Embed the query. The query is sent to the retriever, which converts it to an embedding representation. (3) Compute the distance metric. The embedded query is compared to every embedded document in the database by computing a distance metric, such as cosine similarity (which measures angle only) or dot product (which measures both angle and magnitude). (4) Sort documents. Documents are sorted in descending order based on their respective computed distance metrics. (5) Retrieve the top k documents. The first k documents with the highest calculated distance metric values are returned as the most relevant search results.

3.2   Conversational Question-Answering System

We use the GPT-3.5 API as a domain-adaptive question-answering system. The API was chosen for its ease of use and low hardware and cost requirements for this prototype implementation. This could also be done with self-hosted models that require more resources and optimization. The component follows a systematic process to generate meaningful interactions with users.

Interaction with the API involves the use of three types of messages. User messages can be any kind of prompt that the assistant (the underlying model) should respond to. Assistant messages are model responses. System messages are user-defined and specify how the assistant should respond. Therefore, system messages do not trigger an assistant response, but they influence all assistant responses that are triggered by user messages. The history of all messages within a conversation is sent to the API and returned by the API with each new message.

In our proposed system, the user interacts with an interface that hides the background computation but allows the user to use it as a chatbot. (i) Enter the user query. The entered query is first passed to the semantic search pipeline. This returns the top k documents that match the query. (ii) Initial prompt creation. A prompt pattern is filled with the query and the returned documents. The prompt consists of the task to act as a question-answering model, the top k documents and the user query to be answered within the given context of the documents. (iii) The assistant generates a response that is displayed to the user. (iv) If the user is not satisfied with the response, he or she can enter follow-up questions. The assistant receives the conversation and references can be made to previous messages. From this point on, steps (iii) and (iv) continue in a loop.

4   Experiments

In this section, we will implement the proposed framework with some of the company's data (c.f. Sect. 4.1). Furthermore, we will perform an evaluation by creating a list of questions to be answered by the implemented system (c.f. Sect. 4.2). Finally, the results will be presented (c.f. Sect. 4.3).

4.1   Data Acquisition and Implementation

To demonstrate the proposed framework, we implement the semantic search pipeline and the GPT-3.5 interaction, which can be accessed through a web application. We apply sample enterprise data to this system and then perform an evaluation. The first step is to collect and process the data to be retrieved by the pipeline.

For this showcase, we want to narrow down the search space. Therefore, we limit our data collection to user manuals only. We take the published user manuals that are available for download from the company's website and use that data to populate the database. In total, we collected 131 PDF files containing user manuals in several languages, such as English, German, French, Italian, etc. We extract the textual content of these files and split the content of each document to obtain document splits containing up to 6 passages each. For this evaluation, we do not use a sliding window and we store each document only once, instead of having multiple splits of different sizes. We also clean the documents of blank lines and multiple whitespaces. Otherwise, the documents remain as they are and are not optimized for content to show the effect of using data that is not specifically optimized or even created for this scenario. Finally, the documents are converted to embedding vectors using OpenAI's text-embedding-ada-002-model[2] and stored in an elasticsearch database. Again, the OpenAI-API could also be replaced by a self-hosted model such as those described in Sect. 2.2. We implemented a small web application based on Streamlit[3], Haystack[4], and the OpenAI-API[5]. This application captures the interaction with the semantic

---

[2] https://openai.com/blog/new-and-improved-embedding-model, last accessed 2023-07-24.
[3] https://streamlit.io, last accessed 2023-07-24.
[4] https://haystack.deepset.ai, last accessed 2023-07-24.
[5] https://platform.openai.com, last accessed 2023-07-24.

search pipeline and the GPT-3.5 model. Users can interact with this application to enter queries, view generated answers, and ask follow-up questions.

Figure 2 shows a sample conversation in which the user asks a specific question about the company's industry. Additionally, a follow-up question is asked about the product portfolio, and the system provides the correct context-sensitive answer.

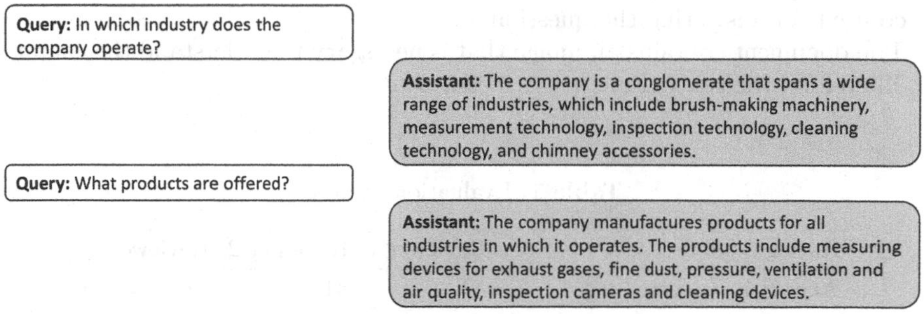

> **Query:** In which industry does the company operate?

> **Assistant:** The company is a conglomerate that spans a wide range of industries, which include brush-making machinery, measurement technology, inspection technology, cleaning technology, and chimney accessories.

> **Query:** What products are offered?

> **Assistant:** The company manufactures products for all industries in which it operates. The products include measuring devices for exhaust gases, fine dust, pressure, ventilation and air quality, inspection cameras and cleaning devices.

Fig. 2. Example of how to answer and continue with a follow-up.

4.2 Evaluation

To evaluate the implemented system, conversations with the system were created and finally evaluated by three independent annotators. For this purpose, documents were first randomly selected from the corpus of user manuals. Then, questions were created manually for each selected document. The questions were created with as much variation as possible so that both simple questions aimed at reproducing specific information and questions whose answers require a comprehensive understanding of the context were included.

The collected questions were submitted to the system. In case of imprecise or incorrect answers, follow-up questions were entered by the user to clarify the question or improve the generated answer. Finally, the completed conversations were stored for later review. The three annotators were presented with a visualization of a stored conversation showing all messages, the initial query, and the retrieved documents, as well as the document used to create the initial query. The goal of the evaluation was to evaluate these generated conversations. Therefore, each annotator received all stored conversations. Their task was to classify whether an initial question was answered correctly, answered incompletely, or not answered. More detailed feedback could be entered as comments.

4.3 Results

For the evaluation, we collected 50 different conversations, which were classified and commented on by three independent annotators. The distribution of ratings per annotator is shown in Table 1. On average, 83% of the total conversations were classified as correctly answering the initial question. In contrast, 4% were incomplete and 13% were incorrect or had no answer at all. Comments focused on incomplete and failed conversations. The main problems identified were as follows:

- The document containing the relevant context was not found. Therefore, the model could not generate an answer.
- An alternative document was found that could only partially serve as the context for answering the question.
- The document contains an image that is necessary to understand the context. Therefore, the textual answer is incomplete.

Table 1. Evaluation results.

Rating	Reviewer 1	Reviewer 2	Reviewer 3
Answer is correct	42	41	41
Answer is incomplete	2	3	1
Answer is incorrect/no answer	6	6	8

5   Discussion

The evaluation of the implemented domain-adaptive question-answering system with user manuals has shown that the system can adapt to domain-specific data and provide accurate answers to user-generated questions. However, there were cases where the system failed to satisfy the user's request. These failures can be caused by several aspects of the system.

The first aspect is the configuration of data processing and database population. Our approach to document splitting did not include more complex solutions that store the same documents in different sizes with overlapping content or use sliding windows. These approaches could improve search performance by storing many more sections for the matching algorithm to find the best match. In contrast to this benefit, there is a storage overhead due to redundancy, and the search pipeline could tend to return either mostly short or long documents, resulting in either very little or too much context.

The second issue is data quality. For this showcase, we did not use optimized content but rather took the existing content as is. Inaccurate wording, missing information, and long sections that are not self-contained and require further information from other documents or document splits can all lead to either poor search performance or poor question-answer performance. In addition, image-heavy documents without descriptions and incompatible table formatting were present in the evaluated corpus. Since the processing steps and models are mostly unable to handle such data, the question-answer system lacks context when answering certain questions.

The third aspect is the configuration of the database query stage. The proposed system does not allow questions to be reformulated to create a new query. Currently, there is an initial query and further user input is sent to the conversational LLM without querying the database again. Therefore, a new conversation must be started if the documents found do not provide enough context. Another problem is the chosen splitting scheme, which divides documents into six passages. Depending on the content, these passages can vary drastically in length. In addition, our chosen conversation model, GPT-3.5, is limited to a certain input length. Therefore, we configured the pipeline to return only the three most similar documents before entering them into the prompt. On the one hand, this ensures that model interactions do not fail, but on the other hand, it is possible that the three documents do not capture all the context that would be necessary to answer the initial question correctly.

6   Conclusion and Future Work

In summary, the emergence of LLMs based on transformer architectures has significantly advanced the state of the art in NLP and NLU, enabling the development of more sophisticated applications and solutions in various domains, including corporate search and information retrieval. This paper demonstrates the potential of combining semantic search and LLMs as a powerful domain-aware question-answering system. By populating a database with document data and corresponding embeddings, the system allows users to enter any data-specific question, then finds the necessary information, and generates appropriate answers, thus making it adaptable to various domains, although its performance is subject to various limitations and considerations. Some of these are data quality, data processing, retrieval configuration, and integration settings. Our approach can improve the customer experience by allowing the user to interact with the entire domain or product knowledge using the conversational question-answering system. Thus, the system is complementary to existing keyword-based search systems, as common product searches will still be necessary and enhanced by the proposed framework.

In future work, the framework can be extended to overcome certain shortcomings, such as the inability to reformulate initial queries to guide the underlying search system to a better result. Furthermore, the data generation for this scenario and the data processing should be further investigated in order to standardize the approaches. Moreover, the framework should be evaluated in other domains with broader document types and content, using different models as retrievers and question-answering systems. For more complex questions, where the answer requires the analysis of multiple documents and the combination of information to produce a report, a deeper and more structured evaluation should be conducted. This could be, for example, an automated analysis of a company's product portfolio to find products, services, or skills that could be leveraged in planned projects. Finally, the trustworthiness of such an application should be further investigated. By self-hosting the models and the application stack, privacy can be ensured. Furthermore, local explanations of model results should be offered, such as providing the cited sources or explaining strange behavior in edge cases.

Acknowledgments. This work was co-funded by the German Federal Ministry of Education and Research under grants 13N16242 and 01IO2208E.

References

1. Almazrouei, E., et al.: Falcon-40B: an open large language model with state-of-the-art performance (2023)
2. Bast, H., Buchhold, B., Haussmann, E.: Semantic search on text and knowledge bases. Found. Trends® Inf. Retrieval **10**(2–3), 119–271 (2016). https://doi.org/10.1561/1500000032
3. Brown, T., et al.: Language models are few-shot learners. In: Larochelle, H., Ranzato, M., Hadsell, R., Balcan, M., Lin, H. (eds.) Advances in Neural Information Processing Systems, vol. 33, pp. 1877–1901. Curran Associates, Inc. (2020). https://proceedings.neurips.cc/paper_files/paper/2020/file/1457c0d6bfcb4967418bfb8ac142f64a-Paper.pdf
4. Cer, D., et al.: Universal sentence encoder for English. In: Proceedings of the 2018 Conference on Empirical Methods in Natural Language Processing: System Demonstrations, pp. 169–174. Association for Computational Linguistics, Brussels (2018). https://doi.org/10.18653/v1/D18-2029. https://aclanthology.org/D18-2029
5. Devlin, J., Chang, M.W., Lee, K., Toutanova, K.: BERT: pre-training of deep bidirectional transformers for language understanding. In: Proceedings of the 2019 Conference of the North American Chapter of the Association for Computational Linguistics: Human Language Technologies, Volume 1 (Long and Short Papers), pp. 4171–4186. Association for Computational Linguistics, Minneapolis (2019). https://doi.org/10.18653/v1/N19-1423. https://aclanthology.org/N19-1423
6. Hirschberg, J., Manning, C.D.: Advances in natural language processing. Science **349**(6245), 261–266 (2015). https://doi.org/10.1126/science.aaa8685
7. Liu, Y., et al.: RoBERTa: a robustly optimized BERT pretraining approach. CoRR abs/1907.11692 (2019). http://arxiv.org/abs/1907.11692
8. Ouyang, L., et al.: Training language models to follow instructions with human feedback. In: Koyejo, S., Mohamed, S., Agarwal, A., Belgrave, D., Cho, K., Oh, A. (eds.) Advances in Neural Information Processing Systems, vol. 35, pp. 27730–27744. Curran Associates, Inc. (2022). https://proceedings.neurips.cc/paper_files/paper/2022/file/b1efde53be364a73914f58805a001731-Paper-Conference.pdf
9. Radford, A., Narasimhan, K., Salimans, T., Sutskever, I., et al.: Improving language understanding by generative pre-training. OpenAI Blog (2018)
10. Radford, A., Wu, J., Child, R., Luan, D., Amodei, D., Sutskever, I., et al.: Language models are unsupervised multitask learners. OpenAI Blog **1**(8), 9 (2019)
11. Raffel, C., et al.: Exploring the limits of transfer learning with a unified text-to-text transformer. J. Mach. Learn. Res. **21**(140), 1–67 (2020). http://jmlr.org/papers/v21/20-074.html

12. Reimers, N., Gurevych, I.: Sentence-BERT: sentence embeddings using Siamese BERT-networks. In: Proceedings of the 2019 Conference on Empirical Methods in Natural Language Processing and the 9th International Joint Conference on Natural Language Processing (EMNLP-IJCNLP), pp. 3982–3992. Association for Computational Linguistics, Hong Kong (2019). https://doi.org/10.18653/v1/D19-1410. https://aclanthology.org/D19-1410
13. Saini, B., Singh, V., Kumar, S.: Information retrieval models and searching methodologies: survey. Int. J. Adv. Found. Res. Sci. Eng. (IJAFRSE) **1**, 20 (2014)
14. Sanh, V., Debut, L., Chaumond, J., Wolf, T.: DistilBERT, a distilled version of BERT: smaller, faster, cheaper and lighter. CoRR abs/1910.01108 (2019). http://arxiv.org/abs/1910.01108
15. Team, M.N.: Introducing MPT-7B: a new standard for open-source, commercially usable LLMs (2023). www.mosaicml.com/blog/mpt-7b. Accessed 24 July 2023
16. Touvron, H., et al.: LLaMA: open and efficient foundation language models (2023)
17. Vaswani, A., et al.: Attention is all you need. In: Guyon, I., et al. (eds.) Advances in Neural Information Processing Systems, vol. 30. Curran Associates, Inc. (2017). https://proceedings.neurips.cc/paper_files/paper/2017/file/3f5ee243547dee91fbd053c1c4a845aa-Paper.pdf
18. Yang, Z., Dai, Z., Yang, Y., Carbonell, J.G., Salakhutdinov, R., Le, Q.V.: XLNet: generalized autoregressive pretraining for language understanding. In: Wallach, H.M., Larochelle, H., Beygelzimer, A., d'Alché-Buc, F., Fox, E.B., Garnett, R. (eds.) Advances in Neural Information Processing Systems 32: NeurIPS 2019, Vancouver, BC, Canada, pp. 5754–5764 (2019)
19. Zhang, S., et al.: OPT: open pre-trained transformer language models (2022)

Synergizing Reinforcement Learning for Cognitive Medical Decision-Making in Sepsis Detection

Lakshita Singh[✉] [ID] and Lakshay Kamra [ID]

Department of Applied Mathematics, Delhi Technological University, Delhi, India
laks1806@uw.edu

Abstract. When the body's defense against an infection damages its own tissues and causes organ malfunction, it develops sepsis, a catastrophic medical illness. Administering intravenous fluids and antibiotics promptly can increase the patient's chances of survival. In order to determine the best treatment plans for septic patients, this study investigates the application of deep reinforcement learning and continuous state-space models. The method produces clinically comprehensible policies that could assist doctors in intensive care in empowering medical professionals to make informed decisions that ultimately enhance the prospects of patient survival.

Keywords: Dueling Double Deep Q Learning Networks (DDDQN) · Sepsis · MIMIC III · Deep-Q

1 Introduction

Sepsis is a clinical syndrome caused by the invasion of bacteria and/or toxins that triggers a harmful reaction in the body, leading to severe morbidity and mortality [1]. Failure to detect and manage this condition early can result in organ failure, septic shock, and death. To improve patient outcomes, it is crucial to detect sepsis as soon as possible, as each hour of delayed treatment after hypotension increases the risk of dying from septic shock by 7.6%. Recent studies have shown that administering a 3-h bundle of care for sepsis patients, including a blood culture, broad-spectrum antibiotics, and lactate measurement, can significantly reduce in-hospital mortality [3]. Therefore, timely and aggressive treatment is essential in managing sepsis. Even experienced professionals face difficulties in diagnosing sepsis early and accurately, as its symptoms can be easily confused with those of other medical conditions. However, the electronic health record (EHR) already captures data that could aid in predicting sepsis, despite the challenges that come with the diagnosis of this condition [2]. Hence, early warning scores that rely on data from the EHR hold great promise in detecting early clinical deterioration in real-time. The National Early Warning Score (NEWS) was developed, validated, and implemented by the Royal College of Physicians to detect patients who are acutely decompensating. NEWS employs six physiological variables and compares them to their expected ranges to produce a single composite score. In addition to antibiotics, intra-venous fluids and vasopressors are used in severe cases. However, patients' mortality rates vary considerably depending on the fluid and vasopressor therapy methods used, highlighting the importance of making the right choices. In the realm of sepsis manage-ment, the absence of tailored real-time decision support has posed significant challenges for healthcare providers despite international efforts to provide general guidelines [13]. In response to this pressing issue, we present a pioneering data-driven approach that leverages advanced deep reinforcement learning (RL) algorithms to optimize sepsis treatment strategies. This study builds upon previous research and seeks to enhance the likelihood of septic patients' survival in the ICU by utilizing continuous- state space models and shaped reward functions to identify the most effective course of action. Our findings represent a crucial contribution to the field of sepsis treatment, as they pave the way for personalized and real-time decision-making strategies that have the potential to transform patient outcomes and reduce mortality rates. We chose RL over supervised learning because there is a lack of consensus in the medical literature on what consti-tutes an effective treatment approach. It is worth noting that RL algorithms enable us to derive optimal strategies from training samples that do not correspond to optimal behav-ior. Our primary emphasis lies in the development of continuous state-space modeling, a sophisticated methodology that utilizes a patient's physiological data from the ICU to represent their current physiological state as a continuous vector at any given instant. We use Deep-Q Learning to determine the appropriate responses. Our study presents remarkable contributions in the realm of patient care, including the generation of treat-ment plans that have the potential to augment patient outcomes and significantly decrease patient mortality rates. We achieved this by implementing advanced deep reinforcement learning models that incorporate continuous-state spaces and precisely designed reward functions [3].

2   Background and Motivation

The initial diagnosis of sepsis poses a daunting challenge owing to its inconspicuous presentation, characterized by clinical manifestations resembling those of less severe ailments [5]. While international initiatives try to offer generic recommendations for managing sepsis, doctors at the bedside still lack effective technologies to offer tailored real-time decision support. Developing and validating early warning scores to forecast clinical deterioration and other related outcomes has been the subject of a significant amount of research. For instance, two of the most popular scores used to gauge overall clinical deterioration are the MEWS score and NEWS score. Additionally, the sys-temic inflammatory response syndrome (SIRS) score (Fig. 1) was a component of the initial clinical definition of sepsis, however more recently, other sepsis-specific scores have gained popularity, including SOFA and qSOFA. The Rothman Index, a more com-plex regression-based method, is also often used to identify general deterioration. In numerous related investigations, multitask Gaussian processes were also used to sim-ulate multivariate physiological time series [15]. Several studies utilized a model that was comparable to ours but placed more emphasis on forecasting vital signs to predict clinical instability.

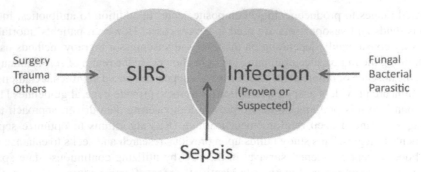

Fig. 1. The systematic inflammatory response syndrome [6].

2.1 SERA Algorithm

The SERA algorithm is a risk assessment tool designed to identify patients who may be at risk for sepsis. The algorithm uses both structured and unstructured data from patient consultations to make a prediction. The algorithm is designed to operate on a patient-by-patient basis, with each consultation serving as an analytical unit. It is composed of two interrelated algorithms: the diagnosis algorithm and the early prediction algorithm. When a patient is examined, the diagnosis algorithm determines if the patient is presently suffering from sepsis.

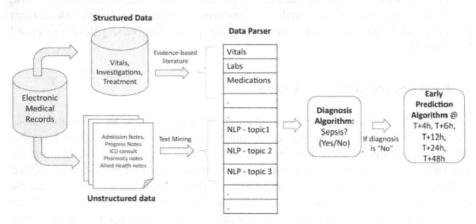

Fig. 2. The development process of the SERA algorithm, a tool that utilizes both structured and unstructured data to diagnose and predict sepsis, is depicted in a flow diagram. The algorithm is designed to function in a standard clinical setting where physicians rely on various data sources to analyze and diagnose patients [4].

On the other hand, the early prediction algorithm ascertains whether sepsis is likely to manifest within the next four hours if the patient does not already have the condition. The algorithm incorporates both structured and unstructured data in its processing. While structured data entails vital signs, investigation results, and treatment details, the unstructured data encompasses clinical notes. Developed to operate in a typical clinical setting, where physicians utilize both types of data to analyze and diagnose patients, the algorithm's construction procedures are illustrated in the elaborate flow diagram presented in Fig. 2.

Supervised learning, particularly in medical applications, has been hindered by the challenge of frequently missing labels per time point in time series datasets. This issue also affects early diagnosis of sepsis. Prior research has addressed the problem of defining resolved sepsis labels by utilizing ad-hoc approaches. These studies have relied on readily available ad-hoc criteria to predict the onset of sepsis and have used a global time series label, such as an ICD illness number designed for billing purposes, to define resolved sepsis labels.

2.2   Algorithms for the Early Detection of Sepsis SERA Algorithm

Over the past 10 years, several data-driven approaches for detecting sepsis in the ICU have been proposed. Numerous methods compare only certain clinical scores, including SIRS, NEWS, or MEWS. None of these ratings, meanwhile, are meant to serve as precise, ongoing sepsis risk scores. Doctors now view the SIRS criteria as being non-specific and out of date for the definition of sepsis. A targeted real-time warning score (TREWS-core) was presented as an alternative to these scores to predict septic shock, which is a common consequence after sepsis [12]. Notably, even though numerous machine learning techniques have outperformed general-purpose or oversimplified clinical schemes, almost no articles have actually made a direct comparison to other machine learning techniques in the literature. It has been demonstrated that using LSTMs is better than using the InSight model. Modern technology Sepsis prevalence numbers range from 6.6% to 21.4%, and real-world datasets with these prevalence values are typically used to build sepsis detection techniques.

2.3   Reinforcement Learning in Medicine

Reinforcement Learning, an intricate framework for optimizing sequential decision-making, has emerged as a game-changing paradigm. In this sophisticated framework, a Markov Decision Process (MDP), which constitutes a 5-tuple (S, A, r, γ, p), serves as the foundation for its seamless operation. Different applications in the field of medicine have used reinforcement learning. References and surveys offer thorough analyses of applications in critical care and healthcare, respectively. Doctors employed dynamic programming-based approaches to construct the best treatment plans for sepsis using a discrete state representation was crafted by leveraging a 25-dimensional discrete action space and clustering patient physiological readouts. Others have thought about partial observability and continuous state representations. Our suggested decision support system makes decisions, based on a preference score (Fig. 3).

2.3.1   Gaussian Process Adapters

It was demonstrated that maximizing a time series end-to-end GP [4] imputation using the gradients of a subsequent classifier outperforms individually improving the classifier and the GP. This technique, also known as GP adapters, is not just for imputed missing data. GP adapters have recently been shown to be a suitable framework for handling the 13 unevenly spaced time series in early sepsis detection. They specifically supported earlier findings that GP adapters outperform traditional GP imputation approaches in time series classification, which call on a separate optimization step unrelated to the classification objective.

2.3.2 Markov Decision Process

Typically, mathematical models for sequential decision problems are formulated as Markov decision processes (MDPs), which consist of a tuple M = (S, A, P, r). In this context, S refers to the possible states of the system, A represents the feasible actions that can be taken, P represents the probability distribution for the next state given the current state and action, and r denotes the reward function that assigns a scalar reward to each state-action pair [6].

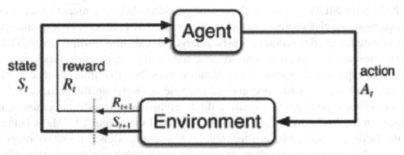

Fig. 3. The proposed approach of deep reinforcement learning boasts a sophisticated network architecture with numerous features and an aesthetically pleasing design [8].

Figure 3 shows the use of Markov Decision Process (MDP) to model time-varying state spaces in reinforcement learning. Amidst the realm of artificial intelligence, the agent observes the state of the environment at each timestep denoted by s(t), and executes an action a(t) followed by earning a reward r(t), leading to a transition to a new state s(t + 1). The ultimate goal of the agent lies in the maximization of the projected discounted future reward, popularly known as the "return", by choosing the most suitable activities. Previous studies have applied reinforcement learning in healthcare contexts, including treating septic patients using models with discretized state and action-spaces. In this study, we used value-iteration procedures to discover an ideal policy, determined by contrasting the Q-values obtained under it with those of a doctor's 14 policy [14]. We improved upon this by utilizing continuous state-space models, deep reinforcement learning, and a clinically oriented reward function. We also evaluated how the learned policies serve patients of varying severity levels.

3   Dataset

We have used the Multiparameter Intelligent Monitoring in Intensive Care (MIMIC-III v1.4) database [7] to conduct this research. It is a freely available dataset which provides us with comprehensive data. This data is generally taken every four hours and the data is recorded, when several data points are present. It yields a feature vector of dimensions 48x1 at a given time 't' and the state at this time is called St. The data provided by MIMIC-III is focused on patients with sepsis-3 symptoms. Since, we must apply multiple queries on the data set, so to filter out relevant data, it is first pre-processed using postgreSQL [9] and relations and tables are built [reference], further the processed data is analyzed to get a MIMIC TABLE, which is directly used as the data source for out RL Algorithm.

4   Hardware/Software Requirements

Our project on Data Analytics was implemented on a Windows operating system with Jupyter Notebook. The experiments have partly been conducted with Ryzen 7 CPU, 16GB RAM, and Nvidia RTX 3050 GPU with 4GB Memory. These requirements were enough to run python and any desired ML algorithm.

The project majorly uses Python. Some important libraries are Matplotlib, NumPy and Pandas and is carried in the Jupyter notebook.

- Python: It is designed to be easy to read and write, with a clean syntax and an emphasis on readability and simplicity. Its popularity stems from its ease of use, powerful standard library, and large number of third-party modules and packages. Python's community development model and open-source license have also contributed to its widespread adoption and continued growth.
- NumPy: A distinguished Python package that caters to the realm of numerical analysis and scientific computing. It endows an unparalleled N-dimensional array object and a vast array of mathematical operations that can be performed effortlessly on these arrays. The versatility of NumPy makes it a quintessential tool for researchers, scientists, and analysts across various fields such as physics, engineering, economics, machine learning, and more.
- Matplotlib: A plotting library for Python that allows users to create high-quality, publishable graphs and visualizations. It provides a range of visualization tools, from simple line charts to 3D charts.
- Pandas: A library for data manipulation and analysis. It provides data structures for efficiently storing and querying large datasets, as well as powerful tools for data cleaning, aggregation, and visualization. Pandas is widely used in data science, finance, and other fields dealing with large amounts of data.
- Scikit-learn: A formidable machine learning library for Python, presents an array of powerful tools beyond just model selection and evaluation. Its rich repertoire boasts of an exquisite set of methods for classification, regression, clustering, and dimensionality reduction, all crafted to elevate the art of machine learning to the next level.
- PostgreSQL: PostgreSQL is a powerful open-source relational database management system. It is widely used in web applications, data science, and other fields that require robust and scalable data storage.

- TQDM: TQDM is a library for creating progress bars in Python. It is often used in long-running processes, such as data processing or model training, to provide users with feedback on the progress of an operation.

5 Research Methodology

5.1 Action Space

We will work with a discrete action space for this research. The action space [10] defined is a 5×5 matrix which will cover maximum vasopressor dose and Intravenous fluids dose over a period of four hours. The action space is defined such that it covers all the non-zero dosages of VP and IV fluids, measured per/dosage and converted into an integer value by the concatenation of dosage, drug and the time stamp. All the zero dosage entries will be represented by 0 bin value. Medical data and records are very uncertain when it comes to finding the appropriate tuples for the action space, that's why we are going forward with the standard i.e., total IV fluid dosage and max Vasopressor dosage as our key tuples for the action space.

5.2 Reward Function

We need a successfully working reward function [10] to map each state-action pair with a numeric value which will intrinsically define the value of that state, which will finally help our model to reach conclusions and not just predictions. We basically measure the lactate levels defining the cell hypoxia and SOFA score which gives a numeric value to measure organ failure in sepsis patients to define the overall health of a sepsis-3 patient. These two measures are the key features of our reward function where increase in SOFA score and lactate levels will result in a negative reward. For a terminal patient, at the time of ending state, the state is rewarded positive if he survives, otherwise negative.

5.3 Model-Used

The model used in this research is Dueling Double Deep Q Learning Networks (DDDQN) [11], which is based on a variant of DQN can be seen in Fig. 5 (Fig. 4).

DDDQN minimizes the error between target and output. We use neural approximation of Q * (s,a) which yields optimal value function. If we include θ in this function, we can easily calculate the output of the networks, i.e., $Q(s, a; \theta)$.

The desired output given by the model is $Q_{target} = r + \gamma * \max_{a'}(s', a', \theta)$ where we have sets of the form $<s, a, r, s'>$. To minimize the expected loss between Q_{target} and Q_{output} we introduce a stochastic batch gradient descent in your model. Moreover, since the target values are highly volatile, addition of an extra network, which is dynamically upgraded, helps to improve the overall yield. The basic Deep Q Networks are not very efficient due to the problem of overestimation, which is very persistent in these networks, which generally leads to incorrect predictions and large error ranges. This problem of overestimation is due to the presence of Max of Q value for the next state in the Q learning update equation. This is solved through a better variant of DQN, i.e., double deep Q networks (DDQN), where we calculate the Q value by a feed-forward pass on the

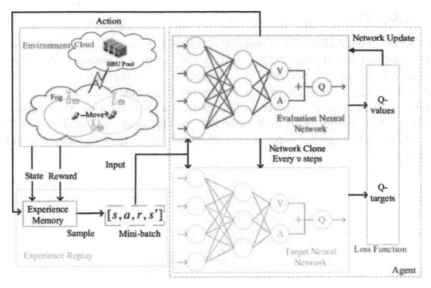

Fig. 4. An illustration of dueling deep-Q-network [16].

main network rather than using the main network directly for calculation of Q values. Now, to solve another problem, i.e., when we find optimal treatments, we have to ignore the influence of the previous state if it has a positive reward and correct action is to be taken at the present time stamp. For this we turn to Dueling deep Q network (DDDQN), where the values of 19 tuples action and state given by Q(s,a) are divided in two parts namely, estimation of advantage of a stage representing the quality of chosen action and estimation of flow of value representing the quality of chosen state. This yields a fully formed Dueling Double-Deep Q Network in Fig. 6 having 2 hidden layers of size 128, combining the above ideas [11]. The training of the model based on this methodology gives us the optimal state of a patient as, $\pi * (s) = \arg \max_a Q(s, a)$.

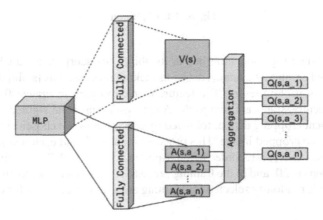

Fig. 5. Architecture of DDDQN [17].

5.4 RL Algorithm

Start with the initialization of two Q networks, D3QN-A network defined as $Q^A(s, a; \theta^A)$ and D3QN-B network defined as $Q^B(s, a; \theta^B)$. Here all the parameters in the networks are defined by θ^A and θ^B. Secondly, the approach involves initializing the Experience Reply with (s_t, s_{t+1}, a_t, r_t). s_t has two components, the first being a comprehensive feature comprising a basic feature and salience map, and the second being a historical experience vector that preserves previously used action indexes. Our approach initializes a 20 * 13d vector to represent historical experience, with a maximum exploring step of 20 and 13 action numbers.

Initialize $Q^A(s, a; \theta^A)$ and $Q^B(s, a; \theta^B)$ with parameters θ^A and θ^B
Initialize Experience Reply pool
for $episode = 1, episode < N_e pisodes$ do
reset the environment and process initial state s_0
    for $t = 1, t < Max_s teps$ do
        select a cropping action a_t according to ε-greedy
        perform action a_t to get $s(t+1)$ and the instant
reward
        put (s_t, s_{t+1}, a_t, r_t) into Experience Reply pool
        randomly choose a set of (s_i, s_{i+1}, a_i, r_i)
        randomly choose the update network of A or B
        if $episode \% update_s tep = 0$ && update A:
$$a^* = \arg\max_a Q^A(s_{i+1}, a, \theta_t^A)$$
$$y_t^A = \begin{cases} r_{i+1}, s_{i+1} ends \\ r_{i+1} + \gamma Q^B(s_{i+1}, a^*; \theta_t^B), else \end{cases}$$
$$loss = (y_t^A - Q^A(s_t, a_t; \theta_t^A))^2 \quad, \quad update \quad \theta^A$$
with gradient descent
        else if $episode \% update_s tep = 0$ && update Bčž
$$a^* = \arg\max_a Q^B(s_{i+1}, a, \theta_t^B)$$
$$y_t^B = \begin{cases} r_{i+1}, s_{i+1} ends \\ r_{i+1} + \gamma Q^A(s_{i+1}, a^*; \theta_t^A), else \end{cases}$$
$$loss = (y_t^B - Q^B(s_t, a_t; \theta_t^B))^2 \quad, \quad update \quad \theta^B$$
with gradient descent
        end if
        $s_t \rightarrow s_{t+1}$
    end for
end for

Fig. 6. RL Algorithm

The art of state representation lies in its ability to incorporate valuable historical experiences and emulate the human decision-making process, thus facilitating informed decision-making in the present. The feature extraction part generates s0 as the initial state. Subsequently, states are sent to the Agent, which uses the ε-greedy algorithm to select the current cropping action, followed by execution of the chosen cropping action and obtaining the cropped image. This process is repeated, and each one-step cropping operation (s_t, s_{t+1}, a_t, r_t) is recorded in the experience reply pool. The maximum number of cropping steps is 20, and in the training process, N_episodes is set to 160,000, with a group of records randomly selected for learning each time. See Fig. 6 for the algorithm steps.

6 Result

On a held-out test set which was accurately on 50 epochs, the y-axis of the graph depicts mortality rates, which fluctuate based on the variance between recommended dosages dictated by the optimal policy and those administered by healthcare providers, which serves as the return of action. This difference was computed and correlated with whether the patient lived or passed away in the hospital for each timestep as shown in

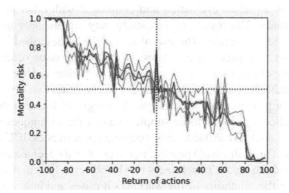

Fig. 7. Plot between the return of the clinician's policy and patients' mortality.

Figure 7, enabling the computation of observed mortality. In Fig. 8, With a 95% confidence level, this bound would always be higher than the clinicians' guideline if enough models were produced. The statistical safety of the novel artificial intelligence (AI) policy in question is a topic of current discourse in theory which is maximized by this model selection method.

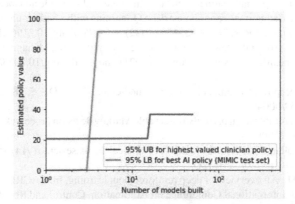

Fig. 8. During the generation of 500 models of MIMIC III, the 95% lower bound of the optimal AI policy is compared with the 95% upper bound of the most esteemed clinician policy established to ascertain the range of values within which they operate.

7 Conclusion

Employing deep learning in this research, the problem of treating sepsis patients is being addressed in a practical manner. The study investigated fully continuous state-space/discrete action space models to discover the most efficient treatment options, learning an estimate for the best action-value function, using Dueling Double-Deep Q networks, Q *(s, a). It was discovered that the resulting continuous state space model generated interpretable regulations that might enhance sepsis treatment. The taught policies will be put through a patient evaluation and contrasted with other investigative algorithms in future study. The results of this study may significantly influence medical practice for sepsis identification. The use of a model like described in the papers can anticipate the onset of sepsis that could lessen the vexing issue of alarm fatigue that plagues the existing clinical scoring systems, improve patient outcomes, and lessen the burden on the healthcare system because sepsis is a condition that is poorly understood and challenging for practitioners to diagnose. Although the focus of this work was on early sepsis identification, it would be simple to adapt the techniques to other clinical events of relevance, such as cardiac arrests, code blue occurrences, ICU admissions, and cardiogenic shock. This will enable practitioner to employ the techniques in a real-world clinical context, and the model's usefulness can be objectively demonstrated by gathering information on the reliability of the warnings it raises and how it is applied on the actual wards.

References

1. Futoma, J.: Gaussian process-based models for clinical time series in healthcare. Doctoral dissertation, Duke University (2018)
2. Raghu, A., et al.: Deep reinforcement learning for sepsis treatment. arXiv preprint arXiv: 1711.09602 (2017)
3. Tardini, E., et al.: Optimal treatment selection in sequential systemic and locoregional therapy of oropharyngeal squamous carcinomas: deep Q-learning with a patient-physician digital twin dyad. J. Med. Internet Res. 24(4), e29455 (2022). https://doi.org/10.2196/29455
4. Goh, K., et al.: Artificial intelligence in sepsis early prediction and diagnosis using unstructured data in healthcare. Nat. Commun. (2021). https://doi.org/10.1038/s41467-021-209 10-4
5. Jonsson, A.: Deep reinforcement learning in medicine. Kidney Dis. 5, 18–22 (2019). https://doi.org/10.1159/000492670
6. Littman, M.L.: A tutorial on partially observable Markov decision processes. J. Math. Psychol. 53(3), 119–125 (2009)
7. Johnson, A., Pollard, T., Mark, R.: MIMIC-III clinical database demo (v14). PhysioNet (2019). https://doi.org/10.13026/C2HM2Q
8. Cao, L., Zhi, M.: An overview of deep reinforcement learning. In: CACRE2019: Proceedings of the 2019 4th International Conference on Automation, Control and Robotics Engineering, pp. 1–9 (2019). https://doi.org/10.1145/3351917.3351989
9. Johnson, A.E.W., et al.: MIMIC-III, a freely accessible critical care database. Sci. Data 3, 160035 (2016)
10. Carew, J.M.: Tech Target blog. Tech Target Enterprise AI. techtarget.com/definition/reinfo rcement-learning

11. Mammen, P.M., Kumar, H.: Explainable AI: Deep reinforcement learning agents for residential demand side cost savings in smart grids (2019)
12. Kim, H.I., Park, S.: Sepsis: early recognition and optimized treatment. https://doi.org/10.4046/trd.2018.0041
13. Barnes, S., Hamrock, E., Toerper, M., Siddiqui, S., Levin, S.: Real-time prediction of inpatient length of stay for discharge prioritization. J. Am. Med. Inform. Assoc. **23**, e2–e10 (2015)
14. Hester, T., et al.: Deep q-learning from demonstrations. In: Thirty-Second AAAI Conference on Artificial Intelligence (2018)
15. Komorowski, M., Celi, L.A., Badawi, O., Gordon, A.C., Faisal, A.A.: The artificial intelligence clinician learns optimal treatment strategies for sepsis in intensive care. Nat. Med. **24**, 1716–1720 (2018). https://doi.org/10.1038/s41591-018-0213-5
16. Guo, B., Zhang, X., Sheng, Q., Yang, H.: Dueling deep-Q-network based delay-aware cache update policy for mobile users in fog radio access networks. IEEE Access 1 (2020). https://doi.org/10.1109/ACCESS.2020.2964258
17. Patel, Y.: Optimizing market making using multi-agent reinforcement learning (2018). https://doi.org/10.13140/RG.2.2.22476.87686

Towards Data Integration for Hybrid Energy System Decision-Making Processes: Challenges and Architecture

Olha Boiko[1,2,3] (iD), Vira Shendryk[1,2,3](✉) (iD), Reza Malekian[1,2] (iD), Anton Komin[3] (iD), and Paul Davidsson[1,2] (iD)

[1] Department of Computer Science and Media Technology, Malmö University, 205 06, Malmö, Sweden
{olha.boiko,vira.shendryk,reza.malekian,paul.davidsson}@mau.se,
{o.boiko,v.shendryk}@cs.sumdu.edu.ua
[2] Internet of Things and People Research Centre, Malmö University, 205 06, Malmö, Sweden
[3] Department of Information Technologies, Sumy State University Sumy, Sumy 40007, Ukraine

Abstract. This paper delves into the challenges encountered in decision-making processes within Hybrid Energy Systems (HES), placing a particular emphasis on the critical aspect of data integration. Decision-making processes in HES are inherently complex due to the diverse range of tasks involved in their management. We argue that to overcome these challenges, it is imperative to possess a comprehensive understanding of the HES architecture and how different processes and interaction layers synergistically operate to achieve the desired outcomes. These decision-making processes encompass a wealth of information and insights pertaining to the operation and performance of HES. Furthermore, these processes encompass systems for planning and management that facilitate decisions by providing a centralized platform for data collection, storage, and analysis. The success of HES largely hinges upon its capacity to receive and integrate various types of information. This includes real-time data on energy demand and supply, weather data, performance data derived from different system components, and historical data, all of which contribute to informed decision-making. The ability to accurately integrate and fuse this diverse range of data sources empowers HES to make intelligent decisions and accurate predictions. Consequently, this data integration capability allows HES to provide a multitude of services to customers. These services include valuable recommendations on demand response strategies, energy usage optimization, energy storage utilization, and much more. By leveraging the integrated data effectively, HES can deliver customized and tailored services to meet the specific needs and preferences of its customers.

Keywords: Hybrid Renewable Energy System · Energy Efficiency · Renewable Energy Sources · Energy Management · Data Flow · Decision-Making · Sustainable Development · Domestic Energy Consumption · Sustainable Growth

© The Author(s), under exclusive license to Springer Nature Switzerland AG 2024
A. Lopata et al. (Eds.): ICIST 2023, CCIS 1979, pp. 172–184, 2024.
https://doi.org/10.1007/978-3-031-48981-5_14

1 Introduction

Population growth and rapid urbanization have led to a significant rise in energy consumption, resulting in increased carbon emissions. However, the implementation of HES technologies is expected to enhance the sustainability of power supply by reducing energy intensity and consumption, thereby mitigating their environmental impact.

The planning and management of the system's structure and energy have crucial social and technological implications for power supply, and the smart system's resilience to social and technical challenges is vital to achieving the Sustainable Development Goals (SDGs) [1]. The term "Sustainable Development" refers to a better and more sustainable future for all. According to the United Nations, it is possible by achieving 17 interconnection goals. One action has an impact on others and there should be a balance among the environmental, societal and economic, components.

In order to meet the goal of SDG 7, which is to ensure an affordable, clean, and reliable energy system, the European Union (EU) has set a target of increasing the share of renewable energy in gross final energy consumption to at least 32% by 2030 [2]. It is important to note that dependency on a single country raises risks, so the EU must increase domestic energy generation, particularly from renewable sources, reduce energy consumption, and invest in updating infrastructure to facilitate the distribution of clean energy throughout the region.

The EU has seen a steadily increase in the use of renewable energy with its share doubling in 2020 when renewables accounted for 22.1% comparing to the share since 2005 that was only 10.2% of gross final energy consumption [3]. This growth can be attributed not only to reductions in investment costs, more efficient technologies, and improvements in supply chains but also to support schemes for renewable energy sources with the introduction of a hybrid energy system.

A hybrid energy system is a system that combines multiple energy sources and technologies to produce energy for electricity, heating, and cooling purposes. It can combine renewable energy sources, such as solar and wind power, with traditional district energy systems. The purpose of a hybrid energy system is to leverage the strengths of different energy sources to achieve a more reliable and cost-effective energy supply.

HESs are intricate, varied, and use a variety of renewable energy sources at different times. It is noteworthy that to use relevant information in support of decision-makings in order to be certain that HES implementation can contribute to increased efficiency, reliability, economic viability and enhance sustainability.

In these conditions, different modeling approaches can be used to predict which type of renewable energy sources is preferable to use [4], and what should be their power. Other research shows that improving information support for decision-making processes can increase the efficiency of HES management [5, 6]. In this condition there is an issue with the diversity and heterogeneity of data sources, which may include data from weather sensors, power meters, energy storage systems, and other sources. These data sources may use different formats, have varying levels of quality and accuracy, and may require different data processing and analysis techniques. This can make it difficult to integrate and analyze data from different sources, leading to inaccurate or incomplete information for decision-making tasks. This is particularly challenging in the context of HESs, which combine different types of energy sources and require complex management strategies to balance their operation.

To address these challenges, it is required to analyze HES models that represent the behavior of the system over time and can provide effective forecasts on consumption and production, as well as insights on how to optimize system operation with a focus on energy efficiency, as well as social and economic aspects.

Thus, we will be able to identify data needed in support of the models and analyses, as well as where it originated from, how it will be used, where information can be duplicated, what another knowledge we need, and how frequently it should be collected.

2 Challenges of Decision-Making Processes in Hybrid Energy Systems

Effective decision-making processes in Hybrid Energy Systems (HES) are crucial for their efficient operation. These processes involve managing system complexity, balancing diverse energy sources, and addressing supply and demand uncertainties. By considering multiple stakeholders and making trade-offs between energy sources, the decision-making aims to achieve the optimal functioning of HES.

One objective of analyzing the challenges related to the decision-making processes in HES is to better understand the difficulties arising from managing the complexity of the system, balancing energy sources, and incorporating data. These challenges encompass issues related to data integration, quality, analysis, and information flow management. Another objective is to identify areas for improvement, such as enhancing data integration techniques, optimizing data analysis methods, improving data accuracy and reliability, and streamlining information flows to ensure efficient and effective operation of HES. However, solving these problems requires an understanding of the system architecture, the processes, and at what level they take place.

2.1 Interaction Layers of Hybrid Energy Systems

The European Committee for Standardization introduced the Smart System Architecture Model (SGAM) to analyze and visualize energy systems use cases in a technology-neutral manner [7]. Therefore, we use this reference model as the basis for the decision-making process for hybrid system management. The SGAM is an architectural framework that provides a structured approach for understanding and designing interoperable smart grid systems. It categorizes interoperability into different levels, reflecting the extent to which components and systems can communicate and interact with one another. As presented in Fig. 1, SGAM's five interaction layers correspond to business goals and processes, functions, information exchange and models, communication protocols, and components [8]. In a HES, data flows from the Business Layer, where goals and requirements are set, to the Function Layer, which utilizes data from the Information Layer. The Communication Layer facilitates this flow, which is implemented through the Component Layer. This interconnected data flow enables efficient operation, informed decision-making, performance optimization, and desired outcomes in the HES.

Figure 1 illustrates connections between objects at the same level, such as physically linking components at the component level, as well as connections between objects at different levels. The connections between layers and the flow of data in a HES can be understood as follows:

- Business Layer to Function Layer: The Business Layer influences functions within the Function Layer by establishing goals and requirements for the HES. It determines the strategic direction and necessary functions for desired outcomes. The SGAM Business Layer connects with the SDGs, supporting sustainability goals. For example, utility and regulatory business models, policies and cost-effective analysis can promote renewable energy, energy efficiency, and demand response for SDGs like climate action, affordable and clean energy, and industry innovation.
- Function Layer to Information Layer: The Function Layer relies on the Information Layer to collect, process, monitor, and manage data related to the operation of the HES. The functions within the HES require access to accurate and timely information about energy demand, supply, weather conditions, performance data, and other relevant parameters. The Information Layer acts as a data provider to enable effective functioning of the functions within the system. In Fig. 1, we specify an number of models useful for the management of hybrid energy system at the Information level.
- Information Layer to Communication Layer: The Information Layer relies on the Communication Layer to facilitate the exchange of data and information between different components and systems within the HES. The Information Layer processes and manages the data, and then the Communication Layer provides the necessary infrastructure and protocols for seamless communication and interoperability.
- Communication Layer to Component Layer: The Component Layer consists of the physical devices and components that make up the HES, such as renewable energy sources, energy storage systems, sensors, and controllers. The Communication Layer enables communication between these physical components, allowing them to exchange data, receive instructions, and coordinate their actions as part of the overall system operation.

In this study, we focus on the information level tasks. The Business Layer defines the business models, which require information systems to support their operation, which is provided by the Information Layer. Information systems collect and process data related to the operation of the HES, such as energy demand, supply, and quality, which are then used by the Business Layer for analysis and making informed decisions.

Several tasks can be considered at the information level at the same time, for instance, this layer can support the development of smart city applications and promote the integration of the HES into urban infrastructure (SDG 11) and enable the monitoring and management of energy consumption and support the integration of renewable energy sources into the HES (SDG 13). Therefore, there is a problem as how to integrate data for different purposes?

2.2 Diversity of Tasks in Hybrid Energy Management

As demonstrated in Fig. 1, the work of Information Layer is implemented by the set of models, which are implemented in appropriate information systems. That work together

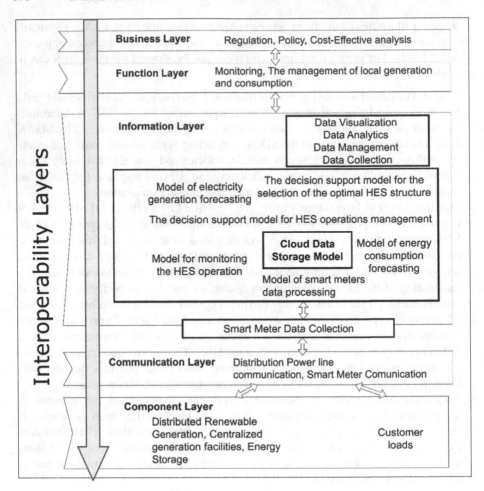

Fig. 1. Interaction layers of Hybrid Energy Systems

to achieve the desired outcome. In the case of an integrated planning system with decision support and management microsystem data flow, there are several subsystems with their own models that are responsible for different aspects of HES management and operation (Table 1). In general, subsystems serve for:

- Planning System provides a centralized platform for data collection, storage, and analysis. It enables the integration of various data sources, including weather data, load data, and energy production data, to support decision-making and management functions.
- Management System provides data and insights on the operation and performance of the microsystem. The system would collect data from various sensors, meters, and other monitoring devices installed throughout the microsystem (power generation sources, energy storage devices, electrical loads, etc.). The system also use data on weather conditions for analysis.

Both systems would include tools for data visualization, reporting, and analysis, allowing for optimal performance, reducing costs, and improving reliability.

Table 1. Tasks that require to make decision in HES.

Stage	Task	Time Frame	Description
Planning	HES structure planning [9–11]	Up to 20 years	We plan for type and amount of PV panels, wind turbines, and accumulator batteries The task is solved by taking into account the operational logic of the hybrid system, historical data on the weather conditions of the area, user consumption, and characteristics of existing installations of renewable sources
Management	Forecasting electricity generation from renewable sources [12–15]	Every hour	To forecast the level of generation from solar panels, we use hourly values of electricity generated during the year, with additional climatic variables: altitude, azimuth, ambient air temperature, precipitation in mm/h, cloud cover
	Forecasting electricity consumption from renewable energy sources for different types of consumers [16–18]		To forecast the level of consumption we use historical data on hourly electricity consumption in kWh. Consider the type of consumer, consumption characteristics for weekdays, weekends, quarantine due to COVID and vacation days, and electricity consumption during the day and night
	The selection of the mode of operation of the hybrid system [19–21]	Every 3 h	From the possible states of operation of the electric network, such a state is chosen in which it is possible to achieve a balance between the production and consumption of electrical energy, and its quality is sufficiently high. The decision-making method uses fuzzy logic The system of fuzzy production rules is formed according to expert assessments, and mathematical models for forecasting the levels of generation and consumption takes into account the operational logic of the power system at a sufficient level of electrical energy quality and is part of the knowledge base

From Table 1, the processes that occur during management can take different lengths of time. There can be operational management, during which current tasks are solved online, and strategic management, during which sustainable development tasks are solved. Moreover, the work considers different processes, and different points of view, considering different sources of data, their change ranges, and time intervals of data collection. Hence, the obvious issue that follows is where and how frequent to store the data? However, there are other issues that come up when dealing with multidimensional tasks.

3   Analysis of Data Flow

The effectiveness and flexibility of the HES rely on its ability to receive and integrate various types of information. This enables accurate predictions and the provision of diverse services to customers. The support offered by the HES is augmented by a combination of direct and indirect information pertaining to power systems, energy consumption prediction, correlation, and management. Direct sources of information include smart meters, sensors on transformers, and distribution stations. Indirect sources of information include historical data, current weather, weather forecasts, user consumption forecasts, and generation forecasts.

The above models of information support for decision-making regarding HES management have different purposes that can be performed in different environments and use different approaches to calculations. However, little research has been done to date on the detailed interdependence of models and methods for their efficient deployment in order to use and give recommendations on power system management modes to independent users at the same time. These users can simultaneously use the information system of the system, and they can be both household consumers and utilities, large enterprises, etc.

A few problems and corresponding tasks arise that need to be solved:

1. One of the main challenges with data is data quality. Decision-makers must ensure that the data used in their decision-making processes is accurate, reliable, and relevant to the problem at hand.
2. The decision is made according to information, calculations in the system and data flows between models in real time. Processed data have different properties and lead to problems related to volume, variety, and speed [22]. The volume of data is constantly growing, some models use the same data, and managing streaming data is a challenge. There is a problem with the efficiency of calculations and the speed of decision-making in the case of big data. The availability of big data in HES requires efficient data management
3. The availability of big data in energy system management tasks requires solving problems related to heterogeneity and incompleteness of data [23, 24]. Thus, additional methods of data analysis may be required before data is used in the modeling of certain processes.
4. Data analysis presents a significant challenge in HES decision-making processes. The study of the operation of the energy system can include different approaches and models, and describe different levels. Data analysis can involve machine learning to

predict consumption or generation, multi-task optimization, statistical analysis, and others. However, in HES, data analysis must take into account the unique characteristics of the HES's elements, including the interplay between different energy sources and the impact of external factors, such as weather patterns, as well as the impact of one model on others.

5. Making intelligent decisions is based on a set of models using historical and operational data that describe user behavior. This leads to problems related to the protection of personal data [25]. In addition, it is not enough to think about protection against cyber-attacks but it is necessary to comply with the current legislation on data security [26]. This may affect what data can be stored in general, and to what extent and frequency

6. Data integration also is a challenge. All generated data can have different types that must be integrated to provide a complete picture of the system. We need to be ensured that data from different sources can be integrated effectively.

According to these problems, before starting the construction of an architectural solution, it is necessary to analyze the entire flow of data circulating in the integrated system and determine the environments of its arrival/existence. This will make it possible to identify for which processes integration of solutions is necessary, how intermediate calculations affect each other, when it is appropriate to have asynchronous access to information, which calculations should be performed on the user's side and which on the server, and how data exchange will take place.

For a visual presentation of the distribution of functions in the system between its parts and their connection, a data flow diagram (Data Flow Diagram) is constructed and shown in Fig. 2. The presented diagram shows the main data flow between external entities, models, and databases. It is conditionally structured into three levels, including management, data layer and planning, each representing different aspects of the HES.

At the lower level i.e., planning level, the diagram includes models that correspond to processes related to planning the hybrid system's structure. These models may involve determining the potential energy generation from renewable energy installations, modelling the planned HES, conducting multi-criteria evaluations, and more.

At the top level, i.e., management layer the diagram showcases models associated with processes related to managing the operation of the hybrid system. These processes can include assessing the quality of energy generated by the real HES, monitoring power system parameters, selecting the appropriate operation mode, etc.

The data layer focuses on processes responsible for processing data and information from external sources, as well as presenting external entities that provide information. It also encompasses the actual storage of data. The diagram shows that data is stored in the operational database as well as in the data warehouse, considering the EU GDPR. The purpose of this distinction is that real-time data is used to inform the management strategy, and historical data from storage is required to train intelligent models on electricity consumption and generation levels.

All the components in the diagram are interconnected through data flows, representing the movement of data between processes, objects, and storage locations. The direction of the data flows indicates the data flow within the system.

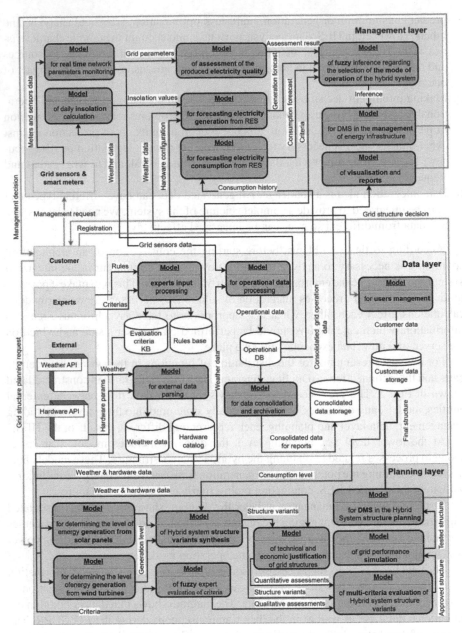

Fig. 2. Data Flow processes during Hybrid System Management

This structured representation of data flows allows a clear visualization of how data moves through the various processes and entities within the hybrid system. It helps to identify the dependencies, interactions, and direction of data flow, facilitating a comprehensive understanding of the system's functioning and supporting decision-making processes.

Operational management takes place online and requires operational data on the current state of the energy system, consumption, and weather conditions. Intelligent forecasting models are used for operational management, which is trained on historical data. Strategic management also requires the collection and accumulation of data, their analysis, and making appropriate decisions based on them. Thus, the data used in the decision-making process must be divided into two streams: operational data and historical data.

The main components of the scheme are highlighted:

- An operational database that users work with in real-time, which receives data from solar panels, electric accumulators, wind turbines, and weather APIs, in other words. All the data needed to support decision-making. External sources of information include data obtained from external sources, such as weather data from APIs, and consumption and generation data from sensors.
- Data repository containing historical data for all models.
- Deployment and storage of data models at each of the levels: planning, and management, taking into account the EU General Data Protection Regulation (GDPR) [27].
- Expert information on the evaluation of socio-economic criteria, as well as on the rules of power system management.
- End users for whom it is necessary to display analyzed, predictive information, and recommendations in a convenient and understandable form.

As a result of the analysis of information flows, it is possible to create a schedule of information flows, in which it is necessary to indicate the sources and destination of information flows, as well as the method of their processing. An architectural solution can be built on the basis of such a schedule.

4 Conclusions

The implementation of optimization, mathematical, and machine learning forecasting models, among others, are the most common areas of information support for decision-making regarding HES management. Overall, this paper contributes to the existing research by highlighting the critical role of data integration in decision-making processes within HES. We provided a framework for understanding the challenges and offered potential avenues for further investigation to overcome these challenges. The challenges associated with data integration, such as data quality, analysis, heterogeneity, and security, were identified and analyzed. By emphasizing the significance of effective data integration, we underscore how effective data integration enables more accurate predictions and enhances the provision of various services to customers.

The rapid and simultaneous deployment of models makes it challenging to ensure the quality of their integration due to the vast amount of data, and various incompatible formats. This leads to increasing the cost and time required for data analysis. In these conditions, it is extremely important to effectively manage information flows. In this paper, a general flow of data has been presented for the decision support system regarding the operation of the HES. Our primary idea was to implement intelligent management decision support by separating data into operational and historical data.

Future work should focus on developing an appropriate architectural solution that offers global and local hierarchical levels of information management. At the global level, there should be processes in charge of analyzing and managing data on electricity generation and making suggestions for management strategies. Data describing consumer behavior must be stored and processed at the local level (or at the edge, closer the end consumer). This approach should enhance not only scalability and flexibility but also security features.

The findings of this study have practical implications for optimizing HES performance, promoting energy efficiency, and facilitating sustainable development in the field of renewable energy systems.

Acknowledgement. This work is supported by the Kamprad Family Foundation for the project *Models of Distributed Information Processing in Smart Grid Systems*, and partially by the Knowledge Foundation (Stiftelsen för kunskaps-och kompetensutveckling) for the project *Intelligent Management of Hybrid Energy Systems* under Grant No. 20220111-H-01, as well as the project *Intelligent and Trustworthy IoT Systems* under Grant No. 20220087-H-01. The authors would like to thank Thomas Höglund at Crossbreed AB and Patrick Isacson at Crossbreed AB and Cetetherm AB for valuable insights in the management of hybrid energy systems.

References

1. The 17 Sustainable Development Goals of the United Nations. https://sdgs.un.org/goals
2. European Commission. Renewable Energy Progress Report. https://eur-lex.europa.eu/legal-content/EN/TXT/PDF/?uri=CELEX:52019DC0225&from=EN
3. Eurostat. Renewable energy statistics. https://ec.europa.eu/eurostat/statistics-explained/index.php?title=Renewable_energy_statistics
4. Judge, M.A., Khan, A., Manzoor, A., Khattak, H.A.: Overview of smart system implementation: frameworks, impact, performance and challenges. J. Energy Storage **49**, 104056 (2022). https://doi.org/10.1016/j.est.2022.104056
5. Vaccaro, A., Pisica, I., Lai, L.L., Zobaa, A.F.: A review of enabling methodologies for information processing in smart systems. Int. J. Electr. Power Energy Syst. **107**, 516–522 (2019). https://doi.org/10.1016/j.ijepes.2018.11.034
6. Antonopoulos, I., et al.: Artificial intelligence and machine learning approaches to energy demand-side response: a systematic review. Renew. Sustain. Energy Rev. **130**, 109899 (2020). https://doi.org/10.1016/j.rser.2020.109899
7. IEC SRD 63200:2021. SGAM smart energy system reference architecture model (2021). https://syc-se.iec.ch/deliveries/sgam-basics/
8. Shendryk, V., Malekian, R., Davidsson, P.: Interoperability, scalability, and availability of energy types in hybrid heating systems. In: Karabegovic, I., Kovačević, A., Mandzuka, S. (eds.) NT 2023. LNNS, vol. 707, pp. 3–13. Springer, Cham (2023). https://doi.org/10.1007/978-3-031-34721-4_1
9. Liu, Z., et al.: Co-optimization of a novel distributed energy system integrated with hybrid energy storage in different nearly zero energy community scenarios. Energy **247**, 123553 (2022). https://doi.org/10.1016/j.energy.2022.123553

10. Haidar, A.M.A., Fakhar, A., Helwig, A.: Sustainable energy planning for cost minimization of autonomous hybrid microgrid using combined multi-objective optimization algorithm. Sustain. Cities Soc. **62**, 102391 (2020). https://doi.org/10.1016/j.scs.2020.102391
11. Khezri, R., Mahmoudi, A.: Review on the state-of-the-art multi-objective optimisation of hybrid standalone/grid-connected energy systems. TIET Gener. Transm. Distrib. **14**(20), 4285–4300 (2020). https://doi.org/10.1049/iet-gtd.2020.0453
12. Aslam, S., Herodotou, H., Mohsin, S.M., Javaid, N., Ashraf, N., Aslam, S.: A survey on deep learning methods for power load and renewable energy forecasting in smart microgrids. Renew. Sustain. Energy Rev. **144**, 110992 (2021). https://doi.org/10.1016/j.rser.2021.110992
13. Sweeney, C., Bessa, R.J., Browell, J., Pinson, P.: The future of forecasting for renewable energy. WIREs Energy Environ. **9**(2) (2019). https://doi.org/10.1002/wene.365
14. Sharifzadeh, M., Sikinioti-Lock, A., Shah, N.: Machine-learning methods for integrated renewable power generation: a comparative study of artificial neural networks, support vector regression, and Gaussian process regression. Renew. Sustain. Energy Rev. **108**, 513–538 (2019). https://doi.org/10.1016/j.rser.2019.03.040
15. Ahmad, T., Zhang, H., Yan, B.: A review on renewable energy and electricity requirement forecasting models for smart grid and buildings. Sustain. Cities Soc. **55**, 102052 (2020). https://doi.org/10.1016/j.scs.2020.102052
16. Seyedzadeh, S., Pour Rahimian, F., Rastogi, P., Glesk, I.: Tuning machine learning models for prediction of building energy load. Sustain. Cities Soc. **47**, 101484 (2019). https://doi.org/10.1016/j.scs.2019.101484
17. Sun, Y., Haghighat, F., Fung, B.C.M.: A review of the-state-of-the-art in data-driven approaches for building energy prediction. Energy Build. **221**, 110022 (2020). https://doi.org/10.1016/j.enbuild.2020.110022
18. Ashouri, M., Haghighat, F., Fung, B.C.M., Yoshino, H.: Development of a ranking procedure for energy performance evaluation of buildings based on occupant behavior. Energy Build. **183**, 659–671 (2019). https://doi.org/10.1016/j.enbuild.2018.11.050
19. Lei, G., Song, H., Rodriguez, D.: Power generation cost minimization of the grid-connected hybrid renewable energy system through optimal sizing using the modified seagull optimization technique. Energy Rep. **6**, 3365–3376 (2020). https://doi.org/10.1016/j.egyr.2020.11.249
20. Wang, J., Qi, X., Ren, F., Zhang, G., Wang, J.: Optimal design of hybrid combined cooling, heating and power systems considering the uncertainties of load demands and renewable energy sources. J. Cleaner Prod. **281**, 125357 (2021). https://doi.org/10.1016/j.jclepro.2020.125357
21. Liu, Z., Cui, Y., Wang, J., Yue, C., Agbodjan, Y.S., Yang, Y.: Multi-objective optimization of multi-energy complementary integrated energy systems considering load prediction and renewable energy production uncertainties. Energy 124399 (2022). https://doi.org/10.1016/j.energy.2022.124399
22. Gungor, V., Lu, B., Hancke, G.: Opportunities and challenges of wireless sensor networks in smart system. IEEE Trans. Industr. Electron. **57**(10), 3557–3564 (2010). https://doi.org/10.1109/TIE.2009.2039455
23. Kaainoa, C.E., Jenkins, S.E.: Foundational challenges and opportunities with turning data into information for system modernization. In International Energy and Sustainability Conference (IESC), Farmingdale, NY, USA, pp. 1–19 (2019). https://doi.org/10.1109/IESC47067.2019.8976771
24. Ibrahim, C., Mougharbel, I., Kanaan, H.Y., Daher, N.A., Georges, S., Saad, M.: A review on the deployment of demand response programs with multiple aspects coexistence over smart system platform. Renew. Sustain. Energy Rev. **162**, 112446 (2022). https://doi.org/10.1016/j.rser.2022.112446

25. Singh, N.K., Mahajan, V.: End-user privacy protection scheme from cyber intrusion in smart system advanced metering infrastructure. Int. J. Crit. Infrastruct. Prot. **34**, 100410 (2021). https://doi.org/10.1016/j.ijcip.2021.100410
26. European Commission. Energy security. https://energy.ec.europa.eu/topics/energy-security_en
27. The General Data Protection Regulation (GDPR). https://gdpr.eu/what-is-gdpr/

Modelling Normative Financial Processes with Process Mining

Ilona Veitaitė[1]([✉]), Audrius Lopata[2], and Saulius Gudas[3]

[1] Institute of Social Sciences and Applied Informatics, Vilnius University, Muitinės str. 8, 44280 Kaunas, Lithuania
ilona.veitaite@knf.vu.lt
[2] Faculty of Informatics, Kaunas University of Technology, Studentų str. 50, 51368 Kaunas, Lithuania
audrius.lopata@ktu.lt
[3] Institute of Data Science and Digital Technologies, Vilnius University, Akademijos str. 4, 08412 Vilnius, Lithuania
saulius.gudas@mif.vu.lt

Abstract. Financial processes are complex procedures related to financial data recording and analysis. Compliance of these processes with the normative rules is important because it is related to the correctness of financial data records, it helps to evaluate the validity of financial processes in the organization. The main issue is that organizations have limited data about how their financial processes run. Based on expert knowledge, normative patterns of financial process types can be developed. Normative rules can be quite complex, and difficult to understand, even if they are systematized in tables or text descriptions. The aim of the article is to present the possibilities of the Process Mining (PM) technology to discover a model of the normative financial process (by the example of the Expenditure cycle). The primary data in this kind of PM project is a list of the meta-events indicating allowed transitions between financial transaction entities (journal types, document types, account names, etc.), i.e. this meta-event-log.

The result of PM is a visualization of the normative rules – the meta-model, convenient to analyze by an expert, to reveal properties of financial processes. The Meta-model of the normative financial process (pattern) could be further used as criteria (restriction) in analyzing financial data records and detecting anomalies in financial data. The experiment results (using the Expenditure cycle as an example) reveal the capability of using meta-models (patterns of financial transactions) in financial data analysis with PM tools.

Keywords: Process Mining · Normative Financial Transaction · Expenditure cycle · Finance Data Space

1 Introduction

Financial processes are the actions organizations take when handling financial activity including accounting and bookkeeping, budgeting, financial planning, financial reporting, forecasting, and strategy.

A. Lopata et al. (Eds.): ICIST 2023, CCIS 1979, pp. 185–197, 2024.
https://doi.org/10.1007/978-3-031-48981-5_15

Financial processes are complex and are divided into several types according to the content of business activities. The data processing of each type of financial process is a transaction that must comply with the rules established by experience. Thus, financial processes are based on normative rules to ensure correct financial data transactions. Normative rules of the financial transactions data recording can be quite complex, and difficult to understand, even if they are systematized in tables or text descriptions.

The aim of the article is to show the possibilities of the Process Mining (PM) technology to discover a typical model of the normative financial process (by the example of the Expenditure cycle). The event log in this kind of PM project is different as it contains not real data records (events linked to timestamp), but a list of normative rules of the financial transaction, i.e. some list of the meta-events indicating allowed transitions between financial transaction entities (journal types, document types, account names, etc.).

The result of process mining using the normative meta-event-log is a kind of meta-model (pattern of the financial transaction type), convenient to analyze with an expert, to reveal its features.

The article is structured into several sections that aim to provide a comprehensive understanding of financial processes and their application in project management. It begins with an introduction, setting the context for the subsequent sections. Section 2 focuses on related works, discussing previous research and literature in the field. Section 3 delves into the exploration of different types of financial processes, highlighting their significance and characteristics. In Sect. 4, the article introduces the concept of a multidimensional financial space for PM project specification, emphasizing its usefulness in analyzing and optimizing financial processes. Section 5 presents an application of process mining in the expenditure cycle, showcasing how it can be applied to uncover insights and improve efficiency. Finally, the article concludes by summarizing the key findings and implications drawn from the previous sections.

2   Related Work

Process mining is a technology to automatically construct a so-called process model that is based on the sequence of events associated with a selected object (entity). Events are listed in a so-called event log, which is stored in the organization's information system.

Process mining is specifically focused on analyzing historical data of process implementation in the form of event logs [1–3]. Many process mining technologies, tools, and applications can grant fact-based support process improvements and solutions. As it is mentioned, process mining is a technology that provides analysis of event logs extracted from the enterprise's information system [1, 2, 11]. Even though process mining has developed very quickly, it is pretty new to the accounting domain, and there are some challenges of its usage in this field, especially for fraud and anomaly detection as well for [4, 5].

Financial data analysis using PM technology is a challenging process, it helps to reveal the flow of the financial activities and their characteristics, to evaluate the validity of financial processes in the organization, to evaluate an organization's performance, and reveal possible fraud in accounting records.

3 Types of Financial Processes

There are many financial types and cycles. There are used these financial transaction (cycles) types in the research [4, 5, 9].

- Expenditure cycle [Purchase-to-Pay Process] – Purchase and payment of goods (Objective to mine the events per transaction line, and understand the regular flow of Purchase)
- Revenue cycle [Order-to-Cash process] – Sale of goods and collection of income (Objective to mine the events per transaction line, and understand the regular flow of Sale).
- Financing cycle – Obtain funding and invest or distribute profits – later on, similar to a funding transaction
- Conversion cycle – Production or assembling of goods, later on, similar to a production "transaction".
- HR/Payroll – Recruit to payment of employees, later on, similar to a payroll transaction.
- Purchase-to-Pay Process [Expenditure cycle] – The Purchase-to-Pay process is also known as PtP, procure-to-pay, or req-to-check. It refers to business processes that cover requisitioning, purchasing, confirming, receiving, paying for, and accounting for goods and services.
- Order-to-Cash process [Revenue cycle] – The Order-to-Cash process, also known as OtC or O2C, refers to a top-level business process that covers all activities between the customer order and order payment. The Order-to-Cash process operates very closely with customers, turning orders into cash.
- Double-entry accounting Requires that every business transaction be recorded in at least two accounts.

Next, there will be examined the application of PM technology by the discovery of only one pattern of the typical financial transaction – the Expenditure cycle normative model. Discovery of the common flow of Expenditure cycle entity types (attributes related to audit objectives), such as Source Documents, JournalNames, Account Names, and other attributes of the Expenditure cycle;

The discovered common flows of the financial transactions are considered to be the normative meta-models (patterns) of accounting data recording, which could be used as a criterion for finding inadequate accounting processes and data.

4 Multidimensional Financial Space for PM Project Specification

Specification of the PM project requires not only financial data content awareness but also specific knowledge of the PM project specification rules as well as PM tool environment.

Specification of PM project includes steps as follows:

- *Preparation of initial data for the PM task, creating an event log;*
- *Identification of some data record attribute as Case ID;*
- *Identification of Activity ID;*
- *Identification of Timestamp;*

● *Assignment of some other data record attributes is as resources or simple attributes;*

There are many PM tools, their environments are very different, so it is too complicated for a financial specialist to use them directly in formulating data analysis tasks. In [6, 7] were presented a user-friendly approach to PM technology implementation for financial data analysis using a multi-dimensional space of financial data.

Figure 1 presents financial data space (FDS) dimensions and their members, which can be covered with particular data from General Ledger prepared for the analysis according to transformation algorithms [6–8, 10]:

● A – Dimension – Financial Statement (FS) categories: a1-FS type (Report), a2-CreditCategory1, a3-CreditCategory2, a4-CreditCategory3, a5-SectionCode;
● B – Dimension – Source documents: b1-Doc-Type, b2-Doc-Subtype1, b3-Doc-subtype2, b4-Doc-subtype3, …;
● C – Dimension – Journals or Sub-Ledgers: c1-Journal, c2-Sub-Journal1, c3-Sub-journal2, c4-Sub-journal3, …;
● E – Dimension – Enterprise Types: e1-Enterprise Type, e2-E-SubType1, e3-E-SubType2, e4-E-SubType3, …;
● L – Dimension – Location: l1-Country, l2-City, l3-Region, l4-Business Unit, l5-Department, l6-Process/Project, …;
● T – Dimension – Time-Period: t1-Year, t2-Month, t3-Day/week day, t4-Day: Hour: min: sec, t5-Hour: min: sec, t6-Period Beginning, t7-Period-Ending;
● D – Dimension – Anomalies: d1-Anomaly type, d2-subtype1, d3-subtype2, d4-subtype3, …;
● K – Dimension – Changes: Internal/External Internal Changes (IC): k1-types, k2-subtype1, k3-subtype2, …; External Changes (EC): k1-types, k2-subtype1, k3-subtype2, ….

According to the user's specific need for financial data analysis, the expert selects in the financial data space which FDS dimensions are relevant (will be visible to the PM tool environment) and which dimension members are important for specifying the PM project.

The next step to apply standard process mining techniques is to prepare financial data for PM, i.e. to create an event log (to) [1–3]. To be able to apply process mining per cell of a specified in the FDS data cube, the classical requirements need to be satisfied [4, 5].

5   Process Mining Application Example: Expenditure Cycle

As mentioned, the expenditure cycle is the purchase and payment of goods. Common rules (normative rules) for expenditure cycle flows are shown in Table 1.

The Expenditure cycle (expenditure transaction) matrix (Fig. 2) is developed, which is based on the Expenditure cycle rules (Table 1) and summarized expert experiences related to the detailed rules. It is necessary to emphasize that in the case of the task we are solving, the aim is to discover the normative financial transaction model (pattern) by the example of the Expenditure cycle).

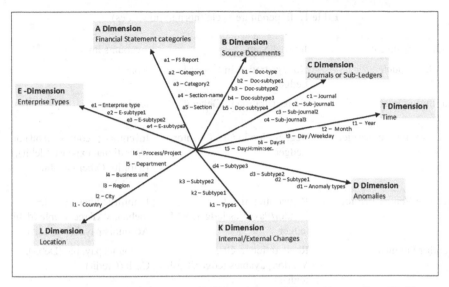

Fig. 1. Financial Data Space (FDS) dimensions and dimension members [6–8]

Expenditure cycle matrix Fig. 2 defines the possible options for how expenditure transaction data can be presented in source document types and indicates the cases in which data records are stored in various journals and corresponding accounts. The role of TimeStamp in this meta-event-log is only symbolic, because meta-event-log defines logical event flow, but not the real-time events. In the case of Expenditure cycle data from Source Document type D1 = Dispatch note can be recorded into journal J1 = GL or journal J2 = Inventory Ledger, and the value of TimeStamp is the same in both records.

Otherwise, if data from some source document type D2 = xx must be written first to J1 = yy and then necessarily to journal J2 = zz in the next step, the timestamp value must be different (be larger) indicating the logical sequence of events.

Based on this systematized matrix of Expenditure cycle rules, a normative event log of expenditure transactions was created for the Process Mining tool.

Matrix of the Expenditure cycle rules (normative events) is used to create the normative event log (meta-event-log), the characteristics of which are as follows:

- the line of this aggregated event log is a record whose attributes are a permitted aggregated event (permitted financial transaction, transaction step), but not a record of actual data,
- the value of the time stamp in the line of this summarized event log is symbolic, it does not indicate the real-time, it is a conditional time,
- the time stamp value can be the same in all records if this event log indicates only permitted financial transactions, where their order is not important,
- in adjacent lines of this summarized event log, the value of the time stamp may differ in the records, if the permissible sequence of financial transactions (group of transaction steps) is specified.

Table 1. Expenditure cycle (normal flow rules)

Source document	Journal Name	Accounts involved
Purchase Quote	No registration in General Ledger	None
Purchase Order	No registration in General ledger	n/a
Receive items or services	Registration in GL, Inventory Ledger	Inventory accounts (debit) or Operational expense (debit), Liability/Other payables (credit)
Receive Vendor Invoice	Registration in GL, Vendor/Payables ledger, VAT ledger	Liability/Other payables (debit), VAT receivable (debit), Accounts payable (credit)
Vendor Payment	Registration in GL, Vendor/payables ledger, Cash register	Accounts payable (Debit), Cash (Credit)
Alternative: Return goods	Registration in GL, Inventory Ledger	Inventory accounts (Credit) or Operational expenses (Credit), Asset/Other receivables (Debit)
Alternative: Credit-invoice Vendor	Registration in GL, Vendor/payables ledger, VAT ledger	Asset/Other receivables receivable (credit), VAT Receivable (credit), Accounts payable (debit)

Experiments with the Expenditure Event Log

The experiment used the well-known Process Mining tool DISCO (Fluxicon BV), which is very convenient and provides visual models of processes and their characteristics in various aspects.

Two process mining projects were created that demonstrate the possibilities of normative financial processes analyzes using PM technology:

- Project 01 – the aim is to reveal the allowed variants of registering source document types (SourceDocument) data to journal types (JournalName).
- Project 02 – the aim is to define the allowed variants of recording the source document types (Source Document) data to journal types (JournalName), linked to the allowed Account names.

The following are the results and explanations of these experiments.

Process mining project 01 specification (importing the matrix in Fig. 2 as an event log):

- *'Source Document'* → *Case ID*
- *'JournalName'* → *Activity ID*
- *'TimeStamp'* → *Timestamp (Pattern: 'yyyy/MM/dd HH:mm:ss')*

Source Document	JournalName	Account names	TimeStamp	AccountNumber	Section (AccountGroup)
Purchase Quote	No GL	None	12:00:00 AM		
Approval	No GL	None	12:00:00 AM		
Purchase Order	No GL	n/a	12:00:00 AM		
Dispatch note (Receive items or services)	GL	Inventory accounts (debit)	12:00:00 AM	AccountID	
Dispatch note (Receive items or services)	GL	Liability / Other payables (credi	12:00:00 AM	AccountID	
Dispatch note (Receive items or services)	GL	Operational expense (debit)	12:00:00 AM	AccountID	
Dispatch note (Receive items or services)	GL	Liability / Other payables (credi	12:00:00 AM	AccountID	
Dispatch note (Receive items or services)	Inventory Ledger		12:00:00 AM	AccountID	
Dispatch note (Receive items or services)	Inventory Ledger		12:00:00 AM	AccountID	Inventory accounts (debit)
Dispatch note (Receive items or services)	Inventory Ledger		12:00:00 AM	AccountID	Liability / Other payables (c
Dispatch note (Receive items or services)	Inventory Ledger		12:00:00 AM	AccountID	Operational expense (debit
Vendor Invoice	GL	Liability / Other payables (credi	12:00:00 AM	AccountID	
Vendor Invoice	GL	VAT receivable (debit)	12:00:00 AM	AccountID	
Vendor Invoice	GL	Accounts payable (credit)	12:00:00 AM	AccountID	
Vendor Invoice	Vendor/Payables ledger	Liability / Other payables (debit)	12:00:00 AM	AccountID	
Vendor Invoice	Vendor/Payables ledger	VAT receivable (debit)	12:00:00 AM	AccountID	
Vendor Invoice	Vendor/Payables ledger	Accounts payable (credit)	12:00:00 AM	AccountID	
Vendor Invoice	VAT ledger		12:00:00 AM	AccountID	VAT receivable (debit)
Vendor Invoice	VAT ledger		12:00:00 AM	AccountID	Accounts payable (credit)
Vendors Credit Invoice	GL	Liability / Other payables (debit)	12:00:00 AM	AccountID	
Vendors Credit Invoice	GL	VAT receivable (debit)	12:00:00 AM	AccountID	
Vendors Credit Invoice	GL	Accounts payable (credit)	12:00:00 AM	AccountID	
Vendors Credit Invoice	Vendor/Payables ledger	Liability / Other payables (debit)	12:00:00 AM	AccountID	
Vendors Credit Invoice	Vendor/Payables ledger	VAT receivable (debit)	12:00:00 AM	AccountID	
Vendors Credit Invoice	Vendor/Payables ledger	Accounts payable (credit)	12:00:00 AM	AccountID	
Vendors Credit Invoice	VAT ledger		12:00:00 AM	AccountID	Liability / Other payables (d
Vendors Credit Invoice	VAT ledger		12:00:00 AM	AccountID	VAT receivable (debit)
Vendors Credit Invoice	VAT ledger		12:00:00 AM	AccountID	Accounts payable (credit)
Vendor Payment Check	GL	Accounts payable (Debit)	12:00:00 AM	AccountID	
Vendor Payment Check	Vendor/Payables ledger	Accounts payable (Debit)	12:00:00 AM	AccountID	
Vendor Payment wire transamision	GL	Accounts payable (Debit)	12:00:00 AM	AccountID	
Vendor Payment wire transamision	Vendor/Payables ledger	Accounts payable (Debit)	12:00:00 AM	AccountID	
Vendor Payment Credit Card	GL	Accounts payable (Debit)	12:00:00 AM	AccountID	
Vendor Payment Credit Card	Vendor/Payables ledger	Accounts payable (Debit)	12:00:00 AM	AccountID	
Vendor Payment Debit Card	GL	Accounts payable (Debit)	12:00:00 AM	AccountID	
Vendor Payment Debit Card	Vendor/Payables ledger	Accounts payable (Debit)	12:00:00 AM	AccountID	
Vendor Payment Cash	Cash register	Accounts payable (Debit)	12:00:00 AM	AccountID	
Vendor Payment Cash	Cash register	Cash (Credit)	12:00:00 AM	AccountID	
Dispatch note (Return goods)	GL	Inventory accounts (Credit)	12:00:00 AM	AccountID	

Fig. 2. Matrix of the Expenditure cycle rules (normative events)

- *Other attributes: 'Account names', 'AccountNumber', 'Section (AccountGroup)'*

After process mining, all Source Documents types (Fig. 4) and all Journal types (Fig. 6) were discovered.

The list of discovered different Source Document types (13 different Case ID = Source Document) is presented in Fig. 4): Purchase Quote, Approval, Purchase Order, Dispatch note (Receive items or services, Vendor Invoice and etc.). There are 6 variants for recording source documents to journal types (JournalName) (Fig. 5).

The normative registration variant of each source document type can be presented in the table and visualized as a process model (normative workflow, see example in Fig. 8).

The resulting dependency diagram of financial entities "journal type" (Activity ID = JournalName) (Fig. 3) shows the allowed options for recording data of source document types to journal types following the rules specified by the experts (by example of recording expenditure transaction data from the source.

The list of discovered different Source Document types (13 different Case ID) is presented in Fig. 4): Purchase Quote, Approval, Purchase Order, Dispatch note (Receive items or services, Vendor Invoice and etc.). List of all allowed Journals types (Activity ID = JournalName) is in Fig. 6.

The normative variants of each source document type recoding to journal types (JournalName) can be presented in the table and visualized as a process model (normative workflow).

There are 6 variants for recording source documents to journal types (JournalName) (Fig. 5).

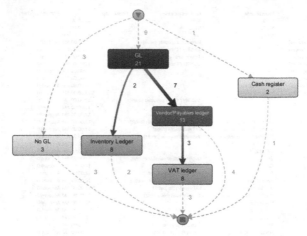

Fig. 3. Dependency graph of financial entities "Journal type" of Expenditure cycle (Project 01)

Case ID	Events	Variant
Purchase Quote	1	Variant 2
Approval	1	Variant 2
Purchase Order	1	Variant 2
Dispatch note (Receive items or services)	8	Variant 3
Vendor Invoice	8	Variant 5
Vendors Credit Invoice	9	Variant 4
Vendor Payment Check	2	Variant 1
Vendor Payment wire transamision	2	Variant 1
Vendor Payment Credit Card	2	Variant 1
Vendor Payment Debit Card	2	Variant 1
Vendor Payment Cash	2	Variant 6
Dispatch note (Return goods)	8	Variant 3
Credit-invoice Vendor	9	Variant 4

Fig. 4. List of Source Document types of Expenditure cycle (Source Document = Case ID)

Variant	▲ Cases	Events
Variant 1	4	2
Variant 2	3	1
Variant 3	2	8
Variant 4	2	9
Variant 5	1	8
Variant 6	1	2

Fig. 5. Variants of recording Source Document types **to Journal types** (Source Document = Case ID; JournalName = Activity ID)

When discovering financial transaction meta-models (patterns), it became clear that standard PM tools provide redundant information. For example, we want to know to which journal types data from the source document type "Dispatch Note" can be registered. From the obtained results in Fig. 7 and Fig. 8 it can be seen that, the source document type "Dispatch Note" (Fig. 7) data recording is allowed to journal types GL and Inventory ledger only (the Activity column stands for JournalName). Options for

Activity	▲ Frequency	Relative frequency	
GL	21	38.18 %	
Vendor/Payables I..	13	23.64 %	
Inventory Ledger	8	14.55 %	
VAT ledger	8	14.55 %	
No GL	3	5.45 %	
Cash register	2	3.64 %	

Fig. 6. List of all allowed Journals types of Expenditure cycle (Activity ID = JournalName)

recording source document types to journal types but GL and Inventory Ledger entries are repeated 4 times each in Fig. 7, although in this case one entry is sufficient.

The process mining tool also represents the discovered knowledge (Fig. 6) of source document type "Dispatch Note" normative recording rules as a process model (Fig. 8). From the obtained results in Fig. 7, it can be seen that GL and Inventory Ledger are repeated several times in the Activity column, so the expert himself has to summarize, that only two types of journals are allowed: GL and Inventory Ledger.

Such a case shows the possible improvements of PM tools (need to filter out duplicates), applying the process pattern discovery based on the knowledge recorded in the meta-event-log.

Activity	Account names
GL	Inventory accounts (debit)
GL	Liability / Other payables (cre..
GL	Operational expense (debit)
GL	Liability / Other payables (cre..
Inventory Ledger	
Inventory Ledger	
Inventory Ledger	
Inventory Ledger	

Fig. 7. Allowed recording of the *Dispatch note (receive items or services)* to journal types (Activity ID = JournalName)

The process mining tool also gives a visualization of the discovered knowledge of source document type "Dispatch Note" recording to journal types normative rules (table in Fig. 7) as a process model (workflow diagram).

Now we will consider a more complicated PM task, when a financial expert wants to extract a more detailed normative model of source documents recording to allowed accounts. In this case, specification of the Project 02 associates journal types and account names, creating a compound Activity ID = JournalName &Account name.

Process Mining Project 02 – The aim is to define the allowed variants of registering the Source Document types into journal types (JournalName), linked to the allowed accounts (Account name).

Event Log data are loaded from the same file – the matrix in Fig. 2, however, Activity ID is composite because it consists of JournalName and Account name pairs:

- *'Source Document'* → *Case ID*
- *'JournalName'* → *Activity ID*
- *'Account names;* → *Activity ID*

- *'TimeStamp'* → *Resource*
- *'AccountNumber'* → *Resource*
- *Other attributes: 'Section (AccountGroup)'*

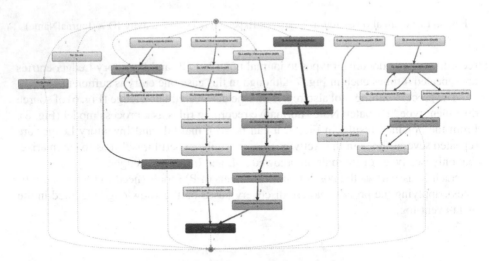

Fig. 8. Dependency map for Activity ID = JournalName & Account name (project 02)

As can be seen in the discovered dependency graph (Fig. 8), it is much more complicated. The list of discovered different Source Document types (13 different Case ID = Source Document) is the same as presented in Fig. 9. Following the rules as specified by the experts). The normative registration variant of each source document type can be presented in the table and visualized as a process model (normative workflow).

Case ID	Events	Variant
Purchase Quote	1	Variant 2
Approval	1	Variant 2
Purchase Order	1	Variant 3
Dispatch note (Receive items or services)	8	Variant 4
Vendor Invoice	8	Variant 5
Vendors Credit Invoice	9	Variant 6
Vendor Payment Check	2	Variant 1
Vendor Payment wire transamision	2	Variant 1
Vendor Payment Credit Card	2	Variant 1
Vendor Payment Debit Card	2	Variant 1
Vendor Payment Cash	2	Variant 7
Dispatch note (Return goods)	8	Variant 8
Credit-invoice Vendor	9	Variant 9

Fig. 9. Types of Source documents (project 02)

There are discovered 9 variants (Fig. 10) of the different normative process models for recording Source Document data to allowed accounts in allowed journal types (Activity ID = JournalName&AccountNames).

For example, Variant 1 contains the normative process model of the Source Document type "Vendors Payment Check" recording (Fig. 11): the rules allow recording (Block 1)

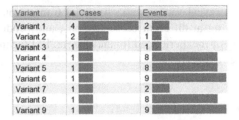

Fig. 10. Variants of the different normative processes

to the journal GL (General Ledger) account Accounts Payable (Debt) and/or (Block 2) to the journal Vendors / payables ledger account Accounts payable (Debt).

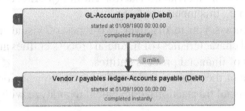

Fig. 11. Source Document type "Vendors Payment Check" data recording process (Variant 1)

Such a case of option 1 shows a possible improvement of PM, because it is possible to specify the type of logical connection between Block 1 and Block 2 - whether it is an OR or AND connection.

For example, Variant 2 is a Source document type Purchase Quote registration normative process model: the Financial Activity Rule does not allow the registration of a Purchase Quote in GL (General Ledger).

For example, Variant 8 is a Source Document with the type Dispatch Note (Return goods) recording process: the financial activity rule allows the Dispatch Note to be recorded in the GL (General Ledger) in the four accounts and in the Inventory Ledger in the four accounts recorded in the Table Dispatch Note (Fig. 12).

Activity	JournalName	Account names
GL-Inventory accounts (Credit)	GL	Inventory accounts (Credit)
GL-Asset / Other receivables (Debit)	GL	Asset / Other receivables (Debit)
GL-Operational expenses (Credit)	GL	Operational expenses (Credit)
GL-Asset / Other receivables (Debit)	GL	Asset / Other receivables (Debit)
Inventory Ledger-Inventory accounts (Credit)	Inventory Ledger	Inventory accounts (Credit)
Inventory Ledger-Asset / Other receivables (Debit)	Inventory Ledger	Asset / Other receivables (Debit)
Inventory Ledger-Operational expenses (Credit)	Inventory Ledger	Operational expenses (Credit)
Inventory Ledger-Asset / Other receivables (Debit)	Inventory Ledger	Asset / Other receivables (Debit)

Fig. 12. Summary of Dispatch Note (Return goods) registrations

The experiments performed and the description of the results allowed us to conclude that PM technology is useful and effective in creating process patterns. Process mining technologies create explicit models – graphical and structured tables of parameters (static indicators) – that reveal variations in financial transactions that are difficult to observe, allow for filtering at different cross-sections, and produce statistical indicators. PM allows training of inexperienced financiers, etc. PM technology discovers new knowledge from a set of expert rules.

6   Conclusions

Normative rules of financial transactions can be quite complex, difficult to understand, even if they are systematized in tables or text description. The Process Mining (PM) technology is used to discover the visual models of the normative financial processes by example of Expenditure cycle.

The event log in this kind of PM project is some list of the meta-events indicating allowed transitions between financial transaction entities (journal types, document types, account names, etc.), i.e., this meta-event-log.

PM technology allows you to discover two types of visual models: dependency models (and statistical characteristics) of financial process entities and workflow models and its characteristics of financial process entities.

Such visualization of the normative flow of financial transactions is a kind of meta-model (pattern of financial transaction), convenient to analyze with an expert, to use its properties.

It is necessary to emphasize that the aim of PM project was to discover the pattern of the financial transaction (meta-model) based on the meta-event log comprising summarized expert knowledge.

The peculiarity of such a PM task is that the timestamp value in this summary event log line is symbolic, it does not indicate real time, it is conditional time, indicates only permitted logical sequence of financial transactions.

When discovering financial transaction meta-models (patterns), it became clear that standard PM tools provide redundant information. From the obtained results in Fig. 7, it can be seen that GL and Inventory Ledger are repeated several times in the Activity column, so the expert himself has to summarize.

Such a case shows the possible improvements of PM tools, applying the process pattern discovery based on the knowledge recorded in the meta-event-log.

The normative meta-model of financial transaction could be further used as a pattern in analyzing validity of financial data records, detecting anomalies in financial transactions.

References

1. Aalst, W.M.P.: Process cubes: slicing, dicing, rolling up and drilling down event data for process mining. In: Song, M., Wynn, M.T., Liu, J. (eds.) AP-BPM 2013. LNBIP, vol. 159, pp. 1–22. Springer, Cham (2013). https://doi.org/10.1007/978-3-319-02922-1_1
2. Aalst, W.V.: Process Mining: Discovery, Conformance and Enhancement of Business Processes. Springer, Heidelberg (2011). https://doi.org/10.1007/978-3-642-19345-3
3. Aalst, W.V., Kees M.V., Werf, J.M.V., Verdonk, M.: Finance process mining auditing 2.0: using process mining to support tomorrow's auditor. Computer **43**(3) (2010). http://www.pad sweb.rwth-aachen.de/wvdaalst/publications/p593.pdf

4. Adriansyah, A., Buijs, J.C.A.M.: Mining process performance from event logs. In: La Rosa, M., Soffer, P. (eds.) BPM 2012. LNBIP, vol. 132, pp. 217–218. Springer, Heidelberg (2013). https://doi.org/10.1007/978-3-642-36285-9_23

5. Alrefai, A.: Audit focused process mining: the evolution of process mining and internal control. Ph.D. thesis (2019). https://rucore.libraries.rutgers.edu/rutgers-lib/60514/PDF/1/play/

6. Gehrke, N., Mueller-Wickop, N.: Basic principles of financial process mining a journey through financial data in accounting information systems. In: Association for Information Systems AIS Electronic Library (AISeL) (2010)

7. Lopata, A., Butleris, R., Gudas, S., et al.: Financial data preprocessing issues. In: Lopata, A., Gudonienė, D., Butkienė, R. (eds.) ICIST 2021. CCIS, vol. 1486, pp. 60–71. Springer, Cham (2021). https://doi.org/10.1007/978-3-030-88304-1_5

8. Lopata, A., et al.: Financial process mining characteristics. In: Lopata, A., Gudonienė, D., Butkienė, R. (eds.) ICIST 2022. CCIS, vol. 1665, pp. 209–220. Springer, Cham (2022). https://doi.org/10.1007/978-3-031-16302-9_16 ISBN 9783031163012

9. Lopata, A., et al.: Financial data anomaly discovery using behavioral change indicators. Electronics 11(10), art. no. 1598, 1–14 (2022). https://doi.org/10.3390/electronics11101598. ISSN 2079-9292

10. Mamaliga, T.: Realizing a process cube allowing for the comparison of event data. Master Thesis. Eindhoven University of Technology (2013)

11. Werner, M., Gehrke, N., Nuttgens, M.: Business process mining and reconstruction for financial audits. In: 45th Hawaii International Conference on System Sciences, pp. 5350–5359 (2012). https://doi.org/10.1109/HICSS.2012.141

Language Technologies and Smart e-Learning Applications

Sentiment Analysis of Lithuanian Youth Subcultures Zines Using Automatic Machine Translation

Vyautas Rudzionis[⊠], Egidija Ramanuskaite, and Ausra Kairaityte-Uzupe

Vilnius University Kaunas Faculty, Muitines 8, Kaunas, Lithuania
vytautas.rudzionis@knf.vu.lt

Abstract. Automatic sentiment analysis is an important technique having a significant impact on many businesses and other fields. Well known fact is that sentiments are culturally dependent phenomena and are differently expressed in various cultural groups. Successful implementation of automatic sentiment identification techniques requires using sentiment corpora. Less widely spoken languages such as Lithuanian often suffer from the lack of corpora, particularly culturally specific corpora. This paper presents the results of an evaluation of the possibilities to apply machine learning techniques and the implementation of other language text corpora for sentiment analysis of texts from representatives of Lithuanian youth subcultures. The results show that quite a high accuracy (about 80–85%) could be achieved at least in some contexts.

Keywords: sentiment analysis · youth subcultures · machine learning · machine translation · zines

1 Introduction

Automatic identification of human sentiments and even emotions from text is a hot and important topic. Sentiment analysis is contextual mining of text which identifies and extracts subjective information in source material [1]. Very often it is understood as the automatic recognition of emotional content hidden in the text. Since human emotions very often are hard to determine precisely and often a matter of discussion even between human experts the task is simplified to the recognition of whether the emotional content of the text message is positive, negative, or not existing. The good working definition of sentiment analysis could be summarized as follows; sentiment analysis is the process of analysing pieces of text to determine the emotional tone they carry, whether they are positive, negative, or neutral. It allows for finding the author's attitude toward the topic of interest described in the message.

The importance of sentiment analysis, in general, was caused by the abundance of data; massive data collection is achievable using various Internet monitoring tools. However, manual analysis of tens of thousands of texts is time and resource-consuming and hence the application of automatic methods of various complexity is very useful. A classical approach to sentiment analysis lies in the simple evaluation of the semantic meaning of words contained in the text. More and more often other and more sophisticated methods are used in sentiment analysis.

Sentiment analysis can help businesses to understand the social sentiment of their brand, product, or service and to improve business and marketing strategies. Not surprisingly businesses became one of the first users of automatic sentiment analysis and the major driving force behind the development of new sentiment analysis methods. But the importance of sentiment analysis is much broader than being only a tool used in marketing strategies. The creative use of advanced sentiment analysis techniques can be an effective tool for doing in-depth research. For example, creative implementation of sentiment analysis techniques could lead to early detection of socially dangerous behaviour in some social groups, identify the cases of mocking even if the victims are reluctant to cooperate, identify potential hate and its sources, etc.

One of the more important sources for sentiment analysis is informal texts created by members of various youth subcultures (e.g., punks, skinheads, metal music fans, etc.) They offer participants a specific identity outside the "traditional cultures" ascribed by social institutions such as family, work and school. These groups often develop a specific type of language with distinct meanings of some words or phenomena as well as a different point of view on various social events and norms. One such example of youth creativity is fanzines, an informal youth press, whose authors "avoid, and often explicitly reject, the sanitised, neutral language of mainstream information, preferring instead to speak from the heart or the gut about sensitive or important issues, not hiding their emotionality or their relationship to knowledge" [2]. Due to their intrinsic conflict with the mainstream culture dominant in society, representatives of the subcultural groups have a higher risk of going into emotionally unstable behaviours that can cause social tensions.

The success of sentiment analysis strongly relies on the existence of sentiment corpora [3]. Sentiment corpora is the typical text corpora supplemented with the emotional meaning and values of the words. The sentiment corpora could have emotional values of the words outside of the context in which they are used or within some semantic context. The development of sentiment corpora is an expensive and time-consuming task. Very often it also requires consensus among human experts assigning emotional values to the words. Not surprisingly that such not widely spoken languages as Lithuanian as well as other relatively narrowly used languages feel a lack of properly developed sentiment corpora. At the same time widely used languages such as English have many sentiment corpora including some freely available ones and the tools to use them. Automatic machine translation techniques achieved significant progress in the recent decade and in some situations achieve close to human translation quality. This could provide new possibilities to use various sentiment analysis tools for such less widely spoken languages as Lithuanian - using automatic translation between the source text in the original language and automatically translated text into language with vast resources of text corpora with emotional text values. This paper aims to investigate the possibilities to apply such an approach for sentiment analysis in less widely spoken languages that suffers from the lack of appropriate sentiment corpora.

Further, the paper is organized as follows. In Sect. 2 the dataset used in the experiments is presented. In Sect. 3 the methodology of experiments and the results are presented. Finally in Sect. 4 conclusions are provided.

2 The Dataset

The speech corpus used in this research has been obtained from Lithuania's Youth Culture Digital Archive (acronym JAUKA) Lithuanian Zine Collection. The Collection has been collected during the project "An open-access database and research of self-published informal Lithuanian youth press (fanzines)" funded by the Research Council of Lithuania. It contains various fanzines published unofficially by representatives of various youth subcultures in Lithuania between 1987 and 2005. The original issues were scanned and transformed into text files using OCR tools. It should be noted that due to various irregularities used by authors, the result of optical character recognition was far below the accuracy usually obtained and manual post-processing often was necessary. The archive is freely available using the address jauka.knf.vu.lt.

Part of the collection was manually labelled assigning the sentiment values for the words contained in the text. The labelling has been performed by a group of semi-experts. This was the group of people without special training in the area of sentiment identification and representing different backgrounds of basic training, but they were instructed on how to label the text and what needs to be taken into account when labelling. It should be noted that the task was more complicated since the OCR processed text contained many errors since original zines were prepared using irregular editing techniques.

Each text was labelled by three different labellers. The idea behind threefold labelling is the fact that because marking sentiments is a highly subjective issue it is necessary to introduce cross-validation of the labelling accuracy. Only labels that are identically labelled by more than one person could be treated as rather objective ones. In this study, labellers marked the word having sentiment value (two options were available - positive sentiment and negative sentiment) and the object associated with the aforementioned sentiment. Trying to ensure the quality of labelling the size of a single labelling session was about 8–10 pages of text in a typical.txt type file.

3 The Experimental Evaluation

As has been explained earlier many widely spoken languages have vast resources of text corpora with assigned sentiment values for different words. There were created general purpose corpora as well specialized corpora. Not surprisingly the biggest number of sentiment corpora were developed for English, Spanish, Chinese, and other very widely used languages. But a large number of resources were developed for the languages that could be called medium popularity languages such as Dutch and similar ones. We can mention the Dutch Sentiment lexicon of general purpose [4], the Subjectivity Lexicon for Dutch Adjectives [5] and such specialised corpora as the Dutch Book Reviews Dataset [6] having 118516 text files with sentiment labelling, and even such tools as the Repustate Dutch Sentiment Analysis API [7] which could be used by the people without prior training in NLP and sentiment analysis. At the same time, there are less well-developed sentiment corpora for such languages as Swedish, Danish, Norwegian and Finnish: we can mention such corpora as ScandiSent [8] or SenSaldo [9] but they are of general purpose and it is not easy to find out how they could be adapted for the use in culturally specific contexts as youth subcultures are. The situation with the Lithuanian sentiment corpora and text sets is significantly worse. Despite the fact that some text sets exist there are no known publicly available sentiment corpora that could be used in third-party research. On the other side, it is unknown how well these text sets could be applied to the analysis of texts written by the representatives of youth subcultures.

In recent years automatic machine translation technologies achieved significant advances. This suggests applying automatic translation technologies to get the possi-bility to use corpora and tools prepared for another language for sentiment analysis in the language of interest. [10] presents the relatively successful attempts to use English sentiment corpora for sentiment analysis in Chinese texts, [11] proposes a multilingual transformer for sentiment analysis in different languages, etc.

In this study, we tried to evaluate the accuracy of sentiment identification by apply-ing automatic machine translation and sentiment corpora in other languages. We used manually labelled original Lithuanian sentiments as a reference. If the manually labelled sentiment in the Lithuanian language was the same as the sentiment identified using auto-matic machine translation and sentiment corpora in another language it was assumed that sentiment identification has been performed correctly. Otherwise, it has been assumed that automatic sentiment identification has been performed badly and identification mis-take has been registered. Only two sentiment values - positive and negative - were used in these evaluations.

It has been selected several texts written by representatives of different youth sub-cultures from the JAUKA archive. The chosen texts had more than 100,000 words and more than 600 sentiment labels. One of the main criteria for text selection was the quality of the language used by the author and the quality of scanning and OCR (original texts often were written using non-typical fonts and layout) to ensure a higher quality of trans-lation. For the automatic translation, Google Translate and Deeplr tools were used. For the sentiment analysis syuzhet package for the R environment [12] has been used. The English, Spanish and Russian languages were selected for the evaluation issues. This means that text in Lithuanian has been translated to one of those languages, sentiment analysis in that language has been performed and the result received has been compared with the sentiment value provided by the human labeller.

Table 1 shows the percent of accurately recognized sentiments using translations to different languages and different translation methods.

Table 1. Sentiment recognition accuracy using different translation methods and different languages

Language	Google Translate, acc %	Deeplr, acc %
English	69	82
Spanish	62	77
Russian	68	84

It is obvious that higher sentiment identification accuracy has been achieved using Deeplr translation tool. This suggests that Deeplr tool is able to transfer better emotional content of the message written in Lithuanian into other languages (we do not try to evaluate the overall translation quality). Comparing the languages, it is seen that the Spanish sentiment identifier generated the worst results. It is difficult to say if this has been caused by cultural-specific or if the Spanish translation engine transfers the emotional content of the message written in Lithuanian not so well.

In the next step, we tried to check how accurately it is possible to identify positive and negative sentiments. Only the Deeplr tool has been used this time. Table 2 shows the results of this experiment.

Table 2. Positive and negative sentiment recognition accuracy using different languages

Language	Positive sentiment acc, %	Negative sentiment acc, %
English	82	83
Spanish	74	79
Russian	84	83

The experiment showed that both using English and Russian translations positive and negative sentiments are recognized with the same accuracy approximately. Using Spanish translation negative sentiments are recognized slightly better than positive sentiments.

4   Conclusions

The possibility to use vast sentiment corpora developed for other languages is an important task and desire for many less widely spoken languages. Advances in automatic machine translation technologies provide additional opportunities at least in some application areas.

The study evaluated the possibilities to use third-language sentiment analysis for Lithuanian youth subcultures text analysis using automatic machine translation. The experimental evaluation showed that the approach can achieve about 80% accuracy compared with the human-based sentiment identification accuracy. These results could be treated as encouraging since could help interested people (ethnologists, anthropologists, etc.) in their work. At the same time, it is unlikely that an automatic approach could completely replace human analytics, but it can help substantially in getting initial insights and going then into deeper analysis. It should be noted that the accuracy of the method depends on many factors: text and translation quality, etc.

Acknowledgement. This project has received funding from the Research Council of Lithuania (LMTLT), agreement No. S-LIP-21-30.

References

1. Bing, L.: Sentiment Analysis: Mining Opinions, Sentiments, and Emotions. Cambridge University Press, Cambridge (2015)
2. Williams, J.P.: Subcultural Theory: Traditions and Concepts, p. 178. Polity, Cambridge (2013)
3. Bhandari, S., Ghosh, G.: An overview of sentiment analysis: approaches and applications. iJRCS – Int. J. Res. Comput. Sci. **03**(04) (2016)
4. Hogenboom, A., Heerschop, B., Frasincar, F., Kaymak, U., de Jong, F.: Multi-lingual support for lexicon-based sentiment analysis guided by semantics. Decis. Support Syst. **62**, 43–53 (2014)
5. Smedt, T., Daelemans., W.: "Vreselijk mooi!" (terribly beautiful): a subjectivity lexicon for Dutch adjectives. In: Proceedings of International Conference on Language Resources and Evaluation (2012)
6. Dutch Book Reviews Dataset. https://github.com/benjaminvdb/DBRD
7. Repustate - Dutch sentiment analysis API for Videos, Reviews & Twitter data. https://www.repustate.com/dutch-sentiment-analysis/
8. ScandiSent - Sentiment Corpus for Swedish, Norwegian, Danish, Finnish. https://github.com/timpal0l/ScandiSent. Accessed 12 Mar 2022
9. Rouces, J., Borin, L., Tahmasebi, N., Eide, S.: SenSALDO: a Swedish sentiment lexicon for the SWE-CLARIN toolbox. In: Selected papers from the CLARIN Annual Conference 2018, Pisa, 8–10 October 2018. Linköping Electronic Conference Proceedings, vol. 159, pp. 177–187 (2018)
10. He, Y., Harith, A., Zhou, D.: Exploring English lexicon knowledge for Chinese sentiment analysis. In: CIPS-SIGHAN Joint Conference on Chinese Language Processing, 28–29 August 2010, Beijing, China (2010)
11. Barriere, V., Balahur., A.: Improving sentiment analysis over non-English tweets using multilingual transformers and automatic translation for data-augmentation. In: Proceedings of the 28th International Conference on Computational Linguistics, Barcelona, Spain, pp. 266–271 (2020)
12. Jockers, M.: Introduction to the Syuzhet Package. https://cran.r-project.org/web/packages/syuzhet/vignettes/syuzhet-vignette.html. Accessed 13 Mar 2022

Chatbots Scenarios for Education

Sirje Virkus[1], Henrique Sao Mamede[2], Vitor Jorge Ramos Rocio[2], Jochen Dickel[3], Olga Zubikova[3], Rita Butkiene[4], Evaldas Vaiciukynas[4], Lina Ceponiene[4], and Daina Gudoniene[4(✉)]

[1] Tallinn University, Tallinn, Estonia
sirje.virkus@tlu.ee
[2] University of Aberta, Edmonton, Canada
Vitor.Rocio@uab.pt
[3] Fachhochschule des Mittelstands University, Bielefeld, Germany
jochen.dickel@fh-mittelstand.de
[4] Kaunas University of Technology, Kaunas, Lithuania
daina.gudoniene@ktu.lt

Abstract. Educational chatbots are digital tools designed to assist learners in various educational settings. These chatbots use natural language processing (NLP) and machine learning algorithms to simulate human conversation and respond to user queries in a way that facilitates learning. They can be integrated into various educational platforms such as learning management systems, educational apps, and websites to provide learners with a personalized and interactive learning experience. Our paper discusses different scenarios for educational purposes and suggests in total four scenarios for educational needs.

Keywords: distance learning · chatbots · learning management

1 First Section

Artificial Intelligence (AI) increasingly integrates our daily lives with the creation and analysis of intelligent software and hardware, called intelligent agents. Intelligent agents can do a variety of tasks ranging from labor work to sophisticated operations. A chatbot is a typical example of an AI system and one of the most elementary and widespread examples of intelligent Human-Computer Interaction (HCI) and can be used as a learning resource (Adamopoulou & Moussiades, 2020; Cahn, 2017; Chaves & Gerosa, 2021). Chatbots are also considered as one of the latest and trendy learning technologies with AI (Vanichvasin, 2021). A chatbot is defined as a tool that combines AI and natural language processing or other technology, which enables it to interact to a certain level of conversation with a human interlocutor through text or voice (Pérez *et al.*, 2020). Dahiya (2017) defines chatbots as a program designed to counterfeit smart communication on a text or spoken ground. Since the inception of the first chatbot, named Eliza, in 1966, the field of natural language processing and human-machine communication has witnessed remarkable advancements. Chatbots have emerged as a prominent application within this domain, experiencing a substantial surge in usage. Furthermore, experts predict a significant upward trajectory in their adoption in the upcoming years (Pérez *et al.*, 2020; Shawar & Atwell, 2007; Weizenbaum, 1966; Zawacki-Richter *et al.*, 2019). Kuhail et al. (2023) found that chatbots hold the promise of revolutionizing education by engaging learners, personalizing learning activities, supporting educators, and developing deep insight into learners' behavior. However, there is a lack of studies that analyze the recent evidence-based chatbot-learner interaction design techniques applied in education.

The aim of this paper is to present four distinct chatbot scenarios designed in the frames of the Challenge Based Learning in AI Enhanced Digital Transformation Curricular programme. The objective was to develop scenarios that directly enhance the study process, ensuring a higher quality of education and promoting the utilization of intelligent technologies in the field of education. The paper has the following structure: Sect. 2 provides a literature review which forms the theoretical framework for this study. Section 3 outlines the research methodology. Section 4 presents the results. Finally, Sect. 5 provides a discussion and conclusion.

2 Methodology

To address the research questions related to the AI in education and chatbots development scenarios, a qualitative research method was selected. The case study was selected in regard to the research questions in order to control research and actual behavioral elements and to focus on contemporary events. To collect relevant data, the research was conducted in the context of studies within the digital transformation curriculum. The research focuses on the approach to develop scenarios for chatbots implementation in education. All data were collected by using the questionnaire for focus groups meeting to find out the need of the targets working with digital transformation curricular.

When providing examples, all details were discussed related to the AI implementation, attitudes, achievements, etc. The theoretical framework was built to be related to the learning process. The case study is based on the reflections, feedback, and assessments of the module's teachers, the students, and the challenge owners. The data used were anonymized and analyzed.

3 Theoretical Background

3.1 Previous Literature Review Findings

Numerous literature reviews have systematically analyzed the body of research investigating the utilization of chatbots in the realm of education (Cunningham-Nelson *et al.*, 2019; Hobert, 2019; Hwang & Chang, 2021; Kuhail *et al.*, 2023; Okonkwo & Ade-Ibijola, 2021; Pérez *et al.*, 2020; Thomas, 2020; Wollny *et al.*, 2021).

For example, Cunningham-Nelson et al. (2019) conducted a review of the relevant literature on chatbots and presented two potential scenarios demonstrating their utility in an educational environment, accompanied by a sample application for each scenario. The first case involves an FAQ chatbot that allows educators to interact with students and answer commonly asked questions. It reduces educators' workload, offers personalized responses, and supports knowledge retention across different instructors. The second case is about a quiz chatbot for students. It helps identify misconceptions, directs students to resources, and allows for error correction and clarifications through dialogue. These chatbots are not standalone resources but rather support mechanisms for handling large student numbers and promoting individualization. They require supervision, support, and maintenance.

The study by Pérez et al. (2020) examined the role of chatbots in education and identified two distinct categories: 1) service-oriented chatbots and 2) teaching-oriented chatbots. Teaching-oriented chatbots have been developed and tested for various age groups, demonstrating their versatility as educational tools. These chatbots can serve as teacher's assistants, complete educators, or trainers in specific subject areas. Notably, there is a significant number of teaching-oriented chatbots designed for language learning, leveraging the effectiveness of conversation in language acquisition. They also suggest that implementing chatbots across multiple platforms can enhance their utility and emphasize the importance of user motivation. Furthermore, certain chatbots possess the capability to detect learners' moods and respond in a way that promotes emotional engagement. Their study also highlights the use of chatbots as a pedagogical tool and their impact on students with disabilities and marginalized groups. It highlights that chatbots have been successful in their applications, with evaluation methods varying based on their purpose. Student questionnaires are commonly used to evaluate chatbots, although other methods such as mixed analysis or usability analysis may be employed. The technology used in chatbot development, including programming language and natural language processing, doesn't significantly influence their educational effectiveness. However, some studies suggest that more current technologies like LSA outperform older ones like AIML. The research indicated a growing trend of using teaching-oriented chatbots as support for teachers, providing benefits such as 24/7 availability, multilingual capabilities, and assistance for students with disabilities. Evaluating chatbots involves various criteria related to technology, conversation, personality, and education.

Thomas (2020) discussed the use of AI in chatbots and highlights the benefits of personalized learning and customized education. The author also explores various applications of chatbots in tutoring, spaced interval learning, assessment of composition skills, student-teacher interaction, easing tasks for tutors, integration of chatbots in classrooms, appealing methods of online education, and language learning. The summary concludes by acknowledging the ongoing research and potential of chatbots in improving education despite some limitations.

Hwang and Chang (2021) found that the research on chatbots in education is deemed to be in the early stages, with great potential for growth and investment. The recommendation for future research includes analyzing teachers' and learners' performance from different perspectives, such as graphical learning behavior analysis and utilizing chatbots to enhance the learning process and effectiveness. They also note that most studies evaluating chatbots' effectiveness in education use pre- and post-tests and questionnaires, neglecting the analysis of students' learning behaviors or causal relationships. However, a few studies have started focusing on students' behavior during the learning process and have found positive outcomes, such as improved speaking performance. They also point out that current chatbot-based educational studies primarily employ a guided learning strategy, indicating a need for incorporating other strategies to enhance student engagement and higher-order thinking.

Okonkwo and Ade-Ibijola (2021) found in their systematic review that most chatbots in education focus on teaching and learning, administration, assessment, advisory, and research. Teaching and learning received the most attention (66%), followed by research and development (19%) and student assessments (6%). The review identified benefits like content integration, quick access, motivation, engagement, and immediate assistance. However, challenges such as ethics, evaluation, user attitudes, supervision, and maintenance can affect chatbot adoption. Suggested future research areas included technological advancements, ethical principles, usability testing, and improving chatbot frameworks and design.

In a systematic literature review on the current state of chatbots in education, Wollny et al. (2021) categorized chatbots into 20 domains based on their pedagogical roles. These roles were grouped into three categories: 1) supporting learning, 2) assisting, and 3) mentoring. The objectives for implementing chatbots were identified as skill improvement, efficiency of education, students' motivation, and availability of education. However, the evaluation procedures used in the studies did not fully align with these objectives. Only a small number of publications addressed chatbot adaptations, mainly within quizzes, indicating a research gap. Three challenges for chatbots in education were identified as research opportunities. The first challenge is aligning chatbot evaluations with implementation objectives, considering cognitive and emotional effects alongside usability and technical correctness. The second challenge involves exploring the potential of chatbots for mentoring students and understanding their information needs. The third challenge is to investigate and leverage the adaptation capabilities of chatbots for education purposes. They found that addressing these challenges could lead to effective educational tools that provide informative feedback.

Kuhail et al. (2023) found that the majority of chatbots were designed on a web platform and used for teaching computer science, language, general education, and other subjects like engineering and mathematics. More than half of the chatbots served as teaching agents, while over a third functioned as peer agents. Many chatbots followed a predetermined conversational path, but some employed personalized, experiential, and collaborative learning approaches. A significant portion of the chatbots underwent evaluation through experiments, and the results indicated improved learning outcomes and subjective satisfaction. Challenges and limitations identified included inadequate dataset training and a lack of emphasis on usability heuristics. The study suggests that future research should investigate the impact of chatbot personality and localization on subjective satisfaction and learning effectiveness.

In conclusion, multiple literature reviews have explored the use of chatbots in education, highlighting their benefits in student support, personalized learning, teaching assistance, and more. They improve engagement, learning outcomes, and accessibility. Evaluation methods vary, and further research is needed to assess cognitive and emotional effects, align evaluation procedures, explore mentoring potential, leverage adaptation capabilities, and consider chatbot personality and localization. Despite challenges, chatbots have proven to be effective educational tools that enhance the learning experience.

3.2   Chatbot Design

Apart from several literature reviews that investigate the utilization of chatbots in education, multiple authors specifically concentrate on chatbot design. Han *et al.,* (2021) highlights the non-trivial nature of crafting an effective interview chatbot, emphasizing the scarcity of tools available to assist designers in iterative design, evaluation, and improvement of such chatbots. Drawing upon a formative study and literature reviews, Han et al. (2021) proposed a computational framework aimed at quantifying the performance of interview chatbots. Their framework served as the foundation for the development of iChatProfile, an assistive chatbot design tool that automatically generates a profile of an interview chatbot with precise performance metrics. Moreover, it offers invaluable design suggestions that leverage these metrics to enhance the chatbot's functionality and user experience.

Anki et al. (2021) conducted a comparative analysis of the performance of a multimodal chatbot implementation based on news classification data. They also provided the chatbot programming flowchart (see Fig. 1).

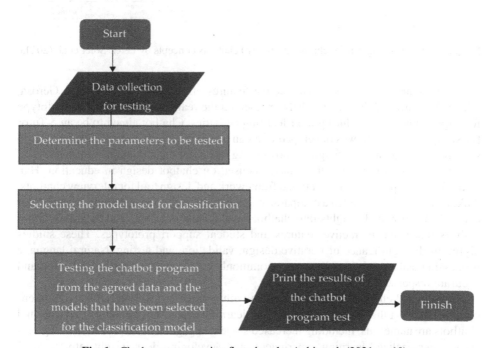

Fig. 1. Chatbot programming flowchart by Anki et al. (2021, p. 10).

Perez-Soler et al. (2021) provide an insightful analysis of the current practices involved in designing chatbots. They present a comprehensive process diagram, depicted in Fig. 2(a), which outlines the key activities entailed in chatbot development. It is worth noting that this process is not strictly linear, often requiring iterations to achieve optimal results. Additionally, the authors emphasize the importance of validation and testing, emphasizing that these activities should be integrated throughout the entire development process. In Fig. 2(b), the authors present a structural diagram, specifically a UML class diagram, showcasing the constituent elements that form a chatbot. The numbers in this diagram identify the process step where the elements are defined.

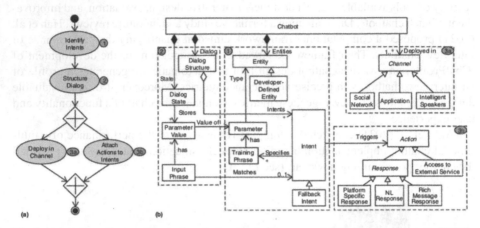

Fig. 2. (a) process diagram for chatbot design (b) chatbots concepts by Perez-Soler et al. (2021).

Several authors discuss the interactive features of the chatbots (Chaves & Gerosa, 2021). Moreover, Colace et al. (2018) presented the realization of a Chatbot prototype for supporting students during their learning activities. Chatbot aimed to be an e-Tutor for students. A system was developed that can detect questions and provide answers to students, utilizing natural language processing techniques and domain ontologies.

In summary, multiple authors have focused on chatbot design in education. Han et al. (2021) proposed a computational framework and design tool for interview chatbots. Anki et al. (2021) conducted a comparative analysis of multimodal chatbots. Perez-Soler et al. (2021) provided insights into chatbot development processes and diagrams. Other authors discussed interactive features and student support prototypes. These studies highlight the significance of iterative design, validation, and testing. Natural language processing and domain ontologies are commonly employed for question detection and accurate responses.

Educational chatbots can help learners with a range of tasks and offer recommendations based on the learner's interests and learning needs. The benefits of educational chatbots are numerous, including increased student engagement, improved learning outcomes, personalized learning experiences, and developing deep insight into learners' behavior (Kuhail *et al.,* 2023). They also provide a scalable and cost-effective solution to educational institutions that may struggle to provide individual attention to each student (Almada *et al.,* 2022).

Educational chatbots can be used for a variety of purposes, including:

1. *Student support*: Chatbots can be used to assist students with coursework and answer questions about subjects (Bala Dhandayuthapani, 2022; Cunningham-Nelson *et al.,* 2019; Srimathi & Krishnamoorthy, 2019).

2. *Administrative support*: Chatbots can be used to automate routine tasks, such as course registration, scheduling, and grading (Ali *et al.*, 2022; Bartneck *et al.*, 2021)

3. *Personalized learning*: Chatbots can be used to provide personalized learning experiences by tailoring content and lessons to individual students' needs and abilities. They can adapt to the student's learning style, pace, and preferences to provide the best possible educational experience (Ashok *et al.*, 2021; Kuhail *et al.*, 2023; Yao & Wu, 2022).

4. *Student engagement*: Chatbots can be used to increase student engagement by providing interactive and gamified learning experiences (Guo *et al.*, 2023; Kuhail *et al.*, 2023; Menkhoff & Lydia Teo, 2022).

5. *Tutoring:* Chatbots can be used to provide students with on-demand tutoring services, including answering questions and providing feedback on assignments. They can help with homework, test preparation, and even offer feedback on writing assignments (Ashfaque *et al.*, 2020; Ji & Yuan, 2022; Koivisto, 2023; Sánchez-Díaz *et al.*, 2018).

6. *Mentoring*: Chatbots can be used to provide mentoring or coaching services to users providing personalized feedback, offering insights into specific areas of interest, and providing guidance on how to achieve goals or overcome obstacles. They can be used to help individuals develop new skills, or provide emotional support. They can provide information on job opportunities, offer advice on career paths, and even provide interview preparation (Mendez *et al.*, 2020; Neumann *et al.*, 2021; Satam *et al.*, 2020; Wollny *et al.*, 2021).

7. *Scaffolding (challenge support)*: Scaffolding (challenge support) chatbots can be used to provide support or guidance to users as they complete a challenging task or process. Scaffolding refers to the use of prompts, hints, or other forms of guidance to help users navigate through a process or complete a task. For example, a scaffolding chatbot might ask a series of questions to help a user troubleshoot an issue with a product, or provide step-by-step instructions for filling out a complex form. Scaffolding chatbots can be particularly useful in situations where users may be unfamiliar with a process or task, or where the process is complex or multi-step. By providing guidance and support, scaffolding chatbots can help to reduce frustration and increase the likelihood of successful completion (Jasin *et al.*, 2023; Zobel & Meinel, 2022).

8. *Student mental health*: Chatbots can be used to provide students with support for their mental health and wellness, including resources for stress management and coping strategies (Crasto *et al.*, 2021; Klos *et al.*, 2021; Rathnayaka *et al.*, 2022).

9. *Distance learning*: Chatbots can be used in distance learning to provide students with instant access to information and support, regardless of their location (Ndunagu *et al.*, 2022; Neto & Fernandes, 2019; Wollny *et al.*, 2021).

10. *Library assistance*: Chatbots can be used to help users to access and utilize library resources and services. Library chatbots can be integrated into library websites, social media platforms, or messaging apps to provide quick and convenient assistance to library patrons. Library chatbots can help users with a variety of tasks, such as finding books or articles, accessing databases, reserving meeting rooms, and getting information about library hours and events. They can also answer frequently asked questions about library policies and procedures. They can provide

24/7 support to library patrons, even when library staff is not available. This can be especially helpful for users who may be unable to visit the library during regular business hours. Library chatbots can improve the user experience by making library services more accessible and convenient, and by reducing the workload of library staff (Kaushal & Yadav, 2022; Meincke, 2018; Thalaya *et al.*, 2022).

11. *Cultural support*: These chatbots are designed to help users learn about different cultures and languages. They can provide historical and cultural context, offer language lessons, and even provide travel recommendations (Wollny *et al.*, 2021; Zhai & Wibowo, 2022).

In conclusion, educational chatbots have emerged as versatile tools that can benefit learners in various ways. They offer personalized support, increase student engagement, provide administrative assistance, and facilitate personalized learning experiences. Chatbots can be utilized for student support, tutoring, mentoring, scaffolding, and mental health support. They also play a role in distance learning, library assistance, and cultural education. The advantages of educational chatbots include improved learning outcomes, scalability, cost-effectiveness, and deep insights into learners' behavior. With their ability to adapt to individual needs and offer timely assistance, chatbots have the potential to revolutionize the educational landscape. We can state that with the continued advancement of machine learning and NLP technologies, educational chatbots are poised to become an increasingly important part of the educational landscape.

4   Results and Discussion

In the research, we followed the Design Science Research (DSR) approach, as defined in Hevner *et al.* (2004). Following DSR, the research aims to create and evaluate new technological artifacts, helping organizations solve problems. Applying this methodology means following a strict procedure, with a certain set of steps and executing a certain number of actions on each step (Peffers *et al.*, 2007), as represented in Fig. 3.

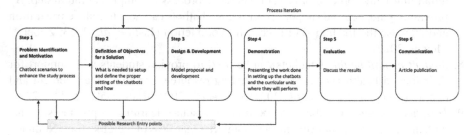

Fig. 3. Six steps from DSR adapted from (Peffers *et al.*, 2007)

As a result, the six step procedure is followed for performing the DSR:

1. Problem Identification and Motivation: Identification and specification of the research problem, definition of the goals for a solution;
2. Definition of the Objectives for a Solution: The issue definition and knowledge of what is achievable and practical are used to infer the objectives of a solution;

3. Design and Development: The required usefulness of the technical product is determined, as well as its architecture. The artifact is then created;
4. Demonstration: Seeks to explain how the artifact created in the preceding stage aids in the resolution of one or more situations of the issue;
5. Evaluation: The observation and measurement of the efficacy of the artifact to support a solution to the problem. This answer is then compared to the demonstration results;
6. Communication: The process concludes with an explanation of the problem and its relevance, as well as the artifact and its usability, distinctiveness, and efficacy to researchers and other relevant audiences.

5   Chatbots Scenarios for Educational Purposes

The authors developed in total four chatbot scenarios *directly related to the study process*, that could assure better quality of education and incensement of using intelligence technologies in education by developing virtual assistant i.e.

1. chatbot for course guiding and support,
2. chatbot for content material support,
3. chatbot for assessment,
4. chatbot for individual tasks support (Fig. 4).

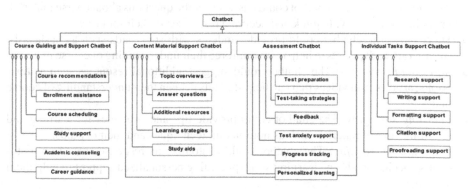

Fig. 4. Four chatbot scenarios directly related to the study process

A course guiding and supporting chatbot would be designed to assist students in navigating their educational journey. The chatbot would be available 24/7 and accessible from any device with an internet connection. It would be programmed with a range of features to support students in achieving their academic goals. Some of the features that a course guidance and support chatbot might include are:

• *Course recommendations*: The chatbot could suggest courses based on a student's interests, academic history, and career aspirations.
• *Enrollment assistance:* The chatbot could help students enroll in courses, answer questions about enrollment requirements, and provide guidance on how to register for classes.

- *Course scheduling:* The chatbot could help students schedule courses in a way that fits their availability, and ensure they are taking the appropriate courses to meet their degree requirements.
- *Study support:* The chatbot could provide tips and resources to help students study effectively, manage their time, and prepare for exams.
- *Academic counseling:* The chatbot could offer advice and support for students who are struggling academically, and connect them with appropriate resources such as tutoring services or academic advisors.
- *Career guidance:* The chatbot could provide information about career options related to different courses, and connect students with career counselors for more personalized guidance.

A course guidance and support chatbot would be a valuable resource for students, providing them with quick and convenient access to information and support that can help them succeed in their academic pursuits.

Chatbot for content material support would be used to assist students with the material covered in their courses. This type of chatbot would be especially useful for students who need additional support outside of the classroom, or who prefer to study independently. Some features that a content material support chatbot might include:

- *Topic overviews:* The chatbot could provide overviews of the topics covered in a course, breaking down complex concepts into easy-to-understand language.
- *Answer questions:* The chatbot could answer specific questions about course material, providing students with quick and accurate responses to their inquiries.
- *Study aids:* The chatbot could provide students with study aids such as flashcards, summaries, and quizzes to help them reinforce their understanding of course material.
- *Additional resources:* The chatbot could suggest additional resources such as textbooks, articles, and videos that can help students deepen their understanding of course material.
- *Learning strategies:* The chatbot could provide tips and strategies for learning and retaining course material, such as note-taking techniques and memory aids.
- *Personalized learning:* The chatbot could customize its responses based on a student's specific needs and learning style, providing personalized support to help them succeed.

A content material support chatbot would be a valuable tool for students who want to enhance their learning experience and succeed in their courses. It would provide quick and convenient access to information and resources that can help students understand and retain course material more effectively.

A chatbot designed to support assessment would be designed to assist students in preparing for exams, quizzes, and other assessments. This type of chatbot would be especially useful for students who struggle with test anxiety, need additional support outside of the classroom, or who want to improve their performance on assessments. Some features that an assessment chatbot might include:

- *Test preparation:* The chatbot could provide students with test preparation resources such as study guides, practice exams, and sample questions.

- *Test-taking strategies:* The chatbot could provide tips and strategies for taking exams, such as time-management techniques, strategies for answering multiple-choice questions, and approaches for tackling essay questions.
- *Feedback:* The chatbot could provide feedback on student performance on practice exams and quizzes, identifying areas where the student needs improvement and suggesting ways to strengthen their knowledge.
- *Test anxiety support:* The chatbot could provide strategies for managing test anxiety and reducing stress before and during exams.
- *Personalized learning:* The chatbot could customize its responses based on a student's specific needs and learning style, providing personalized support to help them succeed on assessments.
- *Progress tracking:* The chatbot could track a student's progress over time, providing insights into their strengths and weaknesses and suggesting areas where they might benefit from additional support.

An assessment chatbot would be a valuable resource for students who want to improve their performance on exams and quizzes. It would provide quick and convenient access to information and resources that can help students feel more confident and prepared, and ultimately achieve better results on their assessments.

A chatbot designed to provide **individual task support** would be used to assist students with specific tasks related to their academic work. This type of chatbot would be especially useful for students who need help with tasks outside of the classroom, such as research, writing assignments, or formatting papers. Some features that an individual task support chatbot might include:

- *Research support:* The chatbot could provide assistance with research tasks such as finding sources, evaluating information, and organizing research materials.
- *Writing support:* The chatbot could provide guidance on writing tasks such as brainstorming, outlining, drafting, and revising essays and other written assignments.
- *Formatting support:* The chatbot could provide guidance on formatting papers according to specific guidelines, such as APA or MLA style.
- *Citation support:* The chatbot could assist students with citing sources in their work, including generating bibliographies and correctly formatting in-text citations.
- *Proofreading support:* The chatbot could provide assistance with proofreading and editing written work, including identifying errors and suggesting improvements.
- *Personalized learning:* The chatbot could customize its responses based on a student's specific needs and preferences, providing personalized support to help them succeed.

An individual task support chatbot would be a valuable tool for students who need help with specific tasks related to their academic work. It would provide quick and convenient access to information and resources that can help students complete their work more efficiently and effectively.

In conclusion, these chatbots offer a range of features and personalized support to assist students in navigating their educational journey, understanding course material, preparing for assessments, and completing academic tasks more efficiently. Thus, these chatbots serve as valuable resources, enhancing the learning experience and improving academic performance for students.

6 Conclusions

1. D Chatbots scenarios will be provided in the digital format with a possibility for downloading and printing and looking at the perspective chatbots will be effectively used for the following courses: (1) Big Data, (2) Digital Education, (3) Artificial Intelligence, (4) Robotics and IoT.
2. The first scenario on a course guiding and supporting chatbot would be designed to assist students in navigating their educational journey to assure a successful learning process inside the course.
3. The second scenario on a Chatbot for content material support would be used to assist students with the material covered in their courses. This type of chatbot would be especially useful for students who need additional support outside of the classroom, or who prefer to study independently.
4. The third scenario on a chatbot designed to support assessment will assist students in preparing for exams, quizzes, and other assessments.
5. The fourth scenario on a chatbot designed to provide individual task support would be used to assist students with specific tasks related to their academic work. This type of chatbot would be especially useful for students who need help with tasks outside of the classroom, such as research, writing assignments, or formatting papers.

Acknowledgement. The paper is developed in the frames of the Erasmus+ project "ASSISTANT - Challenge Based Learning in AI Enhanced Digital Transformation Curricular", No. 2022-1-LT01-KA220-HED-000086555.

References

Adamopoulou, E., Moussiades, L.: An overview of chatbot technology. In: Maglogiannis, I., Iliadis, L., Pimenidis, E. (eds.) AIAI 2020, Part II. IAICT, vol. 584, pp. 373–383. Springer, Cham (2020). https://doi.org/10.1007/978-3-030-49186-4_31

Ali, M.S., Azam, F., Safdar, A., Anwar, M.W.: Intelligent agents in educational institutions: NEdBOT-NLP-based chatbot for administrative support using DialogFlow. In: 2022 IEEE International Conference on Agents (ICA), pp. 30–35. IEEE (2022)

Almada, A., Yu, Q., Patel, P.: Proactive chatbot framework based on the PS2CLH model: an AI-Deep Learning chatbot assistant for students. In: Arai, K. (ed.) IntelliSys 2022. LNNS, vol. 542, pp. 751–770. Springer, Cham (2022). https://doi.org/10.1007/978-3-031-16072-1_54

Anki, P., Bustamam, A., Buyung, R.A.: Comparative analysis of performance between multimodal implementation of chatbot based on news classification data using categories. Electronics 10(21), 2696 (2021)

Ashfaque, M.W., Tharewal, S., Iqhbal, S., Kayte, C.N.: A review on techniques, characteristics and approaches of an intelligent tutoring chatbot system. In: 2020 International Conference on Smart Innovations in Design, Environment, Management, Planning and Computing (ICSIDEMPC), pp. 258–262. IEEE (2020)

Ashok, M., Ramasamy, K., Snehitha, G., Keerthi, S.R.: A systematic survey of cognitive chatbots in personalized learning framework. In: 2021 Sixth International Conference on Wireless Communications, Signal Processing and Networking (WiSPNET), pp. 241–245. IEEE (2021)

Bala Dhandayuthapani, V.: A proposed cognitive framework model for a student support chatbot in a higher education. Int. J. Adv. Netw. Appl. **14**(02), 5390–5395 (2022)

Bartneck, C., et al.: Application Areas of AI. In: Bartneck, C., Lütge, C., Wagner, A., Welsh, S. (eds.) An Introduction to Ethics in Robotics and AI, pp. 71–81. Springer, Cham (2021). https://doi.org/10.1007/978-3-030-51110-4_9

Cahn, J.: CHATBOT: architecture, design, & development. University of Pennsylvania School of Engineering and Applied Science Department of Computer and Information Science (2017)

Chaves, A.P., Gerosa, M.A.: How should my chatbot interact? A survey on social characteristics in human–chatbot interaction design. Int. J. Hum.-Comput. Interact. **37**(8), 729–758 (2021)

Colace, F., De Santo, M., Lombardi, M., Pascale, F., Pietrosanto, A., Lemma, S.: Chatbot for e-learning: a case of study. Int. J. Mech. Eng. Robot. Res. **7**(5), 528–533 (2018)

Crasto, R., Dias, L., Miranda, D., Kayande, D.: CareBot: a mental health ChatBot. In: 2021 2nd International Conference for Emerging Technology (INCET), pp. 1–5. IEEE (2021)

Cunningham-Nelson, S., Boles, W., Trouton, L., Margerison, E.: A review of chatbots in education: practical steps forward. In: 30th Annual Conference for the Australasian Association for Engineering Education (AAEE 2019): Educators Becoming Agents of Change: Innovate, Integrate, Motivate, pp. 299–306. Engineers, Australia (2019)

Dahiya, M.: A tool of conversation: chatbot. Int. J. Comput. Sci. Eng. **5**(5), 158–161 (2017)

Guo, K., Zhong, Y., Li, D., Chu, S.K.W.: Investigating students' engagement in chatbot-supported classroom debates. Interact. Learn. Environ. 1–17 (2023)

Han, X., Zhou, M., Turner, M.J., Yeh, T.: Designing effective interview chatbots: automatic chatbot profiling and design suggestion generation for chatbot debugging. In: Proceedings of the 2021 CHI Conference on Human Factors in Computing Systems, pp. 1–15 (2021)

Hobert, S.: How are you, chatbot? Evaluating chatbots in educational settings–results of a literature review. In: DELFI 2019 (2019)

Hwang, G.J., Chang, C.Y.: A review of opportunities and challenges of chatbots in education. Interact. Learn. Environ. **31**, 1–14 (2021)

Jasin, J., et al.: The implementation of chatbot-mediated immediacy for synchronous communication in an online chemistry course. Educ. Inf. Technol. 1–26 (2023)

Ji, S., Yuan, T.: Conversational intelligent tutoring systems for online learning: what do students and tutors say?. In: 2022 IEEE Global Engineering Education Conference (EDUCON), pp. 292–298. IEEE (2022)

Kaushal, V., Yadav, R.: The role of chatbots in academic libraries: an experience-based perspective. J. Aust. Libr. Inf. Assoc. **71**(3), 215–232 (2022)

Klos, M.C., Escoredo, M., Joerin, A., Lemos, V.N., Rauws, M., Bunge, E.L.: Artificial intelligence–based chatbot for anxiety and depression in university students: pilot randomized controlled trial. JMIR Format. Res. **5**(8), e20678 (2021)

Koivisto, M.: Tutoring postgraduate students with an AI-based chatbot. Int. J. Adv. Corp. Learn. **16**(1), 41 (2023)

Kuhail, M.A., Alturki, N., Alramlawi, S., Alhejori, K.: Interacting with educational chatbots: a systematic review. Educ. Inf. Technol. **28**(1), 973–1018 (2023)

Meincke, D.: Experiences building, training, and deploying a Chatbot in an academic library. Libr. Staff Publ. **28** (2018)

Mendez, S., et al.: Chatbots: A tool to supplement the future faculty mentoring of doctoral engineering students. Int. J. Doctoral Stud. **15** (2020)

Menkhoff, T., Lydia Teo, Y.Q.: Engaging undergraduate students in an introductory ai course through a knowledge-based chatbot workshop. In: Proceedings of the 6th International Conference on Information System and Data Mining, pp. 119–125 (2022)

Ndunagu, J.N., Jimoh, R.G., Chidiebere, U., Opeoluwa, G.D.: Enhanced open and distance learning using an artificial intelligence (AI)-powered chatbot: a conceptual framework. In: 2022 5th Information Technology for Education and Development (ITED), pp. 1–4. IEEE (2022)

Neto, A.J.M., Fernandes, M.A.: Chatbot and conversational analysis to promote collaborative learning in distance education. In: 2019 IEEE 19th International Conference on Advanced Learning Technologies (ICALT), vol. 2161, pp. 324–326. IEEE (2019)

Neumann, A.T., et al.: Chatbots as a tool to scale mentoring processes: individually supporting self-study in higher education. Front. Artif. Intell. **4**, 668220 (2021)

Okonkwo, C.W., Ade-Ibijola, A.: Chatbots applications in education: a systematic review. Comput. Educ.: Artif. Intell. **2**, 100033 (2021)

Pérez, J.Q., Daradoumis, T., Puig, J.M.M.: Rediscovering the use of chatbots in education: a systematic literature review. Comput. Appl. Eng. Educ. **28**(6), 1549–1565 (2020). https://doi. org/10.1002/cae.22326

Perez-Soler, S., Juarez-Puerta, S., Guerra, E., de Lara, J.: Choosing a chatbot development tool. IEEE Softw. **38**(4), 94–103 (2021)

Rathnayaka, P., Mills, N., Burnett, D., De Silva, D., Alahakoon, D., Gray, R.: A mental health chatbot with cognitive skills for personalized behavioral activation and remote health monitoring. Sensors **22**(10), 3653 (2022)

Sánchez-Díaz, X., Ayala-Bastidas, G., Fonseca-Ortiz, P., Garrido, L.: A knowledge-based methodology for building a conversational chatbot as an intelligent tutor. In: Batyrshin, I., Martínez-Villaseñor, M.L., Ponce Espinosa, H.E. (eds.) MICAI 2018, Part II. LNCS (LNAI), vol. 11289, pp. 165–175. Springer, Cham (2018). https://doi.org/10.1007/978-3-030-04497-8_14

Satam, S., Nimje, T., Shetty, S., Kurle, S.: Review on mentoring chatbot. SAMRIDDHI: J. Phys. Sci. Eng. Technol. **12**(SUP 1), 147–150 (2020)

Shawar, B.A., Atwell, E.: Chatbots: are they really useful? J. Lang. Technol. Comput. Linguist. **22**(1), 29–49 (2007)

Sreelakshmi, A.S., Abhinaya, S.B., Nair, A., Nirmala, S.J.: A question answering and quiz generation chatbot for education. In: 2019 Grace Hopper Celebration India (GHCI), pp. 1–6. IEEE (2019)

Srimathi, H., Krishnamoorthy, A.: Personalization of student support services using chatbot. Int. J. Sci. Technol. **8**(9), 1744–1747 (2019)

Thalaya, N., Puritat, K.: BCNPYLIB CHAT BOT: the artificial intelligence Chatbot for library services in college of nursing. In: 2022 Joint International Conference on Digital Arts, Media and Technology with ECTI Northern Section Conference on Electrical, Electronics, Computer and Telecommunications Engineering (ECTI DAMT & NCON), pp. 247–251. IEEE (2022)

Thomas, H.: Critical literature review on chatbots in education. IJTSRD **4**(6), 786–788 (2020)

Vanichvasin, P.: Chatbot development as a digital learning tool to increase students' research knowledge. Int. Educ. Stud. **14**(2), 44–53 (2021)

Weizenbaum, J.: ELIZA - a computer program for the study of natural language communication between man and machine. Commun. ACM **9**(1), 36–45 (1966). https://doi.org/10.1145/365 153.365168

Wollny, S., Schneider, J., Di Mitri, D., Weidlich, J., Rittberger, M., Drachsler, H.: Are we there yet?-a systematic literature review on chatbots in education. Front. Artif. Intell. **4**, 654924 (2021)

Yao, C.B., Wu, Y.L.: Intelligent and interactive chatbot based on the recommendation mechanism to reach personalized learning. Int. J. Inf. Commun. Technol. Educ. (IJICTE) **18**(1), 1–23 (2022)

Zawacki-Richter, O., Marín, V.I., Bond, M., Gouverneur, F.: Systematic review of research on artificial intelligence applications in higher education–where are the educators? Int. J. Educ. Technol. High. Educ. **16**(1), 1–27 (2019). https://doi.org/10.1186/s41239-019-0171-0

Zhai, C., Wibowo, S.: A systematic review on cross-culture, humor and empathy dimensions in conversational chatbots: the case of second language acquisition. Heliyon e12056 (2022)

Zobel, T.E.I., Meinel, C.: Towards personalized, dialogue-based system supported learning for MOOCs. In: Guralnick, D., Auer, M.E., Poce, A. (eds.) TLIC 2021. LNNS, vol. 349, pp. 425–435. Springer, Cham (2022). https://doi.org/10.1007/978-3-030-90677-1_40

Understanding User Perspectives on an Educational Game for Civic and Social Inclusion

Edgaras Dambrauskas[1](✉) ⓘ, Daina Gudonienė[1] ⓘ, Alicia García-Holgado[2] ⓘ,
Francisco José García-Peñalvo[2] ⓘ, Elisavet Kiourti[3], Peter Fruhmann[4],
and Maria Kyriakidou[5]

[1] Kaunas University of Technology, Kaunas, Lithuania
edgaras.dambrauskas@ktu.lt
[2] GRIAL Research Group, Research Institute for Educational Sciences, Universidad de
Salamanca, Salamanca, Spain
[3] Open University of Cyprus, Nicosia, Cyprus
[4] ZB&V - Narrative Research, Esdoornplantsoen 11, 1326 BW Almere, The Netherlands
[5] Educational Association Anatolia, Pylaia, Greece

Abstract. This paper presents a comprehensive analysis of user perspectives on an educational game designed to promote civic and social inclusion. The study employed a questionnaire-based survey with 302 respondents, aimed at gathering insights into the players' experiences, perceptions, and attitudes towards the game. The survey explored various aspects such as game mechanics, educational content, user engagement, and the potential impact on civic and social awareness. The results of the study indicated a generally positive reception of the educational game among the respondents. The majority reported finding the game engaging and enjoyable, with a high level of immersion and interactivity. The educational content was deemed informative and relevant, contributing to the players' understanding of civic and social issues. Furthermore, the game was observed to foster empathy and perspective-taking, enhancing the players' ability to appreciate diverse viewpoints. Overall, this research sheds light on the user perspectives regarding an educational game for achieving societal changes. The findings highlight the game's potential as an effective tool for promoting civic awareness, social empathy, and inclusive education. The insights gained from this study can inform the future development of similar educational games, aiding in the design of more engaging and impactful experiences that facilitate civic and social learning among diverse user populations.

Keywords: user testing · Human-Computer Interaction · young people · serious game · game-based learning · user experience

1 Introduction

In this paper, we explore user perception and skill development through the immersive experience of playing a game created to specifically promote social inclusion and civic involvement. Our research intends to reveal the complex relationships between games,

A. Lopata et al. (Eds.): ICIST 2023, CCIS 1979, pp. 222–234, 2024.
https://doi.org/10.1007/978-3-031-48981-5_18

knowledge absorption, and the growth of abilities necessary for engaging in said areas. We want to provide insight into the effectiveness of such interventions in effecting social change by looking at how users interpret information and learn skills within the setting of an educational game.

We get important insights from the players using a well-designed questionnaire-based method, enabling us to record their experiences and viewpoints regarding the game's influence on their knowledge of civic duties and their capacity to connect with various populations. We employ data analysis to identify patterns and trends, revealing the subtleties of user perception and skill development as they move about the virtual environment created to mimic real-world issues by taking control of a fictional character learning about contemporary societal challenges.

By using an extensive questionnaire, we investigate how the game's mechanics, narrative, and interaction aspects contribute to the participants' cognitive and emotional involvement by investigating their experiences. In order to determine the degree to which players' newly acquired knowledge translates into practical abilities applicable to every-day circumstances, we study the manner in which players interpret and absorb the information offered inside the game. Additionally, we look at the game's ability to promote social inclusion and dismantle impediments to personal growth.

The results of this study have the potential for a deeper understating of game design and its effectiveness on educational initiatives that seek to encourage social inclusion and civic involvement. We offer important insights that can guide the creation of the next games and learning platforms by exposing the fundamental mechanics through which users perceive information and learn new abilities. Furthermore, by showing the potential of well-designed games to achieve real-life effects and even lifestyle or behavioural changes, our research adds to the larger conversation on using technology for achieving social changes.

2   Games for Personal and Societal Growth

Games provide a different and engaging way for players to learn about a variety of topics, allowing them to increase their knowledge and comprehension of several societal concerns. People have the chance to learn more about a variety of subjects and explore difficult ideas in an interactive and pleasant way by playing games [1–4]. Additionally, games have the capacity to motivate players to take action outside of the game by fostering a sense of empowerment and promoting in-person involvement with the issues and allow experiencing it digitally [5, 6]. Games have become an effective tool for developing curiosity, increasing learning, and inspiring people to have a positive influence in their communities and beyond by bridging the gap between enjoyment and education.

Today, among other benefits, games as a tool, do not face the same spatial restrictions as before. Smart gadgets, cloud computing, and game technology have all emerged in the modern period, marking a new beginning in the era of educational possibilities. Therefore, it is now simple to expand classrooms and learning opportunities outside the bounds of conventional brick-and-mortar locations [7]. By utilizing smart devices and access to the massive quantities of data and resources saved in the cloud, it opens new potential for both instructors and students and provides additional flexibility which is becoming increasingly more important. Additionally, the use of gaming technology in educational contexts has transformed how students interact with course material, promoting immersive and interactive learning environments. As a result, it is now easier to create and apply cutting-edge teaching strategies and learning opportunities, improving the whole educational environment.

It has been exceptionally important and prevalent during the COVID -19 which, expectedly, resulted in larger consumption of digital content in general. Here some scholars point out that [8, 9] there was a serious issue regarding students' motivation in the context of the COVID-19 pandemic, where online learning has become the standard because of mandatory constraints. There have been particular difficulties in making the switch to totally remote learning, with studies showing a considerable drop in student enthusiasm and educational games became one of the solutions for increasing engagement and keeping interest. Games as a tool for education serve more functions than simply keeping their audience engaged as scholars notice that they served a broader range of functions besides entertainment [10]. Schrier [11] claims that games also served as digital communities where 'civic deliberation, public demonstration and values sharing took place'. This expanded function of games during the pandemic highlights their potential to facilitate important social interactions and further emphasizes their significance in the digital era. Themistokleous [12] further notices that due to their innate flexibility and receptivity to civic education activities, the literature overwhelmingly supports the idea that civic education primarily targets the younger generation. Particularly young adults interact with others, educate themselves, and pursue personal development on both online and offline venues. As adolescents have a stronger potential to adjust to new situations and learn from a variety of sources, this age group is seen to be more responsive to civic education activities. Youth-focused civic education initiatives may successfully develop their knowledge of civic duties, encouraging active citizenship and involvement in society.

Some authors suggest [13] that games that successfully combine gameplay and instructional material will have the greatest impact on encouraging civic learning. These video games would let players draw links between their in-game behaviour and larger social systems that exist in reality. By combining moral considerations with effective and efficient thinking, such games would also motivate players to make ethical decisions regarding a wide range of social issues, whether local or national politics or environmental challenges. It is anticipated that by including these components, the games will provide players who want to improve their civic consciousness and comprehension of societal dynamics with an engaging and effective learning experience.

Additionally, a major part of modern games is created with certain educational goals in mind, which restricts their potential and range. Greipl [14] takes a simulation game on sustainability that tries to inform players about environmental challenges as an example and argues that while a game like this could provide insightful information, it frequently lacks full information, and some crucial elements might be missed by students. Therefore, in order to overcome this drawback and ensure a more complete and in-depth comprehension of the subject matter, it becomes crucial to combine the experience provided by the game with other teaching techniques, such as group discussions. Teachers can fill in the gaps left by individual games and promote a more thorough learning experience for students by mixing different teaching methods.

3 Expectations for Game Design

The active participation of representative users throughout the design process is a fundamental component of user-centred design in the field of game design [15]. It is commonly known that if this important component is ignored, developed games are under a risk of not fulfilling expectations from both creators and target audiences. Designers of video games make an effort to involve representative users at many phases, from conception to execution, because they understand how important this is. Designers may gain insightful information and user input by incorporating players, ensuring that the game meets their tastes, needs, and expectations. This is especially important when designing educational games that have the aim of educating players and making an impact on real-life behaviour as opposed to providing entertainment. This user-centred design strategy encourages the creation of games that are more engaging, fulfilling, and fun for the intended audience.

Engagement is often achieved via in-game goals, such as scoring points, levelling up or other progress-reward mechanics. Egenfeldt-Nielsen [16] points out that it poses a risk for educational games because it interferes with intended goals. Some students tend to ignore or skim important content, usually provided specifically for learning or context purposes. In such cases, players place more importance on the game's aims than on its educational ones and it becomes a major challenge in finding game designs that successfully combine learning and gaming or, at the very least, guarantee that they do not clash. It's still difficult to determine the appropriate ratio between engaging gameplay and insightful instructional material. Furthermore, the adoption of a learning approach is the first component that has a significant influence on students' acceptance of an educational computer game. This introduction has a significant impact on the reported enjoyment, perceived utility, and attitude toward utilizing the game in addition to the perceived simplicity of use [17]. Therefore, while creating instructional computer games, game creators must include appropriate learning methodologies. By doing this, teachers may not only improve their students' learning efficiency but also increase the likelihood that they would accept and participate in these activities. Students will be more likely to actively participate in playing these games as a consequence, and they will gain a lot from them.

Similarly, both players having limited and those having extensive gaming experience, place a high value on a game's degree of engagement and enjoyment. Casual players, who seldom play games and mostly for entertainment purposes are looking for a smooth, enjoyable, and simple experience. If the primary goal of a game is to provide information or knowledge, players are unlikely to actively seek it out or devote time to it unless the gameplay incorporates educational elements in a pleasant and interesting way. Therefore, some players might not find a convincing reason to play a game that divides gameplay and information into different components. On the other side, experienced players often respect the harmony between the mechanics, the story, and the content. Therefore, it causes a similar problem as with casual players if the information component is blatantly and independently provided from the action [18].

In terms of user expectations, there are a number of motives that can act as a catalyst for a player to continue playing and learning new concepts. Research conducted during the "PaGamO" testing indicates that the following motives were among the most important for players: (1) fun, (2) self-learning, (3) want to get a higher grade in the final examination, (4) challenging, (5) want to get a higher score in the game, (6) enjoyment, (7) I can choose when to play, (8) self-achievement, (9) want to win, and (10) the game has high relevance to my learning [19].

It should be noted that in certain cases, instructional games stray from the traditional strategy of teaching students preset knowledge. Instead, they provide the students with the freedom to direct their own educational path by letting them choose the inquiries and pursuits they are interested in [20]. To improve the learning process, this procedure may include input from instructors, activity leaders, or peers. Furthermore, the task of assessing the learned information falls outside the game's boundaries. Participants and teachers are free to choose how they use the game and how they evaluate their learning outcomes in light of their unique objectives. Within the context of instructional gaming, this learner-centred methodology promotes[1] autonomy, engagement, and individualised progress [xx].

4   User Experience with the INGAME

In this paper, we analyse the data acquired from the questionnaire after testing the In this paper, we analyse the data acquired from the questionnaire after testing the educational game under the INGAME[2] project. The INGAME project initiative places a lot of emphasis on online games and digital literacy for the advancement of young people's abilities and civic literacy. It utilizes the most recent advancements in educational technology and attempts to build the skills and knowledge required for fostering interest in public involvement through online gaming. The game introduces and integrates gaming into school teaching techniques and practices, particularly those relevant to the disciplines of civic literacy and pedagogy, and will, directly and indirectly, improve the digital, language, reading, communication, and cooperation abilities of the users. Users will be encouraged to engage in informal, outside-of-classroom learning and civic involvement thanks to the convergence of innovation and education.

The educational scope of the game encompasses the acquisition of social and civic skills, values, and relevant knowledge through player engagement and interaction. Players are required to possess certain skills to effectively interact with the game, and through their participation, they will acquire new skills and knowledge. It is important to consider the learning outcomes and identify which game activities contribute to their achievement. The narrative and storyline of the gameplay a significant role in shaping the game's world [21]. This includes the background story, character descriptions, behaviours and interactions, settings, action sequences, plot points, ethical dilemmas, conflict resolutions, and the design of the game's challenges. The game does not focus on a single aspect such as puzzles or narrative but also influences the motivations for player actions and

---

[1] https://www.learningliftoff.com/the-benefits-of-video-games-in-education.

[2] https://ingame.erasmus.site/.

the available types of actions. Players are motivated by various factors to take specific actions within the game and learn more about the consequences of these actions.

The questionnaire for evaluating the game was conducted in a number of countries simultaneously, with the majority of respondents being from Lithuania, Italy, Spain, Greece and Cyprus. Total number of respondents – 302. Respondents are working young people. The questionnaire was divided into several categories with each of them dedicated to a different segment of the overall digital product. These categories are as follows:

- Goals of the game

  - Overall game goals were presented in the beginning of the game
  - Overall game goals were presented clearly
  - Intermediate goals were presented in the beginning of each scene
  - Intermediate goals were presented clearly

- Feedback

  - I received feedback on my progress in the game
  - I received immediate feedback on my actions
  - I was notified of new tasks immediately
  - I was notified of new events immediately
  - I received information on my success (or failure) of intermediate goals immediately

- Hints and in-game support

  - The game provided "hints" in text that helped me overcome the challenges
  - The game provided "online support" that helped me overcome the challenges
  - The game provided video or audio auxiliaries that helped me overcome the challenges
  - The difficulty of challenges increased as my skills improved
  - The game provided new challenges with an appropriate pacing
  - The game provided different levels of challenges that tailor to different player

- Sense of being in control

  - I felt a sense of control and impact over the game
  - I knew the next step in the game
  - I felt a sense of control over the game

- Immersion

  - I forgot about time passing while playing the game
  - I became unaware of my surroundings while playing the game
  - I temporarily forgot worries about everyday life while playing the game
  - I experienced an altered sense of time

- I could became involved in the game
- I felt emotionally involved in the game
- I felt viscerally involved in the game

- Knowledge

  - The game increased my knowledge
  - I caught the basic ideas of the knowledge taught
  - I tried to apply the knowledge in the game
  - The game motivated the player to integrate the knowledge taught
  - I want to know more about the knowledge taught

- Open-ended information

  - Indicate any highlights or positive aspects of your experience playing the game (optional)
  - Indicate any problems or negative aspects of your playing experience (optional)

According to Dixon [18], the level of prior gaming experience that players possess has a direct impact on their receptiveness to game content, as well as their expectations. The amount of previous experience individuals have with games in general significantly influences their attitudes towards new game offerings and their overall engagement with the gameplay. Additionally, players' prior experiences shape their perception of what constitutes a satisfying gaming experience, thereby influencing their expectations regarding game mechanics, narrative elements, and overall game design. In the provided figure (Fig. 1), it can be observed that the majority of respondents expressed their infrequency

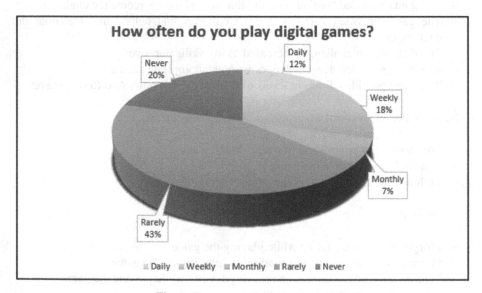

Fig. 1. Frequency of playing games

in playing games in general. Specifically, only 30% of the participants reported engaging in gaming activities on a daily or weekly basis, while a significant proportion of 20% indicated that they do not play games at all. These findings suggest that a substantial portion of the surveyed individuals either have limited interest in or limited access to gaming, highlighting the diversity of preferences and behaviours among the respondents.

Goals of the Game

The initial section of our survey sought input on the game's goals, both intermediate and ultimate, in terms of their clarity. 140 participants responded to our survey, expressing their satisfaction with the overarching objectives laid forth at the start of the game and agreeing or disagreeing with their clarity. In addition, 152 respondents said that during their games, the intermediate goals were well-explained and unambiguous. These results show that the majority of players thought the game's ultimate and intermediate objectives were clear and understandable as well as indicate that the game design is sufficient at explaining its goals to the players so they knew what they were playing for and where they were going. Additionally, the good comments on the clarity of intermediate goals suggest that the game gave players clear direction and instructions as they advanced through different stages of the game that differ in terms of topics and gameplay. Since players could easily comprehend their short-term goals and follow their progress in the game, it allowed them to retain motivation and a sense of accomplishment throughout the experience. Overall, these findings show that the game was successful in communicating its objectives to players, both at the beginning and throughout playtime and the user experience and satisfaction were enhanced by the concise description of these objectives, both overall and intermediate.

Feedback

Based on the results of the questionnaire, a total of 133 respondents agreed that they were provided with feedback during the gameplay (agree/partially agree). Meanwhile, 92 respondents expressed the opposite sentiment about the game. Furthermore, 148 respondents received immediate feedback on their actions within the game, whereas 88 respondents did not. These findings suggest a mixed response in terms of user satisfaction with the game's progress. A significant number of respondents agreed or somewhat agreed with their perceived progress, indicating a positive experience and a sense of advancement within the game. However, a considerable portion of the respondents expressed disagreement or partial disagreement, suggesting that particular game levels require. Additionally, the discrepancy in immediate feedback indicates that a higher proportion of respondents benefited from receiving instant information about their actions compared to those who did not. This suggests that immediate feedback may positively impact the user experience, providing players with a more responsive and engaging gameplay environment. Overall, the data highlights the importance of providing clear and timely feedback to players in order to enhance user satisfaction and improve the gaming experience. Responses also suggest that addressing areas of concern related to progress and incorporating more immediate feedback mechanisms could be beneficial for further enhancing user satisfaction and engagement in the game. It appears that the amount of feedback required for players heavily depends on the experience level as out of 92 respondents 61 also indicated that play digital games rarely or never, therefore, additional efforts should be put into providing additional and well-structured feedback for those with limited game experience.

Hints and In-Game Support

This section of the questionnaire is dedicated to learning whether the in-game support and additional assistance were sufficient for players. According to the results, 132 respondents thought in-game support and additional assistance were sufficient, while 94 said they thought that they were not. Even though this educational game was not supposed to be challenging or difficult in a traditional sense, players experienced varying levels of difficulty provided by the game (Fig. 2) These results are consistent with the opinions expressed regarding in-game feedback provision. In addition, 139 respondents said the game provided auditory or visual aids that helped them get through obstacles, whereas 90 people disagreed. Given that more than half of the respondents said they played video games rarely or never, it is important to note that there is a considerable association between the availability of such auxiliary devices and past gaming experience. These observations highlight the significance of offering thorough in-game assistance, suited to the various demands and skill levels of players, to ensure a positive gaming experience. It becomes important as new players can often benefit greatly from these hints and in-game assistance as they go through a game. They offer important advice and instruction that can help players who aren't familiar with the gameplay, controls, or game mechanics comprehend and advance in the game more quickly. Furthermore, in the case of educational games, they can also be used to explain certain educational aspects and highlight why certain learning material is important, for example, some information regarding recycling provided as part of the game can further be used as part of short quiz and such information on the structure of the game could be beneficial for new players.

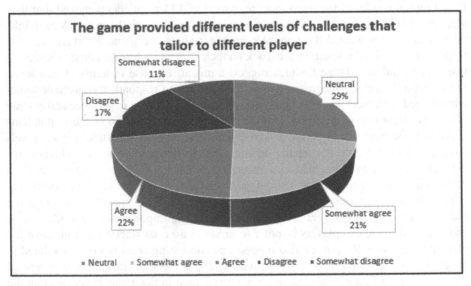

Fig. 2. Tailoring difficulty levels for different players

These clues, which assist novice players in overcoming obstacles and learning essential abilities, might take the form of covert indications, prompts, or explicit directions. Game design containing a sufficient amount of such assistance empowers players to feel more self-assured, engaged, and driven by providing easily accessible and thorough help, enhancing their overall experience and success in the game.

Sense of Being in Control

The analysis of user satisfaction results reveals intriguing insights regarding the perceived level of control among players in the tested game. The data indicates a peculiar trend, with 124 respondents expressing dissatisfaction with the sense of control and impact they experienced while playing. This finding suggests that a significant portion of the players felt limited or constrained in their ability to influence the game's outcome. Furthermore, 129 respondents reported feeling uncertain about the next steps to take within the game, indicating a potential lack of clarity or guidance in terms of gameplay progression. These results shed light on important areas for improvement, emphasizing the importance of enhancing player agency and providing clearer objectives or directions to enhance the overall gaming experience. On the other hand, this presents another issue. A lack of control can foster a sense of discovery and exploration, allowing new players to engage with the game world in a more immersive manner. By encouraging curiosity and experimentation, it can lead to a deeper engagement with the game's narrative, mechanics, and hidden secrets, such as finding interactive objects. This can enhance the overall enjoyment and sense of wonder for new players, as they uncover new possibilities and experiences within the game. At the same time, lack of control, especially for new players, may lead to finding the game and its mechanics overwhelming as something that may seem intuitive for some, may very likely seem confusing for others, therefore linear or semi-linear game attempts to solve this issue making the game more suitable to a wider audience.

Immersion

This category is intended for how immersed players were during the gameplay. 152 respondents did not become unaware of their surroundings while playing the game, 145 did not experience an altered sense of time and 160 did not temporarily forget worries about everyday life while playing the game. These results suggest that the game did not create a distorted perception of time or make it feel either slower or faster, indicating that the game did not provide a strong enough distraction or immersion to divert their attention from real-life concerns. These findings suggest that the tested game may need improvements in terms of creating a more immersive and captivating experience for players, as it currently does not seem to fully engage or captivate their attention. These results point to certain areas where the educational game intended to promote civic involvement and engagement needs to be improved. The game might benefit from additional interactive features that promote active engagement in order to improve user immersion. A more engaging experience may be achieved by including additional obstacles requiring players to put in additional effort and presenting a reasonable challenge for the age of the target audience as well as slight alterations to gameplay systems. Additionally, adding gamification components like achievements, prizes, and a feeling of development might increase player motivation and deepen their immersion. By taking into account these elements, the educational game may provide a more engaging and satisfying setting, encouraging players to finish the game and experience the whole content our game has to offer.

Knowledge

Based on the questionnaire results, the findings reveal encouraging outcomes regarding the knowledge section of the tested game. Out of the total 164 respondents, it was reported that the game effectively enhanced their knowledge, indicating a positive impact on the players' understanding and learning. Additionally, a significant number of 178 participants grasped the fundamental concepts and ideas presented in the educational content of the game. These results hold particular significance for a game that prioritizes the development of new skills and knowledge, as they indicate the game's potential in providing practical and applicable insights for real-life situations. Overall, the findings underscore the game's efficacy in fostering learning and its relevance in offering valuable knowledge for users to apply beyond the digital environment.

These results were also supported by further feedback in at least one country (Greece) where College students who pilot-tested the game, were asked to evaluate it in a separate assignment for their political science class. The feedback that was given in the form of response papers a few days after pilot testing suggests that through exploring the different levels of ENGAME, the main learning points attained are both knowledge-based and skills-based. Students were acquainted with concepts new to them such as gentrification and greenwashing and reflected on similar issues they had experienced and on how important their engagement could be on these matters. In their words, they learned 'how to distinguish a credible from a non-credible sustainable business and how to avoid falling prey to greenwashing'. The learning objectives achieved through the game embrace individual and collective values. Students also connected especially with the levels referring to social equality, ethnic background and housing situation for students and how these can affect their overall performance.

5   Conclusions

The research on piloting the game intended for fostering civic participation and social inclusion as well as data from the questionnaire provided valuable insights for further developing the INGAME content as well as an aspect to pay attention to when developing other educational games. First of all, attention should be paid to the familiarity with playing digital games that the target audience already possesses. This should be regarded as one of the key elements dictating the creation of further content and mechanics as players with prior experience with games intuitively understand simplistic mechanics and additional efforts can be put into the educational aspect and other knowledge-building activities. At the same time, less experienced players may find themselves struggling to learn controls or figure out game mechanics, for example, using bookshelves as platforms for the controlled character in order to reach an interactive object, therefore, this more of a hand-holding approach may discourage experienced players. Secondly, newly acquired knowledge appears to be valued positively, indicating that minor technical issues or lack of familiarity with certain game mechanics are not an obstacle towards obtaining new information. This can be achieved through clear and clever level design as well as well-written in-game content, that, in turn, increase interest and immersion rates as well as keep the player engaged.

References

1. Abrams, S.S.: Emotionally crafted experiences: layering literacies in minecraft. Read. Teach. **70**(4), 501–506 (2017)
2. Ashtari, D., de Lange, M.: Playful civic skills: a transdisciplinary approach to analyse participatory civic games. Cities **89**, 70–79 (2019)
3. Neys, J., Jansz, J.: Engagement in play, engagement in politics: Playing political video games. Playful Citizen **36** (2019)
4. Apperley, T., Walsh, C.: What digital games and literacy have in common: a heuristic for understanding pupils' gaming literacy. Literacy **46**(3), 115–122 (2012)
5. Constantinescu, T., Devisch, O., Huybrechts, L.: Civic participation: serious games and spatial capacity building. School of Architecture, Design & Environment and i-DAT (Institute of Digital Art and Technology), Plymouth University (2015)
6. Dishon, G., Kafai, Y.B.: Connected civic gaming: rethinking the role of video games in civic education. Interact. Learn. Environ. **30**(6), 999–1010 (2022)
7. Papadakis, S., Trampas, A.M., Barianos, A.K., Kalogiannakis, M., Vidakis, N.: Evaluating the learning process: the "ThimelEdu" educational game case study. In: CSEDU (2), pp. 290–298 (2020
8. Krouska, A., Troussas, C., Sgouropoulou, C.: Mobile game-based learning as a solution in COVID-19 era: modeling the pedagogical affordance and student interactions. Educ. Inf. Technol. 1–13 (2022)
9. Nisiforou, E.A., Kosmas, P., Vrasidas, C.: Emergency remote teaching during COVID-19 pandemic: lessons learned from Cyprus. Educ. Media Int. **58**(2), 215–221 (2021)
10. Whitton, N., Hollins, P.: Collaborative virtual gaming worlds in higher education. ALT-J **16**(3), 221–229 (2008)
11. Schrier, K.: We the Gamers: How Games Teach Ethics and Civics. Oxford University Press, Oxford (2021)
12. Themistokleous, S., Avraamidou, L.: The role of online games in promoting young adults' civic engagement. Educ. Media Int. **53**(1), 53–67 (2016)
13. Raphael, C., Bachen, C., Lynn, K.M., Baldwin-Philippi, J., McKee, K.A.: Games for civic learning: a conceptual framework and agenda for research and design. Games Cult. **5**(2), 199–235 (2010)
14. Greipl, S., Moeller, K., Ninaus, M.: Potential and limits of game-based learning. Int. J. Technol. Enhanc. Learn. **12**(4), 363–389 (2020)
15. Tan, J.L., Goh, D.H.L., Ang, R.P., Huan, V.S.: Participatory evaluation of an educational game for social skills acquisition. Comput. Educ. **64**, 70–80 (2013)
16. Egenfeldt-Nielsen, S.: Overview of research on the educational use of video games. Nordic J. Digit. Lit. **1**(3), 184–214 (2006)
17. Huang, Y.M.: Exploring students' acceptance of educational computer games from the perspective of learning strategy. Aust. J. Educ. Technol. **35**(3) (2019)
18. Dixon, M., Gamagedara Arachchilage, N.A., Nicholson, J.: Engaging users with educational games: the case of phishing. In: Extended abstracts of the 2019 CHI Conference on Human Factors in Computing Systems, pp. 1–6 (2019)
19. Cheung, S.Y., Ng, K.Y.: Application of the educational game to enhance student learning. In: Frontiers in Education, vol. 6, p. 623793. Frontiers Media SA (2021)

20. Niederhauser, D.S., Stoddart, T.: Teachers' instructional perspectives and use of educational software. Teach. Teach. Educ. **17**(1), 15–31 (2001)
21. Hopson, J.: Behavioral game design. Gamasutra (2001)

Using Quantum Natural Language Processing for Sentiment Classification and Next-Word Prediction in Sentences Without Fixed Syntactic Structure

David Peral-García[1]([✉])(iD), Juan Cruz-Benito[2,3](iD),
and Francisco José García-Peñalvo[3](iD)

[1] Faculty of Science, Universidad de Salamanca (https://ror.org/02f40zc51),
Plaza de los Caídos s/n, 37008 Salamanca, Spain
`daveral@usal.es`
[2] IBM Quantum, IBM T.J. Watson Research Center,
Yorktown Heights, NY 10598, USA
`juan.cruz.benito@ibm.com`
[3] GRIAL Research Group, Department of Computers and Automatics,
Research Institute for Educational Sciences, Universidad de Salamanca
(https://ror.org/02f40zc51), Paseo de Canalejas, 169, 37008 Salamanca, Spain
`fgarcia@usal.es`

Abstract. Quantum Computing is envisioned as one of the scientific areas with greater transformative potential. Already there exist applications running in quantum devices for different areas, like cybersecurity, chemistry, or machine learning. One subarea being developed under quantum machine learning is quantum natural language processing. Following the promising results existing in problems like sentiment classification or next-word prediction, this paper presents two proofs of concept to demonstrate how these two tasks can be solved using quantum computing. For the first task showcased, sentiment classification, we employ the removal of caps and cups morphisms to make the string diagrams simpler and more efficient. In the case of next-word prediction, we show how to solve the task for sentences with previously unknown syntactic structures by applying a classical Random Forest machine learning algorithm that classifies the syntactic structure and enables our QNLP algorithm to infer the proper string model.

Keywords: Quantum computing · Quantum machine learning · Quantum natural language processing

1 Introduction and State of the Art

The field of quantum computing has emerged as an active area of academic and corporate research and development in the past years. One of the reasons explaining the emergence of quantum computing is that quantum computers could solve specific problems that classical computers could not solve due to computational complexity or the time classical computers would take to resolve. The technical implementation of these quantum computers, albeit it is still not fault-tolerant, is becoming a reality while we enter into the utility era for quantum computers [13]. Companies like IBM, Google, or Rigetti are developing quantum hardware with different approaches, like superconductors, trapped ions, neutral atoms, diamond NV centers, etc. Different approaches exist in the hardware because each implementation has advantages and disadvantages, for example, different decoherence times or gate fidelity. At the same time, the companies and open source community are improving the capabilities that people take advantage of using software libraries like Qiskit [17], Q#, CirQ [8] or Pennylane [3].

The basic unit in quantum computing is the quantum bit, known as qubit. The Bra Ket notation represents it and indicates that we are referring to a quantum state. The state $|0\rangle$ represent the matrix $\begin{bmatrix} 1 \\ 0 \end{bmatrix}$ and the state $|1\rangle$ represent the matrix $\begin{bmatrix} 0 \\ 1 \end{bmatrix}$.

To make operations when the qubits are defined, we use quantum gates. An example of these gates are the X-Gate $\begin{bmatrix} 0 & 1 \\ 1 & 0 \end{bmatrix}$, Y-Gate $\begin{bmatrix} 0 & -i \\ i & 0 \end{bmatrix}$, Z-Gate $\begin{bmatrix} 1 & 0 \\ 0 & -1 \end{bmatrix}$ or H-Gate $\frac{1}{\sqrt{2}} \begin{bmatrix} 1 & 1 \\ 1 & -1 \end{bmatrix}$.

(a) Z Gate   (b) H Gate

Fig. 1. Z Gate applied to a $|0\rangle$ state and H Gate applied to a $|0\rangle$ state

Algorithms theoretically demonstrated in the last century now have a real-world implementation in actual quantum computers. For example, Grover's search algorithm [11], Shor's algorithm [20] for integer factorization in polynomial time or superdense coding, a protocol to communicate a number of classical bits of information by transmitting a smaller amount of qubits (see Fig. 1).

Moreover, quantum computing fields of application have been expanded to other areas like cybersecurity [2,18,24], physics [1,16] or machine learning [4,19] (see Fig. 2), a review of quantum machine learning algorithms and their applications can be found here [10]. One of the subareas of QML, quantum natural language processing QNLP, has been promising studies like Quantum Vision Transformers [5] (see Fig. 3) or the creation of the DisCoPy [9], DisCoCirc [6] and lambeq [12] frameworks. These frameworks already enabled applications in

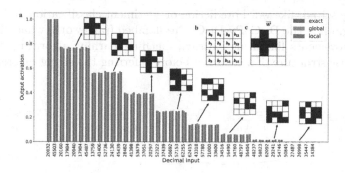

Fig. 2. Classification of 4×4 pixel images [21]

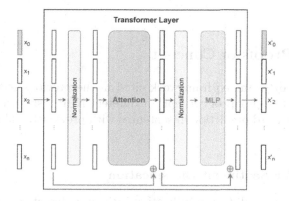

Fig. 3. Quantum Vision Transformer - Single Transformer Layer [5]

fields like word prediction [22], sentiment classification, or interpretable generative music systems [15].

Referring to the DisCoPy-DisCoCirc framework, one of its main aspects is the use of ZX Calculus [7], a graphical calculus for reasoning about quantum phenomena. A ZX-diagram is a graphical representation of a linear map between qubits reminiscent of a conventional quantum circuit diagram [23].

Building on the recent proposal of quantum algorithms for NLP tasks by Zeng and Coecke [48], we take advantage of the tensor structure in order to construct a map from DisCoCat models to variational quantum circuits, where ansatzes corresponding to lexical categories are connected according to the grammar to form circuits for arbitrary syntactic units.

As the authors did in [14], we will try to connect the lexical categories of the sentence with their ansatzes according to the grammar to form circuits for arbitrary syntactic units Fig. 4. This paper aims to achieve classical NLP tasks that are already solved, like word prediction or sentiment classification with quantum computing, using the DisCoPy-DisCoCirc-lambeq frameworks while introducing some improvements like using classical machine learning algorithms to classify the syntactic structure of a sentence before inferring the string diagram.

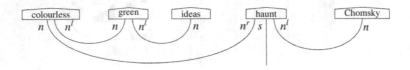

Fig. 4. String Diagram [14]

2   QNLP Proofs of Concept

Using the DisCoPy-lambeq framework cited in the previous section, DisCoPy, we will present two proofs of concept for different NLP tasks: sentiment classification and next-word prediction in sentences with previously unknown syntactic structure.

2.1   QNLP for Sentiment Classification

In this example, we will test classification tasks in different sentences, trying to predict positive or negative sentiment. We present the modeling process, which includes the codification and transformation of the data and model training.

First, the input sentence is encoded into a string diagram using a parser, for example, DepCGG or BobCat parser (see Fig. 5). Second, we removed the cups from the string diagram (see Fig. 6). For the sake of simplifying the string diagram and making it more efficient, we remove the unnecessary cups and caps. The cups and caps are morphisms able to wire an object and its adjoint. Third, we parameterized the diagram and transformed it into a quantum circuit using an ansatz. Some examples of the ansatzes that lambeq provides are SpiderAnsatz (see Fig. 7), IQPAnsatz, Sim14Ansatz (see Fig. 8), Sim15Ansatz or StronglyEntanglementAnsatz. Fourth, when the parameterisable circuit is created, a compatible backend with the model must be defined. We can select a classical device, a quantum simulator, or a real quantum device; when this option is selected, we train the model in the selected device.

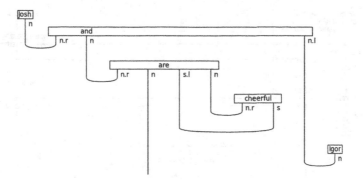

Fig. 5. String Diagram

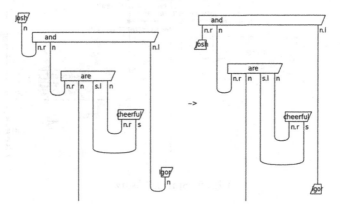

Fig. 6. String Diagram - Remove Cups

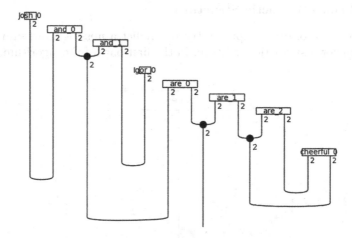

Fig. 7. Spider Ansatz

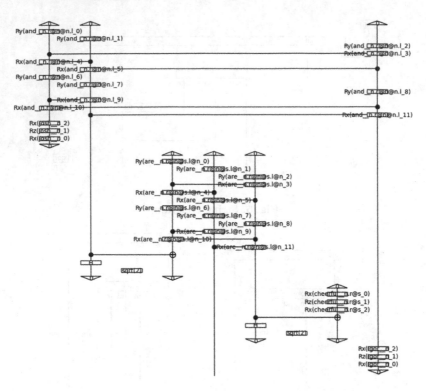

Fig. 8. Sim14 Ansatz

2.2 QNLP for Next Word Prediction in Sentences with Previously Unknown Syntactic Structure

In the second proof of concept, we try to predict a missing word in a sentence with an unknown syntactic structure. In the first part of the algorithm, we train

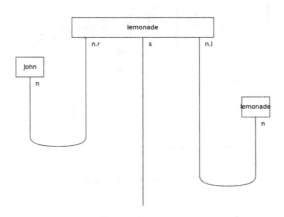

Fig. 9. Prediction Model Input Sentence

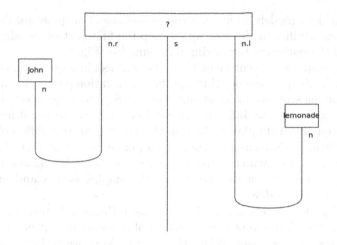

Fig. 10. Prediction Model Missing Value

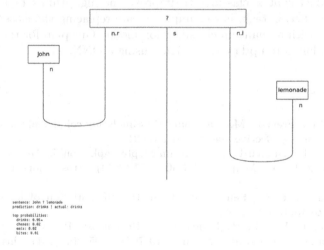

Fig. 11. Prediction Model Results

a Random Forest model to obtain the syntactic structure of a sentence with a missing word. When we have predicted the syntactic structure, we infer it in the DisCoPy string model (see Fig. 10). After converting the sentence into a string diagram, we parameterize it into a model and train it (see Fig. 11).

3   Conclusions and Future Lines

As discussed in the first section, quantum computing is an area with great potential showing promising results in different areas. Regarding QNLP, the conceptual and mathematical basis of this subfield has been established, the creation of hybrid models, models which can run in a classical or quantum device, allow us great compatibility in the way we develop the first part of the algorithm, the encoding of the sentences into string diagrams (see Fig. 9).

We can compute the sentiment classification task in a quantum device using the Discopy-lambeq framework through the classification proofs of concept. First, we transform the sentence into a string diagram. Second, we convert this diagram into an ansatz. Finally, we infer this ansatz into a model and run it in a quantum device or a quantum simulator. As a next step, we can test different ansatz to maximize the model's accuracy. Also, we can increase the number of words that the model can predict, which is the number of words in the whole sentence, and increase the complexity of the sentence with complex syntax and more words, which affects both models.

Regarding the prediction task, first, we use a Random Forest classical model to determine the correct syntactic structure of the sentence. After that, we parse the sentence into a diagram. When this step is done, we train the model with the unknown word and a defined grammatical structure. We intend to use a quantum model syntax classifier to improve the algorithm's first part of the next-word prediction task. For example, we are replacing the classical Random Forest model with a quantum classification model. Our plan for the second step of the algorithm is to update the weights using a QNN.

References

1. Bauer, C.W., Freytsis, M., Nachman, B.: Simulating collider physics on quantum computers using effective field theories (2021)
2. Bennett, C.H., Brassard, G.: Quantum cryptography: public key distribution and coin tossing. Theor. Comput. Sci. **560**, 7–11 (2014). https://doi.org/10.1016/j.tcs.2014.05.025
3. Bergholm, V., et al.: Pennylane: automatic differentiation of hybrid quantum-classical computations (2022)
4. Biamonte, J., Wittek, P., Pancotti, N., Rebentrost, P., Wiebe, N., Lloyd, S.: Quantum machine learning. Nature **549**(7671), 195–202 (2017). https://doi.org/10.1038/nature23474
5. Cherrat, E.A., Kerenidis, I., Mathur, N., Landman, J., Strahm, M., Li, Y.Y.: Quantum vision transformers (2022)
6. Coecke, B.: The mathematics of text structure (2020)
7. Coecke, B., Duncan, R.: Interacting quantum observables: categorical algebra and diagrammatics. New J. Phys. **13**(4), 043016 (2011). https://doi.org/10.1088/1367-2630/13/4/043016
8. Developers, C.: Cirq (2022). https://doi.org/10.5281/zenodo.7465577. See full list of authors on Github: https://github.com/quantumlib/Cirq/graphs/contributors
9. de Felice, G., Toumi, A., Coecke, B.: DisCoPy: monoidal categories in Python. Electr. Proc. Theor. Comput. Sci. **333**, 183–197 (2021). https://doi.org/10.4204/eptcs.333.13
10. García, D.P., Cruz-Benito, J., García-Peñalvo, F.J.: Systematic literature review: quantum machine learning and its applications (2022)

11. Grover, L.K.: A fast quantum mechanical algorithm for database search. In: Proceedings of the Twenty-Eighth Annual ACM Symposium on Theory of Computing, STOC '96, pp. 212–219. Association for Computing Machinery, New York (1996). https://doi.org/10.1145/237814.237866
12. Kartsaklis, D., et al.: Lambeq: an efficient high-level python library for quantum NLP. arXiv preprint: arXiv:2110.04236 (2021)
13. Kim, Y., et al.: Evidence for the utility of quantum computing before fault tolerance. Nature **618**, 500–505 (2023). https://doi.org/10.1038/s41586-023-06096-3
14. Meichanetzidis, K., Gogioso, S., de Felice, G., Chiappori, N., Toumi, A., Coecke, B.: Quantum natural language processing on near-term quantum computers. Electr. Proc. Theor. Comput. Sci. **340**, 213–229 (2021). https://doi.org/10.4204/eptcs.340.11
15. Miranda, E.R., Yeung, R., Pearson, A., Meichanetzidis, K., Coecke, B.: A quantum natural language processing approach to musical intelligence (2021)
16. Nachman, B., Provasoli, D., de Jong, W.A., Bauer, C.W.: Quantum algorithm for high energy physics simulations. Phys. Rev. Lett. **126**(6), 062001 (2021). https://doi.org/10.1103/physrevlett.126.062001
17. Qiskit contributors: Qiskit: an open-source framework for quantum computing (2023). https://doi.org/10.5281/zenodo.2573505
18. Scarani, V., Bechmann-Pasquinucci, H., Cerf, N.J., Dušek, M., Lütkenhaus, N., Peev, M.: The security of practical quantum key distribution. Rev. Modern Phys. **81**(3), 1301–1350 (2009). https://doi.org/10.1103/revmodphys.81.1301
19. Schuld, M., Sinayskiy, I., Petruccione, F.: An introduction to quantum machine learning. Contemp. Phys. **56**(2), 172–185 (2014). https://doi.org/10.1080/00107514.2014.964942
20. Shor, P.W.: Polynomial-time algorithms for prime factorization and discrete logarithms on a quantum computer. SIAM J. Comput. **26**(5), 1484–1509 (1997). https://doi.org/10.1137/s0097539795293172
21. Tacchino, F., Barkoutsos, P., Macchiavello, C., Tavernelli, I., Gerace, D., Bajoni, D.: Quantum implementation of an artificial feed-forward neural network. Quantum Sci. Technol. **5**(4) (2020). https://doi.org/10.1088/2058-9565/abb8e4. arXiv:1912.12486
22. Toumi, A., Koziell-Pipe, A.: Functorial language models (2021)
23. van de Wetering, J.: ZX-calculus for the working quantum computer scientist (2020)
24. Zhang, W., Ding, D.S., Sheng, Y.B., Zhou, L., Shi, B.S., Guo, G.C.: Quantum secure direct communication with quantum memory. Phys. Rev. Lett. **118**(22), 220501 (2017). https://doi.org/10.1103/physrevlett.118.220501

AI-Based IT Solutions

Analyzing the Impact of Principal Component Analysis on k-Nearest Neighbors and Naive Bayes Classification Algorithms

Rafał Maciończyk[ID], Michał Moryc[(⊠) ID], and Patryk Buchtyar[ID]

Faculty of Applied Mathematics, Silesian University of Technology, Kaszubska 23,
44-100 Gliwice, Poland
m60mor@gmail.com

Abstract. Principal Component Analysis (PCA) is a well-known dimensionality reduction technique that has been widely used in various machine learning algorithms. This includes kNN and Naive Bayes algorithms which can be time-consuming. The reduction of dimensions can have positive effects on those two algorithms by reducing the number of related types of data and decreasing the data they need to analyze. Here we present detailed findings about how the PCA algorithm affects them both in time efficiency and accuracy. All calculations regarding those values were carried out in Python programming language. The dataset used in research is the Titanic dataset, on which data cleaning and normalization were done. The data in this paper suggests that it is possible to maintain the same level of accuracy with great improvement in time efficiency. For the kNN algorithm reducing the number of dimensions by one resulted in a 31.09% increase in accuracy and for the Naive Bayes algorithm an 18.18% increase while having an imperceptible effect on accuracy.

Keywords: PCA Algorithm · kNN Algorithm · Naive Bayes Classification Algorithms · analyze · impact · effect

1 Introduction

As the field of Artificial Intelligence (AI) evolves [1, 2], it is evident that the demand for advanced and innovative approaches to data analysis is increasing. The growing complexity and volume of data generated by modern systems require novel solutions and techniques to efficiently handle and interpret them [3, 4]. Consequently, researchers and developers in the field of AI are consistently seeking new avenues to harness the power of AI and machine learning algorithms to devise more precise and effective solutions [5, 6]. Continuous innovation in AI is imperative to address intricate issues and enhance the quality of life for individuals worldwide [7–9]. The combination of Principal Component Analysis (PCA) [10–12] with machine learning algorithms such as k-Nearest Neighbors (kNN) [13, 14] and Naïve Bayes [15, 16] has become a popular approach in the field of data analysis. While previous studies have explored the use of PCA with these algorithms, there is still a need for more in-depth analysis to understand

A. Lopata et al. (Eds.): ICIST 2023, CCIS 1979, pp. 247–263, 2024.
https://doi.org/10.1007/978-3-031-48981-5_20

the influence of PCA on the effectiveness of kNN and Naive Bayes. In this article, we aim to fill this gap by conducting an extensive evaluation of PCA's impact on the classification performance of these algorithms. By examining on Titanic database and varying the number of principal components used, we hope to help everyone select the best approach for their applications of Principal Component Analysis.

Principal Component Analysis (PCA) is a dimensional reduction method that allows us to reduce the dimensions of big data sets. After the implementation of PCA data sets store most of their previous information but requires fewer resources to explore and visualize it. This is accomplished by linearly transforming the data into a new coordinate system where most of the variation in the data can be described with fewer dimensions than the initial data.

2 Methodology

2.1 Dataset

The dataset used comprises 12 columns and 1309 unique records containing ID, information about whether the selected person survived, a proxy for socio-economic status, full name, sex, age, number of siblings/spouses abroad, number of parents/children abroad, ticket number, cost of a ticket, Cabin, and port where they embarked. In order to properly analyze data in the dataset, data cleaning is required. This includes handling columns with non-numeric data, by transforming to proper values or removing them. Handling missing data by either removing records or replacing them with adequate value. Removing duplicates if present, and removing data that significantly stands out.

In the dataset used in the research, 5 columns were dropped, and one was transformed to numeric data. After doing so all records with missing values were removed which left 1045 rows present. Furthermore, all data in the database was randomly shuffled to avoid any patterns and sorting that may be present.

Columns that have been dropped

- Name
- Cabin
- Embarked
- Ticket
- PassengerId

Columns that have been transformed into numeric data

- Sex

The order of the columns was changed in a way that is easier to see

- Pclass - ticket class
- Sex - gender
- Age - age in years
- SibSip - number of siblings/spouses abroad ship
- Parch - number of parents/children aboard the ship
- Fare - cost of the ticket
- Survived - whether survived or not

2.2 Data Normalization

Data normalization is the practice of adjusting values of different types of data measured on various scales so that they are scaled the same way. It is one of the most crucial steps when analyzing a dataset, otherwise, one type of measurement can dominate the other. In the research min-max feature scaling was used as the basis for normalization

$$x' = \frac{x - \min(x)}{\max(x) - \min(x)}$$

2.3 Data Preparations Algorithms

Algorithm 1: Shuffle Data
Result: Data
Data: x = Data
i ← x.length;
while i > 0 **do**
    j ← random(0, i − 1);
    swap(x[i], x[j]);
    i ← i − 1;
end
result ← max(kElems);

Algorithm 2: Split Data
Result: trainingData, validationData
Data: x = Data;
trainingData ← x[0 : x.length ∗ 0, 7];
validationData ← x[x.length ∗ 0, 7 : x.length];

Algorithm 3: Normalize Data
Result: Data
Data: x = Data
while column in Data. columnNames **do**
    data ← x[:, column];
    max1 ← max(data);
    min1 ← min(data);
    while row in x[column] **do**
        xprim ← (x[row, column] − min1)/(max1 − min1);
        x[row, column] ← xprim;

    end
    swap(x[i], x[j]);
    i ← i − 1;
end
result ← max(kElems);

2.4 kNN and Naive Bayes Algorithms

The kNN algorithm is a non-parametric supervised learning method commonly used in data analysis and machine learning. The premise of the algorithm is to classify data points into one of predefined classes. Firstly the algorithm calculates distances from the point to all other data points present in the training dataset which can be done with various types of metrics. After doing so all data is sorted from nearest to furthest distance. Then the k-nearest point is selected, and based on their classes, the datapoint is classified as the most repeated one. In order to find the distance, the Euclidean distance was used in the study. This metric looks for the smallest possible line segment in the space between two unique data points. As a way to do so, the Pythagorean theorem is used.

$$d = \sqrt{\sum_{i=1}^{n}(q_i - p_i)}$$

When searching for k-nearest points k with the value of 4 was used.

Algorithm 4: kNN algorithm

Result: className
Data: x = trainSet, element = dataEntry, k ≥ 1
dist ← [];
i ← 0;
while i < x.length **do**
    sum ← 0;
    j ← 0;
    while j < element.length - 1 **do**
        sum ← sum + $(x[i,j] - element[j])^2$;
        j ← j + 1;
    end
    i ← i + 1;
    dist ← dist + $\sqrt{sum}$;
end
x ← x + dist;
y ← x.sorted(by = "dist");
i ← 0;
kElems ← [];
while i < k **do**
    kElems[y[class]] ← 0;
    end
    i ← 0;
    while i < k **do**
        kElems[y[class]] + = 1;
    end
    result ← max(kElems);

The Naive Bayes classifier is a probabilistic classifier that utilizes principles of Bayes' theorem which states that the probability of a hypothesis A given evidence B is proportional to the probability of the evidence given the hypothesis, multiplied by the prior probability of the hypothesis divided by the probability of the evidence. In other words:

$$P(A|B) = \frac{P(B|A) \times P(A)}{P(B)}$$

The classifier calculates the probability of datapoint being part of one of the predefined classes that are present in the dataset. There is not a single algorithm for training this classifier but all algorithms follow the same premise - that all values of one type are independent from values of another type. That's why this classifier is called naive. The algorithm used in the research is named Gaussian Naive Bayes. It bases on the assumption that all values are distributed according to the Gaussian distribution

$$f(x) = \frac{1}{\sqrt{2\prod\sigma^2}}e^{-0.5\times\frac{(x-\mu)^2}{\sigma^2}}$$

Algorithm 5: Naive Bayes algorithm
Result: className
Data: x = trainset
sample = dataEntry
probability ← [];
while className in x['Survived'].unique() **do**
   p1 ← 1;
   columns.columns − "Survived";
   while column in columns **do**
      data ← data[column];
      mu ← mean(data);
      sigma ← stv(data, mu);
      prob ← gaussP ropability(sample[column], mu, sigma);
      p1 ← p1 ∗ prob;
   end
   p2 ← x['Survived'].valuecounts()[classN ame];
   probability ← probability + [p1 ∗ p2/x.length];
end
maxI ← max(probability);
maxI ← probability.index(maxI);
result ← x['Survived'].unique().tolist()[maxIdx]

2.5 PCA in kNN and Naive Bayes Algorithms

Principal Component Analysis (PCA) is a statistical method for reducing the number of dimensions in a dataset while keeping the majority of the key properties. In order to build a new set of variables that effectively capture the most crucial information in the data, it first determines the directions in which the data fluctuates most. The first step is to normalize the data to ensure, that each variable will contribute equally to the analysis. The next step is to calculate the covariance matrix. The purpose of this stage is to determine the relationship (if any) between the variables in the input data set and how they differ from the mean in relation to one another. Because sometimes variables can be highly correlated to the point where they contain redundant data, we compute the covariance matrix in order to find these associations. The covariance matrix is a p × p symmetric matrix (where p is the number of dimensions) which as entries has covariance between each pair of elements. For example for the 3-dimensional data set, the covariance matrix is as follows:

$$\begin{bmatrix} Cov(a, a) & Cov(a, b) & Cov(a, c) \\ Cov(b, a) & Cov(b, b) & Cov(b, c) \\ Cov(c, a) & Cov(c, b) & Cov(c, c) \end{bmatrix}$$

where $Cov(a,a) = Variance(a)$, and covariance formula is:

$$cov(x, y) = \frac{\sum_{i=1}^{n}(x_i - \mu_x)(y_i - \mu_y)}{n}$$

After doing that, eigenvectors and eigenvalues are computed in order to determine the principal components of the data. Principal components are new variables that are constructed as linear combinations of original variables, chosen to maximize the variance in the data. These combinations are done in such a way that the new variables are uncorrelated and most information is squeezed into the first component. The reason for using principal components is to reduce the dimensionality of the data while retaining most of its important features.

Algorithm 6: PCA Algorithm
Result: xReduced
Data: X = trainingData
numOf Comp = number of components
X M eaned ← X − mean(X);
cov mat ← Covariance(X M eaned);
eigen values ← eigenV al(cov mat);
eigen vectors ← eigenV ec(cov mat);
sorted index ← argsortDesc(eigen values);
sorted eigenvalue ← eigen values[sorted index];
sorted eigenvectors ← eigen vectors[sorted index];
eigenvector subset ← sorted eigenvectors[:, 0 : numOf Comp];
xReduced ← dot(eigenvector subset.transpose(), X_Meaned.transpose());
xReduced ← xReduced.transpose();

3   Experiments

First and one of the most important parts of data analysis is proper data preparation. The Titanic data set used in the research was first simplified by dropping and transforming non-numeric columns for further calculations. Then all records with missing data were removed and the dataset was normalized. In order to get the best results, data was split in 70:30 ratio. This provides enough training data to properly train algorithms and enough validating data for data points to not repeat too often when testing (Fig. 1).

	Pclass	Sex	Age	SibSp	Parch	Fare	Survived
0	0.0	1	0.448829	0.0	0.000000	0.051505	1
1	0.5	0	0.298509	0.0	0.000000	0.025374	0
2	0.0	1	0.498935	0.0	0.000000	0.060508	1
3	0.0	0	0.361142	0.0	0.000000	0.432884	1
4	1.0	0	0.210823	0.5	0.333333	0.015469	1
...	...	...	...	...	...	...	...
1040	0.5	0	0.711888	0.0	0.000000	0.020495	0
1041	1.0	0	0.348616	0.0	0.000000	0.015412	0
1042	1.0	1	0.198296	0.0	0.000000	0.015713	0
1043	1.0	1	0.436302	0.0	0.000000	0.013907	0
1044	1.0	0	0.273456	0.0	0.000000	0.015176	1

1045 rows × 7 columns

Fig. 1. Final dataset, resulting from data cleaning and data normalization

In the study, calculations were carried out to measure the time and accuracy of kNN and Naive Bayes algorithms. First, they were performed for the training and validating data from the dataset that had been previously cleaned. Then PCA algorithm was introduced to reduce more and more dimensions. The full dataset consists of 6 dimensions which is referred to as the state "without PCA", with PCA it is possible to reduce this number to 5 then 4, 3, and 2. The results of the measurements are seen in the tables below (mean of 10 measurements) (Table 1).

The data from tables can then be transferred to graphs where we can conclude whether the relationship between data exists (see Table 2).

The presented graphs clearly show that the more dimensions are removed by the PCA algorithm, the faster the execution time is. Another important factor is that both kNN and Naive Bayes exhibit a linear relationship between time and dimensions removed. In the kNN algorithm, this dependency is much more impactful which we can prove by

Table 1. Mean execution time and mean accuracy for kNN algorithm based on number of dimensions (10 measurements).

Number of dimensions	Time Consumed (s)	Accuracy (%)
2	16.04	82.36
3	28.93	83.63
4	33.84	83.26
5	46.40	83.26
6	*48.54*	82.72

Table 2. Mean execution time and mean accuracy for Naive Bayes algorithm with and without PCA (10 measurements).

Number of dimensions	Time Consumed (s)	Accuracy (%)
2	0.73	84.89
3	0.87	85.62
4	0.99	84.03
5	1.25	84.57
6	1.30	83.93

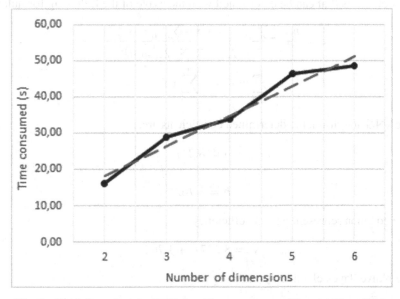

Fig. 2. Graph for a time the kNN algorithm consumes with and without PCA.

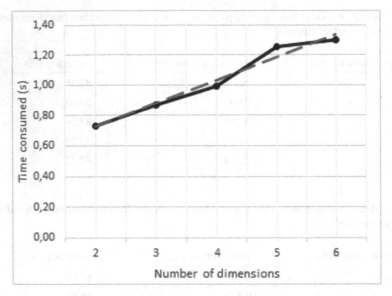

Fig. 3. Graph for a time the Naive Bayes classifier consumes with and without PCA.

using linear regression on collected data. Overall linear regression is method in statistical modeling that help find a model that represents present data the most accurately. In the case of this study, data on both graphs are best represented by linear functions with a and b coefficients that can be determined with the usage of the following formulas:

$$a = \frac{n \times \sum_{i=0}^{n} (x_i \times y_i) - \sum_{i=0}^{n} x_i \times \sum_{i=0}^{n} y_i}{n \times \sum_{i=0}^{n} x_i^2 \times (\sum_{i=0}^{n} x_i)^2}$$

$$b = \frac{1}{n} \times (\sum_{i=0}^{n} y_i - a \times \sum_{i=0}^{n} x_i)$$

For the kNN algorithm, the determined coefficients are:

$$a = 8.247$$

$$b = 1.762$$

The equation representing time efficiency

$$y = 8.247x + 1.762$$

For the Naive Bayes classifier:

$$a = 0.152$$

$$b = 0.42$$

The equation representing time efficiency

$$y = 0.152x + 0.42$$

This brings us to the conclusion that on average removing one dimension with PCA gives us a 31.09% increase in time efficiency for kNN algorithm and only an 18.18% increase for the Naive Bayes classifier (see Figs. 2 and 3).

kNN:

$$\frac{f(3) - f(2)}{f(3)} \times 100\% = 31.09\%$$

Naive Bayes:

$$\frac{f(3) - f(2)}{f(3)} \times 100\% = 18.18\%$$

For accuracy:

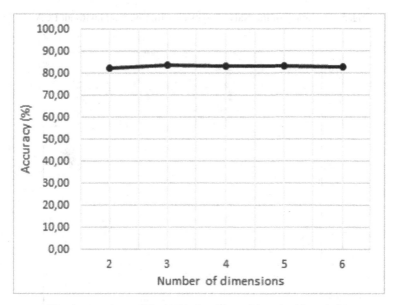

Fig. 4. Accuracy of the kNN algorithm with and without PCA.

From those graphs we can conclude that the titanic dataset with PCA algorithm applied can provide us with accurate prediction even after reducing data from 6 to 2 dimensions. The fluctuation of measured precision for both kNN and Naive Bayes algorithms is negligible and both graphs present us with constant results (see Figs.4 and 5).

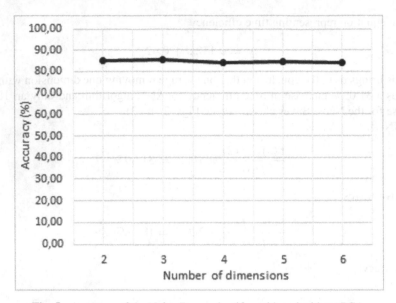

Fig. 5. Accuracy of the Naive Bayes classifier with and without PCA.

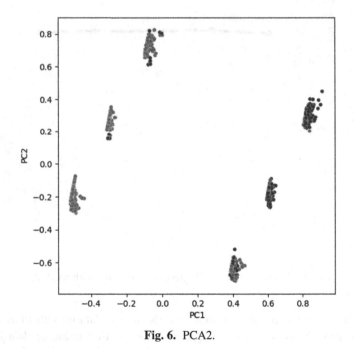

Fig. 6. PCA2.

Above graphs demonstrate the power of the PCA algorithm allowing for a clear grouping of data points based on class. As we can see, data points belonging to each class have been grouped closely together, forming distinct clusters on the plot. This

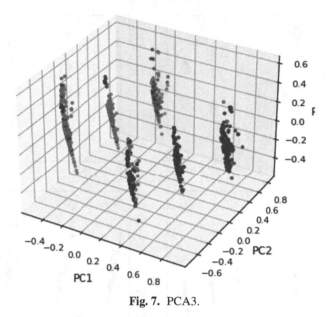

Fig. 7. PCA3.

shows how PCA has allowed for clear grouping making it easier for KNN and Naive Bayes to process the data more efficiently (see Figs. 6 and 7).

While data points are well separated and clearly grouped when plotted in a 2D space using the first principal component (PC1), they are mixed and unclear when plotted in other 2D spaces that do not use PC1. It indicates that PC1 captures the most important information that distinguishes between the different classes. However, when PC1 is not plotted in the graph, the class separation is no longer visible because the remaining principal components do not contain enough information to clearly distinguish between the different classes. Principal components beyond the first one capture less and less of the overall variation in the data, and thus may not be as effective. Therefore, it is important to carefully select the number of principal components to include in the analysis based on how much information they contain and how effectively they can separate the classes (see Figs. 8 and 9).

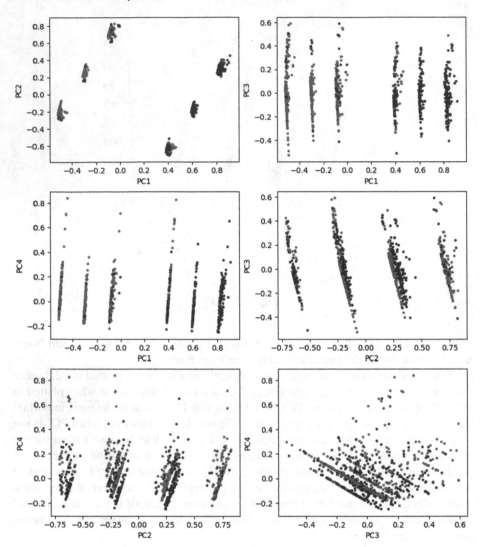

Fig. 8. PCA4.

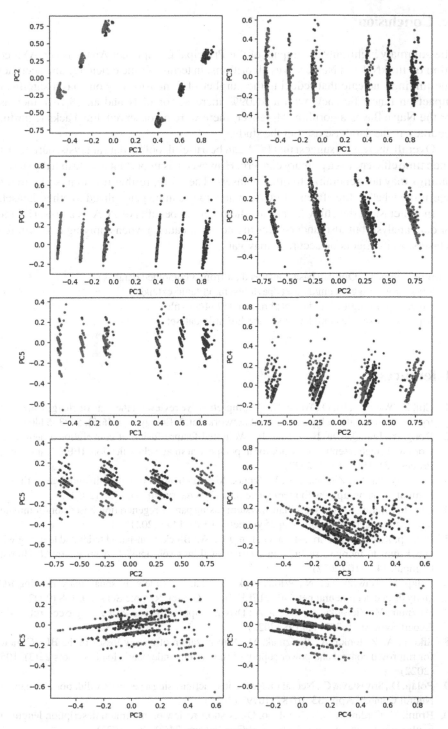

Fig. 9. PCA5.

4 Conclusion

The summary highlights the impact of the Principal Component Analysis (PCA) algorithm on the kNN and Naive Bayes algorithms, in terms of time efficiency and accuracy. The findings indicate that reducing the number of dimensions by one has a significant impact on time efficiency, with a 31.09% increase for kNN and an 18.18% increase for the Naive Bayes algorithm. Moreover, there were no observed drawbacks regarding accuracy in the database used in the study.

Overall, the results suggest that PCA can be a useful tool for data analysis, particularly when time efficiency is a primary concern. However, it is important to note that the study's findings may not generalize to other datasets. Therefore, further research is required to determine whether the effects of PCA on accuracy can be generalized to other datasets.

In conclusion, the study highlights the potential benefits of PCA as a powerful tool for data analysis but also underscores the need for caution when applying it to different datasets, as its effects on accuracy may vary.

Acknowledgment. Our database contains data from 3 combined databases:
https://www.kaggle.com/datasets/pavlofesenko/titanic-extended
https://www.kaggle.com/datasets/brendan45774/test-file
https://www.kaggle.com/datasets/yasserh/titanic-dataset

References

1. Cui, Z., Wang, L., Li, Q., Wang, K.: A comprehensive review on the state of charge estimation for lithium-ion battery based on neural network. Int. J. Energy Res. **46**(5), 5423–5440 (2022)
2. Dong, Y., Liu, Q., Du, B., Zhang, L.: Weighted feature fusion of convolutional neural network and graph attention network for hyperspectral image classification. IEEE Trans. Image Process. **31**, 1559–1572 (2022)
3. Pleszczyński, M., Zielonka, A., Woźniak, M.: Application of nature-inspired algorithms to computed tomography with incomplete data. Symmetry **14**(11), 2256 (2022)
4. Ghosh, G., et al.: Secure surveillance systems using partial-regeneration-based non-dominated optimization and 5d-chaotic map. Symmetry **13**(8), 1447 (2021)
5. Prokop, K., Połap, D., Srivastava, G., Lin, J.C.-W.: Blockchain-based federated learning with checksums to increase security in internet of things solutions. J. Ambient Intell. Human. Comput. **14**, 1–10 (2022)
6. Połap, D., Wawrzyniak, N., Włodarczyk-Sielicka, M.: Side-scan sonar analysis using ROI analysis and deep neural networks. IEEE Trans. Geosci. Remote Sens. **60**, 1–8 (2022)
7. Woźniak, M., Zielonka, A., Sikora, A.: Driving support by type-2 fuzzy logic control model. Expert Syst. Appl. **207**, 117798 (2022)
8. Sikora, A., Zielonka, A., Woźniak, M.: Minimization of energy losses in the BLDC motor for improved control and power supply of the system under static load. Sensors **22**(3), 1058 (2022)
9. Połap, D., Srivastava, G.: Neural image reconstruction using a heuristic validation mechanism. Neural Comput. Appl. **33**, 10787–10797 (2021)
10. Bruni, V., Cardinali, M.L., Vitulano, D.: A short review on minimum description length: an application to dimension reduction in PCA. Entropy **24**(2), 269 (2022)

11. Anaman, R., et al.: Identifying sources and transport routes of heavy metals in soil with different land uses around a smelting site by GIS based PCA and PMF. Sci. Total Environ. **823**, 153759 (2022)
12. Guo, Y., He, F., Liang, C., Ma, F.: Oil price volatility predictability: new evidence from a scaled PCA approach. Energy Economics **105**, 105714 (2022)
13. Zheng, T., et al.: Compositionally graded kNN-based multilayer composite with excellent piezoelectric temperature stability. Adv. Mater. **34**(8), 2109175 (2022)
14. Zhou, Y., Liu, P., Qiu, X.: Knn-contrastive learning for out-of-domain intent classification. In: Proceedings of the 60th Annual Meeting of the Association for Computational Linguistics (Volume 1: Long Papers), pp. 5129–5141 (2022)
15. Vu, D.-H.: Privacy-preserving naive bayes classification in semi-fully distributed data model. Comput. Secur. **115**, 102630 (2022)
16. Zhang, H., Jiang, L.: Fine tuning attribute weighted naive bayes. Neurocomputing **488**, 402–411 (2022)

Comparison of kNN Classifier and Simple Neural Network in Handwritten Digit Recognition Using MNIST Database

Wiktoria Koman[✉] and Kuba Małecki[✉]

Faculty of Applied Mathematics, Silesian University of Technology, Kaszubska 23, 44-100 Gliwice, Poland
{wk303202,km303218}@student.polsl.pl

Abstract. The choice of the appropriate method in the classification task is most often a problem related to the adaptation of the input data to the classifier. However, adaptation alone does not result in high classification scores. In this paper, we present a comparison of two artificial intelligence methods for recognizing and classifying the handwriting of digits. The study was based on the popular MNIST database, and we dug up algorithms such as K-nearest neighbors and also neural networks to conduct the study. The paper presents mathematical models of selected tools and selected network architecture. Then, the results of the research carried out in order to choose a more accurate character classification technique are presented. For the purpose of verification, the accuracy metric and the analysis using the error matrix were used. Article also includes analysis of different variables to used methods, like metrics (Euclidean, Manhattan and Chebyshev) or hyperparameter k.

Keywords: Machine Learning · Neural networks · k-NN · MNIST database

1 Introduction

Machine learning is a field of artificial intelligence that creates algorithms and models to automatically learn from data and take action based on it [1–3]. It is a very important part of artificial intelligence because it allows a great deal of automation and acceleration of many processes [4, 5]. There are a lot of methods that enable machine learning, such as neural networks [6], fuzzy sets [7, 8] or various types of classifiers such as KNN (K-nearest neighbors) and heuristic approaches [9–12]. Neural networks are based on the biological neurons of the brain, and their exact operation will be described later in the article [13]. Again, fuzzy sets make it possible to analyze ambiguous features and conditions and also make inferences based on them [14]. In the case of clustering, they make it possible to assign objects to groups with a certain probability, and not just to one particular class [15]. Thus, they enable a more precise grouping of objects that are hard to classify unambiguously.

Handwriting recognition and its appropriate classification is one of the tasks of image recognition that have attracted the attention of machine learning and computer science

A. Lopata et al. (Eds.): ICIST 2023, CCIS 1979, pp. 264–273, 2024.
https://doi.org/10.1007/978-3-031-48981-5_21

specialists for many years [16]. In the context of digit identification, neural networks are popular methods that allow efficient classification and recognition of digits from different datasets. Such identification can also be done using the K-Nearest Neighbors (KNN) algorithm.

The purpose of this article is to compare the KNN algorithm and neural networks in the context of recognizing and classifying handwritten digits into printed scripts. The principles of these algorithms and their advantages and disadvantages will be presented in the context of their application to digit identification. In particular, their effectiveness in recognizing digits from the MNIST database will be compared. A comparison of image processing time for both algorithms will also be presented, which is of great importance in the context of their practical applications.

2   Methodology

2.1   Algorithm kNN

kNN (k-Nearest Neighbors) is a machine learning algorithm used for classification. It involves searching for the number of "k"-nearest neighbors of a given point in object space. Then, based on the class or numerical value of these neighbors, the point belongs to a certain class or predicted numerical value.

The kNN algorithm consists of a few main steps:

- Data preparation - The first step is to properly prepare the data for analysis. Depending on the problem, this may include normalizing the data, removing outliers, coding categorical variables and other data preprocessing techniques.
- Determining similarity - Similarity between features is then determined based on a chosen metric, such as Euclidean distance or Manhattan distance. The goal is to find the k nearest neighbors of a given feature.
- Selecting the number of neighbors - Once the similarity has been determined, the number of neighbors that will be used for the classification process must be selected. There is no specific rule for selecting the number "k". The value of "k" can be determined by experience or model selection techniques such as cross-validation.
- Classification - The classification of an object is based on the classification of its "k" nearest neighbors.
- Model evaluation - In the last step, the quality of the model is evaluated using various metrics, such as accuracy.

Examples of metrics with descriptions that were used to classify the digits:

- Euclidean distance - calculated as the square root of the sum of the squares of the differences between consecutive elements of the feature vector.

$$d(x, y) = \sqrt{\sum_{i=1}^{n} (x_i - y_i)^2} \qquad (1)$$

○ d($\mathbf{x}$, $\mathbf{y}$) represents the distance between vectors
○ $\mathbf{x}$ and $\mathbf{y}$ in an n-dimensional Euclidean space.

○ x_i and y_i denote the i-th coordinates of vectors **x** and **y**, respectively.

- Manhattan distance - calculated as the sum of the absolute values of the differences between consecutive elements of the feature vector.

$$d(x, y) = \sum_{i=1}^{n} |x_i - y_i| \qquad (2)$$

○ d(**x**, **y**) represents the distance between vectors
○ **x** and **y** in an n-dimensional space using the Manhattan metric.
○ x_i and y_i denote the i-th coordinates of vectors **x** and **y**, respectively.

- Chebyshev distance - calculated as the maximum difference between elements of the feature vector.

$$d(x, y) = \max_{i=1}^{n} |x_i - y_i| \qquad (3)$$

○ d(**x**, **y**) represents the distance between vectors
○ **x** and **y** in an n-dimensional space using the Chebyshev metric.
○ x_i and y_i denote the i-th coordinates of vectors **x** and **y**, respectively.

Choosing the right value of "k" in the KNN algorithm is crucial to achieving good prediction quality. Too small a value of "k" can cause over-fitting, while too large a value of "k" can cause under-fitting. Methods such as the validation curve or learning curve can be used to select the optimal value of "k".

2.2 Artificial Neural Networks

Artificial neuron is function, based on nerve cells in the brain. It has several inputs and gives one output. Inputs have wages, which are the learning element in this model. Those wages are multiplied with their corresponding inputs and summed. This sum goes through the activation function, which translates the sum to the preferred output. Mathematically we can write basic artificial neurons as:

$$y = \phi\left(\sum_{i=0}^{n} x_i w_i\right) \qquad (4)$$

○ y is an output of a neuron
○ Φ is an activation function
○ x_i and w_i are i-th input and wage

Additionally, we often show neurons through diagrams like in Fig. 1

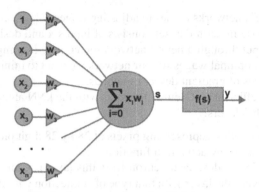

Fig. 1. Representation of artificial neuron

There are a few of the most common activation functions:

- Threshold function - returns 0 up to some constant c, then returns 1. The common function used in linear classification.

$$T(x) = \begin{cases} 0, x <= c \\ 1, x > c \end{cases} \tag{5}$$

- ReLU - returns 0 for negative numbers and x for positive numbers. It's better than the linear function f(x) = x, which is easy to learn but can't learn complex mapping functions. ReLU keeps the derivative simple but is capable of returning true zero.

$$ReLU(x) = \begin{cases} 0, x <= 0 \\ x, x > 0 \end{cases} \tag{6}$$

- Sigmoid/Tanh function - Sigmoid function transforms output to range from 0 to 1, very similarly Tanh function transforms output to range from -1 to 1. These are also better than linear function but uses complex exponential calculations and are only sensitive to changes in the midpoint.

  Sigmoid function:

$$S(x) = \frac{1}{1 + e^{-x}} \tag{7}$$

Tanh function:

$$Tanh(x) = \frac{e^{2x} - 1}{e^{2x} + 1} \tag{8}$$

The artificial neural network is a bunch of neurons connected, often divided into layers. Layers may perform different transformations to their sum of waged inputs, to send it to the next layer of neurons. The first layer is called input, the last is called output and all layers in the middle are called hidden because we don't interact with them during the learning process.

Learning in neural networks comes to adjusting wages, which are randomized at the start. Single learn case in learn dataset consists of inputs **x** and desired output d. After the input of data is put through a neural network, outcome y is compared with d by the cost function. To get optimal wages for our network we want to minimize cost function. We use different types of gradient descent methods.

To compare the efficiency of neural networks with the kNN algorithm, we can use a simple network with 3 layers:

- Input layer of 784 nodes, representing pixels of 28 by 28 digit pictures. Their output is not transformed by any activation function.
- Hidden layer of 784 nodes, each neuron from this layer is connected to every node from the input layer - the layer with that type of connection with the previous layer is called a dense layer. This layer uses the ReLU activation function described above.
- Output layer of 10 nodes, each representing 1 of 10 digits, its another dense layer, so each neuron in this layer is connected to every node in the previous layer. This layer uses the softmax function as activation.

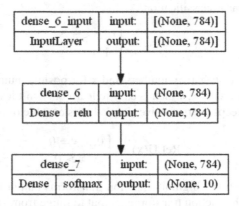

Fig. 2. Diagram of the neural network

The Softmax function works similarly to the Sigmoid function but it takes outputs from the whole layer, and transforms it in a probability distribution.

$$\sigma(x)_i = \frac{e^{x_j}}{\Sigma_{j=0}^{n} e^{x_i}}, \text{ for } i = 0, \ldots, n \tag{9}$$

○ σ is a softmax function
○ **x** is a vector of inputs, in the case of the neural network used in this paper, its a vector of sums of products of inputs and wages from the output layer

The network will give us the output of 10 probabilities for each digit. The cost function in this neural network will be cross-entropy, which suits the output of our network because of its probability form.

$$H(y, d) = -\sum_{i=0}^{n} y_i \log d_i \tag{10}$$

○ H is a cross-entropy

○ **y** is a vector of output from neural network

○ **d** is a vector of desired output (in case of digit classification it's a vector where value 1 for an index of digit the picture represents, 0 for the rest)

Finally, to find a minimum cost function, we use the Adam optimizer, which is a kind of stochastic gradient descent method that uses the first and second moments of gradients to optimize step size for each parameter. The whole network is presented as a diagram in Fig. 2.

3 Experiment

3.1 MNIST Database

MNIST database (Modified National Institute of Standards and Technology database) was created in 1998 combining two NIST databases. It's made of digits written by high school students and United States Census Bureau employees.

MNIST is a dataset of 70000 pictures of handwritten digits. There's even a number of every digits pictures (7000). Images are 28 by 28 pixels. All digits are centered and scaled to a constant size. Figure 3 shows a few examples from this dataset.

This database is well known in the scientific world, to this day specialists are trying to get the lowest error rate possible. People tried with all sorts of algorithms: Random Forests, Linear classifiers, support-vector machines, k Nearest Neighbors, and Neural Networks. In this paper, we will use the basic implementation of the two last methods from the list.

3.2 Results of Digit Recognition Research by kNN

The data presented shows the accuracy of the classification algorithm using different distance metrics (Euclidean, Manhattan, Chebyshev) and a different number of neighbors

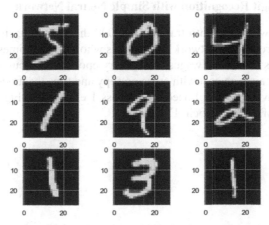

Fig. 3. Few examples of MNIST dataset digits

(from 2 to 24). For the Euclidean metric, the classification accuracy is about 96%, and the best result was obtained for 3–4 neighbors. In the case of the Manhattan index, the accuracy of the classification is also around 96%, with the best result obtained for 3 neighbors. In the case of the Chebyshev metric, the classification accuracy is much lower than in the case of other metrics, it is about 79%, and the best result was obtained for 5–6 neighbors.

In general, using more neighbors does not always improve classification accuracy. It is worth noting that the results obtained for different metrics can vary significantly, and the choice of the appropriate metric depends on the characteristics of the data and the problem we are solving (Fig. 4).

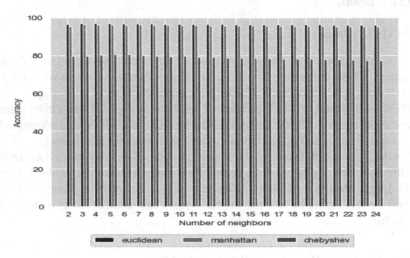

Fig. 4. Result Graph

3.3   Results of Digit Recognition with Simple Neural Network

The MNIST data were split into training (60 000 digits) and testing (10 000 digits) datasets and put through the network. We process whole data 10 times (10 epochs) after every 200 elements we update wages. With every epoch, we calculate model accuracy for the test dataset, average cost with cross-entropy and time the model takes to process 1 epoch, and the average model needs to process 1 element. In Fig. 6 we can see the confusion matrix of the last epoch (Fig. 5).

Fig. 5. Euclidean metric

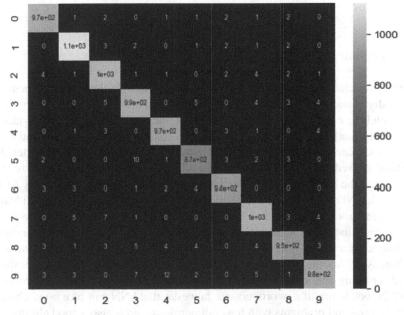

Fig. 6. Confusion Matrix for Neural Network

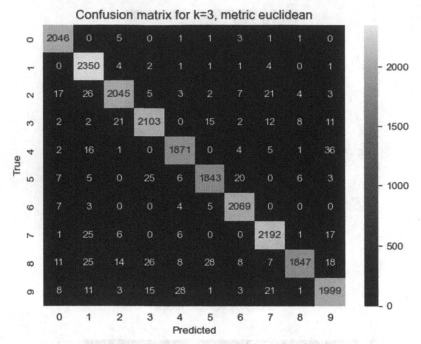

Fig. 7. Confusion Matrix for kNN

4 Conclusion

The article, which compares the K-Nearest Neighbors (kNN) algorithm and neural networks in digit handwriting recognition, aimed to compare the performance of the two methods and the correctness of classification. In the study, the data was divided into 70% (training data) and 30% (test data), and thus consisted of test samples and training samples, where each sample was a 28×28 pixel image representing handwritten digits. The results showed that the neural networks achieved higher performance in recognizing digits than the kNN algorithm. The neural networks achieved an accuracy of about 98.2%, while kNN achieved an accuracy of about 96% considering the Euclidean and Manhattan metrics while using the Chebyshev metric the results dropped as low as about 78%. It follows that neural networks are a more effective tool in recognizing handwriting digits than kNN, especially in the case of a large amount of training data and a large input dimension. Another very important advantage of using neural networks is the time required for fitting and testing. While the neural network for MNIST data needed seconds, kNN took hours. It is worth noting, however, that kNN can be a good choice for smaller data sets and problems with fewer dimensions, and is also a good alternative for those who are just starting to delve into the subject of artificial intelligence and machine learning.

Based on the confusion matrix for the kNN algorithm, we can conclude that the most frequently correctly classified number was the digit 1. It can also be noted that for the kNN classifier, the digit 4 was especially often mistaken for the digit 9. In the case of the confusion matrix for the neural network, we can find that the digit 9 was misclassified twelve times as the digit 4.

The reason for the misclassification may be inaccuracy due to unsightly/fast typing. The digits shared many common features, for this reason the classifier made an error (Fig. 7).

Acknowledgments. We would like to express our gratitude to the creators of MNIST for making this valuable data available on Kaggle. The efforts of the National Institute of Standards and Technology in collecting and curating this dataset are greatly appreciated.

• MNIST Dataset on Kaggle: https://www.kaggle.com/datasets/crawford/emnist.

References

1. Cui, P., Athey, S.: Stable learning establishes some common ground between causal inference and machine learning. Nat. Mach. Intell. **4**, 110–115 (2022)
2. Ke, Q., Siłka, J., Wieczorek, M., Bai, Z., Woźniak, M.: Deep neural network heuristic hiearchization for cooperative intelligent transportation fleet management. IEEE Trans. Intell. Transp. Syst. **23**, 16752–16762 (2022)
3. Esterhuizen, J.A., Goldsmith, B.R., Linic, S.: Interpretable machine learning for knowledge generation in heterogeneous catalysis. Nat. Catalysis **5**, 175–184 (2022)
4. Połap, D., Woźniak, M.: A hybridization of distributed policy and heuristic augmentation for improving federated learning approach. Neural Netw. **146**, 130–140 (2022)
5. Rajeshkumar, G., et al.: Smart office automation via faster RCNN based face recognition and internet of things. Measur.: Sens. **27**, 100719 (2023)
6. Siłka, J., Wieczorek, M., Woźniak, M.: Recurrent neural network model for high-speed train vibration prediction from time series. Neural Comput. Appl. **34**, 13305–13318 (2022)
7. de Andrés-Sánchez, J.: A systematic review of the interactions of fuzzy set theory and option pricing. Expert Syst. Appl., 119868 (2023)
8. Woźniak, M., Zielonka, A., Sikora, A., Piran, M.J., Alamri, A.: 6g-enabled IoT home environment control using fuzzy rules. IEEE Internet Things J. **8**, 5442–5452 (2020)
9. Abualigah, L., et al.: Meta-heuristic optimization algorithms for solving real-world mechanical engineering design problems: a comprehensive survey, applications, comparative analysis, and results. Neural Comput. Appl., 1–30 (2022)
10. Sikora, A., Zielonka, A., Woźniak, M.: Heuristic optimization of 18-pulse rectifier system. In: 2021 IEEE Congress on Evolutionary Computation (CEC), pp. 673–680. IEEE (2021)
11. Marewski, J.N., Gigerenzer, G.: Heuristic decision making in medicine. Dial. Clin. Neurosci. (2022)
12. Połap, D., Srivastava, G.: Neural image reconstruction using a heuristic validation mechanism. Neural Comput. Appl. **33**, 10787–10797 (2021)
13. Prokop, K., Połap, D., Srivastava, G., Lin, J.C.-W.: Blockchain-based federated learning with checksums to increase security in internet of things solutions. J. Ambient Intell. Human. Comput., 1–10 (2022)
14. Kumar, S., Sahoo, S., Lim, W.M., Kraus, S., Bamel, U.: Fuzzy-set qualitative comparative analysis (FSQCA) in business and management research: a contemporary overview. Technol. Forecast. Soc. Chang. **178**, 121599 (2022)
15. Haseeb, J., Mansoori, M., Hirose, Y., Al-Sahaf, H., Welch, I.: Autoencoder-based feature construction for iot attacks clustering. Futur. Gener. Comput. Syst. **127**, 487–502 (2022)
16. Zhang, J., Li, Y., Xiong, H., Dou, D., Miao, C., Zhang, D.: Handgest: Hierarchical sensing for robust-in-the-air handwriting recognition with commodity wifi devices. IEEE Internet Things J. **9**, 19529–19544 (2022)

Comparison of Support Vector Machine, Naive Bayes, and K-Nearest Neighbors Algorithms for Classifying Heart Disease

Bartosz Lewandowicz and Konrad Kisiała[✉]

Faculty of Applied Mathematics, Silesian University of Technology, Kaszubska 23, 44-100
Gliwice, Poland
kk303188@student.polsl.pl

Abstract. Heart disease has been the leading cause of death in the EU for many years. Early detection of this disease increases a patient's chance of survival. The aim of the study is to see if machine learning algorithms can help in the early diagnosis of these illnesses. For this purpose, three classifiers: kNN, Naive Bayes and SVM were implemented and trained on a dataset containing medical data related to the possibility of cardiovascular disease. The result of the study is a comparative analysis of the classifiers that summarises the accuracy and stability of the results in determining the possibility of heart disease. The results show the highest accuracy and stability of the SVM classifier, which achieves an average of 82.47% accuracy in disease prediction, meaning that machine learning algorithms can significantly aid in the early diagnosis of patients based on their basic medical data.

Keywords: Classification algorithms · k-NN · K-Nearest Neighbors · Naive Bayes · SVM · Support vector machine · Heart Disease

1 Introduction

Circulatory diseases have long been the leading cause of death in most EU Member States, accounting for 35% of all deaths. One of the main causes of these diseases is ischaemic heart disease [1]. As various risk factors, including excessive cholesterol, blood pressure, lack of physical exercise, and diabetes are on the rise in several EU nations, the issue has recently grown more serious [2]. Sometimes people are unaware of heart problems until they experience a heart attack or heart failure because the early symptoms may go unnoticed or be confused with other conditions. The most common symptoms of heart disease are chest pain, extreme fatigue, shortness of breath and palpitations [3]. The lifestyle we lead has a significant impact on the state of our cardiovascular system. A lack of healthy habits significantly increases the likelihood of cardiovascular disease. Incorporating activities such as regular exercise, a healthy diet and weight control into your life can reduce the risk of diseases such as cardiovascular disease by more than 80% and diabetes by >90% [4]. Medical organizations around the world collect data on patients with cardiovascular disease. Given the volume of data collected, it's difficult for humans to process it efficiently. The solution to this problem is machine learning algorithms, which can analyze huge amounts of data and predict the presence or absence of cardiovascular disease.

The current state of knowledge indicates that important methods in the field of artificial intelligence are primarily neural networks and the support vector machine. These tools can automatically adapt to the specific databases used in a given classification problem [5–7]. Another method is fuzzy logic, which, through modeled adaptation functions, enables the control of a certain phenomenon like driving control model [8] or consensus in decentralized federated learning [9]. An interesting approach is also to use heuristic algorithms, that returns optimal solution in finite time. An example is the problem of incomplete data in computed tomography [10].

The aim of the study is to determine whether it is possible, and with what accuracy, to predict the likelihood of heart disease using classification methods based on medical data such as cholesterol, blood pressure, etc. Predicting heart disease is a key task requiring the highest precision, so the model should have high accuracy.

2 Methodology

The stages of research are shown in Fig. 1.

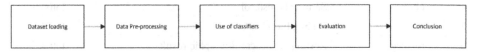

Fig. 1. Flowchart of the research

2.1 Stages of Research

The dataset used in this study was collected through a collaborative effort by Andras Jansoni of the Hungarian Institute of Cardiology in Budapest, William Steinbrunn of the University Hospital in Zurich, Matthias Pfisterer of the University Hospital in Basel and Robert Detrano of the V.A. Medical Centre in Long Beach and Cleveland Clinic Foundation [11]. Dataset attributes are shown in Table 1.

The process of preparing data for future analysis or machine learning is known as preprocessing. This stage includes the following steps: shuffling, normalization and data splitting. Shuffling can reduce overfitting and variation in the data. Normalization is the next stage and its aim is to change the values of the numerical columns in the dataset to a similar scale while preserving the disparities in the value ranges. The data set is then divided into two parts: a test component and a model training component.

The classification algorithms used in this research are k-Nearest Neighbours, Naive Bayes and Support Vector Machine.

Evaluation is the basic process by which we obtain data to determine the effectiveness of the chosen classification method. The conventional metric for measuring a classifier's quality is accuracy, which is simple to interpret. Equation (1) gives the definition of accuracy. We collect the resulting accuracy measures and then compute statistics such as mean and standard deviation.

$$Accuracy = \frac{TP + TN}{TP + TN + FP + FN} \tag{1}$$

The final step is to summarise and assess the results obtained from the classifiers. At this point, it is important to consider what is a satisfactory result. In general, what is a good result depends on the problem we are considering and how critical the possible error is. Since the purpose of our study is to check for early disease detection, we can assume that results greater than the majority classifier can be considered a good result [12].

Table 1. Heart Disease Data Set

No	Attribute name	Description	DType
0	age	Age of patient	Int64
1	sex	Gender of patient	Int64
2	cp	Chest pain type	Int64
3	trestbps	Resting blood pressure	Int64
4	chol	Serum cholesterol	Int64
5	fbs	Fasting blood sugar	Int64
6	restecg	Resting electrocardiographic results	Int64
7	thalach	Maximum heart rate	Int64
8	exang	Exercise-induced angina	Int64
9	oldpeak	ST depression induced by exercise relative to rest	Float64
10	slope	The slope of the peak exercise ST segment	Int64
11	ca	Number of major vessels colored by flourosopy	Int64
12	thal	Thalassemia	Int64
13	num	Diagnosis of heart disease	Int64

2.2 kNN

The K-Nearest Neighbours (kNN) classification algorithm is simple but efficient on small datasets. Since most of the processing takes place during categorization, rather than when it comes into contact with training instances, this is the main reason for kNN's poor performance on big datasets [13]. To create a neighborhood around a data set t and classify it using kNN, we find its k nearest neighbors. Typically, the data sets in the neighborhood decide how to classify t, whether or not distance-based weighting is applied. However, in order to use kNN, an appropriate value of k must be chosen, and the classification result is strongly influenced by this value. In other words, the value of k affects how biased the kNN is [14] (Fig. 2).

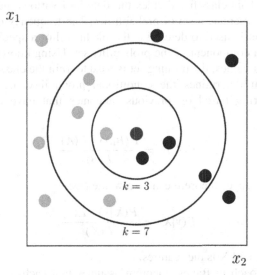

Fig. 2. Visualisation of the kNN algorithm. The red and blue dots represent the classes and the green dot is the classified dot. (Color figure online)

Neighborhoods in kNN are determined by a distance or dissimilarity measure that can be calculated between observations based on their independent variables. The two most commonly used measures are the Euclidean distance and the Manhattan metric. The Euclidean distance is calculated as the square root of the sum of the squared differences between corresponding values of the independent variables:

$$D(x, y) = \sqrt{\sum_{i=1}^{n} (y_i - x_i)^2} \qquad (2)$$

The Manhattan metric, on the other hand, is calculated as the sum of the absolute differences between corresponding values of the independent variables:

$$D(x, y) = \sum_{i=1}^{n} |y_i - x_i| \qquad (3)$$

In addition to these measures, there is also the Minkowski distance, which is a metric in a normed vector space that can be considered a generalization of both the Euclidean distance and the Manhattan distance [15]. The Minkowski distance is defined as the p-th root of the sum of the p-th power of the absolute differences between corresponding values of the independent variables. When p = 1, the Minkowski distance is reduced to the Manhattan distance, and when p = 2, it is reduced to the Euclidean distance:

$$D(x, y) = \left(\sum_{i=1}^{n} (|y_i - x_i|^p) \right)^{1/p} \qquad (4)$$

2.3 Naive Bayes

The Naive Bayes classifier is known for its simplicity, speed and universality, especially on small datasets. This classifier divides the data into various classes and then uses the Bayes theorem to create a set of probabilities. The frequency of each value inside a certain training set is used to determine the likelihood of a specific characteristic in the data, which is a component of the probability set. Using known values to forecast upcoming unknown values, the training set is used to train the classifier [16].

Bayes' theorem determines the conditional probability, i.e. the likelihood of an outcome occurring based on previous outcomes that have occurred in similar circumstances:

$$P(A|B) = \frac{P(B|A) * P(A)}{P(B)} \tag{5}$$

In our case, the Bayes theorem can be rewritten as:

$$P(y|X) = \frac{P(X|y) * P(y)}{P(X)} \tag{6}$$

where y is the class and X is the features.

The naive approach to Bayes' theorem assumes that each feature is independent [17]. Therefore, the denominator does not change for all entries in the data set, so we can remove it and introduce the concept of proportionality:

$$P(y|x_1, \ldots, x_n) \propto P(y) \prod_{i=1}^{n} P(x_i|y) \tag{7}$$

where x_i is the given feature.

The result of the classification will be a class with maximum probability:

$$y = argmax_y P(y) \prod_{i=1}^{n} P(x_i|y) \tag{8}$$

Since our predictor variable takes on continuous values rather than discrete ones, we can make the assumption that these values are drawn from a Gaussian distribution [18]. In this case, the conditional probability formula remains as follows (Fig. 3):

$$P(x_i|y) = \frac{1}{\sigma\sqrt{2\pi}} exp - \frac{(x_i - \mu)^2}{2\sigma^2} \tag{9}$$

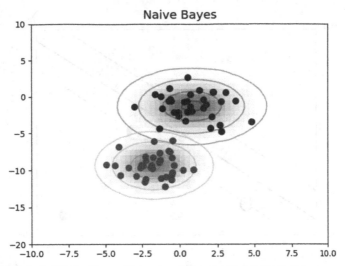

Fig. 3. Visualization of Naive Bayes. The red and blue dots represent the classes, a more intense cluster of colors means a higher probability. (Color figure online)

2.4 SVM

The Support Vector Machine has become a popular classifier in the field of machine learning due to its high performance with a small number of features, its robustness to model errors and its computational efficiency compared to other classifiers [19]. The task of the SVM classifier is to find a hyperplane, in the number of dimensions of the space corresponding to the number of features, that forms boundaries separating objects belonging to other classes. The essence of determining the hyperplane is the process of selecting weights so that the decision boundary is as far away as possible from the extreme points of each class, called support vectors [20]. Determining the hyperplane for two-class data involves finding a straight line with the maximum margin of the given classes. Given a data set x_i ($i = 1, 2 \ldots, n$) and class labels $y_i \in \{-1, 1\}$, we can define the straight line as:

$$w^T x + b = 0 \tag{10}$$

where w is a vector of weights, x is a vector of inputs and b is a bias. This hyperplane must then satisfy the condition of class separation by a maximum margin so that the data is distributed to the left and right of the hyperplane. Which in turn can be written as

$$w^T x + b = \begin{cases} \geq 1\, for\, y_i = 1 \\ \leq -1\, for\, y_i = -1 \end{cases} \tag{11}$$

However, a different region for the hyperplane and different class boundaries can be assumed and the aim of the SVM is to select the values of w and b so that the hyperplane separates the data and maximizes the margin (Fig. 4).

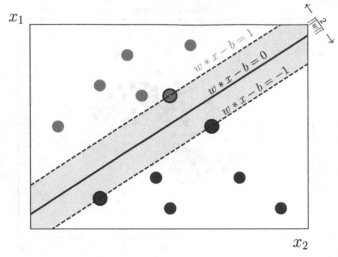

Fig. 4. Visualisation of the SVM. The red and green dots represent the classes separated by the hyperplane. (Color figure online)

3 Experiments

The dataset consists of 303 rows and 14 columns (see Table 1). Each attribute is represented as an integer, excluding the *oldpeak* attribute, which takes a floating point value. The dataset has been checked for noises, such as null values and inaccurate values.

Scale attribute values in the dataset to a range of values [0,1] using the equation:

$$x_{scaled} = \frac{x - x_{min}}{x_{max} - x_{min}} \tag{12}$$

where x is the initial value.

The dataset is split into a training set and a test set, this is a process of randomly dividing the original dataset in a ratio of 70:30, meaning that 70% of the data is used to teach the model and the rest of the data is used to test the performance of the classifier, i.e. to assess its ability to classify new data.

In order to make the analysis as accurate as possible, several pre-tests were carried out before the actual research began in order to determine the optimal number of neighbors used by the kNN algorithm. As a result of these pre-tests, the desired number of neighbors was found to be 7, as shown in the diagram (see Fig. 5).

When using the naive Bayes algorithm, a normal (Gaussian) distribution was chosen. Of the distributions used, it gave the most desirable results during pre-testing (Fig. 6).

The kernel used for the SVM algorithm was the linear kernel, as the results showed that it performed best during pre-testing, compared to other types of kernels. Results are shown in Fig. 7. When conducting the experiments, we used the implementation of the SVM classifier included in the sklearn library. In this implementation, the C parameter defaults to 1. Based on the documentation of the sklearn library, we decided that leaving the default value is a reasonable choice.

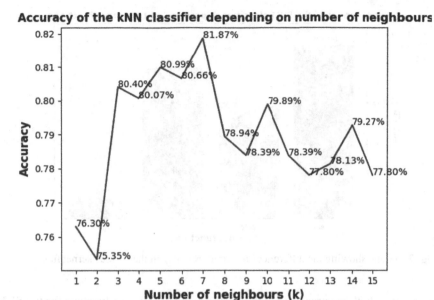

Fig. 5. Graph showing differences in accuracy in relation to the parameter k

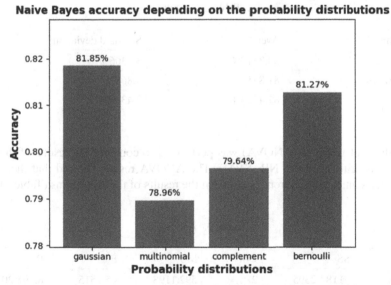

Fig. 6. Graph showing the differences in accuracy between the various probability distributions.

After testing 500 different training samples, the average accuracy was determined to establish which classifier performed best in predicting the presence of heart disease in a patient, as well as the standard deviation to identify which algorithm was most consistent. The results are shown in Table 2.

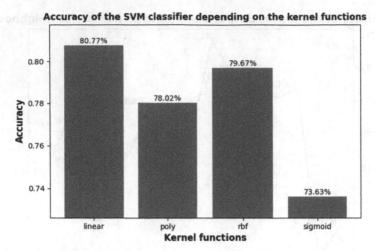

Fig. 7. Graph showing the differences in accuracy between the various kernel functions.

In terms of both accuracy and stability, the results show an advantage for the SVM classifier.

Table 2. Results

Algorithm	Average	Standard deviation
kNN	80.3516%	3.5306%
Naive Bayes	81.8352%	3.8687%
SVM	82.4725%	3.4385%

Analysis of variance (ANOVA) was performed to compare the results of the classification algorithms (kNN, NB, SVM). The ANOVA results showed that there were statistically significant differences between the results of the algorithms (Table 3).

Table 3. ANOVA

	SS	DoF	MS	F	P
Between	1184.2395	2	592.1198	45.2515	8.29e-20
Within	19588.3739	1497	13.0851		
Total	20772.6134	1499			

The p-value is a very small $8.29e-20$ ($p < 0.05$), indicating that there are statistically significant differences between at least two groups.

Post hoc tests are performed after ANOVA analysis, when the overall significance of differences between groups has been confirmed. Post hoc tests can more accurately identify which pairs of groups are statistically significantly different from each other (Table 4).

Table 4. Post-Hoc Test

Groups	Means	Difference	Lower	Upper	P-value	Signif
SVM vs kNN	[82.4725, 80.3516]	−2.1209	−2.6576	−1.5842	0.00000	*****
NB vs SVM	[81.8352, 82.4725]	0.6373	0.1006	1.174	0.01494	*
NB vs kNN	[81.8352, 80.3516]	−1.4836	−2.0203	−0.9469	0.00000	*****

In summary, the confidence interval analysis shows that there are statistically significant differences between the average performance of NB, SVM and kNN classifiers. The SVM algorithm seems to achieve better results than kNN, while NB occupies an intermediate position. The p-values of less than 0.05 indicate that the differences between the means are significant, which means that the results are probably related to the actual differences between the classification algorithms.

4 Conclusion

The aim of the study was to investigate whether it is possible to predict heart disease from medical data and with what accuracy. For this purpose, a comparative analysis was performed in which different classification models were described and implemented. As a result of the study, it was shown that all classifiers showed high accuracy, however, the best performance in both accuracy and stability was achieved by the SVM (Support Vector Machine). In the case of early disease detection, due to the lower criticality of the possible error, the result obtained by the SVM classifier can be considered satisfactory and can significantly contribute to the early diagnosis of the disease. Some of the other studies done with this dataset show a different approach to this problem, using linear regression [11]. In several cases, it achieves better results than those presented here [21].

5 Online Resources

We would like to thank the creators of the dataset used in conducting the research. It is available via:

- Dataset

Source code for the implementation of classifiers is available via:

- GitHub

References

1. OECD, E. Union, Health at a Glance: Europe 2022 (2022). https://www.oecd-ilibrary.org/content/publication/507433b0-en. https://doi.org/10.1787/507433b0-en

2. Katsoularis, I., Fonseca-Rodríguez, O., Farrington, P., Lindmark, K., Connolly, A.-M.F.: Risk of acute myocardial infarction and ischaemic stroke following covid-19 in Sweden: a self-controlled case series and matched cohort study. Lancet 398/10300, 559–607 (2001). https://www.thelancet.com/journals/lancet/article/PIIS0140-6736(21)00896-5/fulltext. https://doi.org/10.1016/S0140-6736(21)00896-5

3. Centers for Disease Control and Prevention, about heart disease (2023). https://www.cdc.gov/heartdisease/about.htm. Accessed 26 Apr 2023

4. Rippe, J.M.: Lifestyle strategies for risk factor reduction, prevention, and treatment of cardiovascular disease. Am. J. Lifestyle Med. **13**(2), 204–212 (2019). https://doi.org/10.1177/1559827618812395

5. Połap, D., Woźniak, M.: A hybridization of distributed policy and heuristic augmentation for improving federated learning approach. Neural Netw. **146**, 130–140 (2022)

6. Ke, Q., Siłka, J., Wieczorek, M., Bai, Z., Woźniak, M.: Deep neural network heuristic hierarchization for cooperative intelligent transportation fleet management. IEEE Trans. Intell. Transp. Syst. **23**, 16752–16762 (2022)

7. Jaszcz, A., Połap, D.: AIMM: artificial intelligence merged methods for flood DDoS attacks detection. J. King Saud Univ.-Comput. Inf. Sci. **34**, 8090–8101 (2022)

8. Woźniak, M., Zielonka, A., Sikora, A.: Driving support by type-2 fuzzy logic control model. Expert Syst. Appl. **207**, 117798 (2022)

9. Połap, D.: Fuzzy consensus with federated learning method in medical systems. IEEE Access **9**, 150383–150392 (2021)

10. Pleszczyński, M., Zielonka, A., Woźniak, M.: Application of nature-inspired algorithms to computed tomography with incomplete data. Symmetry **14**, 2256 (2022)

11. Aha, D.W.: Heart disease data set (1988). https://archive.ics.uci.edu/ml/datasets/heart+disease. Accessed 27 Apr 2023

12. Timbers, T., Campbell, T., Lee, M.: Data Science: A First Introduction. Chapman & Hall, Boca Raton (2022). https://datasciencebook.ca/classification2.html#critically-analyze-performance

13. Guo, G., Wang, H., Bell, D., Bi, Y., Greer, K.: Knn model-based approach in classification. In: Meersman, R., Tari, Z., Schmidt, D.C. (eds.) OTM 2003. LNCS, vol. 2888, pp. 986–996. Springer, Heidelberg (2003). https://doi.org/10.1007/978-3-540-39964-3_62

14. Zhongheng, Z.: Introduction to machine learning: k-nearest neighbors. Ann. Transl. Med. **4**(11) 218 (2016). https://www.ncbi.nlm.nih.gov/pmc/articles/PMC4916348/#r5.https://doi.org/10.21037/atm.2016.03.37

15. Mikulski, B.: Minkowski distance explained (2019). https://www.mikulskibartosz.name/minkowski-distance-explained/. Accessed 27 Apr 2023

16. Dimitoglou, G., Adams, J.A., Jim, C.M.: Comparison of the c4.5 and a Naive Bayes classifier for the prediction of lung cancer survivability. J. Comput. **4**(8) (2012). https://doi.org/10.48550/arXiv.1206.1121. https://arxiv.org/abs/1206.1121

17. Webb, G.I.: Naïve Bayes. In: In: Sammut, C., Webb, G.I. (eds.) Encyclopedia of Machine Learning, pp. 713–714. Springer, Boston (2010). https://doi.org/10.1007/978-0-387-30164-8_576

18. Gandhi, R.: Naive bayes classifier (2018). https://towardsdatascience.com/naive-bayes-classifier-81d512f50a7c. Accessed 28 Apr 2023

19. Gholami, R., Fakhari, N.: Chapter 27 - support vector machine: principles, parameters, and applications. In: Samui, P., Sekhar, S., Balas, V.E. (eds.) Handbook of Neural Computation, pp. 515–535. Academic Press (2017).https://doi.org/10.1016/B978-0-12-811318-9.00027-2. https://www.sciencedirect.com/science/article/pii/B9780128113189000272
20. Huang, S., Cai, N., Pacheco, P. P., Narrandes, S., Wang, Y., Xu, W.: Applications of support vector machine (SVM) learning in cancer genomics. Cancer Genomics Protemics **15**(1), 41–51 (2017). https://doi.org/10.21873/cgp.20063. https://cgp.iiarjournals.org/content/15/1/41
21. Abd Allah, E.M., El-Matary, D.E., Eid, E.M., Tag El Dien, A.S.: Performance comparison of various machine learning approaches to identify the best one in predicting heart disease. J. Comput. Commun. **10**(2), 1–18 (2022). https://doi.org/10.4236/jcc.2022.102001. https://www.scirp.org/journal/paperinformation.aspx?paperid=115134#ref3

Iterative Method of Adjusting Parameters in kNN via Minkowski Metric

Emilia Pawela[(✉)] and Wojciech Olech

Faculty of Applied Mathematics, Silesian University of Technology, Kaszubska 23,
44-100 Gliwice, Poland
ep303242@student.polsl.pl

Abstract. In today's world, where solutions from the last century are no longer enforced, there is a constant demand for newer, more efficient ways to analyze data. An example of such an application is the k-nearest neighbors (k-nn) mechanism. In this article, this mechanism will be proposed, improved by the possibility of finding the optimal number of neighbors and the coefficient m for the Minkowski function used in it to calculate the distance between points. This mechanism is automated, which allows you to use different parameters for the Minkowski function and determine the accuracy for a different number of neighbors in an automatic way. From these accuracies, the ranking system selects the best values for the parameter m, which defines the dimension of the space in the Minkowski function, and the best number of nearest neighbors. The number of nearest neighbors checked and the value of the m parameter can be set independently, which allows you to check various combinations of the m parameter and the number of nearest neighbors.

Keywords: clustering · automatization · k-nn · Minkowski

1 Introduction

The rapid pace of technological advancement in recent years has led to a growing demand for innovative solutions in various industries. Artificial intelligence (AI) is at the forefront of this revolution, offering businesses a range of tools and methods for optimizing operations, improving customer experiences, and gaining a competitive edge. Companies and researchers across multiple sectors, such as data processing [1, 2], healthcare [3–5], and Internet of Things [6–9], are increasingly looking to integrate AI into their operations. They are seeking solutions that can leverage large datasets, automate decision-making processes [10, 11], and provide insights that were previously impossible to obtain. As such, the need for new AI technologies, algorithms, and methods has never been greater [12, 13]. This demand is driving research and development in the AI field, with experts continually exploring new approaches to meet the evolving needs of the market.

As the field of AI expands, so too does the need for reliable and effective algorithms. The k-nearest neighbors (kNN) algorithm is one such algorithm that has proven useful in a range of applications, from image recognition to natural language processing [14]. However, the algorithm's effectiveness is highly dependent on the selection of appropriate parameter values. As such, there is a growing demand for novel approaches to parameter selection that can optimize the performance of kNN in various applications. Our proposed iterative approach for selecting optimal kNN parameters based on the Minkowski distance [15], is one such solution. By enabling the variation of distance calculation order, our approach offers greater flexibility and precision in the selection of parameter values. This can lead to higher classification accuracy and improved performance, addressing the needs of the market for more efficient and accurate AI solutions.

The k-nearest neighbors (kNN) algorithm is a non-parametric algorithm that is widely used in machine learning. The algorithm classifies new data points based on the majority class of their k-nearest neighbors in the training data. However, the effectiveness of the algorithm depends on several factors, including the choice of parameter values. In this paper, we propose an iterative approach to selecting optimal kNN parameters based on the Minkowski distance. The Minkowski distance is a generalization of the Euclidean distance and allows us to vary the order of distance calculation.

Our approach involves testing different values of the k parameter and the order of the Minkowski distance and selecting the values that result in the highest classification accuracy. We evaluate the effectiveness of our approach using the anemia dataset, and compare our approach with the traditional approach of selecting fixed parameter values.

2 Methodology

In this article, the nearest neighbor (knn) algorithm was used, which evaluates new samples according to their data. It determines the type of a sample based on its distance from a certain number of neighbors whose type is specified.

The diagram in Fig. 1 illustrates the k-nearest neighbors algorithm. The new sample is surrounded by its closest neighbors. The number of neighbors whose types will determine the type of the sample is determined. The diagram shows that the type of the new sample will be class A, because two out of three neighbors have this type. Also, when we increase the number of neighbors to six, the sample type remains the same. It can also be seen that above a certain number of neighbors, the accuracy of the sample type determination decreases because, for nine neighbors, four are already of a different class.

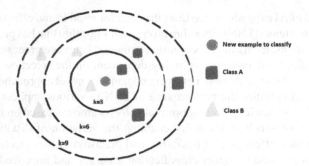

Fig. 1. Diagram that shows k-nearest neighbor

The first step in the algorithm is to calculate the distances between the sample and its potential neighbors. Then all potential neighbors are sorted in ascending order by distance from the sample. In the next step of selecting a specific number of nearest neighbors, their types are counted. Based on the type with the most votes, the sample type is determined. In order to increase the accuracy of determining the type of sample, automation was used to select the number of neighbors and select the m parameter.

The distance between the neighbors and the sample is calculated from the Minkowski metric described by the following formula:

$$L_m(x, y) = \left(\sum\nolimits_{i=1}^{n} |x_i - y_i|^m \right)^{\frac{1}{m}} \tag{1}$$

where:

d - distance between two points,
n - number of dimensions in which two points are defined,
x, y - two points in n-dimensional space,
x_i, y_i - coordinate values of two points in i-dimension,
m - dimension of space.

Automation during the selection of the number of neighbors k and parameter m can be presented in several steps:

1. The accuracy of the algorithm is calculated for different combinations of m and k nearest neighbors.
2. The values of the parameters m and k of the nearest neighbors are selected for which the accuracy is the highest.
   a. If for several k nearest neighbors and a value of parameter m the greatest accuracy is the same, for those k nearest neighbors and a value of parameter m a recalculation of the accuracy is performed using the same nearest neighbor (kNN) algorithm but with a halved validation set.
   b. Next, the k nearest neighbors and the m values with the highest accuracy are selected again. If for several k nearest neighbors and the value of parameter m the greatest accuracy is the same, step 2a. is repeated.

The introduction of automation turns out to be a very useful and necessary solution. This allows you to automatically calculate the accuracy for different combinations of m and k nearest neighbors. This facilitates and speeds up the work because there is no need to manually enter these values and check their accuracy. Also, thanks to the applied ranking system, the best value of the parameter m and k nearest neighbors for a given database is automatically returned, which speeds up the work, because there is no need to manually check and search for which parameters give the best results.

The time complexity for determining the accuracy in a given validation set with the unmodified knn algorithm is as follows:

$$O(n * d)$$

where:

n - is the number of records in the database,
d - number of dimensions in the database.

In the algorithm modified by us (that is shown in Algorithm 2), the time complexity is greater and is represented by the following formula:

$$O(n * d * k * m)$$

where:

n - is the number of records in the database,
d - number of dimensions in the database,
k - number of nearest neighbors to consider,
m - values of parameter m to be considered.

Although more complex, it is possible to specify the accuracy for different combinations of parameters k and m, and the parameters with the best accuracy are selected (see Algorithm 2).

Algorithm 1: KNN Algorithm

---

for Each k **do**
  for Each m **do**
    Counter ← 0
    for Every row in validating sample **do**
      Table_Of _Distances ← []
      for Every row in training sample **do**
        Temporary ← 0
        for Every column in samples minus Result **do**
          $Temporary = Temporary + |Training\_Sample[row][column] -$
          $Validating\_Sample[column]|^m$
        end for
        $Table\_Of\_Distances \leftarrow add\ (Temporary)^{1/m}$
      end for
      Add Column to Training Set with distances
      Sort Training Set by distances
      Dictionary ← {*Ill* ← 0, *Healthy* ← 0}
      for From one to k **do**
        if Result for training sample is ill **then**
          Dictionary[Ill] ← *add* 1
        else
          Dictionary[Healthy] ← *add* 1
        end if
      end for
      return Key of bigger Dictionary
      if Key of bigger Dictionary is the same as Result in Validating Sample **then**
        Counter ← *add* 1
      end if
    end for
    Accuracy_Value ← *Counter/(length of Validating_Set)* * 100%

    print Accuracy: *Accuracy_Value*
  end for
end for

Algorithm 2: Finding the best kNN attributes algorithm

---

if There is more than one highest value **then**
  trainingDataVariable ← *trainingDataVariable / 2*
  Do kNN algh orith m with trainingDataVariable
  Add to table at th e end new Accuracy
  Sort table
  return *New Table*
else
  print *Th e_h igh est_accuracy*
end if

---

3   Experiments

The database used in this article predicts anemia based on certain rates. The database contains columns such as gender, hemoglobin, Mean Corpuscular Hemoglobin Concentration (MCHC), Mean Corpuscular Volume (MCV), Mean Cell Hemoglobin (MCH) and whether the patient is healthy or not. Gender is determined numerically, with a value of 1 for female and a value of 0 for male.

Hemoglobin is the protein that carries oxygen to your body's organs and tissues and transports carbon dioxide from your organs and tissues back to your lungs. The normal range for hemoglobin is 13 g/dL to 18 g/dL for men and 12 g/dL to 16 g/dL for women.

MCH is the average amount in each of your red blood of a protein called hemoglobin, which carries oxygen around your body. The normal range is 27–33 pg.

MCHC is a measure of the average concentration of hemoglobin inside a single red blood cell. The normal range seems to be in the range of 28–31 g/dL.

MCV is an indicator of the average volume of erythrocytes, i.e. the volume of red blood cells. Normal values are in the range of 82–92 fl.

A person with anemia corresponds to a value of 1, and a healthy person a value of 0.

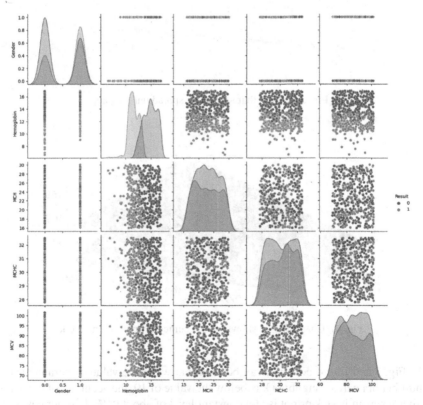

Fig. 2. Charts that show how spread out are data

In Fig. 2 you can see 25 graphs that show the relationships between all the columns in the database used for the experiment. The blue color represents a healthy person, while the orange color represents an anemic person.

In the experiment, accuracy was calculated for the nearest number of neighbors k in the range from 2 to 15, and the values of the parameter m in the range from 1 to 14. In total, 197 results were obtained.

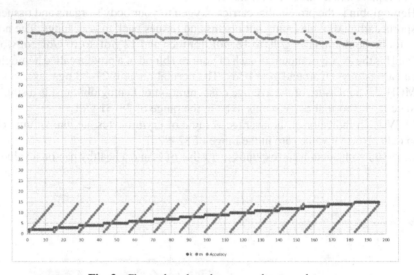

Fig. 3. Charts that show how spread out are data

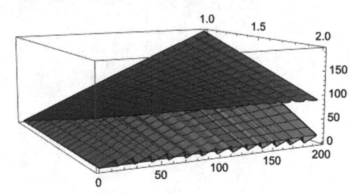

Fig. 4. Chart 3D that shows how accuracy depends on m and k

In Fig. 3 and Fig. 4 below, it can be seen that when the value of parameter m and the number of nearest neighbors k is below the value of 10, the accuracy of determining whether a person is sick or not is at a constant level of about 94%. In other cases, when m is between 1 and 5, the accuracy is the highest. For the value of the parameter m and the number of nearest neighbors k above 10, the accuracy drops below 90%.

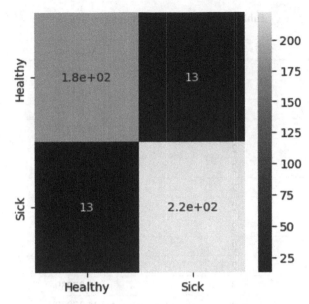

Fig. 5. Matrix Confusion for our results

For the algorithm used in this article, a Confusion Matrix (see Fig. 5) was generated which shows the performance of the algorithm, showing the number of errors of the algorithm to the number of corrects of verified samples. It can be seen that the number of sick people outweighs the number of healthy people with the selected validation set to test the algorithm.

The results contained in the Table 1 show that for the base on which the experiment was carried out, the best number of nearest neighbors is 13 and the best value of the m parameter is 1.

The efficiency of the solution presented by us is better compared to the one where the parameters are chosen randomly. Thanks to this solution, all possible combinations of parameters are checked, and the combination with the best accuracy is automatically selected. This significantly speeds up the search for parameters that are characterized by the highest accuracy for the database.

Table 1. Accuracy with different parameters

m	k	Accuracy
1	13	95.31616
13	2	94.84778
14	2	94.84778
1	11	94.84778
3	2	94.61358
4	2	94.61358
5	2	94.61358
6	2	94.61358
7	2	94.61358
11	2	94.61358
12	2	94.61358
1	3	94.37939
2	4	94.37939
2	5	94.37939
2	6	94.37939
1	14	94.37939
8	2	94.1452
9	2	94.1452
10	2	94.1452
1	15	94.1452
5	3	93.91101
2	8	93.91101
2	11	93.91101
1	12	93.91101

4 Conclusion

We proposed an iterative approach for selecting optimal k-nearest neighbors (kNN) parameters based on the Minkowski distance. Our approach involves testing different values of k and the order of the Minkowski distance, and selecting the values that result in the highest classification accuracy. Our results suggest that the most optimal values of k and the order of the Minkowski distance for the datasets we used are k = 13 and m = 1. These values were found to result in the highest classification accuracy across the anemia dataset we used.

In conclusion, our approach allows for a more flexible and adaptive selection of parameter values, which can result in higher classification accuracy. We hope that our approach will inspire further research in this area and encourage the use of kNN algorithm in various domains.

In addition to the main findings presented in the summary, there are several additional insights and conclusions that can be drawn from the results of the study:

- Our approach demonstrates the importance of carefully selecting optimal parameter values for machine learning algorithms to achieve better accuracy. By testing different values of k and the order of the Minkowski distance, we were able to identify the most effective parameter values for the anemia dataset.
- The use of the kNN algorithm is promising in various domains where the classification accuracy is crucial, such as healthcare, finance, and security. Our findings suggest that kNN algorithm can be a competitive and robust choice in these domains.
- Future research can investigate the applicability of our iterative approach for selecting optimal kNN parameters to other datasets and domains. For instance, exploring the impact of different distance metrics or using feature selection techniques in combination with our approach.
- The optimal values of k and the order of the Minkowski distance can vary depending on the characteristics of the dataset. Therefore, it is essential to evaluate different parameter values for each dataset and domain to obtain the best classification accuracy.

In summary, our study provides an effective approach for selecting optimal parameter values for the kNN algorithm based on the Minkowski distance. Our findings demonstrate the importance of parameter tuning for machine learning algorithms and provide insights into the applicability of the kNN algorithm in various domains.

5 Online Resources

- Used Database
- Code on GitHub

References

1. Ding, H., Chen, L., Dong, L., Fu, Z., Cui, X.: Imbalanced data classification: a kNN and generative adversarial networks-based hybrid approach for intrusion detection. Futur. Gener. Comput. Syst. **131**, 240–254 (2022)
2. Połap, D., Wawrzyniak, N., Włodarczyk-Sielicka, M.: Side-scan sonar analysis using ROI analysis and deep neural networks. IEEE Trans. Geosci. Remote Sens. **60**, 1–8 (2022)
3. Nawaz, M., et al.: Skin cancer detection from dermoscopic images using deep learning and fuzzy k-means clustering. Microsc. Res. Tech. **85**, 339–351 (2022)
4. Połap, D.: Fuzzy consensus with federated learning method in medical systems. IEEE Access **9**, 150383–150392 (2021)
5. Woźniak, M., Połap, D.: Intelligent home systems for ubiquitous user support by using neural networks and rule-based approach. IEEE Trans. Ind. Inf. **16**, 2651–2658 (2019)
6. Abdulzahra, A.M.K., Al-Qurabat, A.K.M.: A clustering approach based on fuzzy c-means in wireless sensor networks for IoT applications, Karbala. Int. J. Mod. Sci. **8**, 579–595 (2022)
7. Woźniak, M., Zielonka, A., Sikora, A.: Driving support by type-2 fuzzy logic control model. Expert Syst. Appl. **207**, 117798 (2022)

8. Sadrishojaei, M., Jafari Navimipour, N., Reshadi, M., Hosseinzadeh, M., Unal, M.: An energy-aware clustering method in the IoT using a swarm-based algorithm. Wirel. Netw. **28**, 125–136 (2022)
9. Woźniak, M., Zielonka, A., Sikora, A., Piran, M.J., Alamri, A.: 6G-enabled IoT home environment control using fuzzy rules. IEEE Internet Things J. **8**, 5442–5452 (2020)
10. Dai, F., Wang, D., Kirillova, K.: Travel inspiration in tourist decision making. Tour. Manag. **90**, 104484 (2022)
11. Alsalem, M., et al.: Multi-criteria decisionmaking for coronavirus disease 2019 applications: a theoretical analysis review. Artif. Intell. Rev. **55**(2022), 4979–5062 (2019)
12. Pleszczyński, M., Zielonka, A., Woźniak, M.: Application of nature-inspired algorithms to computed tomography with incomplete data. Symmetry **14**, 2256 (2022)
13. Ke, Q., Siłka, J., Wieczorek, M., Bai, Z., Woźniak, M.: Deep neural network heuristic hierarchization for cooperative intelligent transportation fleet management. IEEE Trans. Intell. Transp. Syst. **23**, 16752–16762 (2022)
14. Altay, O.: Performance of different kNN models in prediction English language readability. In: 2022 2nd International Conference on Computing and Machine Intelligence (ICMI), pp. 1–5. IEEE (2022)
15. De Amorim, R.C., Mirkin, B.: Minkowski metric, feature weighting and anomalous cluster initializing in k-means clustering. Pattern Recogn. **45**, 1061–1075 (2012)

Predicting Diabetes Risk in Correlation with Cigarette Smoking

Julia Jędrzejczyk(✉), Bartłomiej Maliniecki, and Anna Woźnicka

Faculty of Applied Mathematics, Silesian University of Technology, Kaszubska 23, 44-100 Gliwice, Poland
{jj303182,bm303217,annawoz530}@student.polsl.pl

Abstract. Machine learning is widely utilized across various scientific disciplines, with algorithms and data playing critical roles in the learning process. Proper analysis and reduction of data are crucial for achieving accurate results. In this study, our focus was on predicting the correlation between cigarette smoking and the likelihood of diabetes. We employed the Naive Bayes classifier algorithm on the Diabetes prediction dataset and conducted additional experiments using the k-NN classifier. To handle the large dataset, several adjustments were made to ensure smooth learning and satisfactory outcomes. This article presents the stages of data analysis and preparation, the classifier algorithm, and key implementation steps. Emphasis was placed on graph interpretation. The summary includes a comparison of classifiers, along with standard deviation and standard error metrics.

Keywords: Machine Learning · Naive Bayes classifier · k-NN · Diabetes prediction dataset

1 Introduction

The application of machine learning techniques in disease prediction and diagnosis has seen significant advancements in recent years. Detecting diseases accurately and early is crucial for improving patient outcomes and reducing healthcare costs. Among these diseases, diabetes is a prevalent and chronic condition with serious health implications. The correlation between cigarette smoking and the likelihood of developing diabetes remains an area that requires further investigation.

Understanding the impact of cigarette smoking on diabetes risk is important for several reasons. It can provide insights into the complex interplay between lifestyle factors and disease development, contribute to more accurate predictive models, and inform public health policies. Therefore, this study aims to explore the correlation between cigarette smoking and diabetes using machine learning techniques.

By analyzing the Diabetes prediction dataset, we investigate whether smoking is an independent risk factor for diabetes or if its impact is confounded by other variables. Our hypothesis is that there exists a positive association between cigarette smoking and the likelihood of diabetes, even after controlling for other known risk factors.

A. Lopata et al. (Eds.): ICIST 2023, CCIS 1979, pp. 297–308, 2024.
https://doi.org/10.1007/978-3-031-48981-5_24

Through rigorous data analysis, application of machine learning algorithms, and interpretation of results, this study provides insights into the relationship between smoking and diabetes. The findings contribute to our understanding of disease etiology and can assist in developing targeted interventions and preventive strategies.

In the following sections, we present the methodology, describe the machine learning algorithms employed, discuss the results, and explore the implications for healthcare practice and policy.

1.1 Assumptions of the Project

The program is designed to predict the potential for diabetes risk in correlation with smoking cigarettes based on the 'Diabetes prediction dataset'.

1.2 Description

The main scheme of the algorithm for assessing the possibility of diabetes risk is a combination of test results, characteristics, habits or habits of the person under study. Based on the information provided the algorithm determines how high the chance is that a particular person will develop diabetes.

2 Methodology

2.1 Steps in the Implementation of the Task

1. Selection of the database.
2. Analysis and reduction of the database - removing rows that did not contain key information crucial to achieve the final result.
3. Appropriate preparation of data for testing.
4. Performing tests using a naive Bayesian classifier.
5. Performing the experiment using the KNN classifier.
6. Drawing conclusions.
7. Preparing the report.

2.2 Description of Operation

Naive Bayesian classifier is a simple probabilistic classifier. It is based on the assumption of mutual independence of predictors, i.e. independent variables. Although this assumption often does not reflect reality, it is therefore called "naive". The model of right of probability in naive Bayesian classifiers can be deduced using Bayes' theorem; a theorem of probability theory, binding the weighted probabilities of two events conditioning on each other.

The formula for conditional probability, which determines what kind of decision we will make if we have specific data:

$$P(A|B) = \frac{P(A \cap B)}{P(B)}$$

Bayes' theorem:

$$P(hypothesis|data|) = \frac{P(data|hypothesis)P(hypothesis)}{P(data)}$$

Depending on the accuracy of the model, naive Bayesian classifiers can be effectively trained in supervised learning mode. In many practical applications of parameter estimation of naive Bayes models, the maximum likelihood a posteriori method is used. In other words, it is possible to work with a naive Bayes model without necessarily believing in Bayes' theorem or using specific Bayes methods.

Despite their naive design and highly simplified assumptions, naive Bayes classifiers often perform better in real-world situations than one might expect.

In our calculations, we used a normal distribution, otherwise known as a distribution of Gauss.

The density function of the normal (Gauss) distribution:

$$f(x) = \frac{1}{\sqrt{2\pi\sigma^2}} \cdot e - \frac{(x-\mu)^2}{2\sigma^2}$$

In this formula:

- f (x) denotes the density function for a random variable x,
- μ is the expected (mean) value of the distribution,
- σ is the standard deviation of the distribution

3 Data Analysis

3.1 Libraries Used

- pandas - data management.
- numpy - advanced mathematical calculations.
- seaborn - creating statistical graphics.
- matplotlib - create graphs and numerical extensions of NumPy.
- random - allows you to select a random element from a given sequence.

3.2 Database Analysis

We began our work by analyzing the database (Fig. 1):

```
<class 'pandas.core.frame.DataFrame'>
RangeIndex: 100000 entries, 0 to 99999
Data columns (total 9 columns):
 #   Column             Non-Null Count   Dtype
---  ------             --------------   -----
 0   gender             100000 non-null  object
 1   age                100000 non-null  float64
 2   hypertension       100000 non-null  int64
 3   heart_disease      100000 non-null  int64
 4   smoking_history    100000 non-null  object
 5   bmi                100000 non-null  float64
 6   HbA1c_level        100000 non-null  float64
 7   blood_glucose_level  100000 non-null  int64
 8   diabetes           100000 non-null  int64
dtypes: float64(3), int64(4), object(2)
memory usage: 6.9+ MB
```

Fig. 1. The database consists of 100,000 rows and 9 columns, of which 2 columns have nonnumeric values. These are the *gender* and *smoking history* columns.

We then made sure that no data is missing, i.e. there are no so-called empty cells, which negatively affect the training of the model.

We further checked the contents of the last 5 rows to compare the data before and after the reduction (Fig. 2).

```
data.tail()
```

	gender	age	hypertension	heart_disease	smoking_history	bmi	HbA1c_level	blood_glucose_level	diabetes
99995	Female	80.0	0	0	No Info	27.32	6.2	90	0
99996	Female	2.0	0	0	No Info	17.37	6.5	100	0
99997	Male	66.0	0	0	former	27.83	5.7	155	0
99998	Female	24.0	0	0	never	35.42	4.0	100	0
99999	Female	57.0	0	0	current	22.43	6.6	90	0

Fig. 2. Data before the reduction

The next step was to remove rows that do not contain information necessary for data analysis. In our case, these were rows that in the *smoking history* column contained the value *'No Info'* . (Figs. 3, 4)

```
data.drop(data[data['smoking_history'] == 'No Info'].index, inplace = True)
```

```
data.info()
<class 'pandas.core.frame.DataFrame'>
Int64Index: 64184 entries, 0 to 99999
Data columns (total 9 columns):
 #   Column               Non-Null Count  Dtype
---  ------               --------------  -----
 0   gender               64184 non-null  object
 1   age                  64184 non-null  float64
 2   hypertension         64184 non-null  int64
 3   heart_disease        64184 non-null  int64
 4   smoking_history      64184 non-null  object
 5   bmi                  64184 non-null  float64
 6   HbA1c_level          64184 non-null  float64
 7   blood_glucose_level  64184 non-null  int64
 8   diabetes             64184 non-null  int64
dtypes: float64(3), int64(4), object(2)
memory usage: 4.9+ MB
```

Fig. 3. Deletion of data

```
data.tail()
```

	gender	age	hypertension	heart_disease	smoking_history	bmi	HbA1c_level	blood_glucose_level	diabetes
99992	Female	26.0	0	0	never	34.34	6.5	160	0
99993	Female	40.0	0	0	never	40.69	3.5	155	0
99997	Male	66.0	0	0	former	27.83	5.7	155	0
99998	Female	24.0	0	0	never	35.42	4.0	100	0
99999	Female	57.0	0	0	current	22.43	6.6	90	0

Fig. 4. Data after reduction

After preparing the database in advance, we plotted charts to analyze the data (5, 6).

The data was grouped according to the value in the 'smoking history' column, and then the average value of the 'diabetes' column for each group was calculated (7).

The chart was created to illustrate the relationship between the columns 'smoking history, 'age' and 'diabetes'. We calculate the average value of 'diabetes'. Each line on the graph represents a different 'smoking history' value. The x and y axes, represent respectively 'age' and 'average percentage of diabetes', and the legend indicates which values correspond to which lines on the graph.

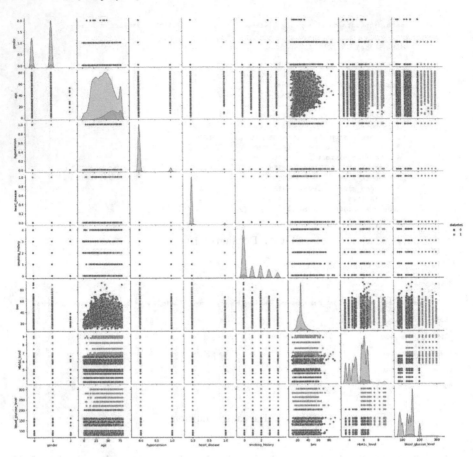

Fig. 5. Correlation of data in the studied database

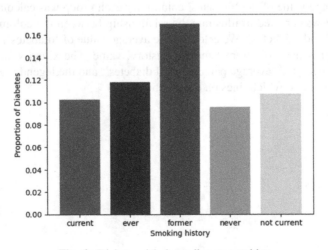

Fig. 6. Diabetes risk depending on smoking

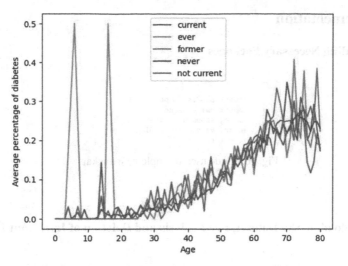

Fig. 7. Relationship between smoking, age and diabetes

In the next step, we took care of changing the 'object' values in the *gender* and *smoking history* to 'numeric' values (Figs. 8, 9, 10, 11 and 12).

```
data.info()
```
```
<class 'pandas.core.frame.DataFrame'>
Int64Index: 64184 entries, 0 to 99999
Data columns (total 9 columns):
 #   Column              Non-Null Count   Dtype
---  ------              --------------   -----
 0   gender              64184 non-null   object
 1   age                 64184 non-null   float64
 2   hypertension        64184 non-null   int64
 3   heart_disease       64184 non-null   int64
 4   smoking_history     64184 non-null   object
 5   bmi                 64184 non-null   float64
 6   HbA1c_level         64184 non-null   float64
 7   blood_glucose_level 64184 non-null   int64
 8   diabetes            64184 non-null   int64
dtypes: float64(3), int64(4), object(2)
memory usage: 4.9+ MB
```

Fig. 8. Data before the change

```
<class 'pandas.core.frame.DataFrame'>
Int64Index: 64184 entries, 0 to 99999
Data columns (total 9 columns):
 #   Column              Non-Null Count   Dtype
---  ------              --------------   -----
 0   gender              64184 non-null   int64
 1   age                 64184 non-null   float64
 2   hypertension        64184 non-null   int64
 3   heart_disease       64184 non-null   int64
 4   smoking_history     64184 non-null   int64
 5   bmi                 64184 non-null   float64
 6   HbA1c_level         64184 non-null   float64
 7   blood_glucose_level 64184 non-null   int64
 8   diabetes            64184 non-null   int64
dtypes: float64(3), int64(6)
memory usage: 4.9 MB
```

Fig. 9. Data after the change

4 Implementation

4.1 Including Necessary Packages

```
import pandas as pd
import numpy as np
import seaborn as sns
import matplotlib.pyplot as plt
import random
```

Fig. 10. Code used to implement packages

4.2 Downloading the Dataset, Pre-analysis and Deletion of Irrelevant Elements

```
df = pd.read_csv('diabetes_prediction_dataset.csv')
data = df.copy()
data.info()
data.tail()
data.drop(data[data['smoking_history'] == 'No Info'].index, inplace = True)
```

Fig. 11. Code used to download dataset, pre-analysis and deletion

4.3 Converting Word Values into Numerical Values and Re-Analyzing the Data

```
data['smoking_history'] = data['smoking_history'].map({'never': 0, 'former': 1, 'current':2, 'not current':3,'ever':4 })
data['gender'] = data['gender'].map({'Male': 0, 'Female': 1, 'Other':2})
data.info()
data.describe()
data.tail()
```

Fig. 12. Code used to convert and analyze the data.

4.4 Data Normalization, Shuffling and Splitting

Data normalization helps to align the value ranges between attributes to avoid distortions and ensure that no attribute dominates over others. We used the Min-Max Scaling method, which transforms the data into a value range from 0 to 1.

We performed data shuffling to increase the diversity of the training data, improve the model's performance, and minimize the impact of input data on the final result. This helps prevent the formation of patterns that could adversely affect the model's performance.

Splitting the data into a training set and a test set allows for obtaining reliable results by working with unused data when measuring the model's accuracy. These data differ in the model training section and the accuracy evaluation section, which is crucial for assessing the model's effectiveness for newly introduced data (Figs. 13, 14, 15, 16 and 17).

```python
def _normalize(self,data):
    for i in data.columns:
        max = data[i].max()
        min = data[i].min()
        try:
            data[i] = (data[i] - min) / (max - min)
        except:
            print("error in column: ", i)
    return data
```

Fig. 13. Code used to normalize data

```python
def _shuffle(self, data: list) -> list:
    for i in range(len(data)):
        j = random.randint(0, len(data) - 1)
        data[i], data[j] = data[j], data[i]
    return data
```

Fig. 14. Code used to shuffle data

```python
def _split(self,data: list, ratio: float) -> (list, list):
    train = data[:int(len(data) * ratio)]
    test = data[int(len(data) * ratio):]
    return train, test
```

Fig. 15. Code used to split data

4.5 Naive Bayes Algorithm

Data: Input: *TrainData*
Result: Bayes classification of the set

stdavg = {};
for *instance* **in** *TrainData* **do**
    Read *label* and instance *attributes*;
    if *label* **not in** *stdavg* **then**
        | Add an empty element to stdavg for *label*;
    end
    for *attribute_index, value* **in** *attributes* **do**
        if *attribute_index* **not in** *stdavg[label]* **then**
            | Initialize stdavg[label][attribute_index] with empty values;
        end
        Add a value to the list of standard deviations for the data *label* attribute_index;
        Add a value to the list of averages for the data *label* attribute_index;
    end
end
for *label, attribute_data* **in** *stdavg_items* **do**
    for *attribute_index, attribute_value* **in** *attribute_data_items* **do**
        Calculate the standard deviation of an attribute;
        Calculate the average of the attribute;
    end
end

Fig. 16. Pseudocode of the Bayes classifier used (algorithm)

```
class Bayes:
    std_avg = {}

    def _gaussian(self, x, avg, std):
        coefficient = 1 / (np.sqrt(2 * np.pi) * std)
        exponent = -1/2 * ((x - avg) / std) ** 2
        return coefficient * np.exp(exponent)

    def eval_accuracy(self, test_data: list):
        correct_count = 0
        for instance in test_data:
            if self.estimate(instance[:-1]) == instance[-1]:
                correct_count += 1
        return correct_count / len(test_data)

    def estimate(self, instance: list):
        probabilities = {}

        for label in self.std_avg:
            probability = 1
            for attrib, attrib_data in self.std_avg[label].items():
                avg = attrib_data["avg"]
                std = attrib_data["std"]
                probability *= self._gaussian(instance[attrib], avg, std)

            probabilities[label] = probability

        return max(probabilities, key=probabilities.get)

    def __init__(self, train_data: list):
        self.std_avg = {}
        for instance in train_data:
            label = instance[-1]
            attributes = instance[:-1]

            if label not in self.std_avg:
                self.std_avg[label] = {}

            for attribute_idx, value in enumerate(attributes):
                if attribute_idx not in self.std_avg[label]:
                    self.std_avg[label][attribute_idx] = {"std": [], "avg": []}

                self.std_avg[label][attribute_idx]["std"].append(value)
                self.std_avg[label][attribute_idx]["avg"].append(value)

        for label, attrib_data in self.std_avg.items():
            for attribute_idx, attrib_values in attrib_data.items():
                attrib_data[attribute_idx]["std"] = np.std(attrib_values["std"])
                attrib_data[attribute_idx]["avg"] = np.mean(attrib_values["avg"])

    def __str__(self):
        return str(self.std_avg)
```

Fig. 17. Code of the Bayes classifier class

5   Experiments

In order to choose the most optimal solution for the problem, we compared the results with another classifier - we conducted experiments with the KNN classifier. Working with this classifier required dividing the database into smaller parts. For 1/5 of the entire dataset, we achieved a result in approximately 3 min. For 1/2 of the dataset, the result appeared after about 15 min. However, we were unable to obtain the result for the entire dataset due to excessively long waiting time (over 30 min of waiting).

The numerical results were satisfactory (accuracy around 88%), but the execution time of the task was decidedly unsatisfactory, leading directly to the rejection of this particular case.

6   Results

The results we obtained using the naive Bayes classifier are: 87.10%, 87.52%, 86.65%, 87.24%, 86.57%. The average standard deviation was: 0.402% and the standard error was: 0.179.

7 Conclusions

The conducted tests clearly indicate that when dealing with a large amount of data, the better solution would be the naive Bayes classifier, which consistently achieved satisfactory results even with different configurations and multiple shufflings. On the other hand, the KNN classifier requires significant computational power and a very long time to execute the assigned task.

We would also like to point out that it is possible to limit the size of the database using hierarchical clustering (e.g., agglomerative clustering), which would significantly reduce the database by grouping similar records and removing rows with very similar values.

8 Summary

In our job we focused on predicting the possibility of diabetes in correlation with cigarette smoking using machine learning techniques. We utilized the Diabetes prediction dataset and implemented the Naive Bayes classifier algorithm to conduct the study. Additionally, we experimented with the k-NN classifier. We emphasized the importance of data analysis and preparation to achieve satisfactory results. The article presents the stages of data analysis, the algorithm of the classifier, and the implementation steps of the code. We also highlighted the interpretation of graphs in the study.

The data analysis phase involved selecting the database, reducing the dataset by removing irrelevant rows, and preparing the data for testing. We also plotted various graphs to analyze the data, including the correlation of variables and the relationship between smoking, age, and diabetes.

The implementation section covered the necessary packages, downloading and pre-processing the dataset, data analysis, converting word values into numerical values, and normalizing and shuffling the data. We split the data into training and test sets for evaluating the model's accuracy.

We also compared the performance of the Naive Bayes classifier with the k-NN classifier through experiments. Although the k-NN classifier yielded satisfactory numerical results (accuracy around 88%), it required significant computational power and a long execution time, making it unsuitable for large datasets.

The results obtained using the Naive Bayes classifier consistently achieved satisfactory accuracy rates, ranging from 86.57% to 87.52% (with the average standard deviation 0.402% and the standard error 0.179).

In conclusion, the study showed that the Naive Bayes classifier is a better choice when dealing with large datasets, as it consistently achieved satisfactory results with different configurations and multiple shufflings. On the other hand, the k-NN classifier was computationally intensive and time-consuming. We suggested the use of hierarchical clustering to limit the size of the database, which could improve efficiency in similar projects.

References

1. Chaki, J., Woźniak, M.: A deep learning based four-fold approach to classify brain MRI: BTSCNet. Biomed. Signal Process. Control **85**, 104902 (2023)

2. Suyanto, S., Meliana, S., Wahyuningrum, T., Khomsah, S.: A new nearest neighbor-based framework for diabetes detection. Expert Syst. Appl. **199**, 116857 (2022)
3. Bilal, A.: Diabetic retinopathy detection and classification using mixed models for a disease grading database. IEEE Access **9**, 23544–23553 (2021)
4. Woźniak, M., Wieczorek, M., Siłka, J.: BiLSTM deep neural network model for imbalanced medical data of IoT systems. Futur. Gener. Comput. Syst. **141**, 489–499 (2023)
5. Le, T., et al.: A novel wrapper–based feature selection for early diabetes prediction enhanced with a metaheuristic. IEEE Access **9**, 7869–7884 (2020)
6. Chaudhary, P., Ram, P.: Automatic diagnosis of different grades of diabetic retinopathy and diabetic macular edema using 2-D-FBSE-FAWT. IEEE Trans. Instrum. Meas. **71**, 1–9 (2022)
7. Chaki, J., Woźniak, M.: Deep learning for neurodegenerative disorder (2016 to 2022): a systematic review. Biomed. Signal Process. Control **80**, 104223 (2023)
8. Siłka, W., Wieczorek, M., Siłka, J., Woźniak, M.: Malaria detection using advanced deep learning architecture. Sensors **23**(3), 1501 (2023)
9. Khademi, F., et al.: A weighted ensemble classifier based on WOA for classification of diabetes, Neural Computing and Applications (2022): 1–9.. 10. F. Haque et al., Machine Learning-Based Diabetic Neuropathy and Previous Foot Ulceration Patients Detection Using Electromyography and Ground Reaction Forces during Gait, Sensors 22.9 (2022): 3507

Soft Inference as a Voting Mechanism in k-Nearest Neighbors Clustering Algorithm

Tomasz Bury, Aleksandra Kacprzak[⊠], and Piotr Żerdziński

Faculty of Applied Mathematics, Silesian University of Technology, Kaszubska 23, Gliwice, Poland
ak303183@student.polsl.pl

Abstract. The rapid growth of IT systems that use artificial intelligence algorithms necessitates increasingly accurate methods. To handle data uncertainty, computer scientists can employ soft sets. One popular classification method in machine learning that utilizes the idea of proximity between data points is the k-NN algorithm. In this paper, we describe a modification to the k-NN algorithm that makes use of soft sets to take into account uncertainty in the classification process. This is achieved by introducing soft inference as a voting mechanism. The authors present a mathematical model with pseudocode for re-implementation purposes and demonstrate and discuss experimental results from conducted tests to show the effectiveness of the proposed approach.

Keywords: k-Nearest Neighbor (k-NN) · soft sets · voting algorithm

1 Introduction

The Internet of Things uses various algorithms to quickly analyze data and use it in various problems such as classification [1] or forecasting [2]. Unfortunately, classic tools quite often do not return very good results or require a lot of computing power and time. For this reason, new algorithms are being modeled [3]. An example of new algorithms is, above all, hybridization with other algorithms [4–6], which makes it possible to achieve better values of evaluation metrics. However, quite often tools are also used that require adaptation to specific data [7]. For this purpose, neural networks [8], heuristic approach [9, 10] and fuzzy logic [11, 12] are mainly used. It is worth noting that the tools allow you to automate activities in the Internet of Things [13], increase data security [14] or speed up calculations [15].

Soft sets [16] and k-NN [17] algorithms are both widely used techniques in machine learning and data analysis. In recent years, researchers have explored the use of soft sets in the k-NN voting algorithm to improve the accuracy of classification models.

Keller et al. [18] in 1985 introduced a k-NN algorithm using fuzzy classifier to assign membership of given object to a cluster. Lashari et al. [19] proposed using k-NN algorithm with soft sets to classify medical data. Soft sets provide a flexible framework for handling uncertainty and vagueness in data, making them particularly useful in scenarios where the data is incomplete or noisy. This paper presents an investigation

A. Lopata et al. (Eds.): ICIST 2023, CCIS 1979, pp. 309–318, 2024.
https://doi.org/10.1007/978-3-031-48981-5_25

into the application of soft sets in the k-NN voting algorithm for classification tasks, using modified Minkowski metric and selection of the best k.

The authors evaluate the effectiveness of this approach on several benchmark datasets and compare the results with the traditional k-NN voting algorithm. In this article, the authors explore the use of soft set voting in the k-NN algorithm, a popular and widely used algorithm for classification in machine learning. The authors demonstrate the effectiveness of the approach on a heart disease dataset, highlighting its advantages over the traditional k-NN algorithm. Results show that the proposed approach can improve the accuracy and robustness of the k-NN algorithm, making it a promising tool for practical applications in machine learning and data mining. The main contribution of this paper are:

- adapting soft set inference to the voting problem,
- hybridization of k-NN with soft sets inference.

2   Mathematical Model

The algorithm presented in the article uses both the k-NN-nearest neighbor algorithm and soft sets.

2.1   k-NN Algorithm

The basic principle of the conventional k-NN approach is to predict the label of a test data point using the majority rule, i.e. by using the main class of k most similar training data points in the space. To create accurate predictions, k-NN uses complex distance measures (e.g. Minkowski metrics) and observable data similarities.

There are two problems associated with its use–the problem of choosing the right number of neighbors to take into account, and the computational complexity, which is $(\mathcal{O}(n^2 \log n))$. It should also be noted that its accuracy depends on the number of objects to be analyzed since a larger number of objects gives the chance to find more similar objects.

Suppose $D = \{(x_i, y_i) : i = 1, ..., m\}$ is the learning data set. For a given unknown sample x, we order D in the form of a sequence, where d represents the calculated distances:

$$\forall j = 1, m - 1. d(x, x_j) \leq d(x, x_{j+1}) \tag{1}$$

The first k elements of the sequence $D(x)$ are defined by $N_k(x)$, the k-element neighborhood of x:

$$N_k(x) = \{(x_1, y_1), (x_2, y_2), ..., (x_k, y_k)\} \tag{2}$$

The algorithm used to determine the distance uses the Minkowski metric for $m = \{1, 2, 3, 4\}$ and returns the maximum of these four values. For any points $x = (x_1, x_2, ..., x_n), y = (y_1, y_2, ..., y_n)$ of space $\mathbb{R}^n$, their Minkowski distance is given by the formula:

$$L_m(x, y) = \left(\sum_{i=1}^{n} |x_i - y_i|^m\right)^{\frac{1}{m}} \tag{3}$$

where:

L_m-the distance in the Minkowski metric for a given m,

m-m is an integer, in this case, a number from 1 to 4 inclusive.

n-the number of dimensions that define two points

Finally, the class with the highest probability is chosen to receive the input x.

$$P(y = j|X = x) = \frac{1}{K} \sum I\left(y^{(i)} = j\right) \qquad (4)$$

2.2 Soft Sets

Soft sets are used to deal with uncertain, fuzzy objects and those that cannot be clearly defined. Soft set theory is similar to fuzzy set theory but is much simplified. For usage in medical expert systems, soft sets have also been applied to the issue of medical diagnosis.

The soft set was described in the following way by Molodtsov. Let E be a set of parameters and U be the initial universe set. Let the power set of U and $A \subset E$ be represented by $P(U)$. A pair (F, A) that has the mapping

$$F : A \rightarrow P(U) \qquad (5)$$

is referred to as a soft set over U. As an example, the soft set describes the features of the cups.

U = the set of cups we are considering

$U = \{c1, c2, c3, c4\}$

E = the set of parameters with which the cups can be described

$E = e1, e2, e3, e4$

$A = \{slim, large, painted, printed\}$

Suppose that:

$F(e1) = \{c1, c3\}$

$F(e2) = \{c2, c4\}$

$F(e3) = \{c2, c3\}$

$F(e4) = \{c3\}$

This can be presented in Table 1.

Table 1. A table of soft set.

U	e1	e2	e3	e4
c1	1	0	0	0
c2	0	1	1	0
c3	1	0	1	1
c4	0	1	0	0

A set P is introduced, which consists of the selected parameters and is a subset of E:

$$P = \{e1, e2, e3\}$$

For any $P \subset E$, (F, P) is a soft subset of (F, E) If by Q we denote the reduct of P, then the soft set (F, Q) is a reduced soft set in (F, P). Then line up the values and find k for which the sum is maximal.

Table 2. A table of soft set.

U	e1	e2	e3	The values
c1	1	0	0	$= 1$
c2	0	1	1	$= 2$
c3	1	0	1	$= 2$
c4	0	1	0	$= 1$

It follows that, for that example under consideration, the best choice would be c2 or c3 (see Table 2).

2.3   k-NN + Soft Set Algorithm

Let X be a set of observations and Y a set of class labels. Let d be a function of the distance between two observations and k be the number of neighbors to be considered.

For each new observation x, compute its distance $d(x, x')$ from each observation x' in the set X. The k observations that have the smallest distances are then selected.

Let V be the set of all possible values of class labels Y, and let $S = \{s_1, s_2, ..., s_n\}$ be the soft set that represents the set of all k neighbors. Then s_j denotes the degree to which the label y_j belongs to the set S, where $y_j \in V$. To assign a label x, determine for each label y_j the set $S_j = \{s_i : y_i = y_j\}$. Then compute the degree of membership of y_j to the set S as:

$$s_j = \sum s_i \qquad (6)$$

for each neighbor $x' \in X$ whose label is y_j. The label to be assigned to x is the one with the highest degree of membership to S.

3   Methodology

3.1   Using Soft Sets to Vote in k-NN Algorithm

The algorithm assigns class membership to a given vector, unlike the usual k-nn algorithm, where a vector is assigned to a class. Every vector sample has a degree of association, which makes it non-arbitrary. The proposed algorithm uses a modified Minkowski metric, finding the maximum distance for $m = 1, 2, ..., 5$ and returning it. Another approaches to modifying the Minkowski metric were explored, such as using mean and minimum distance. All potential algorithm modifications were tested for different values of k. The test results are presented in Fig. 1.

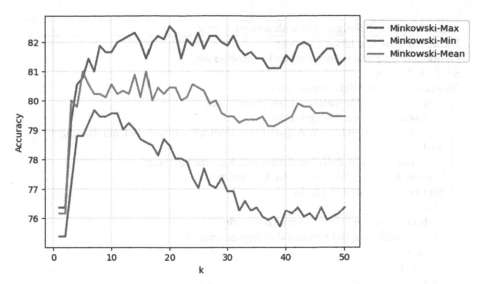

Fig. 1. Tests of potential Minkowski metric modifications

Based on the results, the maximum distance approach was chosen. The algorithm for this solution is presented below.

Algorithm 1: Modified Minkowski Metric

Data: vectors $x = (x1, x2, ..., xn)$, $y = (y1, y2, ..., yn)$

for $m \leftarrow 1$ **to** 5 **do**

$$d_m \leftarrow \left(\sum_{i=1}^{n} |x_i - y_i|^m \right)^{\frac{1}{m}}$$

end

return $\max(d_m)$

Algorithm 2: k-NN algorithm with soft set voting
___
Data: database of n labeled vectors
Divide database into training set and validation set;
Set k, $1 \le k \le n$;
foreach *vector in validation set* **do**
  Choose one sample vector x from training set;
  foreach *vector in training set* **do**
    | Compute distance with **Algorithm 1** from x to all vectors from training set;
  end
  Sort training set by calculated distance in ascending order;
  Choose k vectors from the sorted training set;
  foreach *class c of objects* **do**
    | $m \leftarrow 1$;
    foreach *vector v in chosen k vectors* **do**
      | Calculate $u_i(v)$ membership degree with (7)
    end
    | $i + +$
  end
end

The algorithm proposed in this paper uses the membership function u_i shown in Eq. (7) to calculate the degree of association vector x to a given class.

$$u_i(\mathrm{x}) = \frac{\sum_{j=1}^{k} u_{ij} \left(\frac{1}{\|x-x_j\|}^{\frac{2}{m-1}} \right)}{\sum_{j=1}^{k} \left(\frac{1}{\|x-x_j\|}^{\frac{2}{m-1}} \right)} \tag{7}$$

where:

x–chosen sample vector

k–number of nearest neighbors to x

x_j–jth vector from the labeled set

u_{ij}–membership in the ith class of the jth vector

In Eq. (7), m is an integer value and is chosen arbitrarily. In our results, $m = 2$.

4 Experiments

The used database consists of data of 303 records of medical data of patients that are risked or not risked of having a heart attack created from 4 databases from the Hungarian Institute of Cardiology. Budapest, University Hospital, Zurich, Switzerland, University Hospital, Basel, Switzerland and V.A. Medical Center, Long Beach and Cleveland Clinic Foundation. Every record is defined by 14 parameters:

- Age,
- Patient's sex (0 - female, 1 - male),
- Exercise-induced angina (0 - no, 1 - yes),
- Number of major vessels (0 - 3),

- Chest pain type (1 - typical type 1, 2 - typical type angina, 3 - non-angina pain, 4 - asymptomatic)
- Resting blood pressure (mmHg)
- Serum cholesterol (mg/dl)
- Fasting blood sugar > 120 mg/dl (0 - false, 1 - true)
- Resting ECG results (0 - normal, 1 - having abnormal ST-T wave, 2 - hypertrophy)
- Maximum heart rate achieved (bpm)
- ST depression induced by exercises relative to rest (previous peak)
- The slope of the peak exercise ST segment (1 - upsloping, 2 - flat, 3 - downsloping)
- Thal (3 - normal, 6 - fixed defect, 7–reversible effect)
- Result (0 - lower chance of heart attack, 1–higher chance of heart attack)

The data were preprocessed before using the proposed algorithm. 1 duplicate record was removed from the training dataset. The dataset was divided into training and validation sets by choosing 211 records for the training set and 91 records for the validation set. Data was normalized using the min-max normalization algorithm.

$$x' = \frac{x - \min(x)}{\max(x) - \min(x)} \tag{8}$$

where:

x'–normalized value

x–original value

The primary objective of this study was to achieve higher performance compared to the classic k-NN algorithm, where "classic" refers to the use of the Euclidean metric for distance calculation and voting to assign a new instance to the class that most of its k nearest neighbors belong to. The comparison of the two approaches, in terms of average accuracy, is presented in Fig. 2.

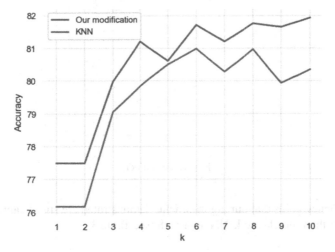

Fig. 2. Comparison of the accuracy (k)

As our dataset pertains to the medical field, inaccurate predictions may result in significant consequences, particularly with false negatives posing a considerable danger. Figure 3 depicts the confusion matrix of a typical outcome, while the recall of our algorithm was calculated based on this matrix, as illustrated in Fig. 4.

$$Recall = \frac{tp}{tp + fn} \tag{9}$$

where:

    tp–true positive

    fn–false negative

As depicted in Fig. 2, our algorithm exhibits a slightly higher accuracy than the classic k-NN approach.

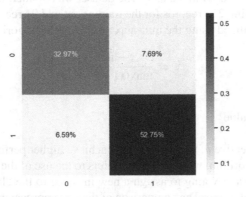

Fig. 3. Confusion matrix for the entire validation set

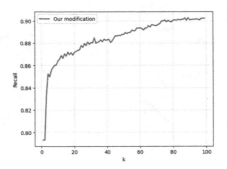

Fig. 4. Recall (k)

The efficiency gains that our algorithm has demonstrated are significant, as it is over 3 times faster than the classic k-NN approach (see Table 3).

Table 3. Time comparison

Algorithm	Time [s]
Our modification	3,37
k-NN	11,3

5 Conclusions

Our modified k-NN algorithm has been shown to improve not only the accuracy of predictions but also their time complexity. We have attempted to optimize these indicators by reducing the number of features, either by keeping the same record size or by reducing them proportionally. However, these attempts did not yield any improvements in average results. While the time complexity continued to decrease, the accuracy was significantly impacted. Nonetheless, our algorithm without reduced feature dimensions was unable to achieve an accuracy greater than 90%. On the other hand, the algorithm with reduced feature dimensions achieved an accuracy greater than 90% on a few occasions. However, this better performance in the maximum case was offset by a greater variance in results.

This paper focuses on a medical dataset, and therefore, the recall metric is more important than accuracy. In future work, attention should be given to improve recall in the algorithm. The dataset used in this study is a subset of the original database, which consists of 76 attributes. To achieve the best possible recall, the next step is to manually select features with an increasing number of instances.

References

1. Revin, I., Potemkin, V.A., Balabanov, N.R., Nikitin, N.O.: Automated machine learning approach for time series classification pipelines using evolutionary optimization. Knowl. Based Syst. **268**, 110483 (2023)
2. Méndez, M., Merayo, M.G., Núñez, M.: Machine learning algorithms to forecast air quality: a survey. Artif. Intell. Rev. **56**, 1–36 (2023)
3. Admon, M.R., Senu, N., Ahmadian, A., Majid, Z.A., Salahshour, S.: A new efficient algorithm based on feedforward neural network for solving differential equations of fractional order. Commun. Nonlinear Sci. Numer. Simul. **117**, 106968 (2023)
4. Siłka, J., Wieczorek, M., Woźniak, M.: Recurrent neural network model for high-speed train vibration prediction from time series. Neural Comput. Appl. **34**, 13305–13318 (2022)
5. Pathak, P.K., Yadav, A.K., Alvi, P.: A state-of-the-art review on shading mitigation techniques in solar photovoltaics via meta-heuristic approach. Neural Comput. Appl. **34**, 1–39 (2022)
6. Mar'i, F., Ubaidillah, H., Mahmudy, W.F., Supianto, A.A.: Hybrid artificial bee colony and improved simulated annealing for the capacitated vehicle routing problem. Knowl. Eng. Data Sci. **5**(2), 109–121 (2023)
7. Połap, D., Wawrzyniak, N., Włodarczyk-Sielicka, M.: Side-scan sonar analysis using ROI analysis and deep neural networks. IEEE Trans. Geosci. Remote Sens. **60**, 1–8 (2022)
8. Bessadok, A., Mahjoub, M.A., Rekik, I.: Graph neural networks in network neuroscience. IEEE Trans. Pattern Anal. Mach. Intell. **45**, 5833–5848 (2022)
9. Pleszczyński, M., Zielonka, A., Woźniak, M.: Application of nature-inspired algorithms to computed tomography with incomplete data. Symmetry **14**, 2256 (2022)

10. Połap, D., Kęsik, K., Woźniak, M., Damaševičius, R.: Parallel technique for the metaheuristic algorithms using devoted local search and manipulating the solutions space. Appl. Sci. **8**, 293 (2018)
11. Khan, M.R., Ullah, K., Khan, Q.: Multi-attribute decision-making using archimedean aggregation operator in t-spherical fuzzy environment. Rep. Mech. Eng. **4**, 18–38 (2023)
12. Woźniak, M., Zielonka, A., Sikora, A.: Driving support by type-2 fuzzy logic control model. Expert Syst. Appl. **207**, 117798 (2022)
13. Woźniak, M., Połap, D.: Intelligent home systems for ubiquitous user support by using neural networks and rule-based approach. IEEE Trans. Industr. Inf. **16**, 2651–2658 (2019)
14. Prokop, K., Połap, D., Srivastava, G., Lin, J.C.-W.: Blockchain-based federated learning with checksums to increase security in internet of things solutions. J. Ambient Intell. Humanized Comput. **14**, 1–10 (2022)
15. Dong, X., Ji, Z., Chu, T., Huang, T., Zhang, W., Wu, S.: Adaptation accelerating sampling-based Bayesian inference in attractor neural networks. Adv. Neural. Inf. Process. Syst. **35**, 21534–21547 (2022)
16. Maji, P.K., Biswas, R., Roy, A.R.: Soft set theory. Comput. Math. Appl. **45**, 555–562 (2003)
17. Zheng, T., et al.: Compositionally graded knn-based multilayer composite with excellent piezoelectric temperature stability. Adv. Mater. **34**, 2109175 (2022)
18. Keller, J.M., Gray, M.R., Givens, J.A.: A fuzzy K-nearest neighbor algorithm. IEEE Trans. Syst. Man, Cybern. SMC **15**(4), 580–585 (1985). https://doi.org/10.1109/tsmc.1985.6313426
19. Lashari, S.A., Ibrahim, R., Senan, N.: Medical data classification using similarity measure of fuzzy soft set based distance measure. J. Telecommun. Electron. Comput. Eng. (JTEC), **9**(2–9), 95–99 (2017)

Online Resources

20. GitHub -https://github.com/PiotrekZe/mod_kNN
21. Database was gathered from Kaggle- https://www.kaggle.com/datasets/johnsmith88 /heart-disease-dataset

The BLDC Motor Efficiency Improvement by Electronical Correction of the Power States Indications

Andrzej Sikora[1] ⓘ, Adam Zielonka[2] ⓘ, and Martyna Kobielnik[2](✉) ⓘ

[1] Faculty of Electrical Engineering, Silesian University of Technology, 44-100 Gliwice, Poland
Andrzej.Sikora@polsl.pl
[2] Faculty of Applied Mathematics, Silesian University of Technology, 44-100 Gliwice, Poland
{Adam.Zielonka,Martyna.Kobielnik}@polsl.pl

Abstract. In this paper an electronic correction of the symmetry of the states is proposed that determines the angular position of the BLDC motor shaft. The results illustrating the measurements of the asymmetry of the states of the Hall effect sensors determining the position of the motor shaft following from the adopted measuring system are presented. The improvement in efficacy by improving the symmetry of the power supply of the motor windings tested resulting from eliminating the asymmetry of signals from the sensors is shown.

Keywords: BLDC motor · Hall sensor · Electronic commutator

1 Introduction

The development of materials engineering enables the usage of rare earth materials in the production of strong magnets. These magnets can be applied in engineering industry to construct modern motors [1, 2], where they play a role in machine excitation. Such a solution allows us to eliminate the excitation winding that can be found in a classical motor, however, it requires some changes in the machine design [3]. In a classic DC motor, the excitation winding is located on the stator and a mechanical commutator is used to power the motor, while in a motor where magnets are used for excitation, they need to be placed on the rotor and an electronic commutator is required [4]. The task of the electronic commutator is to adequately supply the armature winding located on the motor stator. The armature winding must be powered synchronously with the angular position of the rotor, due to the current course of the magnetic field lines generated by the permanent magnets rotating with the rotor. Modern permanent magnet motors can be divided into two main groups: permanent synchronous motor (PMSM) [5, 6], and brushless DC motor (BLDC). In a BLDC motor, there is no excitation winding and therefore there is no excitation current flow, which eliminates the energy losses needed to excite the machine [7, 8]. The use of permanent magnets ensures the excitation of the machine without generating additional losses in the rotor that prevent it from heating up [9].

A. Lopata et al. (Eds.): ICIST 2023, CCIS 1979, pp. 319–328, 2024.
https://doi.org/10.1007/978-3-031-48981-5_26

In comparison of BLDC motors with commonly available asynchronous motors, the advantage of BLDC is evident. Although asynchronous motors are constantly developed and those produced nowadays have much better parameters than their predecessors, in many aspects BLDC motors turn out to be better. Currently, the energy saving and reduction of the fossil fuels usage are very important factors, hence the efficiency of the motor is a significant indicator of the utility for the modern drives. BLDC motor is characterized by higher efficiency due to elimination of losses in the excitation winding. The magnetic flux is produced by a strong magnet located on the rotor of the motor. These issues are considered in [10–12]. The reduction of maximum rotor temperatures also has a positive effect on the bearings of the machine, extending their durability. Compared to asynchronous machines, the time between successive bearing replacements is about twice as long. It makes this type of drive more competitive, greener, and more economical [13]. Moreover, because of their smaller dimensions and lower weight, they seem very attractive for use in modern drive systems. Nowadays, permanent magnet motors are used in various drives, from household appliances with a power of hundreds of watts, through drives of electric vehicles with a power of several dozen kW [14], to drives of rail vehicles with a set of motors with a total power of several MW.

Knowledge of the rotor position is required to control the power transistors. It can be determined indirectly or directly. As rotor position sensors, one can use encoders, Hall effect sensors that utilize additional permanent magnets placed on the measuring system, or Hall effect sensors placed in the grooves of the motor, detecting changes in the magnetic field generated by the motor excitation magnets.

2 Technical Description

The subject of the research is the SMZT 80–6 permanent magnet motor with a rated power of 1 kW and a rated speed of 1000 rpm. The motor is powered with a rated voltage of 48 V. It is connected to a load machine driven by permanent magnets of similar rated power through two couplings and a Dataflex 22/20 torque meter. The research stand is presented in Fig. 1.

Powering a three-phase motor excited by permanent magnets requires sequential switching of transistors through which the motor windings are powered from a DC voltage source. This sequence is strictly determined by the relative position of the magnetic axis of the rotor to the axis of the stator winding bands. This is the reason why it is necessary to know the angular position of the rotor during engine operation. There are two methods to determine the rotor position: sensor and sensorless.

The first method uses sensors attached to the motor (e.g. hall sensors and absolute or incremental encoders), while the second one is based on the signal coming from the motor windings. The sensorless method does not require any additional equipment. Although both methods lead to very similar results, in the case of start and return, a better choice is the sensor method with absolute sensors that determine the position of the rotor at zero speed. It is particularly important in the case of traction drives because they should not step back and require a significant starting torque.

Fig. 1. The research stand: The tested BLDC motor with hall sensors mounted in the stator grooves on the left, and the generator with permanent magnets used to load or drive the BLDC motor on the right. Machines are connected via a Dataflex 22/20 torque meter.

2.1 The Power System

BLDC motor control does not require constant tracking of the rotor position. It is sufficient for the rotor position angle measurement system to give a signal when the voltage should be applied to a given winding band. For this purpose, encoders can be applied. An encoder can give a precise measure of the angular position of the rotor; however, it increases the cost of the drive, while it transmits a lot of unnecessary information, that is not used for the purpose of controlling the BLDC motor. In this paper, encoders are not the subject of interest.

To control the BLDC motor, a hall sensor can be used. In this paper, a method of determining the position of the rotor that uses the Hall effect sensors is discussed. Sensors that detect changes in the magnetic flux generated by the rotor are placed in the grooves of the stator. Alternatively, Hall sensors could be mounted outside the engine. In this setting, they need to cooperate with an additional magnetic transmitter, as shown in [3, 4]. The applied angular position sensor of the motor shaft consisted of six hall sensors placed in the grooves of the stator. The angular distance between successive engine grooves is 10°, and, due to the geometry, this is the optimal location of the hall sensors that enables the detection of 12 symmetric states defining a single control cycle. For a six-pole motor, there are 36 states per shaft revolution (three complete control sequences). Analysis of the signals of the Hall sensors that determine the position of the rotor located in the grooves of the BLDC motor showed that the states determined by these Hall sensors are not symetric.

Here we introduce the description of the test stand. The scheme is shown in Fig. 2. The stand consists of two machines with permanent magnets with a torque gauge placed at the connection of their shafts. An additional sensor was placed on the torque gauge to be able to detect one full rotation of the shaft. The electrical parts present in the scheme are: a source of DC voltage, a system of Hall effect sensors, and a power electronic commutator. The power elements of the power electronic commutator are MOSFET transistors, and the system that performs logical functions is the ATtiny 2313 micro-processor. Measurements exposed the asymetry of the duration of the individual power states of the tested engine when operating at a constant rotational speed. The schematic diagram of the measuring system is presented in Fig. 3.

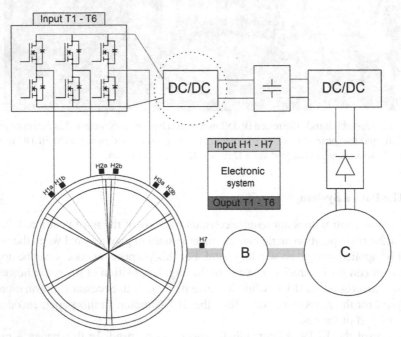

Fig. 2. Scheme of the test stand that consist of the motor with 6 halotrons H1a, H1b, H2a, H2b, H3a, H3b placed in the grooves of the motor stator, and hall sensor H7 placed above the magnetic marker mounted above the motor shaft, B represents the torque meter, and C is the load machine with permanent magnets, a three-phase rectifier system is marked with a diode symbol, next, a DC/DC converter for setting the motor load is placed, a DC voltage source is marked with a capacitor symbol, a DC/DC converter that is surrounded by a dashed line is used to regulate the voltage fed to the electronic commutator, and an electronic commutator is marked with six transistors and control system (electronic system).

Bipolar hall sensors type TLE4935–2 were used as sensors detecting the characteristic points of the motor rotor position, for which the control sequence of power electronic keys should be changed. These sensors placed in the stator grooves cooperate with the motor rotor magnets (they detect the change of the N, S poles). The measurements showed the asymmetry of individual control sequences. In order to improve the operation of the engine, it was decided to implement a software correction of the symmetry of the control states of power electronic keys. This solution affected the efficiency of the entire drive system.

Different durations of individual motor power states cause different current flow times, which translates into different current values in individual motor windings. The resulting current asymmetry in the motor windings cause different losses in individual windings, which leads to the different temperature increases of individual windings.

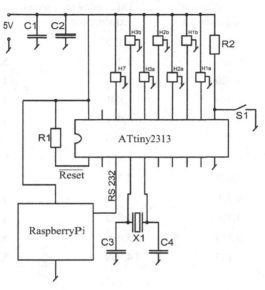

Fig. 3. Schematic diagram of the measurement system used to test the asymmetry of the BLDC motor control states. H1a, H1b, H2a, H2b, H3a, H3b, and H7 are Hall effect sensors connected directly to the pins of the ATtiny2313 measuring microcontroller clocked by a quartz generator marked X1, connected to the RaspberryPi computer via RS232 to record data sent by the micro-controller program. C1 and C2 are the filter capacitors, R1 and R2 are the resistors, and C3 and C4 are capacitors in the quartz generator circuit. S1 is the switch that initialize recording.

A further consequence of this phenomenon is increased energy losses in the motor and its power supply system, increased drive vibrations, and thus greater noise generated by the drive system. To determine the difference in the duration of individual power states caused by the asymmetry of signals obtained from Hall effect sensors placed in the stator grooves, a measurement system was prepared. The recorder was built on the basis of a microcontroller counter clocked by a quartz generator. Using an additional sensor located on the coupling, after a measurement signal, the microcontroller detected the first state of the hall sensor and started to count the pulses for each of the next 36 states per one full revolution of the motor shaft. When the pulses for all states per one revolution are counted, the microcontroller sent the data through the RS232 port to the master unit, that is, the Raspberry PI system. The results were then statistically analyzed. Data were collected for two different states of the machine tested. In the first case, the motor was driven by an external machine and results were registered for two different rotation speeds. In the Table 1. The durations of individual states of the hall effect sensors are presented for the engine rotation speed of 340 rmp. The results presented in the Table 1. Show large disproportions of the duration of states of the Hall effect sensors. Undoubtedly, it has a negative impact on engine efficiency.

Table 1. Hall effect sensor states duration for three consequtive control sequences maing up a full rotation of the motor shaft for the speed of 340 rpm.

Control state number	Duration of the first sequence [ms]	Duration of the second sequence [ms]	Duration of the third sequence [ms]
1	4.202	4.175	4.481
2	5.400	5.422	5.404
3	4.620	4.618	4.620
4	1.560	1.891	1.364
5	8.131	8.071	8.311
6	1.972	1.815	1.835
7	7.812	7.822	7.891
8	5.857	5.741	5.760
9	4.239	4.434	4.293
10	4.326	4.039	4.242
11	5.503	5.696	5.679
12	5.143	4.968	5.136

Similar experiments were carried out for the motor rotation speed of 560 rpm. A summary of statistical results in both cases for two different directions of rotation (0 stands for clockwise and 1 for counterclockwise direction) is presented in the Table 2. The statistical measures used are the following:

$$\bar{x} = \frac{1}{n} \sum_{k=1}^{n} x_k,$$

$$s = \sqrt{\frac{1}{n} \sum_{k=1}^{n} ((x_k - \bar{x}))^2},$$

$$v = 100\% \frac{\bar{x}}{s},$$

$$r = \max \left\{ \frac{|\bar{x} - x_k|}{\bar{x}}, k = 1, \ldots, n \right\}.$$

The second experiment was to test the engine on neutral. In this case, three different spin speeds were used, namely 340, 680, and 1000 rpm. The summary of results for the symmetry of the Hall effect sensors are shown in the Table 3.

Presented results indicate that both in the case of an engine driven by the second machine and for an engine on neutral gear, the Hall effect sensor of the engine shaft position in this settings causes significant differences in the successive states durations in the sequence of states determining the engine shaft position.

Table 2. Summary of statistics for the motor driven by an independent machine for two speeds and two rotation directions.

Motor speed	340 rpm		560 rpm	
Direction	0	1	0	1
x- [ms]	4.902	4.892	2.953	2.938
s	1.902	1.457	1.101	0.712
v	38.80	29.78	37.28	24.23
r	72.17	68.93	71.38	67.76

Table 3. Summary of statistics for engine working on neutral gear for different rotation speeds and directions.

Motorspeed	340 rpm		680 rpm		1000 rpm	
Direction	0	1	0	1	0	1
x- [ms]	4.899	4.430	2.440	2.240	1.652	1.377
s	2.015	1.875	0.957	1.065	0.650	0.794
v	41.124	42.328	39.210	47.558	39.338	57.643
r	70.08	91.27	67.25	90.67	74.63	107.31

3   Hall Effect Sequence States Signals Correction

In previous section, based on the measurements, it was shown that the durations of states of successive sequences read from the Hall effect sensors differ significantly. This phenomenon has a negative impact on the efficiency of the motor controlled with these signals. This research goal is to propose a correction method that is simple to perform, while giving a significant improvement of the control states symmetry. This solution can be implemented by the motor commutator microcontroller. Results showing the advance in the efficiency with comparision to no correction are presented.

Figure 4 Presents the signal waveform of the Hall effect sensors, where n_i i $= 0, \ldots,$ 12 denotes the switching times between changes in the state of the control sequence. The proposed method is based on determining the midpoints of the duration of two successive states. This is a very easy operation from the microcontroller point of view. It only requires to compute a sum of two numbers and a bit shift (which correspond to division by 2). In the figure, the points obtained this way are marked in red and denoted s_i. At least the result is smoothed using the same operation again. The final points are marked green on the figure and are denoted *sic*. These points are switching points of the control sequence of the transistors on the bridge that powers the BLDC motor.

In order to show the improvement resulting from the use of the proposed correction, the engine efficiency tests were carried out for the control with and without correction.

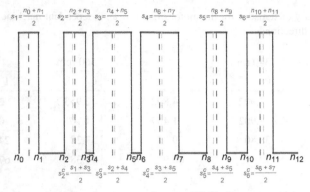

Fig. 4. The waveform of the signal sequence of a set of Hall effect sensors placed in the grooves of the motor, where the averaging of two successive states is marked in red, and their smoothing in green.

Table 4. Summary of motor efficiency determined for control based on the signal from Hall sensors without correction and with correction for three different spin speeds N = 1/3, 2/3. $1n_N$ and for three different loads M = 0.4, 0.8, $1M_N$.

Load	No correction			With correction		
	$n = 1/3\ n_N$	$n = 2/3\ n_N$	$n = n_N$	$n = 1/3\ n_N$	$n = 2/3\ n_N$	$n = n_N$
M = $0.4M_N$	67.905	75.350	76.884	70.305	78.298	97.988
M = $0.8M_N$	50.420	55.948	57.087	52.821	58.082	59.666
M = $1M_N$	47.737	52.970	54.049	49.908	55.479	56.433

Measurements for different motor rotation speeds and motor operation for different loads are presented in the Table 4.

The results presented in the table clearly show that a simple correction of the hall effect signal had a positive effect on improving the efficiency of the BLDC motor in all operating states tested.

4 Conclusions

Simple algorithms that can be implemented in an eight-bit microprocessor of AVR type, the BLDC motor operation can be improved. Such a microprocessor was used as an element of the electronic commutator used to power the BLDC motor. The motor was prepared in a way that enabled the location of the rotor position sensors in the grooves. This solution allows the use of magnetic field emitted by the magnets on the rotor to determine its position, and more precisely to determine the position that requires a change in the control of the electronic commutator keys. The research conducted showed that such a solution causes the measurement inaccuracy, which resulted in asymmetric power states of the motor windings. Power supply imbalances are the cause of vibrations and excessive energy losses that are different in individual windings. Different activation times of the electronic commutator keys result in different values of effective current, and hence different losses in the windings. Also, windings with higher current flows (rms value) tend to heat up more compared to others. The electronic commutator using signals from Hall effect sensors located in the grooves of the motor can be improved with additional algorithm modifying the symmetry of the power electronic commutator key control. This approach results in reducing the uneven heating of the windings by equalizing the rms value of the currents of the individual windings. Another positive effect is in balancing the losses in individual keys of the power electronic commutator. In addition, ensuring symmetrical operation reduces the vibrations of the drive system, hence the niose level is lower. Laboratory measurements of the efficiency of the entire system (BLDC motor with a power electronic commutator) confirmed the effects. The tables show the efficiency measurements of the entire system resulting from tests for two different programs stored in the microprocessor memory. In the first variant, only the signals from the sensors located in the slots of the BLDC motor stator were used to control the power electronic commutator keys. The second, improved variant of the program also used an algorithm to improve the symmetry of the BLDC motor winding power supply states. In this solution, in addition to signals from hall sensors, the microprocessor used measurements of the duration of states from the previous turnover stored in the memory. For the safety of the entire system, the shift could be made by only one state to correct the control state of the electronic commutator keys based on the readings from the hall sensors. The program stored in the microprocessor allowed for a faster change of the existing state in relation to the next state resulting from the reading of signals from the sensors.

The second variant of the correction allowed us to extend the current state despite the change in the signals received from Hall effect sensors placed in the grooves of the engine. This solution improved the efficiency of the entire drive system. The measurements for both control variants for different loads and spinning speeds are attached in tables.

Acknowledgements. Authors would like to acknowledge contribution to this research from the Rector of the Silesian University of Technology, Gliwice, Poland under pro-quality grant no. 05/030/RGJ23/0063.

References

1. Ozturk, S.B., Toliyat, H.: Direct torque control of brushless DC motor with non-sinusoidal back-EMF. In: Proceedings of the 2007 IEEE International Electric Machines & Drives Conference, Antalya, Turkey, 3–5 May 2007, vol. 1, pp. 165–171
2. Jang, G.H., Kim, M.: Optimal commutation of a BLDC motor by utilizing the symmetric terminal voltage. IEEE Trans. Magn. 42, 3473–3475 (2006). http://www.ncbi.nlm.nih.gov. National Center for Biotechnology Information.
3. Sikora, A., Woźniak, M.: Impact of current pulsation on BLDC motor parameters. Sensors **21**, 587 (2021)
4. Sikora, A., Zielonka, A., Woźniak, M.: Minimization of energy losses in the BLDC motor for improved control and power supply of the system under static load. Sensors **22**, 1058 (2022)

5. Maraaba, L.S., Twaha, S., Memon, A., Al-Hamouz, Z.: Recognition of stator winding inter-turn fault in interior-mount LSPMSM using acoustic signals. Symmetry **12**, 1370 (2020)
6. Liu, H., Li, S.: Speed control for PMSM servo system using predictive functional control and extended state observer. IEEE Trans. Ind. Electron. **59**, 1171–1183 (2011)
7. Czerwinski, D., Gęca, J., Kolano, K.: Machine learning for sensorless temperature estimation of a BLDC motor. Sensors **21**(14), 4655 (2021)
8. Usman, A., Rajpurohit, B.S.: Speed control of a BLDC motor using fuzzy logic controller. In: Proceedings of the 2016 IEEE 1st International Conference on Power Electronics, Intelligent Control and Energy Systems (ICPEICES), pp. 1–6. Delhi, India (2016)
9. Zhou, X., Chen, X., Lu, M., Zeng, F.: Rapid self-compensation method of commutation phase error for low-inductance BLDC motor. IEEE Trans. Ind. Inform. **13**, 1833–1842 (2017)
10. Kumar, N.S., et al.: A novel design methodology and numerical simulation of BLDC motor for power loss reduction. Appl. Sci. **12**, 20 (2022)
11. Kumaresan, S., Habeebullah Sait, H.: Design and control of shunt active power filter for power quality improvement of utility powered brushless DC motor drives. Automatica **61**(3), 507–521 (2020)
12. Glowacz, A.: Termographic fault diagnosis of ventilation in BLDC Motors. Sensors **21**, 21 (2021)
13. Zhao, L., Zhang, X., Ji, J.: A torque control strategy of brushless direct current motor with current observer. In: Proceedings of the 2015 IEEE International Conference on Mechatronics and Automation(ICMA), pp. 303–307 Beijing, China (2015)
14. Kumar, B.R., Kumar, K.S.: Design of a new dual rotor radial flux BLDC motor with Halbach array magnets for an electric vehicle. In: Proceedings of the 2016 IEEE International Conference on Power Electronics, Drives and Energy Systems (PEDES)

The Impact of Entropy Weighting Technique on MCDM-Based Rankings on Patients Using Ambiguous medical Data

Antoni Jaszcz[✉][iD]

Silesian University of Technology, Faculty of Applied Mathematics, Gliwice, Poland
aj303181@student.polsl.pl

Abstract. Multi-Criteria Decision Making (MCDM) is a method that allows to make a decision based on many different factors. Such solutions are important from a practical point of view in situations where there are many important criteria to examine. This work considers a situation in which many patients suffer from multiple symptoms, and focus should be on those most in need. For this purpose, publicly available databases related to COVID-19 symptoms were used. The proposition is composed of processing different types of samples and a combination of their numerical values. Then, it is used in selected entropy-weighted MCDM methods for returning a patient's ranking. The proposed solution shows that this approach has great potential due to the possibility of practical use.

Keywords: MCDM · Weighted methods · Rankings · Medical data

1 Introduction

The amount of data we gather and process has been growing exponentially in recent years. This creates a great challenge to find better and more reliable methods of data analysis. Given numerous, ambiguous criteria assessment tasks can be especially demanding, reaching beyond human capability to efficiently make decisions. Over recent years, more and more attention has been brought to MCDM (Multi-Criteria Decision-Making) methods and techniques, facilitating such tasks. From choosing the best and worst option, through highlighting the most important criterion, to ranking all alternatives, MCDM methods have proven to be highly effective and vaguely universal.

MCDM is often found along with federated learning (FL) solutions [9]. FL is based on the aggregation of models in order to obtain a single, common one. However, there is a dire need to filter the malicious agents in such a system. With the development of FL, great attention is being paid to MCDM which helps with

Supported by Rector's mentoring project at the Silesian University of Technology.

A. Lopata et al. (Eds.): ICIST 2023, CCIS 1979, pp. 329–340, 2024.
https://doi.org/10.1007/978-3-031-48981-5_27

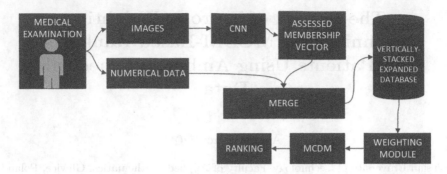

Fig. 1. Visualization of data processing in the proposed method

consensus mechanisms in FL. Another example is using the heuristic approach to increase the efficiency of federated learning [10]. It is important to analyze and compare different solutions that were shown in [2]. The authors analyze different approaches to show the current state of research in this matter. Different approaches can be applied in such applications. An example is fuzzy selection [4]. A similar approach is often used in MCDM applications [1]. MCDM methods are also applied in Internet of Things (IoT) solutions or along with optimization algorithms such as heuristic algorithms. In such algorithms, an optimal solution is found based on a specific objective function [3,15]. The research describes the propositions of using selected heuristic algorithms in multi-criteria problems. Again in [13], a similar idea was shown as an application in IoT.

Quite often, the knowledge used in such decision-making has to be located somewhere. Quite often these are databases, clouds or even blockchains [11,12]. It is worth noting that MCDM methods are mainly used in the operation of the blockchain [5]. Adding a new block involves data analysis as well as assessing the credibility of the adder. The area of MCDM operation and its use is huge due to the universality of the methodology. An important element of scientific research is practical application, which can be seen primarily in the medical area [6,7].

Based on current research, in this paper, I propose a solution based on a real-life scenario, where a medical emergency is considered and patients need to be assessed and ranked based on their need for help, to provide those in the most need with the limited resources. The main contribution of this paper are:

– enhancement of a variety of MCDM methods on ranking ambiguous data,
– a universal solution-outline which can be used for binary ranking problems.

2   Proposed Methodology

The proposed solution is based on the patient performing tests in a medical facility. Data is most often saved as numerical values or an image (e.g. X-ray). For this purpose, I propose to process the image by a convolutional neural network in order to obtain specific numerical data. Then all the data saved in one form are merged and stored in the database. In the case of a sufficient amount of data, an analysis of the weights of individual features is performed, which are used in the selected decision-making method. The final result is the ranking of patients depending on the features recorded in the numerical vector. An example visualization is shown in Fig. 1.

2.1 Creating Multi-criteria Patient Database

To expand the available data and consolidate it into a comprehensive attribute-based database, two or more different datasets can be merged, resulting in a new collection of samples. In order to differentiate the data, medical images showing the lungs, cough-spectrograms and database related to numerical data showing various symptoms, all of healthy and sick patients were selected. For the purposes of this study, I focused on two classes: healthy and ill.

2.2 Criteria Weighting Methods

Consider a decision matrix X, reflecting a set of n alternatives with m criteria. To be able to rank the alternatives, two additional vectors of length m are required:

- O_C objective vector, where each value $o_C \in \{min, max\}$. Each Criterion must be given an objective indicating whether it is beneficial to maximize or to minimize its corresponding value. Each criterion must be manually assigned an objective by an expert. However, this task is not particularly demanding, as there are only two classes to choose from and the criteria are very often transparent in terms of their goal.
- W_C weight vector, where each value $w_C \in [0, 1]$. Each criterion must be assigned a weight value indicating its importance relative to other criteria in the decision matrix. This can be done either manually with expertise or using criteria weighting methods.

$$X = \begin{array}{c} \\ A_1 \\ A_2 \\ \vdots \\ A_i \\ \vdots \\ A_n \end{array} \begin{array}{cccccc} C_1 & C_2 & \cdots & C_j & \cdots & C_m \\ \left(\begin{array}{cccccc} x_{11} & x_{12} & \cdots & x_{1j} & \cdots & x_{1m} \\ x_{21} & x_2 & \cdots & x_{2j} & \cdots & x_{2m} \\ \vdots & \vdots & \ddots & \vdots & \ddots & \vdots \\ x_{i1} & x_2 & \cdots & x_{ij} & \cdots & x_{im} \\ \vdots & \vdots & \ddots & \vdots & \ddots & \vdots \\ x_{n1} & x_n & \cdots & x_{nj} & \cdots & x_{nm} \end{array} \right) \end{array} \quad (1)$$

Entropy weighting method is one of the methods allowing for the weight-assessment based solely on the values in the decision matrix. First, the decision matrix X must be standardized. This can be done by calculating standardized values p for each criterion set. This can be presented as:

$$p_{ij} = \frac{x_{ij}}{\sum_{k=1}^{n} x_{kj}} \tag{2}$$

Then, the entropy value for each criterion C_j is calculated:

$$E_j = -\frac{\sum_{i=1}^{n} p_{ij} \cdot \ln p_{ij}}{\ln n} \tag{3}$$

Finally, each weight is obtained by the formula:

$$w_{C_j} = \frac{1 - E_j}{\sum_{k=1}^{m}(1 - E_k)} \tag{4}$$

2.3 MCDM Methods

MCDM stands for Multi-Criteria Decision Making, which is a field of study that deals with decision-making problems involving multiple conflicting criteria. MCDM methods provide systematic approaches to help decision-makers evaluate and rank different alternatives based on multiple criteria. In this paper, I used MCDM methods to create a ranking of all patients.

A general equation for obtaining rank score R of an alternative A from a decision matrix X (see Eq. 1) using MCDM method denoted as function f can be presented as:

$$\begin{aligned} R_A &= f(X_A, W_C, O_C) \\ X_A &= x_{a1}, x_{a2}, ..., x_{am}, \quad \text{alternative's values} \\ W_C &= w_{C_1}, w_{C_2}, ..., w_{C_m}, \quad \text{criteria weights} \\ O_C &= o_{C_1}, o_{C_2}, ..., o_{C_m}, \quad \text{criteria objectives} \end{aligned} \tag{5}$$

In the experiments, following methods were used:

1. COPARAS
2. MOORA
3. MultiMOORA
4. TOPSIS
5. VIKOR

These methods have been extensively described in [14].

3 Experiments

3.1 Data

Three publicly available datasets were used to generate a database of many different types of data. The first was a collection called the Covid-19 Symptom patient dataset, which contains 2575 samples with five different symptoms: Fever $[94, 108]°F$, Body Pain $\{0, 1\}$, Age $[1, 100]$, Runny Nose $\{0, 1\}$, Difficulties with breathing $\{-1, 0, 1\}$. This data is accessible at *Kaggle*, under this link. The second dataset was the Coughing Mel-Spectrogram Image dataset, which is described under this link. The last dataset contains lung x-ray samples with prepared masks and this dataset is available on *Kaggle*, under this link. Selected samples from these databases are shown in Fig. 2.

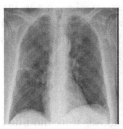  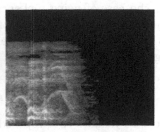

(a) Lung X-ray Image (b) Mask matching   (c) Cough MeL Spectrogram
            X-ray Image   Image

Fig. 2. Example of image data used in the experiments, described in Sect. 3.1

3.2 Convolution Neural Network Models

The image data processing is based on convolutional neural networks that process the image through three types of layers. The first one is convolutional, which is designed to extract the features of the image, pooling, which reduces the size, and dense, which is an interpretation of the classic layer composed of neurons. In this paper, the incoming data can be represented as a lung x-ray (that is given as an original image with a mask) or a cough audio sample that is presented as a spectrogram.

For the x-ray data, the input is two 256×256 gray-scale images: original and mask which indicates the region of interest. For such input, the following architecture has been proposed:

- Convolutional 2D layer (filters = 64, kernel size = 3, activation function = ReLU)
- Max Pooling 2D layer (pool size = 3×3)
- Convolutional 2D layer (filters = 64, kernel size = 3, activation function = ReLU)

- Max Pooling 2D layer (pool size = 3 × 3)
- Convolutional 2D layer (filters = 128, kernel size = 3, activation function = ReLU)
- Max Pooling 2D layer (pool size = 3 × 3)
- Convolutional 2D layer (filters = 256, kernel size = 3, activation function = ReLU)
- Max Pooling 2D layer (pool size = 3 × 3)
- Flatten Layer
- Dense layer (64 neurons, activation function = ReLU)
- Dense layer (8 neurons, activation function = ReLU)
- Dense (1 neuron, activation function = softmax).

The returned value is in the range $\langle 0, 1 \rangle$ indicating the probability of being sick.

This model was trained by ADAM optimizer [8] with 5 epochs.

In the case of using mel-spectrograms, there are no masks, so the input of the above model is based on one image of size $256 \times 256 \times 4$ (where 4 means RGBA color model). In the case of the output layer, the activation function was changed to a sigmoid one.

3.3   Creating Database of Artificial Patients

In order to validate the proposed method, selected databases were modified. The database of symptoms has been extended with an additional attribute, which is the probability table. This was done by assigning a sample from the database to a sample from the table of probabilities (while maintaining the appropriate class). Another database was modified by combining a random set of graphical data with a random numerical sample. Of course, the amount of data in the selected databases was different, so the database was reduced to only combined samples. Finally, after assembling the databases, for each of the datasets (except for the Symptoms database, where 48 samples of each class were chosen) only 1000 positive and 1000 negative samples have been randomly selected for further assessment.

In each dataset, the objective of every single criterion was to maximize the value. That is because the goal was to detect Covid-positive patients and greater values of the criteria were beneficial for such purpose.

4   Results

The result of the experiment was a list of patients. The main objective of that ranking was to distinguish Covid-positive patients from the negative ones and order them by severity of Covid-related symptoms. Thus, the expected ranking would have negative cases at the bottom, and positive ones at the top of the ranking.

TOP x Accuracy Graph

In order to better illustrate and measure the correctness of a ranking, I used TOP x accuracy graphs. Each ranking vector R can be transformed by the function:

$$TOP(x) = \frac{\sum_{i=1}^{x} \begin{cases} 1 & \text{if } R_i \text{ is a positive sample} \\ 0 & \text{if } R_i \text{ is a negative sample} \end{cases}}{x} \tag{6}$$

Consequently, the TOP(x) function graph representing ideal ranking R should look exactly like Fig. 3. Further-described metrics used to assess the models and are derived from this function graph.

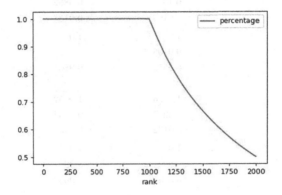

Fig. 3. Ideal TOP(x) graph (for 2000 samples, 1000 healthy and 1000 ill)

4.1   Calculated Weights

Weights obtained by using entropy method (Sect. 2.2) are presented visually in Fig. 4 as a collection of four radar graphs (for each dataset used in the experiments).

4.2   Metrics

All of the obtained results can be listed as:

- Difference between the ideal and the obtained area under the first half of the TOP(x) function.
- Mean Absolute Error (MAE) (for the TOP(x) function).
- Mean Squared Error (MSE) (for the TOP(x) function).
- TOP x% accuracy of the ranking.

Table 1. Comparison table of the obtained results using mean weighting for different MCDM methods and databases

Metrics	Symptoms × Cough × X-ray	Symptoms × Cough	Symptoms × X-ray	Symptoms only
COPRAS				
AreaDiff	10.6	93.69	79.11	22.04
MAE	**0.0102**	**0.0711**	**0.0595**	0.3293
MSE	**0.000318**	**0.0092**	**0.0078**	0.1424
TOP1%	1.0000	1.0000	1.0000	1.0000
TOP5%	1.0000	0.9604	1.0000	0.5000
TOP10%	0.9950	0.9652	0.9900	0.5455
MOORA				
AreaDiff	15.09	154.32	121.14	**20.33**
MAE	0.0140	0.1071	0.0862	**0.3139**
MSE	0.000624	0.0199	0.0138	**0.1269**
TOP1%	1.0	1.0	1.0	1.0
TOP5%	1.0	0.9505	1.0	0.6667
TOP10%	1.0	0.9552	0.9801	0.5455
MultiMOORA				
AreaDiff	12.4	135.25	118.52	23.08
MAE	0.0127	0.0957	0.0834	0.3371
MSE	0.000552	0.0162	0.0131	0.1520
TOP1%	1.0	1.0	1.0	1.0
TOP5%	1.0	0.9901	0.9901	0.5
TOP10%	1.0	0.9701	0.9652	0.5455
TOPSIS				
AreaDiff	**9.15**	**90.09**	**77.35**	23.89
MAE	0.0108	0.0719	0.0655	0.3559
MSE	0.000336	0.0098	0.0082	0.1658
TOP1%	1.0	1.0	1.0	1.0
TOP5%	1.0	0.9703	0.9802	0.5
TOP10%	1.0	0.9851	0.9900	0.4545
VIKOR				
AreaDiff	85.48	203.99	199.45	23.39
MAE	0.0662	0.1531	0.1494	0.3516
MSE	0.009309	0.0365	0.0372	0.1617
TOP1%	1.0	1.0	1.0	0.5
TOP5%	1.0	0.9703	1.0	0.5
TOP10%	0.9950	0.9254	0.9652	0.5455

Table 2. Comparison table of the obtained results using entropy weighting for different MCDM methods and databases

Metrics	Symptoms × Cough × X-ray	Symptoms × Cough	Symptoms × X-ray	Symptoms only
COPRAS				
AreaDiff	**0.605**	30.92	4.476	**22.85**
MAE	0.000837	0.0241	0.00804	**0.3363**
MSE	5.43e−06	0.000806	0.000261	**0.1509**
TOP1%	1.0	1.0	1.0	1.0
TOP5%	1.0	0.9307	1.0	0.5
TOP10%	1.0	0.9552	1.0	0.5455
MOORA				
AreaDiff	0.716	25.45	5.824	24.40
MAE	0.000825	0.0246	0.00971	0.3518
MSE	7.59e−06	0.000799	0.000340	0.1694
TOP1%	1.0	1.0	1.0	1.0
TOP5%	1.0	0.9703	1.0	0.5
TOP10%	1.0	0.9652	1.0	0.4545
MultiMOORA				
AreaDiff	0.834	27.63	6.328	24.02
MAE	0.000898	0.0257	0.01047	0.3598
MSE	7.39e−06	0.000916	0.000369	0.1696
TOP1%	1.0	1.0	1.0	1.0
TOP5%	1.0	0.960396	1.0	0.5
TOP10%	1.0	0.970149	1.0	0.5455
TOPSIS				
AreaDiff	1.168	30.35	4.477	23.99
MAE	0.001425	0.0236	0.00925	0.3482
MSE	7.14e−06	0.000686	00.000293	0.1630
TOP1%	1.0	0.9524	1.0	1.0
TOP5%	1.0	0.9802	1.0	0.5
TOP10%	1.0	0.9602	1.0	0.4545
VIKOR				
AreaDiff	0.816	**21.72**	**3.409**	23.48
MAE	**0.000669**	**0.0188**	**0.00443**	0.3490
MSE	**5.05e−06**	**0.000441**	**0.000122**	0.1630
TOP1%	1.0	1.0	1.0	1.0
TOP5%	1.0	0.9703	1.0	0.6667
TOP10%	1.0	0.9801	1.0	0.4545

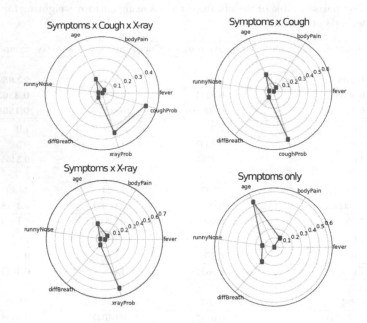

Fig. 4. Entropy weighting values comparison for different databases

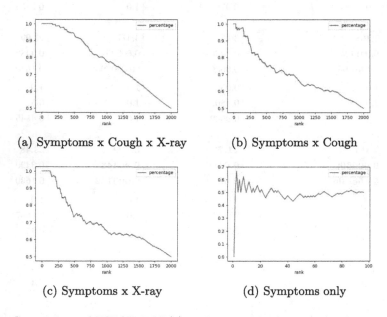

(a) Symptoms x Cough x X-ray

(b) Symptoms x Cough

(c) Symptoms x X-ray

(d) Symptoms only

Fig. 5. Comparison of VIKOR TOP(x) ranking graphs for each database with mean weighting method applied.

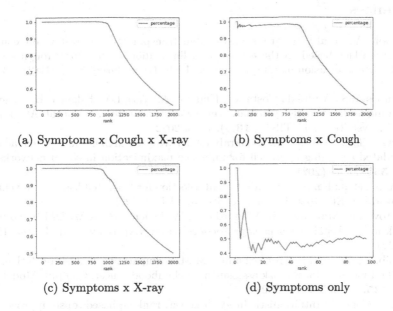

(a) Symptoms x Cough x X-ray   (b) Symptoms x Cough

(c) Symptoms x X-ray   (d) Symptoms only

Fig. 6. Comparison of VIKOR TOP(x) ranking graphs for each database with entropy weighting method applied.

5   Conclusion

The proposed model can be used to solve challenging problems in real life, such as the one considered in the experiment. MCDM methods can serve as an accurate and unbiased ranking agents. Furthermore, they can be greatly enhanced with the use of entropy weighting, prior to the ranking process. Based on the results of this paper, the use of entropy weighting in the VIKOR model was extremely effective as it outperformed every other MCDM method when the weighting method was used (Table 2). Furthermore, VIKOR can be viewed as the worst model with standard weighting, as can be seen in Table 1. This, however, does not mean that the other methods did not perform well, as they all were greatly improved by entropy weighting. This conclusion was drawn by comparing both of two fore-mentioned tables. As VIKOR method showed the best improvement, the relevant graphs were shown in Figs. 5–6.

The proposal can be used in various types of systems where there is a lot of information on which to make a decision, e.g. medical systems or federated learning. In future work, I plan to focus on adapting new multi-criteria methods in the federated learning process.

References

1. Alnoor, A., et al.: Toward a sustainable transportation industry: oil company benchmarking based on the extension of linear diophantine fuzzy rough sets and multicriteria decision-making methods. IEEE Trans. Fuzzy Syst. **31**(2), 449–459 (2022)
2. Antunes, R.S., André da Costa, C., Küderle, A., Yari, I.A., Eskofier, B.: Federated learning for healthcare: systematic review and architecture proposal. ACM Trans. Intell. Syst. Technol. (TIST), **13**(4), 1–23, 2022
3. Biswas, T.K., Abbasi, A., Chakrabortty, R.K.: An MCDM integrated adaptive simulated annealing approach for influence maximization in social networks. Inf. Sci. **556**, 27–48 (2021)
4. Cha, N., et al.: Fuzzy logic based client selection for federated learning in vehicular networks. IEEE Open J. Comput. Soc. **3**, 39–50 (2022)
5. Filatovas, E., Marcozzi, M., Mostarda, L., Paulavičius, R.: A MCDM-based framework for blockchain consensus protocol selection. Expert Syst. Appl. **204**, 117609 (2022)
6. Habib, S., Akram, M., Ali Al-Shamiri, M.M.: Comparative analysis of Pythagorean MCDM methods for the risk assessment of childhood cancer. Comput. Model. Eng. Sci. **135**(3), 2585–2615 (2023)
7. Jin, J., Garg, H.: Intuitionistic fuzzy three-way ranking-based topsis approach with a novel entropy measure and its application to medical treatment selection. Adv. Eng. Softw. **180**, 103459 (2023)
8. Kingma, D.P., Ba, J.: Adam: a method for stochastic optimization. arXiv preprint arXiv:1412.6980 (2014)
9. Lau, H., Tsang, Y.P., Nakandala, D., Lee, C.K.: Risk quantification in cold chain management: a federated learning-enabled multi-criteria decision-making methodology. Ind. Manag. Data Syst. **121**(7), 1684–1703 (2021)
10. Połap, D., Woźniak, M.: A hybridization of distributed policy and heuristic augmentation for improving federated learning approach. Neural Netw. **146**, 130–140 (2022)
11. Prokop, K., Połap, D., Srivastava, G., Lin, J.C.W.: Blockchain-based federated learning with checksums to increase security in internet of things solutions. J. Ambient Intell. Humanized Comput. **14**(5), 4685–4694 (2023)
12. Qahtan, S., et al.: Novel multi security and privacy benchmarking framework for blockchain-based IoT healthcare industry 4.0 systems. IEEE Trans. Ind. Inform. **18**(9), 6415–6423 (2022)
13. Rahmanifar, G., Mohammadi, M., Sherafat, A., Hajiaghaei-Keshteli, M., Fusco, G., Colombaroni, C.: Heuristic approaches to address vehicle routing problem in the IoT-based waste management system. Expert Syst. Appl. **220**, 119708 (2023)
14. Trung, D.D.: Application of EDAS, MARCOS, TOPSIS, MOORA and PIV methods for multi-criteria decision making in milling process. Strojnícky časopis - J. Mech. Eng. **71**(2), 69–84 (2021)
15. Zhao, M., Shen, X., Liao, H., Cai, M.: Selecting products through text reviews: An mcdm method incorporating personalized heuristic judgments in the prospect theory. Fuzzy Optim. Decis. Making, pp. 1–24 (2022)

Author Index

Printed in the United States
by Baker & Taylor Publisher Services